Teacher's Edition

Strategies in Reading B

Ethel Grodzins Romm

HBJ

HARCOURT BRACE JOVANOVICH, PUBLISHERS

Orlando　　New York　　San Francisco
Chicago　　Atlanta　　Dallas

We do not include a Teacher's Edition automatically with each classroom set of textbooks. We prefer to send a Teacher's Edition only when requested by the teacher or administrator concerned or by one of our representatives. A Teacher's Edition can be easily mislaid when it arrives as part of a shipment delivered to a school stockroom, and since it contains answer materials, we want to be sure it is sent *directly* to the person who will use it or to someone concerned with the use or selection of textbooks.

If your classroom assignment changes and you no longer are using or examining this Teacher's Edition, you may wish to pass it on to a teacher who will be using it.

Copyright © 1984 by Harcourt Brace Jovanovich, Inc.

All rights reserved. No part of this publication may be reproduced or transmitted in any form or by any means, electronic or mechanical, including photocopy, recording, or any information storage and retrieval system, without permission in writing from the publisher.
Requests for permission to make copies of any part of the work should be mailed to: Permissions, Harcourt Brace Jovanovich, Publishers, Orlando, Florida.

Printed in the United States of America

ISBN 0-15-337125-0

Contents

Overview	Tiii
Objectives for *Strategies in Reading A-F*	Tv
Notes for Teachers	Txi
The Pupil's Edition, Contents	v

Overview

Strategies in Reading A-F is a series of six reading-skill workbooks for students in grades 7-12. Each workbook provides instruction and practice in twelve important reading-skill categories that improve comprehension: *Sentence Meaning, Relationships, Judgments, Inferences, Main Idea, Dictionary, Context, Structure, Word Origins, Figurative Language, Imagery, Flexibility and Study Skills.* Each workbook contains short motivating selections for students to read. *Strategies in Reading* is completely self-contained. It may be used in conjunction with *Journeys: A Reading and Literature Program* or independently. Since it provides practice in skills essential to all reading, it can be used as a supplement to any literature program. The goal of *Strategies in Reading* is mastery of skills that result in improved reading. The program accomplishes its goal through:

1. A deductive approach that first provides clear definitions and examples and then asks students to apply what they have learned
2. A sequence of skills appropriate to the needs of the students
3. A flexible structure that allows for differences in students' abilities
4. Selections that are short and motivating
5. A format that invites and aids reading
6. An easy-to-follow plan for classroom management

Approach

The approach of *Strategies in Reading* is deductive. Each lesson begins with a clear definition which is printed in **boldface.** This definition is reinforced by examples. At least one written example follows each definition, but *Strategies in Reading* also makes judicious use of comic strips and cartoons to further illustrate the definitions. The definition and examples are followed by one or more exercises that require the students to apply what they have learned. This clear and consistent approach makes it easy for below average students to follow the lessons.

Structure and Sequence of Skills

Each level of *Strategies in Reading* is divided into twelve chapters covering twelve important skill categories: *Sentence Meaning, Relationships, Judgments, Inferences, Main Idea, Dictionary, Context,*

Structure and Sequence of Skills

Structure, Word Origins, Figurative Language, Imagery, and *Flexibility and Study Skills.* Each lesson in each chapter focuses on only one aspect of the skill category. For example, a lesson in the relationships chapter will focus on understanding cause and effect. By having each lesson focus on only one aspect of the skill category, *Strategies in Reading* ensures that students will not be given more information than they can handle at one time.

Skills progress from simple to complex wherever appropriate. Many skills are taught at each level of *Strategies in Reading.* For these skills, the level of material that students read to apply these skills becomes more complex as students progress through the program.

Each lesson in *Strategies in Reading* is completely self-contained. Because of this, *Strategies in Reading* can be used for self-teaching. We suggest teachers have their better students use *Strategies in Reading* on their own. For their below average students, we suggest teachers read aloud the beginning part of the lesson, which contains the definition and examples, or have their students read it aloud. Once teachers are sure their students have understood this material, they can have them complete the exercises.

Some exercises require students to read selections. Better students should be able to read these selections on their own. We suggest that teachers have below average students read these selections orally and then have these students answer the questions on their own.

Some lessons contain more than one exercise. Teachers may find that they want their below average students to complete only the first exercise and their better students to complete all of the exercises.

Every chapter ends with a *Practice* lesson which requires students to read a complete selection and apply the skills they learned in the chapter. This *Practice* lesson can be used to review the skills from the chapter and to test mastery.

Classroom Management

When *Strategies in Reading* is used with *Journeys: A Reading and Literature Program,* teachers may follow one of two plans.

1. Teach a unit in the literature anthology. Use the *Test Booklet* for *Journeys* to determine which students need additional skill instruction. Teach chapter in *Strategies in Reading* as needed. Use *Practice* lesson at end of chapter for evaluation.
2. Teach a lesson in the literature anthology. Use the *Test Booklet* for evaluation. Teach a corresponding lesson in *Strategies in Reading.*

When *Strategies in Reading* is used independently, teachers should teach a chapter in *Strategies in Reading.* Use the *Practice* lesson for evaluation.

Teacher's Edition

The *Teacher's Edition* contains the complete objectives for the program and notes for teaching the chapters. It also contains the complete *Pupil's Edition* with all the answers.

Objectives for Strategies in Reading A-F

Sentence Meaning

Teaching Objective: *Students will recognize sentence parts and use them to gain meaning from sentences.*

Level where taught

A, B, C, D, E, F	1. Students will interpret punctuation marks as aids to gaining meaning from sentences in prose and poetry.
A, B, C, D	2. Students will use quotation marks to gain meaning from dialogue.
A, B, C, D, E, F	3. Students will identify core parts in simple sentences.
E, F	4. Students will identify core parts in compound sentences.
A, B, C, D, E	5. Students will identify and interpret modifiers in sentences.
A, B, C, D, E	6. Students will read sentences with pronouns and identify the words to which the pronouns refer.
A, B, C, D, E, F	7. Students will understand the function of word order in sentences and read and interpret sentences with complicated word order.
C, D	8. Students will read and interpret sentences with words left out.

Relationships

Teaching Objective: *Students will develop an understanding of relationship patterns in writing.*

A, B, C, D, E, F	1. Students will identify time order and be able to place events in their proper time order.
A, B, C, D, E, F	2. Students will identify listing and be able to place items in a list.
A, B, C, D, E, F	3. Students will identify spatial order and be able to determine the spatial relationship of one object to another.
A, B, C, D, E, F	4. Students will identify cause and effect and see how it functions in sentences and in a selection.
A, B, C, D, E, F	5. Students will identify comparison and contrast and see how it functions in sentences and in selections.
A, B, C, D, E, F	6. Students will read various sentences and identify the relationship pattern of each sentence.
C, D, E, F	7. Students will identify order of importance and see how it functions in a selection.
C, D, E, F	8. Students will identify sentences containing more than one relationship pattern.

Judgments

Teaching Objective: *Students will read critically and will evaluate statements in writing.*

Level where taught

Levels	Objective
A, B	1. Students will identify reliable sources and use them to determine the validity of information.
A, B, C, D, E, F	2. Students will identify statements of fact and statements of opinion.
A, B, C, D, E, F	3. Students will identify and interpret mixed statements of fact and opinion.
A, B, D	4. Students will recognize and form valid opinions and conclusions and identify unsupported judgments.
A, B, C, D, E, F	5. Students will recognize stereotypes.
A, B, C	6. Students will identify and recognize the effect of loaded words.
A, B, C, D, E, F	7. Students will recognize faulty reasoning (e.g., statements of opinion disguised as fact, irrelevant evidence, hidden assumptions, arguing in circles, name-calling).
C, D, E, F	8. Students will distinguish between primary and secondary sources of information.
C, D, E, F	9. Students will make generalizations and distinguish between valid generalizations and hasty generalizations.

Inferences

Teaching Objective: *Students will find the meaning of material when it has not been directly stated.*

Levels	Objective
A, B, C, D, E, F	1. Students will make inferences based on evidence and identify evidence that supports inferences.
A, B, C, D, E, F	2. Students will make inferences about what characters are like, what their motives are, and what their feelings are.
A, B, C, D, E, F	3. Students will make inferences about past, present, and future actions and events.
A, B, C	4. Students will make inferences about time and place.
A, B, C, D	5. Students will make inferences about realistic and fantastic details.
A, B, C, D, E, F	6. Students will make inferences about tone.
C, D, E	7. Students will make inferences about mood.
D, E, F	8. Students will make predictions as they read.
D, F	9. Students will make inferences about irony.
E, F	10. Students will make inferences about satire.
A, E, F	11. Students will make inferences about exaggeration.
F	12. Students will identify incorrect inferences.

Main Idea

Teaching Objective: *Students will identify and interpret main ideas both when they are stated and when they are implied.*

Level where taught

A, B, C, D, E, F	1. Students will read paragraphs and identify their topics.
A, B, C, D, E, F	2. Students will distinguish between the topic and the main idea of a paragraph.
A, B, C, D, E, F	3. Students will read paragraphs and find the topic sentence for each paragraph.
A, B, C, D, E, F	4. Students will identify the implied main idea of a paragraph.
A, B, C, D, E, F	5. Students will state the implied main idea of a paragraph.
A, B, C, D, E, F	6. Students will find supporting details when the main idea is stated and when it is implied.
A, B, C, D, E, F	7. Students will order the importance of ideas.
A	8. Students will understand the changes signaled by paragraphs.
A	9. Students will read and interpret paragraphs with conflicting main ideas.
B	10. Students will find the main idea in dialogue.
B, C, D, E, F	11. Students will paraphrase the main idea of a paragraph.

Dictionary

Teaching Objective: *Students will develop an understanding of the function of a dictionary and interpret the information they find in a dictionary.*

A, B, C, D, E, F	1. Students will recognize guide words and develop an understanding of their function.
A, B, C, D, E, F	2. Students will interpret the information in a dictionary entry.
A, B, C, D, E, F	3. Students will read a complete dictionary entry and choose from the definitions the one that fits the context.
A, B	4. Students will use a dictionary to select the homophone that fits the context.
A, C, D	5. Students will use a dictionary to select the homograph that fits the context.
A, B	6. Students will use a dictionary to find the correct spelling of a word.
A, B, C, D, E, F	7. Students will interpret the symbols in a pronunciation key and use them to pronounce words.
B, C, D, E, F	8. Students will use a dictionary to find the principal parts of a verb.
A, B, C, D, E, F	9. Students will use a dictionary to find the part of speech of the entry word.
B, C, D, E, F	10. Students will use a dictionary to divide words into syllables.

Level where taught

B, C, D, E, F	11. Students will use a dictionary to find derivatives.
A, B, C, D, E, F	12. Students will find synonyms and antonyms in a dictionary.
C, D, E, F	13. Students will interpret synonym information that shows the differences in meaning among synonyms.

Context

Teaching Objective: *Students will use the context of a word to find its meaning.*

A, B, C, D, E, F	1. Students will recognize that words have more than one meaning and then choose the meaning that fits the context.
A, B, C, D, E, F	2. Students will identify words used as nouns and verbs and recognize that their meaning within a sentence depends on how they are used.
A, B, C, D, E, F	3. Students will recognize direct context clues and use them to find the meaning of unfamiliar words.
A, B, C, D, E, F	4. Students will recognize indirect context clues and use them to find the meaning of unfamiliar words.
C, D, E, F	5. Students will recognize when context helps and when it doesn't.
B, D, F	6. Students will choose synonyms that fit the context.
B	7. Students will choose antonyms that fit the context.
B, C, D, E, F	8. Students will use context to interpret jargon.
C, D	9. Students will use context to choose the correct homophone.
C, D	10. Students will use context to interpret words from Spanish.

Structure

Teaching Objective: *Students will identify prefixes, suffixes, and root words and use word structure to find the meaning of words and to build new words.*

A, B, C, D, E, F	1. Students will identify root words and use them to build new words.
A, B, C, D, E, F	2. Students will identify prefixes and use them to build new words and to find the meaning of unfamiliar words.
A, B, C, D, E, F	3. Students will identify suffixes and use them to build new words and to find the meaning of unfamiliar words.
A, B, C, D, E, F	4. Students will identify Latin and Greek roots and use them to build new words and to find the meaning of unfamiliar words.
A, B, C, D, E, F	5. Students will identify compound words and use their structure to find their meaning.
A, B, C	6. Students will identify contractions and understand their meaning.

Level where taught

C, D, E, F	7. Students will use suffixes to change the part of speech of a word.
C, D, E, F	8. Students will gain an understanding of how the pronunciation of words changes when affixes are added.
E, F	9. Students will gain an understanding of companion forms.

Word Origins

Teaching Objective: *Students will gain an understanding of the origin of words.*

A, B, C, D, E, F	1. Students will find word origins in a dictionary.
A, B, C, D, E, F	2. Students will read and interpret information about the origins of words based on names of people and places.
A, B, C, D, E, F	3. Students will gain an understanding of how words have changed in meaning.
A, B	4. Students will read and interpret information about the origins of words from the American Indians.
A, B, C, D, E, F	5. Students will read and interpret information about the origins of words from foreign languages.
C, D, E, F	6. Students will gain an understanding of how words have become shortened through use.

Figurative Language

Teaching Objective: *Students will identify and interpret figurative language.*

A, B, C, D, E, F	1. Students will distinguish between figurative and literal language.
A, B, C	2. Students will read and interpret figurative expressions.
A, E, F	3. Students will read and interpret idioms.
A, B, C, D, E, F	4. Students will identify and interpret similes.
A, B, C, D, E, F	5. Students will identify and interpret metaphors.
C, D, E, F	6. Students will find suitable figurative comparisons.
C, D, E, F	7. Students will interpret symbols in literature.

Imagery

Teaching Objective: *Students will identify and interpret imagery.*

A, B, C, D, E, F	1. Students will read and interpret sensory language in prose and in poetry.
A, B, C, D, E, F	2. Students will use imagery to visualize a setting.
A, B, E	3. Students will identify vivid verbs and see how they create strong images.

Level where taught

A, C, D	4. Students will identify modifiers and see how they create strong images.
A	5. Students will gain an understanding of how sounds create vivid impressions.
B	6. Students will identify and interpret words that stand for sounds.
B, E, F	7. Students will gain an understanding of connotation and denotation.
C, D	8. Students will read selections with words from other languages and gain an understanding of how these words create vivid images.
E, F	9. Students will use imagery to visualize a character.
E, F	10. Students will gain an understanding of how imagery affects mood.
F	11. Students will recognize alliteration and gain an understanding of its effect.

Flexibility and Study Skills

Teaching Objective: *Students will select the appropriate method and rate of reading and gain an understanding of how to use study aids available to them.*

A, B, C, D, E, F	1. Students will set a purpose for reading and gain an understanding of how to adjust their rate to their purpose.
A, B, C, D, E, F	2. Students will scan an article for facts.
A, B, C, D, E, F	3. Students will skim an article.
A, B, F	4. Students will gain an understanding of the importance of following directions.
A, C, D	5. Students will take notes as they read.
A, B, C, D, E, F	6. Students will gain an understanding of the outline form and organize information in an outline.
A, B	7. Students will gain an understanding of how to use the frontmatter and backmatter of a book.
A, B, C, D, E, F	8. Students will select the reference book that is appropriate to their needs.
A, B, C, D, E, F	9. Students will read and interpret the information in a graph.
A, B, C, D, E, F	10. Students will read and interpret the information in a time line.
C	11. Students will read and interpret the information in a table.
B, C, D, E, F	12. Students will read an article intensively.
C, D	13. Students will gain an understanding of how books are arranged in the library.
E, F	14. Students will read and interpret maps.

Tx

Notes for Teachers

**Chapter 1
Sentence Meaning
pp. 1–26**

This chapter focuses on mastering strategies for finding the meaning of sentences. **Lesson 1** (pp. 1–3) concentrates on punctuation marks as clues to meaning. It explains the function of the period, the exclamation mark, the question mark, the comma, the dash, the colon, and the semicolon. **Lesson 2** (pp. 3–5) expands the information in the first lesson on punctuation marks. It shows how punctuation marks provide help for reading sentences in poetry. It explains that the end of a line in poetry does not always signal the end of a sentence; therefore, it is essential to pay attention to punctuation marks which tell you when to pause and when to stop. **Lesson 3** (pp. 5–7) focuses on using quotation marks to find the exact words of a speaker. It also explains how to identify the speaker by noting the order in which the characters speak. **Lesson 4** (pp. 8–10) deals with finding core parts in sentences. Core parts are the simple subject, the simple predicate, and the word or words that complete the simple predicate. Finding core parts is a useful strategy for gaining the basic meaning of a sentence. This lesson also introduces the concept of the verb phrase and explains that the helping word may be separated from the main verb in a verb phrase. **Lesson 5** (pp. 10–13) explains compound subjects and compound verbs. It provides strategies for reading sentences that are slightly more complicated than those the students have been reading up until now. **Lesson 6** (pp. 13–17) concentrates on word order. It explains natural word order, and provides a strategy for reading a sentence that has a group of words before the subject. **Lesson 7** (pp. 17–20) focuses on reading sentences with interrupters. It explains that an interrupter may cause reading problems because it sometimes separates the main parts of a sentence. **Lesson 8** (pp. 21–23) provides instruction and practice in understanding pronoun reference. It defines the pronoun and lists commonly used pronouns. It emphasizes the problem of ambiguous pronoun reference. **Lesson 9** (pp. 23–26) is a *Practice* lesson. Students read "Is Our Capitol Haunted?" by Henry N. Ferguson and complete the exercise applying skills from the chapter.

**Chapter 2
Relationships
pp. 27–56**

This chapter concentrates on showing how people, things, events, and ideas are connected or joined in writing. **Lesson 1** (pp. 27–29) introduces the concept of spatial order. It points out words that show the spatial relationship of one object to another. **Lesson 2** (pp. 29–32) provides instruction and practice in understanding time order. It shows that events may be connected in three ways: one event may happen before another event, one event may happen after another event, or two events may happen at the same time. **Lesson 3** (pp. 33–35) introduces the concept of the list. It explains the difference between the simple list and the significant list. **Lesson 4** (pp. 35–37) focuses on identifying words that signal cause and effect. It helps students distinguish between the cause and the effect in a sentence. **Lesson 5** (pp. 37–41) applies the skill of understanding cause and effect to a short story. **Lesson 6** (pp. 42–44) deals with identifying words that signal contrast. It has students read a short selection comparing roller coasters today with those of the past and show how they differ. **Lesson 7** (pp. 45–48) explains that a comparison shows how things are alike, while a contrast shows how they are different. It asks students to compare and contrast two characters in a story. **Lesson 8** (pp. 48–51) provides a review of time order, spatial order, cause and effect, and comparison and contrast. It provides practice in identifying each of these relationship patterns. **Lesson 9** (pp. 51–56) is a *Practice* lesson. Students read "Lifeboat in Space" by Gurney Williams III and complete an exercise applying skills from the chapter.

**Chapter 3
Judgments
pp. 57–80**

This chapter focuses on skills that help students read critically. **Lesson 1** (pp. 57–60) sets up three criteria for students to use to determine whether or not someone is a reliable source. **Lesson 2** (pp. 60–62) defines a statement of fact and a statement of opinion and asks students to distinguish between the two. **Lesson 3** (pp. 63–66) reviews the definitions of a statement of fact and a statement of opinion. It explains that some statements contain both fact and opinion. These statements are called mixed statements of fact and opinion. **Lesson 4** (pp. 66–67) explains that a valid opinion is an opinion based on facts. It asks students to identify facts that back up opinions. **Lesson 5** (pp. 68–69) defines a stereotype. It points out that the words *all, always, only,* and *never* are often implied in a stereotype, even if they are not stated. **Lesson 6** (pp. 69–72) deals with identifying unsupported judgments. It shows how jumping to conclusions can lead to mistakes. **Lesson 7** (pp. 73–75) introduces the concept of loaded words. It shows how some loaded words create positive impressions, while others create negative impressions. **Lesson 8** (pp. 75–77) focuses on identifying faulty reasoning. It highlights three traps that can cloud your thinking and make your reasoning faulty. These traps are opinions disguised as facts, evidence that doesn't fit the opinion or conclusion, and name-calling or appeals to the emotions. **Lesson 9** (pp. 78–80) is a *Practice* lesson. Students read "Dinosaur Hunting" by Robert Makela and complete the exercise applying skills from the chapter.

**Chapter 4
Inferences
pp. 81–112**

This chapter concentrates on helping students make inferences while they read. **Lesson 1** (pp. 81–83) defines an inference as an intelligent guess based on evidence. It points out how we use evidence every day to make inferences. **Lesson 2** (pp. 83–86) deals with making inferences about characters. It shows how to read between the lines to determine what a character is like and what a character is thinking and feeling. **Lesson 3** (pp. 86–89) concentrates on making inferences about motives. It shows how to use clues in a selection to determine the reason behind a character's actions. **Lesson 4** (pp. 90–

92) points out how to use clues to make inferences about past events and present events. **Lesson 5** (pp. 92–94) then shows how to use clues to make inferences about future events. **Lesson 6** (pp. 95–98) deals with making inferences about time. It explains how to make inferences about three types of time: the time of day, the time of year, and the time period. **Lesson 7** (pp. 99–102) concentrates on making inferences about place. It points out clues that help you determine where events occur. **Lesson 8** (pp. 102–104) explains the difference between realistic details and fantastic details. **Lesson 9** (pp. 105–108) focuses on making inferences about tone. It defines tone as the author's attitude or feeling toward what he or she has written or said. It asks students to decide whether the tone of a paragraph is humorous or serious. **Lesson 10** (pp. 108–112) is a *Practice* lesson. Students read "Johanna" by Jane Yolen and complete an exercise applying skills from the chapter.

**Chapter 5
Main Idea
pp. 113–141**

This chapter develops strategies for reading for main ideas. **Lesson 1** (pp. 113–115) focuses on identifying the topic of a paragraph. It explains that the topic can be expressed as one word or as several words, but not as a sentence. **Lesson 2** (pp. 115–118) distinguishes between the topic of a paragraph and the main idea. **Lesson 3** (pp. 118–120) introduces the concept of the topic sentence. It explains that the topic sentence is often found at the beginning of a paragraph, but may appear near the middle or at the end of a paragraph. **Lesson 4** (pp. 120–122) explains the concept of supporting ideas. It asks students to identify supporting ideas when the main idea is stated. **Lesson 5** (pp. 122–124) focuses on paraphrasing. It asks students to paraphrase the main idea of a paragraph. **Lesson 6** (pp. 124–126) explains that the main idea of a paragraph is not always stated. Sometimes it is implied. It asks students to choose the statement that best states the main idea of a paragraph. **Lesson 7** (pp. 127–128) reviews the concept of the implied main idea. It asks students to write a sentence expressing the main idea of a paragraph. **Lesson 8** (pp. 129–131) provides instruction and practice in identifying supporting details when the main idea is implied. **Lesson 9** (pp. 131–133) focuses on ordering the importance of ideas. It distinguishes between the most important idea and the less important ideas. **Lesson 10** (pp. 134–138) provides instruction and practice in finding the main idea in dialogue. **Lesson 11** (pp. 139–141) is a *Practice* lesson. Students read "Using Solar Energy: It's Not All That Easy!" by Jack Myers and complete the exercises applying skills from the chapter.

**Chapter 6
Dictionary
pp. 143–168**

This chapter develops skills for using a dictionary. **Lesson 1** (pp. 143–145) explains the function of guide words. **Lesson 2** (pp. 145–147) shows how to read a dictionary entry. It points out the different information that can be found in the entry. **Lesson 3** (pp. 148–150) focuses on using a pronunciation key. It explains how to pronounce the symbols used in the key and how to interpret the accent marks. **Lesson 4** (pp. 150–151) defines the principal parts of a verb and shows how to find them in a dictionary. **Lesson 5** (pp. 152–153) concentrates on using a dictionary to find parts of speech. It explains that when a word can be used as different parts of speech, the dictionary entry usually contains definitions for the word used as these parts of speech. **Lesson 6** (pp. 154–155) shows how to use a dictionary to divide words into syllables. **Lesson 7** (pp. 156–158) concentrates on finding the correct meaning. It explains that since most words have more than one meaning, the dictionary entry usually contains more than one definition for each entry word. When you read, you select the definition that fits the sentence. You may also have to adapt the definition slightly to fit the sentence. **Lesson 8** (pp. 159–161) shows how to use a dictionary to find the homophone that fits the sentence. **Lesson 9** (pp. 161–163) defines a derivative and explains how to find derivatives in a dictionary. **Lesson 10** (pp. 164–166) explains how to use the spelling chart in a dictionary. **Lesson 11** (pp. 166–168) is a *Practice* lesson. Students read "The Two Kings" by Helen Pierce Jacob and complete the exercise applying skills from the chapter.

**Chapter 7
Context
pp. 169–192**

This chapter focuses on developing skills for using context to find the meaning of words. **Lesson 1** (pp. 169–171) introduces the concept of context. It shows how to use context clues both in a sentence and in a passage to find the meaning of an unfamiliar word. **Lesson 2** (pp. 171–174) explains that most words have more than one meaning. It demonstrates that when you read, you must choose the meaning that fits the context. **Lesson 3** (pp. 174–177) concentrates on understanding direct context clues. It explains that sometimes writers provide definitions of words they think their readers may not know. **Lesson 4** (pp. 178–180) provides instruction and practice in using indirect context clues to find the meaning of unfamiliar words. **Lesson 5** (pp. 180–182) explains that many words can be used as both nouns and verbs. Their meaning in a sentence depends upon which part of speech they are used as. **Lesson 6** (pp. 183–184) shows how to use context to choose the correct synonym. **Lesson 7** (pp. 185–188) concentrates on using context to understand dialect, and **Lesson 8** (pp. 188–190) deals with using context to understand jargon. **Lesson 9** (pp. 190–192) is a *Practice* lesson. Students read a selection from *Lame Deer: Seeker of Visions* by John (Fire) Lame Deer and Richard Erdoes and complete an exercise applying skills from the chapter.

**Chapter 8
Structure
pp. 193–220**

This chapter demonstrates how to use word structure to find the meaning of unfamiliar words and to build new words. **Lesson 1** (pp. 193–195) focuses on identifying root words. **Lesson 2** (pp. 195–197) introduces the prefix and lists prefixes that show number. **Lesson 3** (pp. 198–199) explains that some prefixes show position and lists four of these. **Lesson 4** (pp. 200–201) concentrates on prefixes that add a negative meaning to words. **Lesson 5** (pp. 202–203) introduces the suffix and explains the function of comparative and superlative suffixes. **Lesson 6** (pp. 203–205) explains that while some suffixes add a different meaning to the root word, others change the function of a word. These include -*age*, -*ment*, -*tion*, -*able*, -*ible*, and -*ly*. **Lesson 7** (pp. 206–208) shows that some roots come from Latin. It focuses on the roots *anim*, *vid*, *vis*, and *port*. **Lesson 8** (pp. 208–209) shows that some roots come from Greek. It focuses on the roots *geo*, *auto*, and *onym*. **Lesson 9** (pp. 210–212) defines the compound word and provides strategies for understanding them. **Lesson 10** (pp. 212–216) focuses on understanding contractions. It points out that some contractions have one letter missing, while others have more than one missing. **Lesson 11** (pp. 217–220) is a *Practice* lesson. Students read "How To Improve Your Vocabulary" by Tony Randall and complete an exercise applying skills from the chapter.

Chapter 9
Word Origins
pp. 221–241

This chapter encourages an appreciation of word histories and shows students how to use a dictionary to find word origins. **Lesson 1** (pp. 221–223) explains that some words are based on the names of places. It shows how to find information about word origins in a dictionary. **Lesson 2** (pp. 223–224) shows that some words are based on the names of people. **Lesson 3** (pp. 225–227) introduces the idea that over the years words change in meaning. **Lesson 4** (pp. 227–228) concentrates on words that have come from the American Indians. **Lesson 5** (pp. 228–232) shows how words have come into English from foreign languages. **Lesson 6** (pp. 232–241) is a *Practice* lesson. Students read a selection from *Words from the Myths* by Isaac Asimov and complete exercises applying skills from the chapter.

Chapter 10
Figurative Language
pp. 243–268

This chapter focuses on interpreting and appreciating figurative language. **Lesson 1** (pp. 243–248) explains the difference between literal and figurative language. **Lesson 2** (pp. 248–251) concentrates on interpreting figurative expressions. **Lesson 3** (pp. 252–255) introduces similes and points out how to identify and interpret them. It also asks students to complete similes. **Lesson 4** (pp. 255–257) provides instruction and practice in interpreting similes in poetry. **Lesson 5** (pp. 257–260) introduces metaphors and explains how to identify and interpret them in prose and in poetry. **Lesson 6** (pp. 260–262) provides additional practice in interpreting figurative language. **Lesson 7** (pp. 263–268) is a *Practice* lesson. Students read "The Boy Who Found Fear," which is a medieval tale collected by Ignaz Künos. Then they complete an exercise applying skills from the chapter.

Chapter 11
Imagery
pp. 269–288

This chapter concentrates on imagery and shows how it creates vivid pictures. **Lesson 1** (pp. 269–271) shows how sensory language contains words and phrases that appeal to the senses. **Lesson 2** (pp. 272–273) focuses on understanding image-making words. **Lesson 3** (pp. 274–275) deals with understanding words that stand for sounds. **Lesson 4** (pp. 276–277) defines the verb and explains how verbs can be particularly vivid and sharp. **Lesson 5** (pp. 278–281) focuses on details in writing that help readers visualize a setting. **Lesson 6** (pp. 281–282) introduces the concept of connotation and denotation and

Txv

demonstrates how this concept functions in poetry. **Lesson 7** (pp. 283–284) provides instruction and practice in finding and interpreting imagery in poetry. **Lesson 8** (pp. 285–288) is a *Practice* lesson. Students read "Prairie Fire" by Laura Ingalls Wilder and complete an exercise applying skills from the chapter.

**Chapter 12
Flexibility and
Study Skills
pp. 289–312**

This chapter focuses on developing skills that help students read more efficiently and study more effectively. **Lesson 1** (pp. 289–291) explains how to set a purpose for reading. **Lesson 2** (p. 292) demonstrates how to adjust rate to purpose. **Lesson 3** (pp. 292–295) explains the techniques of scanning and asks students to scan an article. **Lesson 4** (pp. 295–297) explains the techniques of skimming and asks students to skim an article. **Lesson 5** (pp. 298–299) introduces the technique of reading intensively and asks students to read an article in this manner. **Lesson 6** (pp. 300–302) focuses on the importance of following directions precisely. **Lesson 7** (pp. 302–303) concentrates on outlining. It explains the parts of the outline form and asks students to complete an outline. **Lesson 8** (pp. 304–306) demonstrates how to use a table of contents and an index. **Lesson 9** (p. 307) deals with reference books and how to use them. **Lesson 10** (p. 308) explains how to read a graph and asks students to interpret information in one. **Lesson 11** (p. 309) explains how to read a time line and asks students to interpret information in one. **Lesson 12** (pp. 310–312) is a *Practice* lesson. Students read "The Mystery of Tornadoes" by Sandra Henneberger and complete an exercise applying skills from the chapter.

Strategies in Reading B

Ethel Grodzins Romm

HBJ

HARCOURT BRACE JOVANOVICH, PUBLISHERS
Orlando New York San Francisco
Chicago Atlanta Dallas

Copyright © 1984 by Harcourt Brace Jovanovich, Inc.

All rights reserved. No part of this publication may be reproduced or transmitted in any form or by any means, electronic or mechanical, including photocopy, recording, or any information storage and retrieval system, without permission in writing from the publisher. Requests for permission to make copies of any part of the work should be mailed to: Permissions, Harcourt Brace Jovanovich, Publishers, Orlando, Florida.

Printed in the United States of America

ISBN 0-15-337119-6

Acknowledgments

For permission to reprint copyrighted material, grateful acknowledgment is made to the following sources:

Archie Comic Publications, Inc.: "Archie" cartoon from 6/13/80. Copyright © 1980 by Archie Comic Publications, Inc.

Associated Book Publishers Ltd. and J.B. Lippincott Company: "Smells" from *Chimney Smoke* by Christopher Morley, published by Methuen & Co., Ltd., London.

Atheneum Publishers: "Vulture," copyright © 1961 by X.J. Kennedy in *One Winter Day in August and Other Nonsense Jingles* by X.J. Kennedy. Copyright © 1975 by X.J. Kennedy. A Margaret K. McElderry Book. From *River Runners: A Tale of Hardship and Bravery* by James Houston. Copyright © 1979 by James Houston. A Margaret K. McElderry Book. "Snowy Morning" in *I Thought I Heard the City* by Lilian Moore. Copyright © 1969 by Lilian Moore.

Blassingame, McCauley and Wood: From "Code of the Underworld" by Jim Kjelgaard, from *Popular Publications* Magazine, January 1979. Copyright © 1979 by Jim Kjelgaard.

Thomas A. Blumenfeld: From "Arthritis: It's Not Just a Grownup Disease" by Thomas A. Blumenfeld in *Science World* Magazine. Copyright © 1982 by Thomas A. Blumenfeld, M.D.

Boy Scouts of America: From "Communication" in *Boys' Life* Magazine, December 1981. Published by the Boy Scouts of America, August 1981.

Curtis Brown, Ltd.: From "Moon Change" by Ann Warren Turner, copyright © 1978 by Ann Warren Turner. "Johanna" by Jane Yolen. Copyright © 1978 by Jane Yolen. From "The Crossover" by Edna Corwin from *Boys' Life* Magazine, January 1983. Copyright © 1983 by Edna Corwin.

John Burger: From "Danger—Mudslides!" by John Burger from *Science World* Magazine, April 1982. Copyright © 1982 by John Burger.

Hugh B. Cave: "Two Were Left" by Hugh B. Cave, from *American Magazine*, June 1942. Copyright 1942 by The Crowell-Collier Publishing Company.

Children's Television Workshop: The following selections taken from *Contact* Magazine: "The History of Roller Coasters" by Barbara Seuling, June 1982; from "Manatees: Gentle Giants of the Sea" by Richard Thiel, June 1982; "Nerves" by Kim Solworth Merlino, October 1982; from "Fighting Fires! New Equipment to the Rescue" by Carole G. Vogel and Kathryn A. Goldner, September 1982. Copyright © 1982 by Children's Television Workshop.

Marchette Chute: From "The Wonderful Winter" by Marchette Chute. Copyright © 1954 by Marchette Chute.

Cobblestone Publishing, Inc.: "A Family Coat of Arms" by Beth Schapira from *Cobblestone*, January 1983 issue: American Immigrants, Part 2. Copyright © 1983 by Cobblestone Publishing, Inc., Peterborough, NH 03458.

James Collier: From "How to Survive a Fire" by James Collier in *Boys' Life* Magazine, October 1982. Copyright © 1982 by James Collier.

Don Congdon Associates, Inc.: From "The Naming of Names" in *Thrilling Wonder Stories* by Ray Bradbury. Copyright © 1949, renewed 1977 by Ray Bradbury.

Curriculum Innovations, Inc.: Adapted from "The Buck Stops Here: Learning to Manage Money" in *Current Consumer*, January 1982. © Curriculum Innovations, Inc., Highland Park, IL.

The Borden Deal Family Trust (Borden Deal, Trustee): From "Antaeus" by Borden Deal. Copyright © 1961 by Southern Methodist University Press.

Delacorte Press: Excerpted from the book *The Lucky Stone* by Lucille Clifton. Copyright © 1979 by Lucille Clifton.

Dial Books for Young Readers, a Division of E.P. Dutton, Inc.: From *Roll of Thunder, Hear My Cry* by Mildred D. Taylor. Copyright © 1979 by Mildred D. Taylor.

Dodd, Mead & Company, Inc.: From *Chappie and Me* by John Craig. From "Midnight" from *Sam Savitt's True Horse Stories* by Sam Savitt.

Doubleday & Company, Inc.: "Haiku" from *The Pregnant Man* by Robert Phillips. Copyright © 1976 by Ernest and Cis Stefani. Originally appeared in *Thistle*.

Dove Publications: "Eye Protectors for Chickens and Improved Burial Case" from *Absolutely Mad Inventions* by A.E. Brown and H.A. Jeffcott, Jr. Copyright 1932, and © 1960 by A.E. Brown and H.A. Jeffcott, Jr.

Deanna B. Durbin: From "Dog Story" by Deanna B. Durbin, originally appeared in *Young Miss* Magazine, October 1982. Copyright 1982 by Parents Magazine.

E.P. Dutton, Inc.: From *Nigger: An Autobiography* by Dick Gregory with Robert Lipsyte. Copyright © 1964 by Dick Gregory Enterprises, Inc.

Ebony Jr!: The following selections taken from *Ebony Jr!* Magazine: "Winter Trees" by Leonard Burch, December 1981, copyright © 1981 by Johnson Publishing Company, Inc.; from "Ray Billingsley is Lookin' Fine" by Debra M. Hall, April 1982; "Life is a Dance" by Karen Odom, October 1982; from "Libraries Long Ago" by Mary Lewis, November 1982. Copyright © 1982 by Johnson Publishing Company, Inc.

Farrar, Straus and Giroux, Inc.: From *Tuck Everlasting* by Natalie Babbitt. Copyright © 1975 by Natalie Babbitt.

Raoul Lionel Felder, esq. and Sheldon Abend of N.Y.C.: "Doc Brackett" by Damon Runyon. © 1978 by Mary Runyon McCann.

Henry Ferguson: From "Is Our Capitol Haunted?" by Henry Ferguson in *Boys' Life* Magazine, July 1982.

Field Newspaper Syndicate: "Marvin" cartoon by Tom Armstrong. © 1982/1983 by Field Enterprises, Inc.

Four Winds Press, a division of Scholastic Inc.: "The Case of the Missing Garlic Bread" by Donald J. Sobol from *Encyclopedia Brown Takes the Cake!* by Donald J. Sobol with Glenn Andrews. Copyright © 1982, 1983 by Donald J. Sobol and Glenn Andrews.

Benjamin Franklin Literary & Medical Society, Inc.: The following selections taken from *Child Life* Magazine: From "The World Under Our Feet" by Renee Bartowski. Copyright © 1968 by Review Publishing Company, Indianapolis, Indiana. From "Our Mysterious Past" by M. Regina Lepore, June/July 1979. Copyright © 1979 by Benjamin Franklin Literary & Medical Society, Indianapolis, Indiana. From "Where Bats Look Like Smoke" by Aubrey B. Haines, March 1979. Copyright © 1979 by The Saturday Evening Post Company, Indianapolis, Indiana. From "A Tale of Tails" by Shirlie Burriston, March 1981; from "The Earth Moves" by Dennice DeGirolamo, February 1981. Copyright © 1981 by Benjamin Franklin Literary & Medical Society, Indianapolis, Indiana. From "Nature's Medicines" by Lois Wickstrom, July 1982; from "The Better to Hear You With, My Dear" by Carol Pado, February 1982; from "Hannah and the Redcoats" by Carolyn B. Cooney, June/July 1982; from "The Mystery of Tornadoes" by Sandra Henneberger. Copyright © 1982 by Benjamin Franklin Literary & Medical Society, Indianapolis, Indiana. The following selections taken from *Children's Digest:* From "If You Went to School in France" by Peggy Kagan, September 1981; from "The Safety Corporation" by Jane Priewe, June/July 1981; from "Cashewing" by Mary Gores, December 1981; from "Fresh if Best" by M. Regina Lepore, January 1981; from "Ben's Battle" by Carole Osborne Cole, January 1981. Copyright © 1981 by Benjamin Franklin Literary & Medical Society, Indianapolis, Indiana. From "A Field Guide to Vampires" by Paul B. Janeczko, October 1982; from "Stage Fright" by Betty Winn Fuller, September 1982; from "The ABZ's of Sleep" by Tom Slear, October 1982; from "Is Weight Lifting for You?" by Jean Barbieri, April/May 1982. Copyright © 1982 by Benjamin Franklin Literary & Medical Society, Indianapolis, Indiana. From "My Dad, the Drummer" by Joan E. Lynn in *Young World* Magazine. Copyright © 1978 by The Saturday Evening Post Company, Indianapolis, Indiana.

Girl Scouts of the U.S.A.: "The First Light" by Susan Goldsmith from *American Girl* Magazine, December 1976.

P.A. Haddock: From "Moon Madness" by Patricia Haddock from *Odyssey* Magazine, July, 1982.

Harcourt Brace Jovanovich, Inc: From *The HBJ School Dictionary*, copyright © 1977 by Harcourt Brace Jovanovich, Inc. From *English Writing and Language Skills*, Second Course, by W. Ross Winterowd and Patricia Y. Murray, © 1983 by Harcourt Brace Jovanovich, Inc. From *Your Speech*, Third Edition, by Francis Griffith, Catherine Nelson, and Edward Stasheff, © 1979 by Harcourt Brace Jovanovich, Inc. From *American Civics*, Fourth Edition, by William H. Hartley and William S. Vincent, © 1983 by Harcourt Brace Jovanovich, Inc. From *Language for Daily Use*, Grade 8 (Gold), Phoenix Edition, by Dorothy Strickland, © 1983 by Harcourt Brace Jovanovich, Inc. "The Wonders Our Eyes Can See" from *Going to the Zoo With Roger Caras* by Roger Caras. "Snow Toward Evening" from *So That It Flower* by Melville Cane. Copyright 1926 by Harcourt Brace Jovanovich, Inc.; renewed 1954 by Melville Cane. "Bee Song" from *Wind Song* by Carl Sandburg. Copyright © 1960 by Carl Sandburg.

Harper & Row, Publishers, Inc.: From pp.13-14 in *Black Boy* by Richard Wright. Copyright 1937, 1942, 1944, 1945 by Richard Wright. From pp. 183-184 in *Sea Glass* by Laurence Yep. Copyright © 1979 by Laurence Yep. From pp. 1-2 in *Child of the Owl* by Laurence Yep. Copyright © 1977 by Laurence Yep. From *Vampires* by Nancy Garden (J.B. Lippincott Co.). Copyright © 1973 by Nancy Garden. From p. 12 in *Sour Land* by William H. Armstrong. Copyright © 1971 by William H. Armstrong. "Prairie Fire" from pp. 276-283 in *Little House on the Prairie* by Laura Ingalls Wilder. Copyright 1935 by Laura Ingalls Wilder; renewed 1963 by Roger L. MacBride.

Highlights for Children, Inc.: The following selections taken from *Highlights for Children* Magazine: "How to Drill an Oil Well" by Bob Winston, October 1980; "Using Solar Energy: It's Not all That Easy!" by Jack Meyers, December 1980. Copyright © 1980 by Highlights for Children, Inc., Columbus, Ohio. From "Making a Dirt House" by Ardath Hunt, February 1981; "Dinosaur Hunting" by Robert Makela, May 1981; from "Eland: Africa's Biggest Antelope" by George Frame, February 1981; from "Competitive Badminton" by Donna Judd, April 1981; from "Bighorn Medicine Wheel" by Jay Ellis Ransom, August/September 1981. Copyright © 1981 by Highlights for Children, Inc., Columbus, Ohio. "Baseball's World Series" by Mike Klodnicki, October 1982; from "Eggs" by George Frame, October 1982. Copyright © 1982 by Highlights for Children, Inc., Columbus, Ohio.

Barbara Hunley Hill: "The Hunley Submarine" by Barbara Hunley Hill from *Boys' Life* Magazine, August 1982.

Holiday House, Inc.: From *Jimmy Yellow Hawk* by Virginia Driving Hawk Sneve. Copyright © 1972 by Virginia Driving Hawk Sneve.

Houghton Mifflin Company: From *The American Heritage Dictionary of the English Language*. Copyright © 1982 by Houghton Mifflin Company. From *Words of the Myths* by Isaac Asimov. Copyright © 1961 by Isaac Asimov. "Snow" from *The Children Sing in the Far West* by Mary Austin. Copyright 1928 by Mary Austin. Copyright renewed 1956 by Kenneth M. Chapman and Mary C. Wheelwright. "Jacob" from *The Collected Stories of Jack Schaefer*. Copyright © 1966 by Jack Schaefer. From *The Spanish Smile* by Scott O'Dell. Copyright © 1982 by Scott O'Dell. From *A Summer to Die* by Lois Lowry. Copyright © 1977 by Lois Lowry. From *Anastasia Again* by Lois Lowry. Copyright © 1981 by Lois Lowry.

Monica Hughes: From "Lights Over Loon Lake" by Monica Hughes from *Owl* Magazine, Summer 1982.

The Hutchinson Publishing Group Ltd.: From "The Fire" in *A Waltz Through the Hills* by G.M. Glaskin, published by Barrie & Jenkins. Copyright © 1961 by Barrie & Jenkins.

International Paper Company: "How to Improve Your Vocabulary" by Tony Randall.

Helen Pierce Jacob: "The Two Kings" by Helen Pierce Jacob, from *Cricket* Magazine, March 1979. Copyright © 1979 by Helen Pierce Jacob.

Hank Ketchum Enterprises, Inc.: "Dennis the Menace" cartoon (March 11, 1982). © 1982 by Field Enterprises, Inc.

Alfred A. Knopf, Inc.: "Mother to Son" from *Selected Poems of Langston Hughes*. Copyright 1926 by Alfred A. Knopf, Inc. and renewed 1954 by Langston Hughes. "In Time of Silver Rain" from *Selected Poems of Langston Hughes*. Copyright 1938 and renewed 1966 by Langston Hughes. From *Soup and Me* by Robert Newton Peck. Copyright © 1975 by Robert Newton Peck. From "Putting It On For Juanita," from *Stories from El Barrio* by Piri Thomas, edited by Fabio Coen. Copyright © 1978 by Piri Thomas.

George Laycock: From "Leave Room for the Grizzly" by George Laycock, from *Boys' Life* Magazine, January 1983.

iii

From "Equipment for a Lifetime" by George Laycock, from *Boys' Life* Magazine, May 1979. From "Mile-a-Minute Vine" by George Laycock, from *Boys' Life* Magazine, August 1982.

Shirley Lee: "The Cake Icing Caper" by Shirley Lee, from *Boys' Life* Magazine, June 1977.

Lothrop, Lee & Shepard (A Division of William Morrow & Company): Adapted from *Morning Arrow* by Nanabah Chee Dodge. Copyright © 1975 by Nanabah Chee Dodge.

Macmillan Publishing Company: "The Open Door" from *Away Goes Sally* by Elizabeth Coatsworth. Copyright 1931, 1933, 1934, 1935, 1936, 1938, 1942 by Elizabeth Coatsworth. "Forest Fire" from *Summer Green* by Elizabeth Coatsworth. Copyright 1948 by Macmillan Publishing Company, renewed 1976 by Elizabeth Coatsworth Beston.

Zoltan Malocsay: From "Shark" by Zoltan Malocsay in *Boys' Life* Magazine, May 1976 and from "Down the Drain" by Zoltan Malocsay in *Boys' Life* Magazine, March 1976. Copyright © 1976 by Zoltan Malocsay.

Scott Meredith Literary Agency, 845 Third Avenue, New York, New York 10022 and Arthur C. Clarke: From *Summertime on Icarus* by Arthur C. Clarke. Copyright © 1960 by The Condé Nast Publications, Inc.

Eve Merriam: "Onomatopoeia" from *It Doesn't Always Have to Rhyme* by Eve Merriam. Copyright © 1964 by Eve Merriam. Published by Atheneum.

Julian Messner, a Simon & Schuster division of Gulf & Western Corporation: "Frisbee Beginnings" from *Frisbee Fun* by Margaret Poynter. Copyright © 1977 by Margaret Poynter. From *How Old Stormalong Captured Mocha Dick* by Irwin Shapiro. Copyright © 1942, 1969 by Irwin Shapiro.

Modern Curriculum Press: "A Modern Dragon" from *Songs From Around a Toadstool Table* by Rowena Bastin Bennett. Copyright © 1967 by Rowena Bastin Bennett.

William Morrow & Company: "About Motion Pictures" in *St. Ann's Gut* by Ann Darr. Copyright © 1968, 1971 by Ann Darr.

National Galleries of Scotland, The Mound, Edinburgh: On p. 96, picture *The Reverend Robert Walker Skating on Duddingston Loch* by Sir Henry Raeburn.

National Shooting Sports Foundation, Inc.: "What the Outdoors Means to Me" by Ron Guidry from *Boys' Life* Magazine, September 1982.

National Wildlife Federation: The following selections taken from *Ranger Rick's Nature Magazine*: From "King and the Copperhead" by Betty N. Meisner, September 1981. Copyright © 1981 by National Wildlife Federation. From "The Case of the Fallen Eagle" by Bet Hennefrund, January 1982; "The Day I Forgot Crocodiles" by Beverly McLoughland, April 1982; "Jed and the Gray Jay" by Robert H. Redding, April 1982. Copyright © 1982 by National Wildlife Federation. "March of the Army Ants" by Julia Fellows, November 1979. Copyright © 1979 by National Wildlife Federation.

The Aaron M. Priest Literary Agency, Inc.: From "Who Is I. Dunno?" from *If Life Is a Bowl of Cherries, What Am I Doing in the Pits?* by Erma Bombeck. Copyright © 1978 by Erma Bombeck. From "Living Cheap" from *Aunt Erma's Cope Book* by Erma Bombeck. Copyright © 1979 by Erma Bombeck. Published by McGraw-Hill.

Read Magazine: "Foul Shot" by Edwin Hoey from *Read* Magazine. Copyright © 1982 by Xerox Corp. "Dr. Heidegger's Experiment" by Steven Otfinoski from *Read* Magazine. Copyright © 1975 by Xerox Corp.

The Register and Tribune Syndicate, Inc.: "The Family Circus" cartoon by Bil Keane.

Deborah Rogers Ltd.: "The Day It Rained Cats and Dogs" by Linda Allen from *Cricket* Magazine, April 1978. Copyright © 1978 by Linda Allen.

Saturday Review: On p. 258, cartoon from *The Saturday Review* Magazine, September 1976. Copyright © 1976 by Saturday Review Magazine Co.

Scholastic Inc.: From *UFO Encounters* by Rita Gelman and Marcia Seligson. Copyright © 1978 by S & R Gelman Associates, Inc. and Marcia Seligson.

Anne E. Schraff: "What a Great Report Needs: People" by Anne E. Schraff from *Young Miss* Magazine, January 1981.

Charles Scribner's Sons/Sierra Club Books: "How to Make a Rush Mat" and another excerpt from *The Long Ago Lake* by Marne Wilkins. Copyright 1978 by Marne Wilkins.

Simon & Schuster, a Division of Gulf & Western Corporation: From *Listening to America* by Stuart Berg Flexner. Copyright © 1982 by Stuart Berg Flexner. From *Lame Deer: Seeker of Visions* by John Fire/Lame Deer and Richard Erdoes. Copyright © 1972 by John Fire/Lame Deer and Richard Erdoes.

Triangle Communications: From "Are You a Bore?" by Sharon Carter from *Seventeen* Magazine, May 1979. Copyright © 1979 by Triangle Communications, Inc.

Tribune Company Syndicate, Inc.: "Kudzu" cartoon by Marlette.

Universal Press Syndicate: "For Better or For Worse" cartoon by Lynn. Copyright © 1983 by Universal Press Syndicate. All rights reserved.

Vanguard Press, Inc.: From *Meet the Austins* by Madeline L'Engle. Copyright © 1961 by Madeleine L'Engle.

Waldman Publishing Corp.: From "Weird and Wonderful Hobbies" in *Know Power* by Steven Otfinoski. Copyright © 1981.

Franklin Watts, Inc.: "A Lifeboat in Space" and from "How You Can Survive" from *True Escape and Survival Stories* by Gurney Williams, III. Copyright © 1977 by Gurney Williams, III. From "Bad-tempered—But Useful" from *The Real Book About Amazing Animals* by Alec Dickinson. From "A Bird That Cannot Fly" from *The Real Book About Amazing Birds* by Eve Merriam.

Western Publishing Company, Inc.: "Colt in the Pasture" by Elizabeth Coatsworth. Copyright 1943 by Story Parade, Inc. Copyright renewed 1971.

The Westminster Press, Philadelphia, PA.: From *Who Do You Think You Are? Digging for Family Roots* by Suzanne Hilton. Copyright © 1976.

Young Miss: From "The Big Change" by Janey Montgomery from *Young Miss* Magazine. Copyright © 1975 by Parents Magazine Enterprises, a division of Gruner & Jahr, U.S.A., Inc.

COVER: © Joan Hadden, Photo Researchers, Inc.

Photo Credits: Page 42, a. Culver Pictures, b. H. Armstrong Roberts; 45, a. and b. H. Armstrong Roberts; 159, UPI; 221, a. © Florence Harrison—Taurus, b. © Walter Chandoha, c. © Engelhard—Monkmeyer, d. © Walter Chandoha

We wish to thank the following critical readers who helped to evaluate materials for this book.

Charles Bier
Bullhead City Schools
Mohave County, Arizona

Marilyn Brown
Wilson Junior High School
Cedar Rapids, Iowa

James Mills
Cleveland Public Schools
Cleveland, Ohio

Contents

Chapter 1. Sentence Meaning

LESSONS

Gr. p.211   **1**   Using Punctuation Marks As Clues to Meaning   1
Gr. p.211   **2**   Using Punctuation Marks To Read Sentences in Poetry   3
Gr. p.211   **3**   Using Quotation Marks   5
Gr. p.215-222   **4**   Finding Core Parts   8
Gr. p.227-9   **5**   Understanding Compound Subjects and Compound Verbs   10
  6   Understanding Word Order   13
  7   Reading Sentences with Interrupters   17
  8   Understanding Pronoun Reference   21
  9   Practice   23

Chapter 2. Relationships

1   Understanding Spatial Order   27
2   Understanding Time Order   29
3   Understanding Listing   33
4   Identifying Words That Signal Cause and Effect   35
5   Understanding Cause and Effect   37
6   Identifying Words That Signal Contrast   42
7   Understanding Comparison and Contrast   45
8   Identifying Relationship Patterns   48
9   Practice   51

Chapter 3. Judgments

1   Identifying a Reliable Source   57
2   Recognizing Statements of Fact and Statements of Opinion   60
3   Understanding Mixed Statements of Fact and Opinion   63
4   Forming Valid Opinions   66
5   Recognizing Stereotypes   68
6   Identifying Unsupported Judgments   69
7   Identifying Loaded Words   73
8   Identifying Faulty Reasoning   75
9   Practice   78

Chapter 4. Inferences

1. Making Inferences Based on Evidence   81
2. Making Inferences About Characters   83
3. Making Inferences About Motives   86
4. Making Inferences About Past and Present Events   90
5. Making Inferences About Future Events   92
6. Making Inferences About Time   95
7. Making Inferences About Place   99
8. Making Inferences About Realistic and Fantastic Details   102
9. Making Inferences About Tone   105
10. Practice   108

Chapter 5. Main Idea

1. Identifying Topics   113
2. Distinguishing Between the Topic and the Main Idea   115
3. Finding the Topic Sentence of a Paragraph   118
4. Finding Supporting Details When the Main Idea Is Stated   120
5. Paraphrasing   122
6. Finding the Implied Main Idea   124
7. Stating the Implied Main Idea   127
8. Identifying Supporting Details When the Main Idea Is Implied   129
9. Ordering the Importance of Ideas   131
10. Finding the Main Idea in Dialogue   134
11. Practice   139

Chapter 6. Dictionary

1. Using Guide Words   143
2. Understanding an Entry   145
3. Using a Pronunciation Key   148
4. Finding Principal Parts in a Dictionary   150
5. Using a Dictionary to Find Parts of Speech   152
6. Dividing Words into Syllables   154
7. Finding the Correct Meaning   156
8. Finding Homophones   159
9. Finding Derivatives in the Dictionary   161
10. Finding the Correct Spelling of a Word   164
11. Practice   166

Chapter 7. Context

1. Understanding Context   169
2. Finding the Meaning That Fits the Context   171
3. Understanding Direct Context Clues   174
4. Understanding Indirect Context Clues   178
5. Understanding Words Used as Nouns and Verbs   180
6. Using Context To Choose the Correct Synonym   183 *(Gr. p.10)*
7. Understanding Dialect   185
8. Using Context To Understand Jargon   188
9. Practice   190

Chapter 8. Structure

1. Identifying Root Words   193
2. Understanding Prefixes That Show Number   195
3. Understanding Prefixes That Show Position   198
4. Understanding Negative Prefixes   200
5. Understanding Comparative and Superlative Suffixes   202
6. More About Using Suffixes To Determine Meaning   203
7. Understanding Latin Roots   206
8. Understanding Greek Roots   208
9. Understanding Compound Words   210
10. Understanding Contractions   212
11. Practice   217

Chapter 9. Word Origins

1. Understanding Words Based on Place Names   221
2. Understanding Words Based on People   223
3. Understanding That Words Have Changed in Meaning   225
4. Understanding Words from the American Indians   227
5. Understanding Words from Foreign Languages   228
6. Practice   232

Chapter 10. Figurative Language

1. Identifying Figurative and Literal Language   243
2. Understanding Figurative Expressions   248
3. Understanding Similes   252
4. Interpreting Similes in Poetry   255
5. Understanding Metaphors   257
6. Interpreting Figurative Language   260
7. Practice   263

Chapter 11. Imagery

1. Recognizing Sensory Language   269
2. Understanding Image-Making Words   272
3. Understanding Words That Stand for Sounds   274
4. Understanding Vivid Verbs   276
5. Visualizing a Setting   278
6. Understanding Connotation and Denotation   281
7. Finding Imagery in Poetry   283
8. Practice   285

Chapter 12. Flexibility and Study Skills

1. Setting a Purpose for Reading   289
2. Adjusting Rate to Purpose   292
3. Scanning   292
4. Skimming   295
5. Reading Intensively   298
6. Following Directions   300
7. Outlining   302
8. Understanding the Parts of a Book   304
9. Using Reference Books   307
10. Reading Graphs   308
11. Reading Time Lines   309
12. Practice   310

Name _____

Chapter 1
Sentence Meaning

A sentence is a group of words expressing a complete thought. A sentence may be a statement, a question, or an order. In this chapter you will learn to understand the meaning of sentences that you read.

Lesson 1
Using Punctuation Marks As Clues to Meaning

Punctuation marks help you read sentences. They tell you when to pause and when to stop. Three punctuation marks tell you to come to a full stop, since a sentence is ending. These are the period (**.**), the question mark (**?**), and the exclamation mark (**!**). For example:

   Many people collect unusual items**.**
   Do you know anyone who collects comic books**?**
   It's a great discovery**!**

The period ends a sentence that is a statement. The question mark ends a sentence that asks a question. The exclamation mark ends a sentence that shows strong emotion or feeling. It also ends a sentence that gives a command. For example:

   Don't touch it**!**

The comma separates parts of the sentence. It tells you to take a brief pause before reading the rest of the sentence. For example:

   Anne Marie, Billy Joe, and Karen collect comic books.
   Anne, Marie, Billy, Joe, and Karen collect comic books.

In the first sentence the commas tell you there are three people collecting comic books. In the second sentence the commas tell you there are five people collecting comic books.

In the next sentence, the comma tells you to pause after the word *matchbooks*.

   Since we decided to collect restaurant matchbooks**,** we made a list of restaurants in our city.

A dash and a colon also tell you to take a brief pause before reading the rest of the sentence. Sometimes a dash indicates a break

Copyright © 1984 by Harcourt Brace Jovanovich, Inc. All rights reserved

in thought. Sometimes both the dash and the colon indicate a list follows. For example:

> She had matchbooks from many restaurants in her collection—O'Leary's, The Great Panda, Upjohn House, McGill's, Seasons, and The Maxwell House.
> He bought the following comic books: *Superman, Wonderwoman, The Hulk,* and *Spiderman.*

A semicolon (;) separates two complete ideas that are closely related. It tells you to take a longer pause than you would for a comma, a dash, or a colon. For example:

> He sold the comic book for five dollars; he sold the matchbook for twenty dollars.

Exercise. Read the following paragraphs from "Weird and Wonderful Hobbies" by Steven Otfinoski. Answer the questions that follow each paragraph. Write your answers in the blanks at the right.

(1) Don't throw away that comic book! Don't toss out that old soda bottle! Don't even crumple up that gum wrapper! Why? Because one day some of these items might become valuable—valuable, at least, to someone who collects comic books, soda bottles, or gum wrappers.

a. How many sentences are in paragraph 1?   *5*

b. How many sentences express a command?   *3*

c. Which sentence asks a question? (Write *first, second, third,* etc.)   *fourth*

d. The last sentence uses two different punctuation marks to tell you to take a brief pause before reading the rest of the sentence. What are these two marks?   *dash and comma*

(2) Collecting has become a mania in America today. People collect everything and anything, and they're having fun doing it.

e. How many sentences are in paragraph 2?   *2*

(3) The world's first serious collectors were the Egyptians, who collected and sealed into the tombs of their dead kings examples of everything produced by their culture. Later, in the Middle Ages, collectors believed they were actually preserving their civilization by keeping the multitude of things people had made: tapestries, books, and handcrafted implements of silver and gold. In more recent years, people have come to believe that even the more disposable products of our culture are of value and well worth saving.

f. The second sentence in paragraph 3 contains a punctuation mark that signals a list follows. What is this punctuation mark?   *colon*

Name _____

(4)   If you're going to start collecting something, there are a few things you ought to think about first. You should be selective in what you collect and try to zero in on just one specific area of interest. For example, bottle collecting is a popular hobby. But if you tried to collect every bottle you came across, pretty soon you'd have a houseful of glass! You should choose one special kind of bottle to collect, such as ink bottles, milk bottles, soda bottles, or patent medicine bottles.

g. The last sentence in paragraph 4 gives examples of special kinds of bottles to collect. How many special kinds does it mention?   __4__

(5)   Next, you should learn everything you can about your hobby, so that you don't waste time or money collecting worthless items or forgeries. For instance, if you collect old postcards, you ought to know that of the millions issued before 1914, only about 5% are worth anything more than the paper they're printed on.

h. How many times should you pause briefly while reading the first sentence in paragraph 5?   __2__

(6)   Finally, don't let money be your main reason for collecting; collecting should be fun and educational, just like any other hobby. However, there *is* a possibility that the longer you hold on to what you've collected, the more it's going to be worth. Just think—if you were around in the 1930s, when the first *Action Comics* comic book came out with the very first Superman story, you would have paid 10 cents for a copy. Today, because this edition is so rare, it is worth around $2,000! But before you start turning your attic or basement upside down, you should know that only nine copies of that comic book are known to exist today!

i. Which sentence in paragraph 6 contains a punctuation mark that separates two closely related ideas? (Write *first, second, third,* etc.)   *first*

j. Which sentence contains a punctuation mark that indicates a break in thought? (Write *first, second, third,* etc.)   *third*

Lesson 2

Using Punctuation Marks to Read Sentences in Poetry

Punctuation marks help you to read poems with expression. They tell you when to pause, to stop, and to change the pitch of your voice.

Copyright © 1984 by Harcourt Brace Jovanovich, Inc. All rights reserved

Commas (,) and dashes (—) tell you to take a brief pause. Semicolons (;) tell you to take a slightly longer pause. Periods (.), question marks (?), and exclamation marks (!) tell you to stop. A question mark also tells you to raise the pitch of your voice. An exclamation mark tells you to say something with emphasis.

When you read poetry, it is important to pay attention to punctuation marks. The end of a line does not always signal the end of a sentence. You have to look for the period to find where the sentence ends. For example, the poem below is "Snow" by Mary Austin. It has eight lines, but it has only three sentences.

> I come more softly than a bird,
> And lovely as a flower;
> I sometimes last from year to year
> And sometimes but an hour.
>
> 5 I stop the swiftest railroad train
> Or break the stoutest tree.
> And yet I am afraid of fire
> And children play with me.

Exercise. The poem below is "The Day I Forgot Crocodiles" by Beverly McLoughland. Read this poem. Then answer the questions that follow each stanza. Write your answers in the blanks below.

> Usually after I've been to the zoo,
> The animals I remember most
> Are lions, tigers, and kangaroos,
> Grizzlies, elephants,
> 5 And chimpanzees,
> Giraffes and pygmy hippos.
> But I especially remember—
> The scaly, creeping,
> Fierce-jawed, dragon-eyed,
> 10 Slyly-grinning crocodiles!

a. How many sentences does the first stanza contain?   _2_

b. You should take a brief pause at the end of how many lines?   _7_

c. Which line should you say with emphasis?   _l. 10_

> The last time I went to the zoo
> Was different.
> Behind a window,
> Curled up in a corner
> 15 Against the glass I saw—
> A soft-brown, furry-bodied,
> Ordinary mouse.
> Lying beside her in the straw
> Were three wiggly-new mouse babies;
> 20 Pink and hairless, and small enough
> To fit into a spoon.

Name _____

<pre>
        No heavier than a lump of sugar,
        Little squirmy suggestions of life,
        Looking as if they'd been born too soon,
     25 More like smooth, pink erasers than mice;
        Blind and deaf to the world around them,
        Sleep and suck were all they knew.
</pre>

d. How many sentences does stanza 2 contain? _____4_____

e. You should take a brief pause at the end of how many lines? _____7_____

f. You should take a slightly longer pause at the end of how many lines? _____2_____

<pre>
        I pressed my nose against the glass
        To watch the little mouse family;
     30 I forgot lions, tigers, and kangaroos,
        Grizzlies, elephants,
        And chimpanzees,
        Giraffes and pygmy hippos.
        And I even forgot—
     35 The scaly, creeping,
        Fierce-jawed, dragon-eyed,
        Slyly-grinning crocodiles!
</pre>

g. How many sentences does stanza 3 contain? _____2_____

h. You should take a brief pause at the end of how many lines? _____6_____

i. You should take a slightly longer pause at the end of how many lines? _____1_____

j. Which line should you read with emphasis? _____*l.* 37_____

Lesson 3

Using Quotation Marks

Opening (") and closing (") quotation marks set off the exact words a character says from the rest of the story. For example, notice the quotation marks around Jessie's exact words in the following:

> Jessie turned to her cousin Howard and said, "I'll show you where two bald eagles are roosting."

Jessie's exact words are:

> "I'll show you where two bald eagles are roosting."

In the following paragraph from "The Case of the Fallen Eagle" by Bet Hennefrund, Jessie and Howard find a wounded bald eagle.

Copyright © 1984 by Harcourt Brace Jovanovich, Inc. All rights reserved

"Stop!" said Jessie, grabbing Howard's arm. "It's too dangerous to get near it. If it gets its talons in us, we'll be in trouble. I'll get Mom and Dad, Howard. You wait here." She looked at her wide-eyed cousin. "Don't worry. Just stand here till I get back." She hurried to the woodpile where Sherlock was excitedly sniffing and scratching. "Come on, Sherlock," she said, and together they raced away through the woods.

First Jessie says, "Stop!" Then her exact words are: "It's too dangerous to get near it. If it gets its talons in us, we'll be in trouble. I'll get Mom and Dad, Howard. You wait here." After Jessie looks at her cousin, her exact words are: "Don't worry. Just stand here till I get back." Finally, she says to her dog, Sherlock: "Come on, Sherlock."

Exercise 1. Read the following paragraphs from "The Case of the Fallen Eagle" by Bet Hennefrund. For each paragraph, underline the exact words of the speaker. Then write the name of the speaker in the blank at the right.

Speaker

a. As they passed behind the Morgans' farmhouse, Ray charged out the door again. "What's going on?" he demanded loudly.
a. **Ray**

b. "One of the eagles has been hurt," Mr. Dobbs said. "We're taking it up to our barn. Doc Ames should be there by now. He can look the bird over and see if he can help it."
b. **Mr. Dobbs**

c. On the workbench in the barn, Dr. Ames checked the bird carefully. Finally he looked up. "It's been shot," he said. "Looks like a wound from a .22 bullet."
c. **Dr. Ames**

d. "Shot!" Jessie gasped. "But . . . but . . . why would anyone shoot a bald eagle?"
d. **Jessie**

e. Jessie's mom looked really mad. "I don't know, but you can be sure I'll find out! Whoever shot it broke the law!"
e. **Jessie's mom**

f. Howard stared at the eagle. "I sure hope it doesn't die!" he said, gulping.
f. **Howard**

g. Mr. Dobbs took hold of Howard's shoulders and pulled him away. "You look kind of shaky, Howard," he said. "I guess you haven't seen much of this sort of thing."
g. **Mr. Dobbs**

h. Just then Ray Morgan burst into the barn. He was out of breath. He stood for a moment looking at the bird on the bench. "Will it die?" he asked a little gruffly.
h. **Ray**

i. "Don't know yet, Ray," Dr. Ames said. "But if it does die, The National Wildlife Federation will offer a reward of $500 for any information that might lead to the arrest of the person who shot this bird. Right, Lila?"
i. **Dr. Ames**

j. Jessie's mom nodded. "Right," she said.
j. **Jessie's mom**

Name _____

Exercise 2. Sometimes the speaker's exact words are quoted, or given, but the speaker is not identified. You can identify the speaker by noting the order in which the characters speak. In the paragraphs below, from *Black Boy* by Richard Wright, a boy is talking with his mother. For each paragraph, underline the exact words of the speaker. Write the name of the speaker in the blank to the right of each paragraph. If the paragraph contains no quoted words, write *No* in the blank. (The first two paragraphs are done for you.)

			Speaker
1.	"<u>Mama, I'm hungry,</u>" I complained one afternoon.	1.	*Son*
2.	"<u>Jump up and catch a kungry,</u>" she said, trying to make me laugh and forget.	2.	*Mama*
a.	"What's a kungry?"	a.	*Son*
b.	"It's what little boys eat when they get hungry," she said.	b.	*Mama*
c.	"What does it taste like?"	c.	*Son*
d.	"I don't know."	d.	*Mama*
e.	"Then why do you tell me to catch one?"	e.	*Son*
f.	"Because you said that you were hungry," she said, smiling.	f.	*Mama*
g.	I sensed that she was teasing me and it made me angry.	g.	*No*
h.	"But I'm hungry. I want to eat."	h.	*Son*
i.	"You'll have to wait."	i.	*Mama*
j.	"But I want to eat now."	j.	*Son*
k.	"But there's nothing to eat," she told me.	k.	*Mama*
l.	"Why?"	l.	*Son*
m.	"Just because there's none," she explained.	m.	*Mama*
n.	"But I want to eat," I said, beginning to cry.	n.	*Son*
o.	"You'll just have to wait," she said again.	o.	*Mama*
p.	"But why?"	p.	*Son*
q.	"For God to send some food."	q.	*Mama*
r.	"When is He going to send it?"	r.	*Son*
s.	"I don't know."	s.	*Mama*
t.	"But I'm hungry!"	t.	*Son*

Lesson 4
Finding Core Parts

The core parts of the sentence contain the basic message. The other parts of the sentence give additional information about the core parts. Most sentences have at least two core parts. One part, the simple subject, answers the question "Who?" or "What?" The second part, the simple predicate, or verb, answers the question "Did what?" or "Does what?" For example, notice the two core parts in the following sentences. The simple subject is underlined once. The simple predicate is underlined twice.

Carol bicycles.

After school Carol bicycles.

After school Carol bicycles home.

After school fourteen-year-old Carol bicycles home.

Chris Pederson jogs.

In the morning Chris Pederson jogs.

In the morning Chris Pederson jogs ten miles.

In the morning Chris Pederson jogs ten miles around the park.

In some sentences the simple predicate is made up of a verb plus one or more helping verbs. For example:

Anita was skating in the park.

Mark had skated in the park yesterday.

Mark will be skating in the park tomorrow.

Some common helping verbs are:

am	have	shall	can	do
is	has	will	could	does
are	had		should	did
was			would	
were				
being				
been				

Some sentences have a third core part that completes the meaning of the predicate. For example, in the following sentences, the subject is underlined once, the predicate twice, and the word that completes the meaning of the predicate three times.

Michael was playing softball in the yard.

Elaine invited her friends to the softball game.

Name _____

Exercise 1. Read each sentence below. Underline the simple subject once and the simple predicate twice.

a. The best <u>players</u> <u><u>compete</u></u> at Wimbledon.

b. Each day many <u>games</u> <u><u>begin</u></u> at the same time.

c. The important tennis <u>stars</u> <u><u>play</u></u> in the center court.

d. Fifteen-year-old <u>Andrea Jaeger</u> <u><u>played</u></u> on Wimbledon's center court.

e. After the match, <u>she</u> <u><u>qualified</u></u> for the quarterfinals.

Exercise 2. Read each sentence below. For each sentence, underline the simple subject once, the simple predicate twice, and the word that completes the simple predicate three times.

a. A happy <u>crew</u> <u><u>sails</u></u> the <u><u><u>boat</u></u></u> on the Hudson River.

b. The <u>crew</u> <u><u>teaches</u></u> the <u><u><u>people</u></u></u> aboard about the river.

c. The big oval <u>cockpit</u> <u><u>seats</u></u> fifteen to twenty <u><u><u>guests</u></u></u>.

d. Six <u>sailors</u> <u><u>handle</u></u> all <u><u><u>lines</u></u></u>.

e. The <u>crew</u> <u><u>rows</u></u> the <u><u><u>sloop</u></u></u> to port.

Exercise 3. In each sentence below, the simple predicate is made up of a verb plus one or more helping verbs. Read each sentence. Then write the predicate in the blank at the right.

	Predicate
a. Some swimmers were wearing snorkling equipment.	*were wearing*
b. One snorkler was looking at a fish below him in the water.	*was looking*
c. The fish had been frightened by a larger fish.	*had been frightened*
d. Now it was swimming very quickly.	*was swimming*
e. Louis had asked his parents for snorkling equipment.	*had asked*
f. With a snorkle, he could breathe with his face underwater.	*could breathe*
g. With fins, he could move quickly through the water.	*could move*
h. With a mask, he could see underwater.	*could see*
i. Today his parents were shopping for the equipment.	*were shopping*
j. At dinner tonight they will give their present to Louis.	*will give*

Lesson 5

Understanding Compound Subjects and Compound Verbs

The subject of a sentence answers the question "Who?" or "What?" A **compound subject is made up of two or more subjects.** These subjects have the same verb. Often these subjects are joined by the word *and*. In each example below, the subjects are underlined once and the verb twice.

Felicia Kerns and Cathy Robertson flew their Frisbees in the park.

Felicia's poodle and Cathy's hound chased the disc.

The two girls and their friends have played in Frisbee competitions.

The predicate, or verb, of a sentence answers the question "Does what?" or "Did what?" or is a form of the word *to be*. A **compound verb is made up of two or more verbs.** These verbs have the same subject. In each example below, the subject is underlined once and the verbs twice.

The disc hovered for a moment and then dropped to the ground.

Felicia's dog ran after the disc, caught it in its mouth, and returned the disc to her.

Not once did the dog bark or drop the disc.

Exercise 1. Read the following selection, "Frisbee Beginnings" by Margaret Poynter. Then follow the directions at the end of the selection.

Darting, sailing, hovering, floating—the sky is filled with flying saucers of blue, red, yellow, green, white. But they aren't *UFO*'s. They're very Familiar Flying Objects indeed. They're Frisbees!

Where did frisbees come from? To go back to the beginning, we'll have to start with Fred Morrison. He was visiting in Bridgeport, Connecticut, one day in 1948. Passing the Frisbie Pie Company, he slowed down to watch two truck drivers throwing empty pie pans back and forth in the parking lot.

Fred remembered his childhood in Utah. He and his friends used to throw pie pans—and paint-can lids, and cookie-tin lids.

As he watched, a wind sprang up. The pie pans wobbled and fell to the ground. They were not heavy enough to stay in flight for long.

Fred continued on his way, his inventive mind working on an idea.

When he returned to his home in Los Angeles, Fred went to work. He wanted to make something round and flat, something that would fly through the air even on windy days. He attached a steel ring to the inside rim of a pie pan. This added extra weight.

Fred practiced throwing the pan at a tree trunk. The weight gave the pan enough stability, or steadiness, to sail straight to a target. There was one problem. His invention was heavy enough to fly to the target all right. It was also heavy enough to give someone a good hard knock on the head.

What material would be heavy enough to fly through the air, yet be light enough not to clobber someone who happened to get in the way?

The answer was not long in coming. Plastics were just beginning to be widely used in the late 1940s. Fred studied and read and tested. He found that a simple plastic circle didn't work.

Fred worked out the design—a disc, round and flat on the bottom, but with a sloped top. Then he curved the rim under and put small rounded projections on the top of the disc. Finally he had a toy that would fly and that would not harm people who wandered into its flight path. He used a plastic which was soft and resilient, or "bouncy." The disc made with this plastic held up under everything Fred did to it.

He named the disc "Morrison's Flyin' Saucer." Now he had to try to sell it! He tried to think of a "gimmick" to catch people's attention.

He came up with a good one. Fred and a friend went to the County Fair in Pomona, near Los Angeles. They each had a carton of the Flyin' Saucers. They also had something else—bundles of "invisible wire"! Of course, there wasn't any wire. The boxes were empty.

"Make way! Make way for the invisible wire!" Fred called as he made his way through the crowd.

"Invisible wire." "What is he talking about?" "Is he crazy?" Fred heard the people murmuring to each other as he set up two posts several yards apart. He looked very serious as he strung his "wire" between the posts.

The audience quieted down as Fred stood at one post and his friend stood at the other.

"Now I shall throw my flyin' saucer along the length of the wire right into my partner's hand," Fred announced.

Sure enough, the saucer sailed straight as an arrow to his friend's outstretched hand. Over and over again Fred threw the saucer. Not once did it wobble or fall to the ground.

"It sure looks as if that disc is attached to something," said a man. "How much is that wire?"

"One cent a foot," answered Fred. "And I'll give you my Flyin' Saucer free with every hundred feet of wire that you buy."

Every day of the Fair, Fred and his partner did a lot of "invisible wire" business!

After the County Fair closed, Fred decided to improve the design of his Flyin' Saucer. He had noticed that it sailed well when twirled in one direction, but did not work as well in the reverse direction. The projections on the top caused the problem. Off came the projections and Fred had a new toy—the Pluto Platter.

One day Fred was demonstrating his toy in Los Angeles. Rich Knerr and "Spud" Melin from the Wham-O Company were watching. They liked what they saw and asked Fred to come out to their factory in San Gabriel, California, to talk about manufacturing more Pluto Platters. Within two years Pluto Platters were being sold in many parts of the United States.

On a visit to Harvard University in Cambridge, Massachusetts, Rich Knerr was pleased to see some students throwing Pluto Platters. They told him how they used to throw Frisbie Company pie tins. In fact, "Frisbie-ing" was what they were calling their Pluto Platter games.

Rich remembered Fred Morrison telling him about the Frisbie Pie Company. When he returned to San Gabriel, he talked to Fred and the people at Wham-O. Everyone agreed that it was a great name for their flying disc—but changed the spelling to "Frisbee."

And Frisbee it has been since. Many models have been developed, including a Moonlighter Frisbee which glows in the dark, and a Professional Model.

Frisbee's popularity grew rapidly. Exhibitions by experts, tournaments, and the International Frisbee Association (IFA) helped make it the exciting sport it is today.

Now the Frisbee is soaring outside the borders of the United States. Russian cosmonauts and Chinese Ping-Pong champions have played catch with the Frisbee. Peace Corps members have taught people in South America and Africa how to play Frisbee. Two United States college students went to the People's Republic of China with their Frisbees, delighting audiences there. And astronauts tossed a plastic disc around on the moon!

Frisbee is played by 30,000,000 people in twenty-eight different countries. And you may be one of them.

Maybe you will spend a lot of time playing Frisbee by yourself. Target practice is always a good way to pass the time. Or how about forming a Frisbee team? A little competition can make a game exciting. Or what about the Rose Bowl World Frisbee Championships? Would you like to play Frisbee with 20,000 people cheering you on?

Play Frisbee any way you want. Fun and good exercise are in your hands!

Name _____

Directions. Each sentence below has a compound subject. Draw one line under the words that make up the compound subject. Draw two lines under the verb.

a. "Fred and a friend went to the County Fair in Pomona, near Los Angeles."

b. "Every day of the Fair, Fred and his partner did a lot of 'invisible wire' business!"

c. "Rich Knerr and 'Spud' Melin from the Wham-O Company were watching."

d. "Russian cosmonauts and Chinese Ping-Pong champions have played catch with the Frisbee."

e. "Fun and good exercise are in your hands."

Exercise 2. Each sentence below has a compound verb. For each sentence, draw one line under the subject. Draw two lines under the words that make up the compound verb.

a. Fred Morrison invented Frisbees and sold the flying discs at county fairs.

b. "The pie pans wobbled and fell to the ground."

c. "Fred studied and read and tested."

d. "Then he curved the rim under and put small rounded projections on the top of the disc."

e. "Not once did it wobble or fall to the ground."

Lesson 6
Understanding Word Order

Word order is the order of words within a sentence. Many sentences begin with the subject. For example, the two sentences below are from "Shark!" by Zoltan Malocsay. The subject of each sentence is underlined.

The shark turned toward him and didn't even pause. He just banked like an airplane turning and came right on, attacking!

Sometimes a group of words appears before the subject. For example, read the next sentence from "Shark!"

Copyright © 1984 by Harcourt Brace Jovanovich, Inc. All rights reserved

Biting down on the snorkel, Bert recoiled* with a shudder and clenched his fist hard around that dull chisel they call an abalone iron.

Here is a useful strategy for reading a sentence with a group of words before the subject. First locate the subject. Then take out the group of words that appears before the subject. For example:

Bert recoiled with a shudder and clenched his fist hard around that dull chisel they call an abalone iron.

Once you are sure you understand the meaning of this sentence, look again at the group of words that appeared before the subject. Ask yourself what additional information this group of words gives you about the subject or verb. For example, the words "biting down on the snorkel" tell you what Bert was doing when he recoiled with a shudder.

Exercise. Continue reading the excerpt below from "Shark!" by Zoltan Malocsay. Then follow the directions at the end.

All he could do was bluff. Thrusting forward the useless iron, Bert aimed it as if it were some kind of nuclear warhead. With his whole body he tried to communicate one idea: *I'm not your dinner, buddy! I'm another hunter just like you and I like the taste of shark!*

Suddenly the shark stopped just a couple of feet away. Bert growled into the snorkel, and he flicked the iron forward.

The shark flinched, wondering now; he moved to the side, giving himself more room and then more. Eyes locked with him, Bert finned slowly.

Five minutes to shore. Slowly, slowly, he finned as gracefully as he could, trying not to make any irregular vibrations. Struggling fish make such vibrations and they act like a dinner bell for sharks.

Lisa was only a few yards away with the inner-tube net they had rigged to float back the abalone. She had been watching it all, and now the shark moved out of sight.

Bert grabbed the inner tube and lifted his face out of the water just long enough to lunge for the spear gun they had fixed to the float with rubber bands. When he did, he heard her gasp past her snorkel, "That won't work!"

Of course it won't, he thought, not daring to keep his face out of water long enough to talk about it. It was a three-rubber gun and pretty powerful, but nothing like he'd want for shark killing. Sticking a shark with something like that would only make him mad, and he didn't want that shark mad. But he did want to have something meaner looking to hold in his hands. He ripped down the gun and stretched the rubbers, notching them into the shaft. *One, two, three, ready.*

---

*recoiled (rĭ-koil'd) v.: Shrunk back in fear.

They abandoned the float and started for the beach. It was hard to swim slowly with his heart pounding at a gallop, but he knew it might be dangerous to hurry. People just can't swim fast in the water. The harder a person tries, the more helpless he looks to a shark. Lisa did a quiet breaststroke ahead of him—no splashing—and Bert followed with the gun.

Then, up ahead, he saw Lisa stare into the distance to her right. Finning closer, he saw the shark again, lurking almost out of view. Bert held the gun aimed at him as they finned wide. The surf lay just ahead and soon Lisa disappeared into the swirling sand kicked up by the waves.

Bert hung back in the clear water just a second to see if the shark was following. He was breathing hard, too excited and downright scared to feel tired, but then his left leg told him how exhausted he really was. The cramp hit like an arrow. The muscle of his calf seemed to split in two and pull apart. *Oh, no!* he groaned. *Not now!*

Shoving the spear gun under his arm, he freed both hands to rub at the cramp. His abalone iron fluttered to the sand below, and he rode the swells up and down at the edge of the surf, rubbing and hoping. *Relax, relax,* he told the leg. *If that shark comes along now . . .*

And then the shark did come along and Bert let go of the leg. Taking up his gun, he tried to swallow the pain and pretend that nothing was wrong.

The act didn't work. The shark quickened his swim, growing more and more excited.

Grimly, Bert snapped the spear gun off safety, ready to fire. He wasn't about to go down without a fight, but he shuddered, knowing that he didn't really have a chance with that gun.

Maybe if I get him in the mouth? Bert wondered. No way to kill him and there'd only be one shot from his gun. No chance to reload. One useless shot and he'd have an angry shark after him and no weapon at all.

But he had to do something and the spear gun was all he had. The shark turned toward him and came on like a torpedo, faster and faster. The jaws opened.

Bert pressured his finger at the trigger, but suddenly he knew how hopeless it was and he stopped. With the shark coming fast, he found himself thumbing at the safety lever. It was just a flick of the thumb, but with those teeth coming in, it was just about the hardest thing he'd ever done. He put the gun on safety so it wouldn't fire, and he jabbed out with it.

The trident point struck the shark's nose. Water slowed the blow and the shark flinched, his tough hide pricked but not pierced by the steel. It felt like hitting a huge lump of gristle bound up in a sandpaper skin, but the points were there to be felt and the shark jerked and twisted away.

Now Bert still had a weapon. Because he hadn't fired, he still had the same weapon when the shark turned and came back for another try. Again the jab of sharp steel turned him. Bert tried for the surf, but the cramp came back and so did the shark.

All right, come on then, Bert resolved, lunging the spear gun at him again. *We can do this all day, but you won't get me. Not me!*

When the shark backed off again, Bert took down the rubbers so the gun couldn't be jarred into firing. He rubbed at the cramp while the shark circled. With his mind as much as his fingers, he worked out the cramp and slowly got back the use of his leg.

Now he started swimming, not into the surf where he couldn't see the next attack coming, but parallel to the beach in the clear water. He could never get out unless the shark let him, so he swam slowly and gracefully and fended off the shark every time he came close.

I'm OK now, Bert tried to show him. *If you're hungry, you'll have to find something else. I'll fight you all day.*

For a while the shark kept watch, but finally a school of mullet came by and the shark picked up speed to follow them out into deep water. Bert turned into the surf then and rode a swell into white water. When he got to the shallows, he stood up and ran, flippers and all.

"What took you so long?" Lisa screamed at him. She looked scared.

Bert dropped down on the sun-warmed sand and told her all about it—how he decided at the last second not to fire, how the spear worked to fend off the attacks.

Her tan seemed to leave her then. She looked more frightened now than before. "I'm—I'm glad you didn't count on that gun to fire. I told you it wouldn't work, remember? I tried it on a fish while you were getting the first abalone. Bert . . . it's jammed!"

A chill of horror spread over him as he grabbed up the gun, drew back the rubbers, snapped off the safety, pointed it at the sand, and pulled the trigger. It didn't budge.

Directions. Draw one line under the subject in each sentence.

a. "Thrusting forward the useless iron, Bert aimed it as if it were some kind of nuclear warhead."

b. Stopping suddenly, the shark eyed Bert.

c. Looking at the terrible scene in the water, Lisa felt powerless to help.

d. "Finning closer, he saw the shark again, lurking almost out of view."

e. "Shoving the spear gun under his arm, he freed both hands to rub at the cramp."

16   Copyright © 1984 by Harcourt Brace Jovanovich, Inc. All rights reserved

f. "Slowly, slowly, he finned as gracefully as he could, trying not to make any irregular vibrations."

g. Staring into the distance to her right, Lisa saw the shark again.

h. Lurking behind a rock, the shark prepared for the attack.

i. "With the shark coming fast, he found himself thumbing at the safety lever."

j. "With his mind as much as his fingers, he worked out the cramp and slowly got back the use of his leg."

Lesson 7
Reading Sentences with Interrupters

An interrupter is an expression or phrase that interrupts a sentence. An interrupter often separates the core parts of a sentence. Usually it is set off by two commas or two dashes. For example, read the two paragraphs below from "Stage Fright" by Betty Winn Fuller.

> Stage fright—that awful, terrifying, tied-in-knots feeling in the pit of the stomach that makes your voice quiver and your knees shake—is a universal experience. Everyone who performs or speaks in public has suffered from it. You stand up in front of an audience, feel suddenly afraid that you will faint, and then just hopeful that you'll drop dead instead!
>
> Recently on the "Today" show, actress Joanne Woodward, wife of Paul Newman, confessed that she is extremely nervous on every opening night. "Isn't everyone?" she asked. Actor Jimmy Stewart, one of the best-loved and most respected actors of recent years, admitted to being almost paralyzed with fear on opening nights. So, if you have qualms about getting up in front of an audience to perform or give a speech, remember that you are in good company.

Look again at the first sentence from "Stage Fright." The interrupter is underlined. The subject is *stage fright*. The verb is *is*.

> Stage fright—that awful, terrifying, tied-in-knots feeling in the pit of the stomach that makes your voice quiver and your knees shake—is a universal experience.

In the sentence below, the interrupter is underlined. The subject of this sentence is *Joanne Woodward*. The verb is *confessed*.

> Recently on the "Today" show, actress Joanne Woodward, wife of Paul Newman, confessed that she is extremely nervous on every opening night.

If you have trouble reading a sentence with an interrupter separating the core parts, take out the interrupter to get the main meaning of the sentence. For example, in the sentence below, the interrupter is underlined.

Actor Jimmy Stewart, <u>one of the best-loved and most respected actors of recent years,</u> admitted to being almost paralyzed with fear on opening nights.

The main meaning of the sentence is:

Actor Jimmy Stewart admitted to being almost paralyzed with fear on opening nights.

The interrupter gives you additional information. Who is Jimmy Stewart? He is "one of the best-loved and most respected actors of recent years."

Exercise 1. Read the following selection, "The Hunley Submarine" by Barbara H. Hill. Then follow the directions at the end of the selection.

Major Gen. D. H. Maury, Confederate commander of Mobile Bay on the Alabama coast, looked out at a floating flatboat target. Suddenly it blew apart, sending wooden fragments into the air.

As the last pieces fell back to sea, a small black object appeared on the water, turned and came slowly to the wharf. It was a small submarine. Its inventor, 35-year-old Horace L. Hunley, smiled as he climbed out an opened hatch. He had just proved the sub would work, and he was sure this secret weapon could help the South win the Civil War.

It was 1863, and for two years the Union Navy had blockaded* southern ports, keeping out the weapons and supplies the largely agricultural Confederacy needed to buy from other countries.

Hunley's sub was a 30-foot-long steam boiler with two tapered† ends and a rudder‡ added, and two hatches welded over holes in the top. Eight crewmen turned a propeller shaft to move the boat through the water (her best speed was 4 miles per hour, in calm water). The captain turned a wheel at the stern to control the rudder. The sub's only other equipment was a depth gauge and a candle that provided light and flickered when the oxygen ran low. When that happened, the sub had to surface and open its hatches for air.

Close to the surface, the captain could see through glass plates in the raised sides of the hatchway; at a lower depth, he steered by guess. Hand-operated ballast§ tanks in the ends (that

---

*__blockaded__ (blŏ-kād′d) *v.*: Closed off.
†__tapered__ (tā′pərd) *adj.*: Forming a gradual point.
‡__rudder__ (rŭd′ər) *n.*: A vertical plate at the stern, or back, of a ship that helps direct the ship's course.
§__ballast__ (băl′əst) *adj.*: Heavy material that helps steady a ship.

could be filled with water or air by valves), detachable (removable) weights, and five-foot diving planes allowed the ship to dive and surface.

For torpedoes, Horace L. Hunley adapted a floating copper mine filled with 90 pounds of gunpowder, towed on a 200-foot line behind the sub. To attack enemy ships, the sub would dive under them and surface on the far side, dragging the torpedo right into the ship. (Hunley's sub was one of several used by the Confederates. The *David* had tried to sink a Yankee ship in Charleston Harbor in October 1863, but its torpedo had exploded too soon.)

Sent by train to Charleston, S.C., to try to break the Union blockade, Hunley's sub was plagued by bad luck. While lying at wharf with hatches open and her crew inside, she was twice swamped by swells from passing steamers. Fourteen men drowned in the accidents.

Hunley and a new crew continued to test the ship in Charleston before attacking the Union blockaders. For several days the crew dived, then returned the sub to its dock. On Oct. 15, 1863, though, with a large crowd watching, the Hunley crew submerged but failed to surface. Apparently Hunley had flooded the forward tanks too rapidly, and the sub plunged nose down into the mud. Horace L. Hunley had gone down with his ship.

Gen. P.G.T. Beauregard, commander of Charleston, discouraged over so much loss of life, wanted to drop the submarine project. However, Charleston had been bombarded for 41 consecutive days and nights, and the general had to do something.

Two engineers who had helped Hunley build the sub convinced Beauregard to raise the ship and try again. They promised to run it near the surface and to attach the torpedo to a spar in front in order to ram an enemy ship.

On the night of Feb. 17, 1864, manned by a volunteer crew, the C.S.S. *H.L. Hunley*, named after its inventor, set out to sink the Union ship U.S.S. *Housatonic* in Charleston Harbor. As the sub approached, the deck officer on the Yankee warship noticed some rippling in the water and gave orders to raise anchor and back the engines, in order to move away from any danger. Moving would take about 12 minutes. In the meantime, the Union crew began shooting at the *Hunley* with rifles and pistols.

Suddenly a great explosion ripped through the *Housatonic's* stern. With a groan the big ship sank into the shallow bay, her crew clinging to the masts, looking for the enemy. They never saw any. The tiny sub, caught beneath the Union warship, also had gone down.

But the little *Hunley* had become the first sub to sink a warship, revolutionizing naval warfare. No longer would the enemy be just another ship, or guns fired from shore. The enemy could also be under the sea.

Directions. Write each sentence below without its interrupter.

a. "Major Gen. D. H. Maury, Confederate commander of Mobile Bay on the Alabama coast, looked out at a floating flatboat target."
Major Gen. D. H. Maury looked out at a floating flatboat target.

b. "Its inventor, 35-year-old Horace L. Hunley, smiled as he climbed out an opened hatch."
Its inventor smiled as he climbed out an opened hatch.

c. "Gen. P.G.T. Beauregard, commander of Charleston, discouraged over so much loss of life, wanted to drop the submarine project."
Gen. P.G.T. Beauregard wanted to drop the submarine project.

d. "On the night of Feb. 17, 1864, manned by a volunteer crew, the C.S.S. H.L. *Hunley*, named after its inventor, set out to sink the Union ship U.S.S. *Housatonic* in Charleston Harbor."
On the night of Feb. 17, 1864, the C.S.S. H.L. Hunley set out to sink the Union ship U.S.S. Housatonic in Charleston Harbor.

e. "The tiny sub, caught beneath the Union warship, also had gone down."
The tiny sub also had gone down.

Exercise 2. An interrupter usually gives you additional information about the main parts of the sentence. Reread each sentence in Exercise 1. Study each interrupter. Then answer the following questions.

a. Reread 1a. Who was Major Gen. D. H. Maury?
He was Confederate commander of Mobile Bay.

b. Reread 1b. Who was the inventor of the submarine?
The inventor was Horace L. Hunley.

c. Reread 1c. Who was Gen. P.G.T. Beauregard?
Beauregard was commander of Charleston.

d. Reread 1d. After whom was the submarine named?
It was named after its inventor.

e. Reread 1e. Why did the tiny sub go down?
It was caught beneath the Union warship.

Name _____

Lesson 8
Understanding Pronoun Reference

A noun is a word that names a person, place, thing, or idea. For example, the words *child, town, bookcase,* and *happiness* are nouns. A pronoun is a word used in place of a noun or nouns. Some common pronouns are:

I, me, my, mine, myself
you, your, yours, yourself
he, him, his, himself
she, her, hers, herself
it, its, itself

we, us, our, ours, ourselves
they, them, their, theirs, themselves
anybody, somebody, nobody
either, neither
none

Pronouns help you to shorten sentences and make them read more smoothly. For example, read the sentence below.

Betty followed *Betty's* dog along the trail as *Betty and the dog* took an afternoon walk.

Notice how much easier it is to read the sentence above when you replace some of the nouns with pronouns.

Betty followed *her* dog along the trail as *they* took an afternoon walk.

Read the two sentences below. Notice the *italicized* nouns in the first sentence. These nouns are replaced by pronouns in the second sentence.

Anne's dog Reginald thought that *Reginald* was *Anne's* master and *Anne* was *Reginald's* pet.
Anne's dog Reginald thought that *he* was *her* master and *she* was *his* pet.

Be careful, though. When you read, it is important to understand to which word each pronoun refers. For example, read the following comic strip.

Copyright © 1984 by Harcourt Brace Jovanovich, Inc. All rights reserved

ARCHIE

Veronica says, "How're *they* biting today?" She means the pronoun *they* to refer to the noun *fish*. Archie and Jughead think the pronoun *they* refers to mosquitoes.

Exercise. In the selection below, the narrator, or character telling the story, is Reginald, Anne's dog. Read this selection from "Dog Story" by Deanna B. Durbin. Pay special attention to the pronouns printed in **boldface.** Write the word or words each boldface pronoun refers to in the blanks at the right.

I have decided it is time for Anne to get a new boyfriend.
Anne is my owner, Anne Thompson. Well, she thinks she's my owner, and I don't intend to tell her the truth. We dogs have to show some tact in these matters, you know.
I have found just the right boyfriend for her, too. **His** name is Joe Greenfield. He's 17, a year older than Anne. He moved in across the street just about two weeks go. Anne and I have seen him several times out in the yard. **They** say hi to each other, and I wag my tail politely.
I've asked around about him, of course. All the dogs in the neighborhood speak well of him. He knows just where to scratch behind a dog's ears. But charm isn't everything, and I can't be too careful about choosing Anne's boyfriend.
So one evening, when I was out walking with Anne, I slipped away from her and poked my nose through Joe's screen door. I sneaked in—Joe was busy raking leaves in the backyard—and looked around inside.
It was a nice house. A comfortable, lived-in house with good solid furniture. Nothing chrome. **I** hate chrome; nothing to sink your teeth into. There was a picture of Joe and his parents on the coffee table in the living room. **They** were standing in front of a big house in the country, surrounded by dogs and trees. Good breeding shows every time, I always say. Even in humans.
Now all I had to do was get rid of Steve. **He** lives down the street, and he's in the same class at school as Anne. I didn't trust him from the start. He tries to pretend he likes dogs, but he smells all wrong. I hate to say this about anybody, but I suspect he's a secret cat lover. And if he parks in front of the house and

a. *Reginald*

b. *the boyfriend's*

c. *Anne and Joe*

d. *Reginald*

e. *Joe and his parents*

f. *Steve*

honks for Anne one more time, I am going to bite **his** tires. Anne's mother and father don't care much for him, either. **They** know better than to say that, of course, but I can always sense these things.

g. _____ *Steve's*
h. _____ *Anne's mother and father*

Tonight, Anne had a date with him for the Homecoming dance. In fact, I had been busy trying to figure out how to get rid of Steve and at the same time encourage Joe, when the doorbell rang. Anne's mother had run next door, and Anne's father was downstairs in **his** workshop, so Anne herself answered the door. She was wearing a beautiful, new royal-blue dress, and she looked like a princess, if I do say so myself.

i. _____ *father's*

And there stood Steve, with a big tabby cat in **his** arms. Which just goes to show, you can always trust your instincts.

j. _____ *Steve's*

Lesson 9
Practice

Of course, we all know that ghosts do not exist. However, this fact has not stopped people from telling stories about strange meetings with ghostly figures. Read the following selection. Then complete the exercise at the end of the selection.

Is Our Capitol Haunted?
Henry N. Ferguson

On a spring evening in 1977, Fred Twomby, a guard at the nation's Capitol building in Washington, D.C., was walking along an upper corridor. He entered a side hallway and stopped in his tracks—horrified.

He saw (he later reported) a black cat approaching, increasing in size with every step—until it became larger than a tiger. Suddenly, the stunned guard saw the terrifying creature spring at him. Twomby quickly covered his eyes with his arms and screamed in terror.

When he opened his eyes, the cat had vanished—leaving him unmarked.

Twomby has not been the only guard to report seeing the mysterious cat. Guards and other night workers at the Capitol call the bone-chilling creature the "Demon Cat." The legendary figure has been reported lurking in the halls of Congress for years.

Capt. Allen P. Powers, night supervisor at the Capitol for more than a decade, says, "We have men on the force who are so uptight about the Demon Cat that they won't patrol the building alone at night. The more superstitious ones consider the cat an evil force that deliberately stalks its victims, making sure they are alone. No one, however, has ever been harmed. Nevertheless, many on the Capitol force are certain the building is haunted."

Many buildings in all parts of the United States have had strange noises, movements, or sightings that caused people to say they are haunted. Despite study by reporters and scientists, many cases have never been proven true or false. They remain unexplained.

The nation's Capitol—perhaps because so many public figures have spent much of their lives there—seems to have more than its share of such strange occurrences.

Take the case of William Taulbee, a congressman from Kentucky. He was gunned down in 1890 by a newspaper reporter during an argument on the steps to the House gallery.

Taulbee's blood spattered over the marble steps. Although the marks were quickly cleaned up, they reappeared a few days later, and despite repeated attempts to erase them, they can still be seen. Some Capitol employees insist Taulbee's ghost haunts the stairway.

At night, when most "ghost" sightings are reported, the Capitol building can be scary. A favorite haunt of nightly phantoms is Statuary Hall, which once was the House of Representatives chamber. It's a spooky place after dark with its row of silent, stone statues of men who once walked the halls as living lawmakers. Some watchmen have reported hearing the footsteps of, they assume, the sixth President, John Quincy Adams. In this chamber, Adams (who became a congressman after being President) suffered a fatal stroke in 1848.

Guards call another ghost the "Solitary Stroller." Some report hearing his slow pacing in the basement beneath the House of Representatives. Those who say they have seen him think the stroller might have been a foreign diplomat. Others are certain he is the ghost of Maj. Pierre L'Enfant, the designer of the city of Washington, D.C.

Through the years, Capitol employees have reported other apparitions wandering through the halls. Among these have been what witnesses said appeared to be President Abraham Lincoln and Frances Willard, founder of the Women's Christian Temperance Union. Some claim to have heard the voices of former House Speakers Joe Cannon and Champ Clark raised in debate.

Guides give no hint to visitors of the phantoms that have created so many legends in the vast Capitol building. They don't want to alarm anyone.

Fred Schwengel, a former Iowa congressman and now president of the U.S. Capitol Historical Society, is familiar with the secrets of the four-acre building. He doesn't believe in ghosts, Schwengel says, but he admits that many reliable people have reported seeing or hearing what seemed to be ghosts or ghostlike apparitions.

Name _____

Aside from its famous "ghosts," the Capitol building has many other unusual features. These include the unoccupied tomb in the crypt, directly below the rotunda. It was planned to transfer the remains of George and Martha Washington there in 1832. But the Washington family heirs refused, insisting the bodies remain in a vault at Mount Vernon.

The most secret place in the Capitol is a musty underground passage where as many as 5,000 loaves of bread were baked daily for Union soldiers during the Civil War. To visit this area, one must crawl through a manhole, then clamber down an iron ladder into a tunnel built under the West Front. The tunnel was sealed off after the war and was only rediscovered 10 years ago.

Exercise. Complete each item below.

a. The paragraph below contains how many sentences?

On a spring evening in 1977, Fred Twomby, a guard at the nation's Capitol building in Washington, D.C., was walking along an upper corridor. He entered a side hallway and stopped in his tracks—horrified.

2

b. When you read the first sentence in the paragraph above, how many times should you pause?

4

c. Read the sentence below. Underline the subject once and the predicate twice.

<u>Guards</u> <u>call</u> another ghost the "Solitary Stroller."

d. Underline the interrupter in the sentence below.

Fred Schwengel, <u>a former Iowa congressman and now president of the U.S. Capitol Historical Society</u>, is familiar with the secrets of the four-acre building.

e. Underline the exact words of the speaker in the paragraph below.

Capt. Allen P. Powers, night supervisor at the Capitol for more than a decade, says, "<u>We have men on the force who are so uptight about the Demon Cat that they won't patrol the building alone at night. The more superstitious ones consider the cat an evil force that deliberately stalks its victims, making</u>

sure they are alone. No one, however, has ever been harmed. Nevertheless, many on the Capitol force are certain the building is haunted."

f. For the sentence below, draw one line under the subject and two lines under the compound verb.

He <u>entered</u> a side hallway and <u>stopped</u> in his tracks—horrified.

g. For the sentence below, draw one line under the subject and two lines under the compound verb.

Twomby quickly <u>covered</u> his eyes with his arms and <u>screamed</u> in terror.

h. For the sentence below, draw one line under the compound subject and two lines under the verb.

Guards and other night workers at the Capitol <u>call</u> the bone-chilling creature the "Demon Cat."

i. Underline the subject of the sentence below.

Aside from its famous "ghosts," the Capitol <u>building</u> has many other unusual features.

j. What word does the pronoun *they* stand for in the following sentence?

Many buildings in all parts of the United States have had strange noises, movements, or sightings that caused people to say they are haunted.

buildings

Name _____

Chapter 2
Relationships

What is a relationship? A relationship is the way in which two or more things, events, people, or ideas are connected or joined. This relationship often adds meaning to the individual items. In this chapter you will study several relationship patterns. These are: spatial order, time order, listing, cause and effect, and comparison and contrast.

Lesson 1
Understanding Spatial Order

Spatial order tells you where one object is in relation to other objects. For example, one object may be *in front of, in back of, over, under,* or *next to* another. Read the sentence below.

The winding trail was next to Five Springs Creek.

Where was the trail in relation to the creek? The trail was *next to* the creek.

The paragraph below is from "Bighorn Medicine Wheel" by Jay Ellis Ransom. Ransom tells about a trip he made in 1924 when he was a boy. He traveled with his father and a group of men from Bighorn Basin in Lovell, Wyoming, to near the top of Medicine Mountain. There they saw an ancient Indian monument called the Medicine Wheel. Read the paragraph below. The words that help you see spatial order are printed in **boldface.**

By late afternoon we made the final crossing **at the mouth of** Five Springs Canyon and began the long, twisting climb to a camping place **in** the lower forest **above** the falls of the creek. With evening settling **over** the mountains and the stars twinkling **in** the trench of sky **overhead,** we quickly made camp. **In** the timber an owl hooted, and **far away** a coyote yapped mournfully. **High above** us **in** a hidden basin a bull elk bugled.

Copyright © 1984 by Harcourt Brace Jovanovich, Inc. All rights reserved

Exercise. Continue reading "Bighorn Medicine Wheel" by Jay Ellis Ransom. Pay special attention to the spatial relation of one object to another. Then answer the questions that follow the selection.

Medicine Rim loomed above Hidden Basin like a great white wall of high limestone cliffs. The last rise we made was just about straight, going hand over hand through a sort of chimney in the face of the cliffs. When we topped out, utterly exhausted in the thin air almost two miles above sea level, I was so tired that I plopped down under a timberline spruce. Wheezing in agony, I could hardly catch my breath. Finally, with my legs trembling from exhaustion, I followed the men a mile east along the drop-off of the rim overlooking the Bighorn Basin. Slowly we climbed over a narrow plateau that was covered with white limestone rocks.

Not until we were a hundred yards away from the prehistoric monument could we see it. It was not a giant stone wheel standing on edge, the way I had imagined it, but a huge circle of loose rocks lying flat on the ground. Panting, I walked around it and counted twenty-eight spokes that connected the unbroken rim with a large central stone cairn* that had caved in. Almost equally spaced along the rim were five smaller caved-in cairns. On an offset southeasterly spoke and about twelve feet outside the rim lay another broken-down pile of rocks that also had once been a covered cairn.

I found several crude arrowheads and a quartz spear tip that were several thousands of years old. Ancient Indians had come this way. Their rock shelters and campsites have now been carbon-dated to be more than eleven thousand years old.

Those who study the ancient Indians of America (Paleo-Indians) estimate that they had migrated from Asia about thirty to forty thousand years ago. The Medicine Wheel is not so old as that but was built a long time ago—maybe as much as two thousand years.

We may never know which Indians built this unique rock structure, nor why they built it near the top of Medicine Mountain at an elevation of 9,642 feet. Some persons think that perhaps they were early astronomers, for the twenty-eight spokes of the wheel are equal to the average number of days in the moon's revolution around the earth. Some of the spokes seem to point directly to certain bright stars that rise in the east each year on the summer solstice, June 21.

Questions
a. Where is Medicine Rim in relation to Hidden Basin?
   It is above Hidden Basin.

b. The group walks a mile east along the drop-off. Where is this drop-off in relation to Bighorn Basin?
   It is overlooking Bighorn Basin.

---

*cairn (kârn) n.: A mound of stones set up as a landmark or memorial.

Name _____

c. How far away from the monument are the men when they first see it?
They are a hundred yards away from it.

d. Ransom had expected the stones of the monument to be standing on edge. How is the relation of the rocks to the ground different from what he had imagined?
The rocks are lying flat on the ground.

e. Ransom walks around the huge circle of flat rocks. How is this circle connected to the central cairn?
It is connected by twenty-eight spokes.

f. Ransom sees five smaller cairns. Where are they located in relation to the rim?
They are almost equally spaced along the rim.

g. On which spoke does Ransom see what had once been another cairn?
He sees it on the southeasterly spoke.

h. Where is this caved-in cairn in relation to the rim?
It is about twelve feet outside the rim.

i. Where is the Medicine Wheel located in relation to Medicine Mountain?
It is near the top of Medicine Mountain.

j. To where do some of the spokes of the wheel seem to point?
Some seem to point directly to certain bright stars.

Lesson 2

Understanding Time Order

Time order tells you when one event happened in relation to other events. Time order answers the question "When?" It tells you the sequence of events. For example, the events in the following paragraph, from *Sour Land* by William H. Armstrong, are arranged according to time order. You learn what Ruth does first, what she does second, what she does third, and what she does last.

Sitting in church between her father and David that Sunday, she followed her regular routine. First she leafed through the hymnbook—that didn't have any pictures last Sunday or the Sunday before and wouldn't have any this, but she leafed anyway. Then she counted the windows on both sides of the church, and wished Mrs. Leech's baby would start crying as it always did. Then she twisted her head all the way around to count the four round pillars that held up the balcony.

Sometimes events are not arranged in their normal time order. For example, read the paragraph below from "Two Were Left" by Hugh B. Cave.

> On the third night of hunger, Noni thought of the dog. Nothing of flesh and blood lived upon the floating ice island with its towering berg except those two.
>
> In the breakup, Noni had lost his sled, his food, his furs, even his knife. He had saved only Nimuk, his great devoted husky. And now the two, marooned on the ice, eyed each other warily—each keeping his distance.
>
> Noni's love for Nimuk was real, very real—as real as hunger and cold nights and the gnawing pain of his injured leg in its homemade brace. But the men of his village killed their dogs when food was scarce, didn't they? And without thinking twice about it.
>
> And Nimuk, he told himself, when hungry enough would seek food. "One of us will soon be eating the other," Noni thought. "So . . ."
>
> He could not kill the dog with his bare hands. Nimuk was powerful, and much fresher than he. A weapon, then, was essential.

First, the ice broke up. Second, Noni saved his dog's life. Third, Noni decided he had to kill his dog for food.

Exercise 1. Continue reading "Two Were Left." Then follow the directions at the end of this part of the selection.

> Removing his mittens, he unstrapped the brace from his leg. When he had hurt his leg a few weeks before, he had fashioned the brace from bits of harness and two thin strips of iron.
>
> Kneeling now, he wedged one of the iron strips into a crack in the ice, and began to rub the other against it with firm, slow strokes.
>
> Nimuk watched him intently, and it seemed to Noni that the dog's eyes glowed more brightly as night waned.
>
> He worked on, trying not to remember why. The slab of iron had an edge now. It had begun to take shape. Daylight found his task completed.
>
> Noni pulled the finished knife from the ice and thumbed its edge. The sun's glare, reflected from it, stabbed at his eyes and momentarily blinded him.
>
> Noni steeled himself.
>
> "Here, Nimuk!" he called softly.
>
> The dog suspiciously watched him.
>
> "Come here," Noni called.

Name _____

Nimuk came closer. Noni read fear in the animal's gaze. He read hunger and suffering in the dog's labored breathing and awkward, dragging crouch. His heart wept. He hated himself and fought against it.

Closer Nimuk came, wary of his intentions. Now Noni felt a thickening in his throat. He saw the dog's eyes and they were wells of suffering.

Now! Now was the time to strike!

A great sob shook Noni's kneeling body. He cursed the knife. He swayed blindly, flung the weapon far from him. With empty hands outstretched he stumbled toward the dog, and fell.

Directions. Arrange the events below in their proper time order. Write 1 by the event that happened first, 2 by the event that happened second, 3 by the event that happened third, 4 by the event that happened fourth, and 5 by the event that happened last.

__3__ **a.** Noni finished sharpening the iron into a knife.
__2__ **b.** Noni made a brace for his leg.
__5__ **c.** Noni threw the knife away.
__4__ **d.** Noni called his dog to him.
__1__ **e.** Noni hurt his leg.

Exercise 2. Finish reading "Two Were Left." Then follow the directions at the end of the selection.

The dog growled ominously (in a threatening way) as he warily circled the boy's body. And now Noni was sick with fear.

In flinging away the knife, he had left himself defenseless. He was too weak to crawl after it now. He was at Nimuk's mercy, and Nimuk was hungry.

The dog had circled him and was creeping up from behind. Noni heard the rattle of saliva in the savage throat.

He shut his eyes, praying that the attack might be swift. He felt the dog's feet against his leg, the hot rush of Nimuk's breath against his neck. A scream gathered in the boy's throat.

Then he felt the dog's hot tongue caressing his face.

Noni's eyes opened, incredulously staring. Crying softly, he thrust out an arm and drew the dog's head down against his own. . . .

The plane came out of the south an hour later. Its pilot, a young man of the coast patrol, looked down and saw the large floating floe, with the berg rising from its center. And he saw something flashing.

It was the sun gleaming on something shiny, which moved. His curiosity aroused, the pilot banked his ship and descended, circling the floe. Now he saw, in the shadow of the peak of ice, a dark, still shape that appeared to be human. Or were there two shapes?

He set his ship down in a water lane and investigated. There were two shapes, boy and dog. The boy was unconscious but alive. The dog whined feebly but was too weak to move.

The gleaming object which had trapped the pilot's attention was a crudely fashioned knife, stuck point first into the ice a little distance away, and quivering in the wind.

Directions. Arrange the events below in their proper time order. Write 1 by the event that happened first, 2 by the event that happened second, 3 by the event that happened third, 4 by the event that happened fourth, and 5 by the event that happened last.

____4____ a. A pilot saw something flashing in the ice.
____3____ b. Noni hugged the dog.
____2____ c. The dog licked Noni's face.
____5____ d. A pilot rescued Noni and Nimuk.
____1____ e. The dog, Nimuk, circled Noni's body.

Name _____

Lesson 3
Understanding Listing

A list is a collection of items, all of which fit into a particular category. For example, Sharon decided to make a list of books she had read during the summer. This is what her list looked like.

Books Read During Summer

Zeely by Virginia Hamilton
Black Hearts in Battersea by Joan Aiken
A Swiftly Tilting Planet by Madeleine L'Engle
Child of the Owl by Laurence Yep
National Velvet by Enid Bagnold
Then Again, Maybe I Won't by Judy Blume
Little Women by Louisa May Alcott
Island of the Blue Dolphins by Scott O'Dell

In some lists, the items are arranged in a significant order. For example, they may be arranged from biggest to smallest, from most important to least important, or from nearest to farthest. Although Sharon enjoyed all the books on her list, she decided to arrange them according to preference. She started with the book she liked the most. Here is what this list looked like.

Books Read During Summer

A Swiftly Tilting Planet by Madeleine L'Engle
Then Again, Maybe I Won't by Judy Blume
Child of the Owl by Laurence Yep
Zeely by Virginia Hamilton
Black Hearts in Battersea by Joan Aiken
National Velvet by Enid Bagnold
Island of the Blue Dolphins by Scott O'Dell
Little Women by Louisa May Alcott

After Sharon read the books, she gave them to her cousin Tillie. Tillie also made a list. She too arranged this list according to preference. Her list, though, looked very different from Sharon's.

Books Read During Summer

Black Hearts in Battersea by Joan Aiken
National Velvet by Enid Bagnold
Island of the Blue Dolphins by Scott O'Dell
Little Women by Louisa May Alcott
Zeely by Virginia Hamilton
A Swiftly Tilting Planet by Madeleine L'Engle
Child of the Owl by Laurence Yep
Then Again, Maybe I Won't by Judy Blume

Copyright © 1984 by Harcourt Brace Jovanovich, Inc. All rights reserved

Exercise 1. Make two lists from the items below. Ten items will fit in the category called "Cities in the United States." The remaining ten items will fit in the category called "Countries in Europe." (If you are not sure of an answer, use your dictionary to help you.) Arrange your lists in alphabetical order.

Boston	Portugal	Spain	Charleston
Miami	Houston	Belgium	West Germany
Denmark	Milwaukee	Phoenix	San Francisco
The Netherlands	Switzerland	Italy	Sweden
Detroit	Norway	Philadelphia	Memphis

Cities in the United States	Countries in Europe
Boston	*Belgium*
Charleston	*Denmark*
Detroit	*Italy*
Houston	*The Netherlands*
Memphis	*Norway*
Miami	*Portugal*
Milwaukee	*Spain*
Philadelphia	*Sweden*
Phoenix	*Switzerland*
San Francisco	*West Germany*

Exercise 2. Read each list below. One item does not fit in each list. Write this item in the blank at the right.

a. football   baseball   soccer   television   tennis — *television*

b. dress   sweater   skirt   slacks   oven — *oven*

c. ocean liner   sailboat   yacht   cabin cruiser   car — *car*

d. milk   apples   oranges   grapes   bananas — *milk*

e. cereal   eggs   pancakes   kitchens   muffins — *kitchens*

f. kitchen   living room   stove   bedroom   dining room — *stove*

g. paper   notebook   pen   pencil   perfume — *perfume*

h. toothpaste   toothbrush   dental floss   gloves   mouthwash — *gloves*

i. snowshoeing   skiing   dancing   ice-skating   bobsledding — *dancing*

j. noun   verb   map   pronoun   adjective — *map*

Name _____

Lesson 4

Identifying Words That Signal Cause and Effect

A cause makes something happen. An effect is what happens. Many ideas and events are connected in a cause and effect relationship. For example, read the two sentences below.

Mark was unable to concentrate on his homework. He had not slept well the night before.

Now let's connect these two sentences to show a cause and effect relationship.

Mark was unable to concentrate on his homework because he had not slept well the night before.

The cause is *he had not slept well the night before.* The effect is *Mark was unable to concentrate on his homework.*

The following words may signal a cause and effect relationship.

accordingly	in order that
as	since
as a result	so
because	so that
consequently	therefore
for	thus

In the following sentences, the signal word is printed in **boldface**, the cause is underlined once, and the effect is underlined twice.

Carla was tired at bedtime **since** she had worked very hard during the day.

Because she was tired, Lila took a nap in the afternoon.

Chris went to bed very late last night; **as a result,** he was tired the next morning.

Exercise 1. Read the selection below from "The ABZ's of Sleep" by Tom Slear. Then follow the directions at the end of the selection.

A Regular Sleep Schedule. The most important rule is to have a regular sleep schedule, or at least a consistent wake-up time. Our bodies thrive on routine because many important functions depend on careful timing. If we constantly ask our systems to rearrange their schedules to meet our changing sleep habits, a few things are bound to break down.

Most noticeable, we feel tired even though we are spending enough time in bed. Concentrating on schoolwork becomes difficult, and sports become a chore rather than fun. Policemen, for example, typically suffer from sleep problems for they often shift between daytime and nighttime work. The irregularity throws their systems off; as a result, they may spend eight hours sleeping and still feel tired.

"That's because *when* you sleep is as important as *how long* you sleep," says Monte Stahl, associate director of the Presbyterian Hospital sleep lab in Oklahoma City. "If you are sleeping late one day and getting up early the next, you are bound to feel a little tired. The most important advice I can give for healthy sleep is to go to bed and get up at the same time every day."

The Right Amount. The proper sleep amount is not as uniform as many people think. We need less sleep as we grow older, but some of us adapt sooner than others. Your friend may need only seven hours of sleep a night to feel alert during the day. You may need nine hours at night and an hour nap in the afternoon.

Once again Dr. Lindsley says the test is how we feel during the day. "Because of popular notions about the 'right' amount of sleep, many people believe they should sleep more than they need to," she says. "The 'right' amount is how much our system demands. It's different for each one of us, though as we get older it usually ranges from six to ten hours a night, with possibly a nap."

However, napping is not well accepted in our society since our daily schedules are busy and allow for sleeping only at night. Still, sleep experts say that an afternoon snooze can be helpful for those who do not fit well into the common long-sleep/long-wake pattern.

"Not everyone is designed for a long sleeping period followed by a long waking period," says Dr. Jim Minard, a sleep researcher at the New Jersey Medical School in Newark. "Naps are a means of tiding us over. But be careful. Don't let them last too long or take them close to evening bedtime."

Directions. Read the sentences below from "The ABZs of Sleep." Circle the signal word in each sentence. Then draw one line under the part of the sentence that is the cause. Draw two lines under the part of the sentence that is the effect.

a. "Our bodies thrive on routine (because) many important functions depend on careful timing."

b. "Policemen, for example, typically suffer from sleep problems (for) they often shift between daytime and nighttime work."

c. "The irregularity throws their systems off; (as a result,) they may spend eight hours sleeping and still feel tired."

d. "However, napping is not well accepted in our society (since) our daily schedules are busy and allow for sleeping only at night."

e. "(Because) of popular notions about the 'right' amount of sleep, many people believe they should sleep more than they need to."

Exercise 2. Read each sentence below. Circle the signal word in each sentence. Then underline the cause once and the effect twice.

a. Karen could not sleep (since) she was excited about tomorrow night's party.

b. Sam watched the late movie last night; (as a result,) he fell asleep in class the next day.

c. Crystal took a warm bath; (accordingly,) she was relaxed when she went to bed.

d. Colas contain caffeine; (consequently,) some people who drink colas in the evening have trouble sleeping.

e. Bruce tossed and turned all night (for) he had had too many colas at the party.

Lesson 5
Understanding Cause and Effect

Many ideas and events are connected in a cause and effect relationship. The cause is what makes something happen. The effect is the result, or what happens. For example, read the paragraph below from *The Long Ago Lake* by Marne Wilkins.

> Another cousin came from Texas to visit in the summer. He taught me how to catch snakes because he collected them. We learned about all the snakes that lived around us at the lake, where their homes were, and what they ate. I was going to make a collection too, but I wasn't much of a scientist. One day I found three nice snakes, but I was in a hurry to go swimming, so I wrapped them snugly in a bandanna and put them into my dresser drawer. The next thing we all heard was a yowl and a crash! My unsuspecting mother had opened my drawer to put the laundry away, and the three snakes were there to greet her. She fainted dead away! That ended my collection, but after my cousin went home, I mailed him three special snakes in a carefully made cage-box. He wrote and thanked me for *the* snake, and that was how I learned that king snakes eat other snakes—

even rattlers. Since my "Texas cousin" summer, I have continued to see snakes. They are probably some of the most beautiful creatures on earth.

Cause and effect plays an important part in the paragraph above. Why did Marne's cousin teach her to catch snakes? He taught her this because he collected them. Why did Marne wrap the snakes in a bandanna? She did this because she was in a hurry to go swimming. Why did Marne's mother scream? She screamed because she opened the drawer and was shocked to find three snakes there. Why did Marne's cousin find only one snake, although Marne had sent him three? He found only one because the king snake had eaten the other two.

Now look at the comic strip below.

MARVIN **by Tom Armstrong**

Why does Marvin think it's time his mother changed the water in the pool? He thinks this because a frog is living in the water.

Exercise. Read the following selection from "The Case of the Missing Garlic Bread" by Donald J. Sobol. Then answer the questions that follow it. Make sure each answer contains the word *because*.

From fall to spring, Encyclopedia helped his father capture crooks. When school let out for the summer, he helped the children of the neighborhood as well.

Every morning he hung his sign outside the garage:

Brown Detective Agency
13 Rover Avenue
Leroy Brown, President
No Case Too Small
25¢ Per Day
Plus Expenses

One morning in late June, Encyclopedia and Sally Kimball, his partner, were seated in the garage when Josh Whipplewhite entered. Josh wore a mad and hungry look.

"You missed breakfast?" asked Encyclopedia.

"No," grumbled Josh. "Lunch."

"It's only 10 o'clock in the morning!" exclaimed Sally. "You must have just flown in from France!"

"Naw, I never left Idaville," Josh replied. "But part of my lunch took off."

He explained. His mother had been fixing the food for his birthday party at one o'clock. She had made a big loaf of garlic bread and a chocolate cake. She had put them on the windowsill for a minute to get them out of the way.

"The cake and the garlic bread disappeared as if they'd flown—pffft!" Josh said. "My party's ruined!"

"You can have a party without garlic bread," Encyclopedia pointed out.

"But not without a birthday cake," declared Sally.

"Uh-huh," corrected Josh. "It's the garlic bread I'll miss. I'd rather have it than cake anytime."

He put a quarter on the gasoline can beside Encyclopedia. "I want to hire you," he said. "Find the thief!"

"Did you see anyone around your house at the time?" asked Encyclopedia.

"Three or four big boys," said Josh. "I didn't pay much attention. But one of them was called Bugs."

"Bugs—Bugs Meany!" cried Sally. "I knew it."

Bugs was the leader of a gang of tough older boys. They called themselves the Tigers. They should have called themselves the Razors. They were always in some kind of scrape.

Encyclopedia had dealt with Bugs before. Almost every week he had to stop the Tigers from cheating the children of the neighborhood.

"I'm pretty sure the Tigers made off with your garlic bread and birthday cake," said Encyclopedia. "Come with us."

The Tiger's clubhouse was an unused tool shed behind Mr. Sweeney's auto body shop. Bugs Meany, Duke Kelly, Spike Larson and Rocky Graham were inside, sitting on orange crates and chewing parsley.

Bugs chewed a little faster when he saw Encyclopedia, Sally and Josh approaching.

"What's this?" he called. "Winter must have come early this year. The nuts are falling out of the trees."

Encyclopedia was used to Bugs' greetings. He ignored the remark.

"This is Josh Whipplewhite," he said. "Earlier this morning you four stole a birthday cake and a loaf of garlic bread from his kitchen windowsill."

"Stole?" exclaimed Bugs. He smote his forehead as if he couldn't believe anyone would accuse him of stealing. "We've been right here in the clubhouse all morning eating rabbit food. Got to get our vitamins."

"You're lying, you big ape," said Sally.

Bugs tilted his nose. "What makes you so sure, Miss Smarty?"

"Your lips are moving," snapped Sally.

Bugs grew red. "You prove I'm not honest in word and deed, and us Tigers will buy this little whipple-dipple kid another cake and a loaf of garlic bread."

"Agreed," said Encyclopedia quickly. He moved off to the side and powwowed with Sally and Josh.

"All we have to do is sniff their breaths," whispered Josh. "Garlic leaves a terrible smell."

"They thought of that," said Sally. "They're chewing parsley on purpose. Parsley will sweeten even a camel's breath."

"Well, somebody ought to take a whiff just the same," Josh said. "But not me. It's my 10th birthday, and I want to live to be 11."

Sally looked at Encyclopedia. The boy detective looked away. He had no desire to have his nose bitten.

"Boys," Sally said disgustedly. "All right, I'll do it."

She marched up to Bugs. "Open your mouth if you dare."

Bugs seemed to be waiting for the command. He opened his mouth confidently.

Sally put her nose close. She did the same with Duke, Spike and Rocky. They breathed heavily into her face and grinned.

She returned to Encyclopedia and Josh, defeated.

"The parsley got rid of the evidence, darn it," she said. "Bugs' breath is better than usual."

"There goes my party lunch," groaned Josh.

"Not yet," said Encyclopedia. "I think I can prove the Tigers stole the garlic bread and birthday cake."

HOW CAN ENCYCLOPEDIA PROVE THE TIGERS STOLE THE BREAD AND CAKE?

SOLUTION TO "THE CASE OF THE MISSING GARLIC BREAD"

The Tigers knew if you eat parsley, it will take away bad breath, even the smell of garlic.

But they forgot they had eaten with their hands.

Unfortunately for them, Encyclopedia was on the case. He told Sally to sniff each Tiger's hands.

"Garlic," she said over and over as she went from Bugs to Duke to Spike to Rocky. "Yuk!"

"You Tigers nearly got away with it," said Encyclopedia. "If you had washed your hands with strong soap, the garlic smell would have disappeared."

Sally laughed. "The Tigers wash their hands? Never!"

Trapped by their mistake, the Tigers bought the ingredients for chocolate cake and garlic bread. Then Sally and Encyclopedia prepared the food for Josh's birthday lunch.

40 Copyright © 1984 by Harcourt Brace Jovanovich, Inc. All rights reserved

Name _____

Questions

a. At the beginning of the story, why is Josh angry and hungry?
Josh looks angry and hungry because he missed lunch.

b. Why does Sally say, "You must have just flown in from France!"?
She says this because it is only 10 o'clock in the morning, certainly not lunchtime in Idaville.

c. Why did Josh's mother make a chocolate cake and garlic bread?
Because it is Josh's birthday, his mother made a chocolate cake and garlic bread for his party.

d. Why did Josh's mother put the chocolate cake and garlic bread on the windowsill?
She put them there because she wanted to get them out of the way.

e. Why does Josh hire Encyclopedia?
Josh hires Encyclopedia because he wants him to find the thief.

f. When he hears Josh's tale, why does Encyclopedia immediately suspect Bugs Meany and his gang?
Encyclopedia immediately suspects them because Bugs and his gang were always getting into some kind of trouble. In addition, Josh had heard the name of one boy—Bugs.

g. Why does Sally try to smell Bugs Meany's breath?
Sally tries to smell Bugs' breath because garlic leaves a distinctive smell.

h. Why are Bugs and his gang chewing parsley?
They are chewing parsley because parsley covers up the smell of garlic.

i. Why does Encyclopedia tell Sally to sniff the hands of each member of the Tigers?
He tells this because, if the boys ate the garlic bread, the scent of garlic will be on their hands.

j. At the end of the story, why do the Tigers buy the ingredients for chocolate cake and garlic bread?
They do this because Bugs had said, "You prove I'm not honest in word and deed, and us Tigers will buy this little whipple-dipple kid another cake and a loaf of garlic bread."

Lesson 6
Identifying Words That Signal Contrast

When you contrast two things, you show how they are different. For example, the two photographs below contrast early roller coasters with roller coasters today.

How are these roller coasters different? Early roller coasters had single cars and simple paths. Today's roller coasters have several cars and complicated paths.

Certain words signal a contrast relationship. For example:

although	nevertheless
but	nonetheless
however	on the contrary
in contrast	on the other hand
in spite of	whereas
instead	while
	yet

Name _____ 43

The sentence below uses a signal word to contrast early roller coasters with roller coasters today.

Early roller coasters had single cars and simple paths, whereas today's roller coasters have several cars and complicated paths.

Exercise. Read the selection below, "The History of Roller Coasters" by Barbara Seuling. Then follow the directions at the end of the selection.

The "Switchback Railway" opened nearly 100 years ago at the Coney Island amusement park. It was the first American railroad built just for fun. People in its railroad car coasted a few hundred feet. At the end of the line, workers turned the car around. They pushed it over a switch and up a hill. At the top, the force of gravity did the rest. The car coasted back along another track.

The "Switchback Railway" was the idea of La Marcus Thompson. He had seen people paying to ride in coal cars in an old coal mine. Why not try the same thing at an amusement park? Because he did, Thompson is given credit for building the first U.S. roller coaster.

Since Thompson's time, people have been improving on his design. First a machine was built to replace the workers who pushed the car. Each coaster car was attached by a series of gears to a chain underneath the tracks. The machine then pulled the car uphill. Soon, taller coasters, with extra dips, twists and turns, were built. By the 1930s, the first loop was added. Cars zoomed down a steep hill into a somersault. The speed of the coaster car created enough force to hold the upside-down riders safely in their seats. The loop helped make coasters one of the most popular amusement park rides of all.

Today's roller coasters are bigger and faster than ever. Computers monitor their speed and safety. Flat metal tracks have been replaced by rails made of steel tubes. Cars with nylon wheels are more comfortable for riders. The curves are banked, or tilted, so that the cars can make smooth turns at top speeds.

Right now the roller coaster is very popular. Dozens of new ones have been built in the last few years. They have names like *The Corkscrew, The Mind Bender* and *The Great American Scream Machine*. Some fans meet each year for a "Coaster Culture Conference." A Florida disc jockey likes roller coasters so much that he set a record by riding one for 168 hours. He covered a distance of 1,946 miles (3,131 km).

Copyright © 1984 by Harcourt Brace Jovanovich, Inc. All rights reserved

One of the biggest, fastest roller coasters of all is *The American Eagle* in Gurnee, Illinois. Built in 1981, it climbs 12 stories high. Then it plunges 147 feet (44 m) into an underground tunnel at a speed of more than 60 miles (96 km) per hour. Other coasters have dazzling double and triple loops. Some swoop down through fog or total darkness. There are six roller coasters in a park in Sandusky, Ohio, that is called the "roller coaster capital of the world."

La Marcus Thompson's simple roller coaster was fun in the 1880s. But now better equipment and people's demand for new thrills have turned the modern roller coaster into an exciting Space Age ride.

Directions. For each sentence below, circle the word that signals contrast.

a. People riding the "Switchback Railway" coasted only a few hundred feet, (while) people riding today's roller coasters ride over a very long track.

b. Early roller coasters were propelled by the pull of gravity; (in contrast,) today's roller coasters are propelled by electricity.

c. (Although) the "Switchback Railway" was a straight path, modern roller coasters have lots of loops.

d. Early roller coasters ran on flat metal tracks, (but) today's roller coasters run on steel tubes.

e. At the end of a ride on an early roller coaster, workers pushed the car over a switch and up a hill; (however,) on today's roller coasters, machines do all the work.

Exercise 2. Write your answers to the questions below on the blanks.

a. Exercise 1a says that people riding the "Switchback Railway" coasted only a few hundred feet. What idea is contrasted with this?
People riding today's roller coasters ride over a very long track.

b. Exercise 1b says that early roller coasters were propelled by the pull of gravity. What idea is contrasted with this?
Today's roller coasters are propelled by electricity.

c. Exercise 1c says that the "Switchback Railway" was a straight path. What idea is contrasted with this?
Modern roller coasters have lots of loops.

d. Exercise 1d says that early roller coasters ran on flat metal tracks. What idea is contrasted with this?
Today's roller coasters run on steel tubes.

e. Exercise 1e says that at the end of a ride on an early roller coaster, workers pushed the car over a switch and up a hill. What idea is contrasted with this?
On today's roller coasters, machines do all the work.

Name _____ 45

Lesson 7
Understanding Comparison and Contrast

When you compare things, you show how they are alike. When you contrast things, you show how they are different. For example, look at the photographs below.

First, let's compare these two people. How are they alike? They are both girls, they both have brown hair, and they both have brown eyes.

Now, let's contrast these two people. One is older than the other, one has long hair while the other has shorter hair, and one has straight hair while the other has curly hair.

Exercise 1. In the paragraphs below, Meg tells about her sister, Molly. Read these paragraphs from *A Summer to Die* by Lois Lowry. Then follow the directions at the end.

>   It was Molly who drew the line.
>   She did it with chalk—a fat piece of white chalk left over from when we lived in town, had sidewalks, and used to play hopscotch, back when we both were younger. That piece of

Copyright © 1984 by Harcourt Brace Jovanovich, Inc. All rights reserved   45

chalk had been around for a long time. She fished it out of a little clay dish that I had made in last year's pottery class, where it was lying with a piece of string and a few paper clips and a battery that we weren't quite sure was dead.

She took the chalk and drew a line right on the rug. Good thing it wasn't a fuzzy rug or it never would have worked; but it was an old, worn, leftover rug from the dining room of our other house: very flat, and the chalk made a perfect white line across the blue—and then, while I watched in amazement (because it was unlike Molly, to be so angry), she kept right on drawing the line up the wall, across the wallpaper with its blue flowers. She stood on her desk and drew the line up to the ceiling, and then she went back to the other side of the room and stood on her bed and drew the line right up to the ceiling on that wall, too. Very neatly. Good thing it was Molly who drew it; if I had tried, it would have been a mess, a wavy line and off center. But Molly is very neat.

Then she put the chalk back in the dish, sat down on her bed, and picked up her book. But before she started to read again, she looked over at me (I was still standing there amazed, not believing that she had drawn the line at all) and said, "There. Now be as much of a slob as you want, only keep your mess on your side. *This side is mine.*"

When we lived in town we had our own rooms, Molly and I. It didn't really make us better friends, but it gave us a chance to ignore each other more.

Funny thing about sisters. Well, about us, anyway; Dad says it's unacademic to generalize. Molly is prettier than I am, but I'm smarter than Molly. I want with my whole being to *be* something someday; I like to think that someday, when I'm grown up, people everywhere will know who I am, because I will have accomplished something important—I don't even know for sure yet what I want it to be, just that it will be something that makes people say my name, Meg Chalmers, with respect. When I told Molly that once, she said that what *she* wants is to have a different name when she grows up, to be Molly Something Else, to be Mrs. Somebody, and to have her children, lots of them, call her "Mother," with respect, and that's all she cares about. She's content, waiting for that; I'm restless, and so impatient. She's sure, absolutely sure, that what she's waiting for will happen, just the way she wants it to; and I'm so uncertain, so fearful my dreams will end up forgotten somewhere, someday, like a piece of string and a paper clip lying in a dish.

Being both determined and unsure at the same time is what makes me the way I am, I think: hasty, impetuous, sometimes angry over nothing, often miserable about everything. Being so well sorted out in her own goals, and so assured of everything happening the way she wants and expects it to, is what makes Molly the way she is: calm, easygoing, self-confident, downright smug.

Name _____

    Sometimes it seems as if, when our parents created us, it took them two tries, two daughters, to get all the qualities of one whole, well-put-together person. More often, though, when I think about it, I feel as if they got those qualities on their first try, and I represent the leftovers. That's not a good way to feel about yourself, especially when you know, down in the part of you where the ambition is, where the dreams are, where the logic lies, that it's not true.

Directions. Write *Compare* in the blank at the right next to each sentence that shows how the two girls are alike. Write *Contrast* in the blank at the right next to each sentence that shows how the two girls are different.

a. Molly draws a straight line, whereas Meg would have drawn a crooked line.   *Contrast*

b. Both Meg and Molly live in the bedroom at the end of the hall.   *Compare*

c. Meg liked things better when she had her own room, and Molly had preferred having her own room, too.   *Compare*

d. Molly is neat, but Meg tends to be sloppy.   *Contrast*

e. Each girl has a dream of what she wants her future to be like.   *Compare*

Exercise 2. Since Meg and Molly are sisters, they are like each other in many ways. But they are also unlike each other. Answer each of the questions below. Write your answers on the blanks provided.

a. Both girls long to be treated with respect when they grow up. Meg wants people to say her name with respect. How is Molly's goal different?
Molly wants to have a different name, a married name, when she grows up, and she wants her children to call her Mother with respect.

b. Both girls have a dream, but Molly is content to wait to realize her dream. How is Meg different?
Meg is restless and impatient.

c. Molly is absolutely sure that her dream will turn out as she wants. How is Meg different?
Meg is uncertain and fearful.

d. Meg is often impetuous, or hasty. How is Molly different?
Molly is calm and easygoing.

e. Meg is often angry and miserable. How is Molly different?
Molly is self-confident and "downright smug."

Copyright © 1984 by Harcourt Brace Jovanovich, Inc. All rights reserved

Exercise 3. Compare and contrast two people you know. List four ways they are alike. List four ways they are different.

Alike

a. *Students' answers will vary.*

b. _____

c. _____

d. _____

Different

a. *Students' answers will vary.*

b. _____

c. _____

d. _____

Lesson 8

Identifying Relationship Patterns

People, things, events, and ideas may be related in several different ways. These include time order, spatial order, cause and effect, and comparison and contrast.

A time order relationship answers the question "When?" It tells you when one event happened in relation to another event. For example:

> After Fran won the tennis match, she shook hands with Debbie.

A spatial order relationship answers the question "Where?" It tells you where one object is in relation to other objects. For example:

> She hit the ball over the net.

A cause and effect relationship answers the question "Why?" The cause is what makes something happen. The effect is what happens. For example:

> Because she exercised regularly, Fran was in good condition for the match.

A comparison and contrast relationship answers the questions "How are they alike?" and "How are they different?" A comparison shows how things are alike. A contrast shows how they are different. For example:

> Both girls hoped to win the match. Debbie won the first set, but Fran won the next two sets.

Name _____

So far in this chapter we have looked at these relationship patterns separately. However, they are combined in most writing.

Exercise. Comparison and contrast is the most important relationship pattern in the selection below, but other relationship patterns are at work, too. Read the selection, "If You Went to School in France" by Peggy Kagan. Then follow the directions at the end of the selection.

Going to a new school means more than making new friends and finding your way home. The new school may have different ways of doing things. Think how different the customs would be if you went to school in another country, such as France.

In French schools the grades are numbered backward. The youngest children are in the highest grades, and the older you get, the lower your grade. Third grade, American style, is the same as ninth grade in France. Our fifth grade is their seventh grade. Sixth grade is the same in both countries, but American eleventh grade is French first grade.

After the French finish their first grade, they go to school another year to prepare for their final high-school exam, the *baccalauréat*. But they don't call it kindergarten—they call it *last* grade.

In a French school:
- You leave your shoes outside the classroom door and wear bedroom slippers in class.
- You do not say the pledge of allegiance in the mornings, because the French don't have one. The school day begins when the teacher comes in after the bell rings. The whole class stands up and says, *"Bonjour, madame,"* or *"Bonjour, monsieur"* ("Good morning, ma'am," or "Good morning, sir").
- You don't drink at a water fountain, because there aren't any. But many students bring snacks to eat at the ten o'clock recess.
- Of course you speak French all day long, but you start to learn a foreign language in seventh grade (American fifth). It might be English—the English that the British speak, not American English. The two are somewhat different.
- In arithmetic, French students put commas where we put decimal points and decimal points where we put commas. 1,592.64 is written 1.592,64. It's just a different custom.
- Test scores are based on twenty points rather than on one hundred points. Nineteen is a very good score indeed!
- You have some homework every day. The French believe that homework builds character.

Copyright © 1984 by Harcourt Brace Jovanovich, Inc. All rights reserved

In France, school might begin at 8:00 in the morning and end at 4:00 in the afternoon, but lunchtime lasts two hours. Most families eat lunch together at home, since it is the big meal of the day.

French students go to school on Saturday mornings, but not on Wednesdays. The other school days are Mondays, Tuesdays, Thursdays, and Fridays. The schedule is sometimes especially convenient. If a holiday falls on Monday, schools often "build the bridge," which means that they take Tuesday off, too. That way the students have a vacation lasting from Saturday afternoon until Thursday morning!

Some French people would like to change the school schedules so that they are like ours. They want the lunch break to last just one hour so that school can end earlier in the day. They would rather have school on Wednesdays than on Saturdays. But most of the French students are happy with their schools. They feel sorry for the poor American students, who have to go to school five days in a row.

Directions. Read the sentences below. In the blanks at the right, put T next to any sentence that shows a time order relationship. Put S next to any sentence that shows a spatial order relationship. Put CE next to any sentence that shows a cause and effect relationship. Put CC next to any sentence that shows a comparison and contrast relationship.

a. Third grade, American style, is the same as ninth grade, French style. — *CC*

b. Although sixth grade is the same, American eleventh grade is French first grade. — *CC*

c. After French students finish their first grade, they go to school for another year. — *T*

d. French students leave their shoes outside their classroom door. — *S*

e. French students do not say a pledge of allegiance because the French do not have one. — *CE*

f. The school day begins after the bell rings. — *T*

g. French test scores are based on twenty points; however, American test scores are based on one hundred points. — *CC*

h. Because the French believe that homework builds character, French students have homework every night. — *CE*

i. Many French families eat lunch together at home. — *S*

j. French students do not attend school on Wednesdays, unlike American students, who attend school five days in a row. — *CC*

Name _____

Lesson 9
Practice

The selection below is about the Apollo 13 mission. Pay special attention to relationship patterns as you read it. Then answer the questions at the end of the selection.

Lifeboat in Space
Gurney Williams III

The spaceship carrying three men to the moon shuddered as if it had bumped into something.

The shudder made no sense. There was nothing to bump into, 205,000 miles away from earth in black space. Astronaut Fred W. Haise was floating between two cabins in the ship when he felt the bump. He pulled himself quickly into the main cabin, called the command module. The ship continued to shake up and down. Haise's heart was beating twice as fast as usual.

There was no gravity in space, so Haise appeared to be floating through the air. Quickly he pulled himself to his seat. Another astronaut, John L. Swigert, slammed the door shut, sealing off the cabin.

Now all three were sitting in a small compartment, about as big as a three-man tent. It was a little after 9:00 P.M. on Monday, April 13, 1970, somewhere between earth and the moon.

Sealed into their cramped quarters, the men tried to figure out what had happened by reading dials in front of them. The whole ship was wobbling now, something like a car with a flat tire. The men's eyes raced over the lighted boards.

A few of the dials were behaving wildly. Some showed the ship was losing electrical power. Capt. James A. Lovell tried to stop the wobbling by firing small rockets outside the ship. It didn't work. Then suddenly he hit on the problem. One of the instruments was like a fuel gauge on a car. It showed how much fuel—called oxygen—was left in one of the large tanks. The fuel was used to make electrical power to run the ship. Just as important, it helped fuel the men: oxygen was a vital part of the air they breathed. Without fuel, the ship—and the men running it—would die.

Lovell radioed the earth about what he had found. "Our oxygen number two tank is reading zero," he said.

Then Lovell got out of his seat and glided to a window so he could see the outside of Apollo 13. He turned to the section of the ship called the service module. That was a large cylinder containing the fuel tanks and the main rocket engine. The service module was connected to one end of the command module where the men lived. In the black night of space, Lovell saw

Copyright © 1984 by Harcourt Brace Jovanovich, Inc. All rights reserved   51

a ghostly cloud coming out of the side of the service module.

Lovell got back on the radio, flashing the news to the gray-walled mission control room in Texas. "It looks to me that we are venting something," he said.

The ship, Apollo 13, pride of America, had soared into the sky two days before. Now like an old boat it was leaking, or "venting." One of its round, silvery fuel tanks had exploded, blasting a hole right through the side of the service module. Fuel was disappearing into space. Every two seconds the ship moved a mile closer to the moon, farther from earth.

Dozens of people on the ground tried to figure out what to do. What they needed was a lifeboat, another rocket ship with its own supply of oxygen, its own rocket engine, to bring the men home.

Well, in a way, Apollo 13 had a lifeboat. Its name was Aquarius. Aquarius was a small but complete rocket ship attached to the command module where the men lived. It had been designed to break away from the command module and carry two men to the surface of the moon, and then back up to the command module. It had its own air supply. It had its own rocket engine.

What it didn't have was space. There was no room to sit down in Aquarius. It had about as much space as a small closet. Aquarius also lacked strength. It was built to land on the moon—not on the earth. If the astronauts tried to ride it all the way home into the earth's air, it would burn to cinders. The command module was the only part of Apollo 13 designed to survive the fiery plunge back to earth.

The people on the ground argued and sweated over what to do. Finally, they agreed on a plan. They radioed the idea into space: Turn off everything in the command module to save what fuel is left. Climb into Aquarius. Use the Aquarius air supply and the Aquarius rocket to get home. Then when you get close to earth, climb back into the command module to protect yourselves when things get hot during landing.

Haise was the first to enter Aquarius. There were no lights except his flashlight. He floated into the dark little cabin. Closer and closer he moved to instruments covering the walls, closer to two triangular windows that had been designed for a view of the moon's surface. There were no seats. Haise turned on some of the switches. Soon the cramped lifeboat was filling with its own supply of oxygen.

Lovell joined Haise. Swigert stayed behind in the command module for a few minutes. He turned everything off, saving the little fuel left for the earth landing. Then he followed the other two into Aquarius. There was no chance now that Aquarius would land on the moon. It now had a new mission, a more important one: to keep three men alive.

Apollo 13, its crew huddled in one end, hurtled on toward the moon. The ship curved around the back side of the moon, out of sight of the earth. The gray lunar surface, pocked with craters, unrolled beneath the ship at about ten times the speed of a fast jet plane on earth. Then the earth, a blue green ball, appeared again. It was time to see whether the small rocket on Aquarius could blast the whole ship into a good course back home to earth. If the course adjustment failed, Apollo could miss the earth completely. The crew wouldn't survive long, and the ship would carry their bodies on an endless trip through space.

"Mark!" said a man in Texas, telling Lovell he had forty seconds to go before firing. Lovell put his hand on the firing button. "Five . . . four . . . three . . . two . . . one." At exactly the right time, the rocket began to fire. No one could hear the explosion. Sound couldn't pass through empty space. But the astronauts could feel the movement. The little rocket on Aquarius kept pushing the whole ship into line. It fired on, a four-minute explosion. Then a computer took over. It turned the rocket off at precisely the right instant.

Men in space and on the ground anxiously checked the course. The rocket had done its job. The ship was aimed for a landing in the Pacific Ocean, a quarter of a million miles away. At least the ship was headed in the right direction. Whether it would splash down safely, no one knew.

Other problems crowded in on the men in the crippled ship.

Since fuel was low, there was not enough energy to keep Aquarius warm. The temperature was dropping. And there were no winter clothes on Apollo 13.

Fuel had been used to make water, so now water supplies were low, too. Like desert explorers, the men had carried some of the water from the main supply in the command module to Aquarius in plastic juice bags. But the supply was still low. Their constant thirst was making it hard for the men to concentrate.

The air was bad. Back in the command module, a machine cleaned the air of dangerous gases. Aquarius had no such machine. Scientists on the ground suggested that the men try to build an air cleaner out of scraps aboard the ship—plastic bags, a hose, some cards, and tape. No one knew whether the contraption would work.

By now, millions of people on earth were worried about the voyagers from the moon. Concern had spread around the world. Thirteen countries offered to help in recovering the ship if it made it back to earth. People gathered on streets to watch TV reports, and in churches and synagogues to pray.

In space, it was cold and quiet. By early Wednesday morning, the temperature in Aquarius had dropped to fifty-five degrees. No one aboard could sleep. The men stayed awake, thirsty, tired, cold, moving around restlessly like animals in a small cage.

"You got up kind of early, didn't you?" the ground radioed.

The men said it was impossible to sleep. Temperatures were headed for the forties.

The air got worse. Before noon on Wednesday, a yellow light in Aquarius warned suddenly that it wasn't safe to breathe. Lovell turned on the taped-up contraption. It began to suck air through the filter.

Clean air flooded the cabin. The light went off. They would be okay as long as the makeshift air cleaner worked.

The double impact of thirst and cold was making it ever more difficult to think. At one point, Lovell was looking out the window. "The moon passed by," he said, watching a ball move slowly in front of the window. Then he corrected himself. "No, that's the earth." For an instant, the astronaut hadn't been able to tell them apart.

A sharp mind was now critical. The ship bore in on the earth like a bullet. The men had to begin moving back into the command module to prepare to land. Landing was complicated because most of Apollo 13 had to be thrown away in space before it was safe to come down. The command module had a solid round shield on its bottom to help it survive the heat when it plunged into the earth's air. The service module and Aquarius had no such protection. One of the astronauts' first jobs was to separate the command module from Aquarius and the service module.

The service module was the first to go. Explosive charges pushed it away from the command module. The module was spinning away into space when Lovell spotted the damage caused by the fuel tank explosion. "There's one whole side of that spacecraft missing," he said. Haise saw it too. "It's really a mess," he reported. The service module shrank to a dot in the blackness.

As it disappeared in the distance, the crew aboard Apollo began to worry about something else, more dangerous than anything that had happened. The fuel tank explosion had damaged the service module just a few feet from the heat shield that would protect the men during the last few minutes of the flight. Suppose the explosion had also damaged the heat shield. Would the command module stand the shock of re-entering earth's atmosphere? No one talked about the possibility. The earth seemed to grow steadily, a big, blue ball out the spaceship's window.

Lovell was the last to leave Aquarius. By the time he had eased his way back through a tunnel into the command module, Aquarius was filled with debris from the flight. The men switched over to the remaining oxygen in the command module. They sealed off the compartment in Aquarius. Then they blasted away from their lifeboat.

They were falling now, in the command module cone, at about 15,000 miles an hour. In less than an hour, they would either land, or burn up.

No one was talking much. Men on the ground were plotting the cone's course. There was little that could be done now. The command module was picking up speed. 17,000 miles an hour. 18,000. In a few minutes it reached 20,000 miles an hour. That meant the end of radio contact was near. The ship-to-ground radios couldn't work through the fire that would soon surround the command module. People on the ground talked nervously with the astronauts about a party they would have after the mission was ended. Swigert said he wished he could be there for it.

About 400,000 feet above the earth, the capsule began heating up. Soon flames whipped around it and the radio went dead. Ground scientists expected radio contact to be broken for about three and a half minutes.

But at the end of three and a half minutes, there was still no word. Another half-minute ticked by. Apollo 13 remained silent. And then another half-minute. Some people began to lose hope.

"Okay, Joe." The voice was Swigert's. He was on the air again. Within minutes, white-and-orange parachutes rose like giant party balloons over the little command module. It splashed into the sea and the men were picked up from their bobbing ship, still so cold inside you could see your breath. They had survived.

And what of Aquarius? The lifeboat had continued to send radio signals long after it had been separated from the men it had saved. "Where did she go?" one of the astronauts had asked just before radio contact was broken.

"Oh, I don't know," replied one of the ground crew. "She's up there somewhere." A radio aboard the deserted lifeboat sputtered out one dying signal. Then lifeboat Aquarius plunged into the earth's atmosphere and burned to ashes.

Exercise. Refer to "Lifeboat in Space" to answer the questions below. Write your answers on the blanks provided.

a. On April 13, 1970, at about 9 P.M., the astronauts in Apollo 13 feel the spaceship shudder, "as if it had bumped into something." Why doesn't this shudder make any sense?
There is nothing to hit 205,000 miles away from earth in space.

b. When does astronaut Lovell first radio earth?
He does this after he notices that the oxygen number two tank is reading zero.

c. As Apollo 13 travels farther and farther from earth, the spaceship leaks fuel. Every two seconds, how much closer does Apollo 13 move toward the moon?
Every two seconds it moves a mile closer to the moon.

d. The astronauts use Aquarius as a lifeboat, since it has its own air supply and rocket engine. On the other hand, what two things does Aquarius lack?
It lacks space and strength.

e. Why does Swigert stay behind for a few minutes in the command module when the other astronauts enter Aquarius?
He stays behind to turn everything off.

f. After they orbit the moon, the astronauts set off a small rocket on Aquarius in order to set the craft on a course back to earth. Why do the astronauts not hear the explosion caused by the rocket's firing?
Sound cannot pass through empty space.

g. If the spacecraft stays on course, where will it land?
It will land in the Pacific Ocean.

h. List three problems the astronauts have in the cramped Aquarius module.
It is cold, the water supply is low, and the air is bad.

i. After the men move back into the command module, they separate the service module from the ship. What problem do they now begin to worry about?
The men worry that the heat shield may have been damaged. If it was damaged, the command module may not withstand the shock of re-entering earth's atmosphere.

j. After radio contact is broken, ground scientists expect to hear from the astronauts within three-and-a-half minutes. When do they actually hear from the astronauts?
They hear after four-and-a-half minutes.

Name _____

Chapter 3
Judgments

You make judgments in order to choose wisely. In this chapter you will learn how to identify a reliable source of information. You will learn how to recognize statements of fact and statements of opinion. You will practice forming valid opinions and drawing sound conclusions. In addition, you will learn to spot stereotypes, unsupported judgments, and loaded words. Finally, you will practice identifying faulty reasoning.

Lesson 1
Identifying a Reliable Source

A reliable source is likely to give you accurate information about a topic. When you read, try to determine whether or not the author is a reliable source. Ask yourself three questions.

1. *Is the author qualified?* Usually, you can trust an author with training and experience in one field to give you accurate information about *this* field.

2. *Is the author presenting the information fairly?* Some authors try to be fair and present all the information truthfully. Others, however, may not tell you the whole story. They may stress only the good parts (or only the bad parts) in order to persuade you to do something that will benefit them.

3. *Is the information accurate?* If you doubt that the information in an article is accurate, or correct, check another source. You might check an encyclopedia, another book on the subject, or an expert in the field.

For example, imagine that your family has bought a boat. Your parents have asked you to find out which life jackets they should buy. You go to the library and find an article on life jackets in an issue of a consumer magazine. The author of the article is an experienced sailor who heads a government agency on water safety. The author describes the various types of life jackets on the market. She mentions the good and the bad points of each. Then she recommends one brand as being superior. Is the author a reliable source of information? Let's look at our three questions.

Copyright © 1984 by Harcourt Brace Jovanovich, Inc. All rights reserved

Is the author qualified? The author is an expert. She is an experienced sailor and she heads a government agency on water safety. By training and experience, she is qualified to give reliable advice.

Is the author presenting the information fairly? The author describes several types of life jackets and points out the good and the bad points of each. She seems to have nothing to gain by recommending one brand over another. In a store, however, the clerk may tell you only the good points of the merchandise. The clerk may not tell you of better products if they are not for sale in that store.

Is the information accurate? The author has tested various kinds of life jackets. You can compare her results with another expert's results. For example, you might go to a boat or yacht club and ask experienced sailors what they use.

The author of this article is a reliable source. Now look at the comic strip below. Neither of these Viking sailors knows enough about lifesavers to be a reliable source.

HAGAR THE HORRIBLE by Dik Browne

Exercise 1. Read each quotation below. Then read the occupations that follow each quotation. Which occupation would give the writer the training and experience necessary to be a reliable source of information for this quotation? Put an X next to this occupation.

a. "Those sneakers are not good for your feet. If you continue wearing them, you will develop fallen arches."

　_____　bus driver

　_____　mechanic

　__X__　foot doctor

b. "Although the two students play guitar at the same level right now, Bobby will develop into the finer musician."

　_____　nurse

　__X__　music teacher

　_____　bridge builder

Name _____

c. "The *Easy-Touch* is the best typewriter on the market for high-school students."

_____ actor

__X__ high-school typing instructor

_____ bookkeeper

d. "Mary's skin is dry and flaky. She needs extra vitamins."

__X__ doctor

_____ hair stylist

_____ singer

e. "This American history book gives you a comprehensive and accurate view of our past. It is filled with details of everyday living that make you feel you are experiencing the events of our past yourself."

_____ television producer

_____ medical doctor

__X__ well-known historian

Exercise 2. Read the following statements. Each is followed by three sources. Check the one who is the most reliable source.

a. "This used stereo system is in excellent condition. You will not regret buying it."

_____ your best friend Mike

_____ owner of the stereo system

__X__ radio, television, and stereo repair person

b. "Anita is an excellent dancer. She should consider going to a high school with special dance courses."

_____ Anita's uncle

__X__ Anita's dance teacher

_____ Anita's music teacher

c. "If used regularly, this shampoo will help clear up even the worst cases of dandruff."

__X__ school nurse

_____ clerk in a drug store

_____ actress in a Broadway play

Copyright © 1984 by Harcourt Brace Jovanovich, Inc. All rights reserved

d. "We all need to exercise. The *Fit for Life Health Club* offers excellent exercise classes in a pleasant environment. I advise you to join now."

__X__ the National Evaluation of Health Clubs

_____ salesperson at the Fit for Life Health Club

_____ member of the Fit for Life Health Club

e. "Maria takes marvelous pictures. She should enter the next photography contest sponsored by the newspaper. She stands a good chance of winning."

_____ Maria's tennis instructor

_____ person who delivers the newspaper to Maria's family

__X__ professional photographer

Lesson 2

Recognizing Statements of Fact and Statements of Opinion

A statement of fact contains information that can be proved true or false. It contains information about things that have happened in the past or are happening in the present. For example, here are three statements of fact.

> Elton John was born on March 25, 1947, in Piener, England.
> The earth is revolving around the sun.
> Five pounds of feathers weighs as much as five pounds of rocks.

A statement of opinion expresses a personal belief or attitude. It contains information that cannot be proved true or false. A statement about the future is a statement of opinion, since it contains information that cannot be proved true or false at this time. A statement about personal likes and dislikes is a statement of opinion.

Sometimes a statement of opinion contains words like "Everyone knows that" or "The truth is that" or "It's a fact that." Don't let these words mislead you into thinking a statement of opinion is a statement of fact.

Here are three statements of opinion.

> Tokyo is the most exciting city in the world.
> Everyone knows that Sue will win the trophy.
> It's the truth that cats make better pets than dogs.

Name _____

Exercise 1. Look at the invention below and read the description following it. Then read the five lettered statements. Write *Fact* in the blank next to each statement of fact. Write *Opinion* in the blank next to each statement of opinion.

No. 730,918. PATENTED JUNE 16, 1903.

EYE PROTECTOR FOR CHICKENS.
APPLICATION FILED DEC. 10, 1902.

NO MODEL.

UNITED STATES PATENT OFFICE
EYE PROTECTOR FOR CHICKENS

No. 730,918 Patented June 16, 1903

Specification forming part of Letters Patent No. 730,918, dated June 16, 1903
Application filed December 10, 1902. Serial No. 134,679.
(No model.)

... This invention relates to eye protectors, and more particularly to eye protectors designed for fowls. This invention protects the eyes of fowls from other fowls that might attempt to peck them. A further object of the invention is to provide a construction that may be easily and quickly put on and removed. These eye protectors will not block the sight of the fowl. ...

a. This is the funniest thing ever invented. *Opinion*

b. Some chickens try to peck other chickens' eyes. *Fact*

c. The description claims that chicken eye protectors are easy to take off. *Fact*

d. Chicken eye protectors were patented in 1903. *Fact*

e. It's the truth that glasses make chickens look more attractive. *Opinion*

Copyright © 1984 by Harcourt Brace Jovanovich, Inc. All rights reserved

Exercise 2. Look at the invention below and read the description following it. Then read the five letter statements. Write *Fact* in the blank by each statement of fact. Write *Opinion* in the blank by each statement of opinion.

No. 81,437. Coffin. Patented Aug. 25, 1868.

UNITED STATES PATENT OFFICE
IMPROVED BURIAL-CASE
Specification forming part of Letters Patent No. 81,437, dated August 25, 1868

... The nature of this invention consists in placing on the lid of the coffin, and directly over the face of the body laid therein, a square tube. This tube extends from the coffin up through and over the surface of the grave. It contains a ladder and a cord. One end of the cord is placed in the hand of the person laid in the coffin. The other end of the cord is attached to a bell on the top of the square tube. If a person is buried before he is dead, he can climb out of the grave and the coffin by the ladder. If he is not able to use the ladder, he can ring the bell, thereby giving an alarm, and thus save himself from premature burial and death. If, on inspection, the person is dead, the tube is withdrawn, the sliding door closed, and the tube used for a similar purpose. ...

a. This invention will sell well in Transylvania. _____Opinion_____
b. The tube contains a ladder and a cord attached to a bell. _____Fact_____
c. It's a fact that the tube can be used for another grave. _____Fact_____
d. This device was invented to prevent a person from being buried alive. _____Fact_____
e. Everyone can see that this device is worthless. _____Opinion_____

Name _____

Lesson 3

Understanding Mixed Statements of Fact and Opinion

A statement of fact contains information that can be proved true or false. For example, read the statement below.

> Scientists investigate many cases in which people claim to have seen flying saucers.

This is a statement of fact. You can prove this information is true. There are reports of the actual investigations.

A statement of opinion expresses a personal belief or attitude. For example, read the statement below.

> One day scientists will find that life exists on other planets.

Since the information in this statement predicts the future, it is a statement of opinion.

Some statements mix facts and opinions. They are called mixed statements of fact and opinion. For example, read the following sentence.

> In the field I saw an unusual light; **I know I will find that it was caused by a spaceship from another planet.**

The first part of this statement is a statement of fact. The second part, printed in boldface, is a statement of opinion, since it predicts the future.

Now read the next mixed statement of fact and opinion.

> When he saw the light in the field, the man started jumping up and down, shouting wildly, and doing other foolish things.

It is a fact that the man started jumping up and down and shouting wildly when he saw the light. It's an opinion that these and the other things he did were foolish.

Exercise 1. Read the following selection from *UFO Encounters* by Rita Golden Gelman and Marcia Seligson. Then follow the directions at the end of the selection.

> Life in the Universe?
> One thing we know for sure: There *is* life on the planet Earth. The star that we call the sun gives light and warmth and life to our planet.
> Suppose you were to make a tiny dot on this page and call it the sun. Then suppose you were to keep on making dots and never stop. No time out for parties or dinners, no more school, no more sleeping—just dot-making for the rest of your life.

Copyright © 1984 by Harcourt Brace Jovanovich, Inc. All rights reserved

By the time you are eighty years old, if you have covered your house, your neighborhood, your city, and all of the United States with dots, you will still not have made as many dots as there are stars in just the *Milky Way* galaxy. There are billions and billions and billions of stars out there. Our sun is only one of them.

And most of these stars *could* be suns for other planets of living things—even intelligent beings.

Maybe beings like us—with arms and noses and language and clothing. Or beings that are nothing at all like us—like nothing we've ever seen—like nothing we can even imagine.

If they *are* out there—those other beings—what are they doing? What are they like? Do they think about us? Do they want to get together with us?

Maybe some of them are far more advanced than we are. Maybe some of them have figured out ways to travel through space and time. Perhaps they have already visited Earth in their spaceships. Perhaps they have even been seen by some of our Earth people.

Which brings us to UFOs: Unidentified Flying Objects.

It's moving.
It's glowing.
It's streaking across the sky.
It must be a UFO!

Probably not. The sky is full of things—and most of them are not UFOs. During the day we can see birds and planes and clouds. At night we can see stars, the flashing lights of planes, and the glowing trails of meteors. All of these sky-things can be mistaken for UFOs.

There are also things happening up there that are more complex and harder to recognize. The planet Venus, for example, sometimes looks so much brighter than anything else in the heavens that it seems to be a giant, unexplainable ball of light. And as it moves westward, Venus takes on an eerie red glow— much like many people's UFOs.

Venus fools a lot of people. Astronomers know that on certain nights, when Venus is especially bright, hundreds of people will phone the police or the Air Force and say, with a lot of excitement, that they are sure they have seen a UFO.

People-made satellites fool a lot of us, too. There are dozens of them orbiting the Earth. They can be seen without binoculars . . . and they *do* look like unnatural objects in the sky. When someone reports a UFO, scientists check their satellite charts.

They check the weather balloons, too. There are thousands of them up there sending down weather reports. And some of them have lights which are often mistaken for UFOs.

Strange clouds sometimes appear like mysterious flying craft. So do tornadoes. And certain kinds of lightning can seem to be fiery, fast-moving balls.

People are often confused by all those things in the sky. The scientists are not. They can easily determine that many UFOs are not UFOs at all.

When a UFO is reported, scientists, the police, the military, and ordinary citizens whose hobby it is to study UFOs come to the spot and check out the possibilities. Seventy percent of all UFO reports turn out to be natural effects or people-made objects. A few turn out to be hoaxes—stories that people make up.

But one out of five of all these reported sightings of UFOs turn out to be *real* UFOs—abnormal things in the sky that cannot be explained or identified.

There have been 70,000 or more reported sightings from all over the world. Some of them are reports of distant objects in the sky. Some of them are of craft that have landed in places very close to the witness. And some are strange tales of alien creatures who walk and talk.

Many of the stories are carefully investigated. In some cases there are pictures. In some, investigators have found holes in the ground or burnt spots on trees. Many of the cases sound absurd, many convincing.

But remember: a UFO has never landed on the south lawn of the White House. News people have never been given an interview with a being from a spacecraft. And a UFO has never crashed in the desert so that we could examine it.

We don't know whether UFOs exist. We know that cocker spaniels and television sets exist, but not UFOs.

And, if they do exist, we really don't know what they are, where they come from, or what they're doing here. UFOs are a huge mystery.

Directions. For each mixed statement of fact and opinion, draw one line under the part that is an opinion.

a. There is life on the planet Earth, and <u>there will always be life on the planet Earth</u>.

b. There are billions and billions of stars and even more planets circling those stars; <u>surely life exists somewhere else in the universe</u>.

c. The man said he looked at the night sky and saw a spaceship <u>that was more beautiful than any craft built on Earth</u>.

d. People who believe that life exists only on Earth <u>will be proved wrong</u>, just as people who believed that the world was flat were proved wrong.

e. We saw three men who were so extraordinary <u>they could only be creatures from outer space</u>.

Exercise 2. Read the mixed statements of fact and opinion below. One word in each statement expresses an opinion. Write this word in the blank at the right.

a. The ugly creature asked us to come along with him.   *ugly*

b. The ship flashed its lights, played music, and did other enchanting things.   *enchanting*

c. The door of the ship opened and out walked a beautiful woman.   *beautiful*

d. The foolish people claimed to have seen UFOs.   *foolish*

e. In the haze he saw the terrible face of the alien.   *terrible*

Lesson 4
Forming Valid Opinions

A valid opinion is a judgment or belief supported by facts. You form valid opinions every day. For example, you hear that the rock group *The Candles* has a new album. You decide that you will like it. You base your judgment on facts. When you heard a cut from the album, you liked it. You enjoyed their two other albums. Your friend Mike, who has heard the album, likes the album.

Exercise 1. Read each opinion below. Then read the statements that follow each opinion. Write *Yes* next to each statement that backs up the opinion. Write *No* next to each statement that does not.

a. *Opinion:* Jack will not be re-elected as president of our club.

   Yes — I questioned fifteen of the twenty members of our club, and they all said they would not vote for Jack.

   Yes — All fifteen members said they prefer Shirley, who is running against Jack.

   No — Shirley is a smart dresser.

   No — When I asked Jack if he thought he would be re-elected, he said, "Of course I will!"

b. *Opinion:* The new restaurant, *The Spot*, will be a success.

   No — The owner of *The Spot* is a good friend of my father.

   Yes — Reporters from our local newspaper reviewed the restaurant and wrote that the food tastes great and the prices are reasonable.

   Yes — *The Spot* has been filled every night since it opened last week.

   Yes — The owner of *The Spot* is very friendly and makes people feel welcome.

Name _____

c. Opinion: My brother Lee will become a professional athlete.

Yes   For the last three years, Lee has attended an Olympics training camp.

_No_   Lee looks very handsome in his basketball uniform.

Yes   Lee has been an outstanding member of the school basketball team.

Yes   Lee has been selected to compete in the next Olympics Games.

d. Opinion: The school football game next weekend will be well attended.

_No_   My boyfriend is on the football team.

Yes   If our team wins this game, we will go on to the championship.

Yes   Football is very popular at our school.

Yes   We are playing our traditional rival, Piermont Junior High School.

Exercise 2. Read each opinion below. Then, on the blanks provided, list two facts that would support each opinion.

a. Opinion: Jake will be elected junior class president.
  (1) *Students' answers will vary.*
  (2) _____

b. Opinion: Christine's model will win the model airplane contest.
  (1) *Students' answers will vary.*
  (2) _____

c. Opinion: It will snow tomorrow.
  (1) *Students' answers will vary.*
  (2) _____

d. Opinion: The airport will be crowded on the day before Thanksgiving.
  (1) *Students' answers will vary.*
  (2) _____

Lesson 5
Recognizing Stereotypes

A stereotype is an opinion about a group of people that does not allow for individual differences. A stereotype is not based on proof. Two common stereotypes are "All bank presidents are white-haired men" and "All real men watch football and hockey." A stereotype can cloud your judgment and prevent you from seeing the worth of an individual.

In the comic strip below, Bridget holds an opinion that is a stereotype. She believes that real Viking boys are cruel and tough. This opinion prevents her from seeing the worth of the boy she is with.

HAGAR THE HORRIBLE by Dik Browne

When you read a statement of opinion, watch out for words like *all*, *always*, *only*, and *never*. Often they signal a stereotype. For example, the following statement is a stereotype:

> All children love comic books.

In a stereotype, the words *all*, *always*, *only*, and *never* are often implied even if they are not stated. For example, "Children love pizza" means the same as "All children love pizza" or "Children always love pizza." In fact, some children don't like pizza very much.

Be careful, however. The words *all*, *always*, *only*, and *never* are also used in statements of fact. For example:

> All home owners in our town must pay a property tax.

Exercise 1. If the statement below is a stereotype, write *Yes* in the blank at the right. If the statement is not a stereotype, write *No*.

a. All professional athletes exercise regularly. _____ *No*

b. All models are tall and beautiful. _____ *Yes*

c. Secret agents lead glamorous lives. _____ *Yes*

d. Everyone knows that all children enjoy the circus. _____ *Yes*

e. Everyone in our class wrote a book report. _____ *No*

f. Presidential elections always fall on even-numbered years. — *No*

g. All people from Sweden have blond hair and blue eyes. — *Yes*

h. Girls like boys who play football. — *Yes*

i. Several of my friends are dating members of the football team. — *No*

j. Anyone who works for a living is a wage earner. — *Yes*

Exercise 2. Try again. If the statement below is a stereotype, write *Yes* in the blank. If the statement is not a stereotype, write *No*.

a. I don't like several people at that junior high school. — *No*

b. The students at that junior high school are loud and destructive. — *Yes*

c. Anyone over sixty-five is too old to work. — *Yes*

d. Some seventy- and eighty-year-olds play golf and tennis. — *No*

e. Politicians avoid telling you what they really believe. — *Yes*

f. A politician who speaks the truth will never get elected. — *Yes*

g. Many politicians work hard to represent the people fairly. — *No*

h. My brother enjoyed the three years he spent in the army. — *No*

i. Men make the best soldiers. — *Yes*

j. The best doctors are always women because women are kind and sensitive to the needs of others. — *Yes*

Lesson 6

Identifying Unsupported Judgments

An unsupported judgment is not backed up by facts. Have you ever been accused of jumping to conclusions? Perhaps your parents said that the family was moving to a new town. You immediately decided that you weren't going to like the new town and that you wouldn't be able to make any friends. Later you found that the town wasn't so bad after all; in fact, it was quite nice. You also found that you still liked your old friends, but you were making new friends.

When you first heard the news of your family's moving, you had jumped to a conclusion, or made a judgment not supported by facts. Making judgments not supported by facts can lead to costly mistakes. The more facts you have to back up a judgment, the more likely it will be that your judgment is sound.

Copyright © 1984 by Harcourt Brace Jovanovich, Inc. All rights reserved

In the comic strip below, the sergeant jumps to a conclusion. When he sees the colonel pushing against his desk, he doesn't try to find out any of the facts. He immediately jumps to the conclusion that the colonel has "just about had it." In fact, the colonel is simply exercising.

BEETLE BAILEY by Mort Walker

Exercise. In the selection below, the real estate agent jumps to many conclusions. Read this selection, from *Anastasia Again!* by Lois Lowry. Then answer the questions at the end of it.

Anastasia didn't even hear him. She was looking at the house, and her stomach felt as if she had been kicked by someone wearing cowboy boots. Her mother had once told her that it was painful to fall in love, and now, suddenly, she knew what that meant. She had expected to feel it for the first time when she fell in love with a *boy*, for pete's sake. But now she was feeling it—the pain in her stomach, her heart beating funny, Mantovani violin music in her ears, and aching behind her eyes as she tried not to cry—because she was falling in love with a *house*.

It was because the house had a tower.

And it happened to all of them as if it were a contagious disease. The main symptoms were speechlessness and silly grins.

The real estate lady didn't understand that. She thought something was wrong. She became confused when none of them said anything, and she began to apologize for the house.

The study was lined from floor to ceiling, on every wall, with bookcases. And it had a fireplace. Anastasia's father stood in the center of the study with a silly grin and said nothing.

"I know you wanted a study," said the real estate lady. "Of course this room seems small, I know. But you could have all these shelves torn out, and that would open up the room quite a bit and make it larger, and . . ."

Her voice drifted away in confusion, because no one was listening to her. Anastasia could read her father's mind. In his mind he was arranging all his books, alphabetically, in the shelves. In his mind, he had a roaring fire in the fireplace; he was sitting in front of it, smoking his pipe, reading.

They moved on to another room, a huge octagonal room stuck onto the side of the house. It was all windows. They stood there, silently, with the same silly grins, and Anastasia read her mother's mind. Her mother was setting up easels in the room. She was doing huge paintings with sweeping brush strokes. She was hiring models to stand there in the brilliant light. She was doing sculpture. Murals.

The real estate lady began to talk very fast, trying to mend the silence. "Of course, in the Victorian era, when this house was built, they always had these strange rooms that they called solariums. Useless, now. You could close it off to conserve heat. Or, in fact, you could even have this room torn down. It does stick out rather awkwardly, from the side of the house, I know. The yard would be bigger if you just had this room taken off, and . . . "

But no one was listening to her. She stopped talking, midsentence, confused, and they moved on.

Upstairs, they moved from one bedroom to another. Big bedrooms, with fireplaces and huge closets for playing hide-and-seek. Their feet echoed in the empty rooms: the heavy, decisive steps of Dr. Krupnik's size-twelve shoes; the staccato taps of the real estate lady's high heels; the duet of Anastasia's sneakers and her mother's sandals; and behind them, the pad, pad, pad of Sam's little feet.

Now not even the real estate lady was saying much. She was embarrassed. She thought they hated the house. Halfheartedly, in a bathroom, she said, "New plumbing. Wonderful copper pipes," but then she fell silent.

Finally, she opened a door on the second floor and gestured toward the narrow, curving staircase behind it.

"You could just close this off," she said.

Anastasia scuttled up the little staircase alone to the tower room and stood there looking out and down, at the green lawns, the huge elms, the curving streets, and in the distance, the Charles River and the buildings of Cambridge and Boston.

Her parents didn't come up the stairs. They had read her mind and knew that she wanted to be in the tower room alone.

But after a moment she could hear Sam's small feet climbing the stairs. He appeared in the room, looking puzzled, and said, "Do you want me to cry again? Do you want to do the plot now?"

But Anastasia said no and took his hand. They went back downstairs just in time to hear her father tell the real estate lady that they would buy the house.

Questions

a. At the beginning of this selection, the real estate agent sees that the members of Anastasia's family are speechless and that they have silly grins on their faces. She jumps to a conclusion. What does she conclude?
She concludes something is wrong.

b. What is the real reason for their being speechless?
They have fallen in love with the house.

c. When Anastasia's father sees the study, he stands in the center of it and says nothing. Again, the real estate agent jumps to a conclusion. What does she conclude?
She concludes that he thinks the room is too small and that he doesn't like the bookcases.

d. What does Anastasia believe her father is really thinking?
Anastasia concludes he is thinking about how he would arrange all the books and is picturing himself sitting in front of the fireplace.

e. When the family walk into the sun room, they again say nothing. The real estate agent jumps to a conclusion. What does she conclude?
She concludes they do not like the room.

f. What does Anastasia believe her mother is thinking?
She believes her mother is picturing herself painting and sculpting in this room.

g. Once upstairs, the real estate agent stops saying very much. She jumps to a conclusion about the tower room. Why does she suggest they close off the staircase to the tower room?
She assumes they would not want a tower room.

h. How does Anastasia feel about the tower room?
Anastasia very much likes the tower room.

i. The real estate agent jumps to a conclusion about the family's buying the house. What does she conclude?
She concludes they will not buy the house.

j. How does the family prove her wrong?
Mother and Father buy the house.

Lesson 7

Identifying Loaded Words

Loaded words color, or slant, writing. They are charged with emotion and arouse strong feelings. Often, they express the writer's judgment of things.

Some loaded words arouse negative feelings. For example, the word *car* is neutral. This means that it does not arouse either positive or negative feelings. However, if you describe a car as a *jalopy*, you arouse negative feelings. The word *jalopy* carries the meaning of old and dilapidated.

On the other hand, some loaded words arouse positive feelings. For example, an advertisement may call a new car a "distinctive motorcar," creating a positive impression of prestige and dignity.

In the same way, a horse could be described as a *nag*, which creates the impression of a pathetic, broken-down animal that no one would want to own. In contrast, a horse could be described as a *thoroughbred*, creating the impression of a beautiful, expensive, and spirited animal.

In the comic strip below, Hagar and his wife each use a loaded word for rest and relaxation. Hagar's wife calls it "slothfulness." Hagar thinks of it as "leisure."

HAGAR THE HORRIBLE by Dik Browne

Copyright © 1984 by Harcourt Brace Jovanovich, Inc. All rights reserved

Exercise. The puzzle on page 75 contains twenty loaded words. These words may be written from left to right, from right to left, from top to bottom, from bottom to top, or diagonally. Read each clue below. Then find the word in the puzzle that matches each clue. Circle it and write it in the blank next to the clue. (You may use your dictionary to help you.)

Clues

a. Negative word for gift — *bribe*

b. Positive word for play — *recreation*

c. Negative word for group — *mob*

d. Negative word for jargon or technical language — *gobbledygook*

e. Positive word for thin — *slender*

f. Negative word for cautious — *chicken*

g. Positive word for graveyard — *cemetery*

h. Positive word for old and used belongings — *antiques*

i. Two words for pale that create a negative impression — *washed out*

j. Two words for stubborn that create a positive impression — *strong willed*

k. Two words for stubborn that create a negative impression — *pig headed*

l. Negative word for quiet — *mousey*

m. Positive word for bossy — *assertive*

n. Two words for big voiced that create a negative impression — *loud mouthed*

o. Positive word for cheap — *thrifty*

p. Negative word for sharp and cunning — *sneaky*

q. Negative word for government worker — *bureaucrat*

r. Negative word for fearless — *foolhardy*

s. Positive word for baby — *cherub*

t. Negative word for cry — *whine*

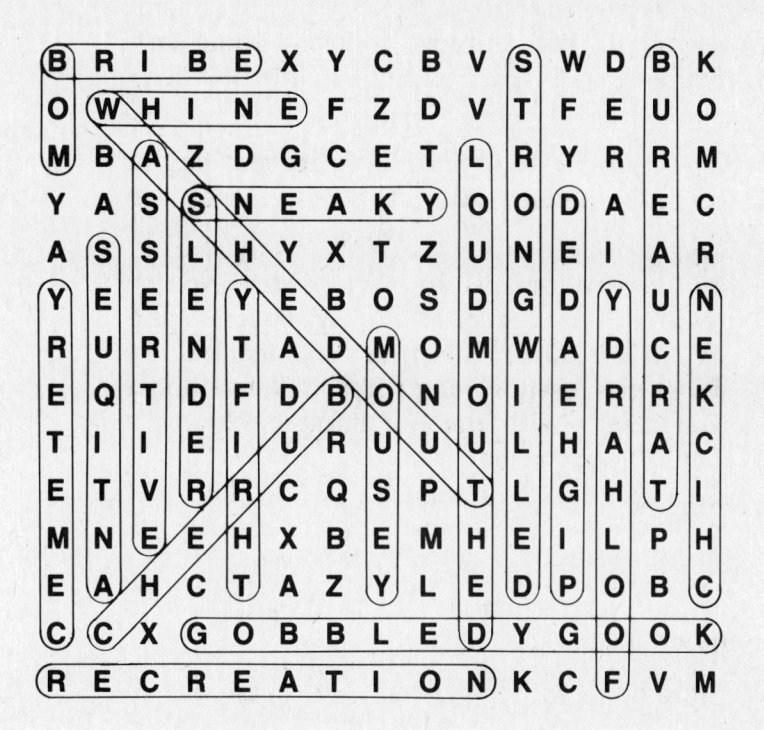

Name _____

Lesson 8
Identifying Faulty Reasoning

Faulty reasoning is thinking that is not sound. Several traps can cloud your thinking and make your reasoning faulty.

First, a writer may disguise a statement of opinion as a statement of fact. For example, the writer may say:

> Everyone knows that ten years from now we will all be using solar energy to power our homes.
> It's a fact that Tommie Browne will win the election.

All statements that make predictions about the future are statements of opinion. Do not be fooled by the words "everyone knows" and "it's a fact."

Second, a writer may use evidence that doesn't fit or support the opinion or conclusion. For example, a writer may say:

> Some people say that the ghost of Peter Stuyvesant haunts his former estate in lower Manhattan. They claim he walks on his pegleg through the site of his manor house. At times, they say, he pounds the walls of his tomb. It's really an exciting story. Late last night I thought I heard someone walking in the living room. When I looked, no one was there. Surely my house must be haunted just as Peter Stuyvesant's estate is.

Copyright © 1984 by Harcourt Brace Jovanovich, Inc. All rights reserved

75

At the end of the paragraph you just read, the writer states that her house must be haunted just as Peter Stuyvesant's estate is. The evidence she gives, the fact that some people believe Peter Stuyvesant's former estate is haunted, does not support, or back up, this judgment.

Third, the writer may cloud your thinking by using name-calling, or appeals to your emotions. For example, the writer may say:

> No self-respecting American will permit savage coyotes to roam at will. Only soft-headed fools want to protect these killer creatures.

We all want to be considered "self-respecting Americans." No one wants to be thought of as a "soft-headed fool." "Savage coyotes" and "killer creatures" are emotional terms chosen to make us afraid of these animals. The writer has used name-calling and emotional appeals to encourage you to agree with him and disagree with those who feel the coyote should be protected.

Exercise 1. Write *F* next to each statement of fact. Write *D* next to each statement of opinion disguised as fact.

a. Everyone agrees that Roberto will be elected class treasurer.   *D*

b. Almost everyone knows that George Washington was our first President.   *F*

c. Everyone knows that our football team will win the game on Friday.   *D*

d. It's a fact that Marcia will become a professional dancer.   *D*

e. It's a fact that Marcia wants to become a professional dancer.   *F*

Exercise 2. In each of the following items, the opinion or conclusion is printed in **boldface.** If the evidence in the paragraph fits, or supports, the judgments, write *Yes* in the blank at the right. If the evidence does not, write *No*.

a. **Everyone knows that it's more fun to live in the city than in the country.** I lived in the country for a year when I was eight. I had a hard time making friends my own age. My school was several miles from my home, so my parents had to drive me there each day. My teacher's name was Mrs. Cedar. I liked her very much. The country was pretty, but I was glad when we moved back to the city.   *No*

b. There are 350 students in the eighth grade at our school. I asked 100 of these students what their favorite color is. Thirty-nine students said blue. Only five students said yellow. I asked these same students what their least favorite color is. Twenty-eight said yellow. Only two said blue. **In conclusion, I feel that the eighth-grade class meeting room should be painted blue, not yellow.**   *Yes*

c. The eighth grade class meeting room should be painted blue, not yellow. Blue makes me think of a summer day at the beach with blue skies and a calm sea. I love going to the beach. Last summer I spent a week at Virginia Beach with my family. I had a great time. The ocean was warm and the weather was perfect for the entire week. Of all the things I did last summer, I enjoyed spending a week at Virginia Beach the most. _____*No*_____

d. There is no such thing as a haunted house. Investigators have found that most seemingly supernatural events have quite natural causes. For example, when two people living in an old house saw a picture fall off the wall for no apparent reason, they yelled "Ghost!" An investigator found that the picture fell because of an earth tremor, not because of a ghost. As one man was walking toward an old house at night, he claimed he saw a ghost in the window. An investigator found that what the man saw was simply a curtain that had blown up against a lampshade. A woman in an old house claimed she heard a ghost moaning every night. An investigator found that the ghost was really an owl that had set up a nest near the house. _____*Yes*_____

Exercise 3. Read each statement below. If the statement contains name-calling or appeals to your emotions, write *Yes* in the blank at the right. If the statement does not, write *No*.

a. Only a fool would believe in ghosts. _____*Yes*_____

b. Many people believe that supernatural events have quite natural causes. _____*No*_____

c. Only closed-minded and dull people refuse to believe in the supernatural. _____*Yes*_____

d. No intelligent person would take a ghost story seriously. _____*Yes*_____

e. Many intelligent people admit that science still has a lot to learn about life on this planet. _____*No*_____

f. Only an unfeeling Scrooge would refuse to donate money to this cause. _____*Yes*_____

g. Many people feel his cause is wrong, and they refuse to support him. _____*No*_____

h. If you don't want to be witty and bright, don't see *The July Girls*. If you do, buy tickets today. _____*Yes*_____

i. *Celestial Shoes* get taken to the best dances. Buy a pair today. _____*Yes*_____

j. Twenty-seven out of one hundred students surveyed wear *Shadowland Jeans*. _____*No*_____

Lesson 9
Practice

Use your judgment skills to read the selection below. Then complete the exercise that follows it.

Dinosaur Hunting
Robert Makela

I teach science at Rudyard High School, which is very close to the Canadian border in northern Montana. Each summer I have a job which some of you would hate, but some of you would do just for the fun of it. I hunt dinosaurs.

No living dinosaurs have been around for something like 100 million years. Hunting them means looking for their fossil bones. There are a number of good hunting grounds in northern Montana. Most of these areas are in desolate-looking country which is sometimes called the badlands. Therefore, dinosaur hunting means camping out for the summer. Our camp life is full and exciting, for we never know what we will find or what will happen next.

Our hunting is done by a crew, usually seven of us, who camp and work together. Each person's idea of how camping is done is different. Some of our tents are small, just for one person. I have a large one, about 18 feet across and built like a tepee. We can all get inside and still have room enough to build a fire for warmth and light.

We get up early each morning so that we have finished breakfast and are ready for work at eight o'clock. Hunting dinosaurs takes sharp eyes and lots of patience. Any rock that looks a little bit strange is examined carefully to see if it may be a dinosaur bone. The hard work comes after finding part of a bone sticking out of the ground. Usually this means digging it up with small tools like the ones your dentist uses. We use soft paintbrushes to clean off the little pieces of rock that are carefully scraped away. Once a large part of the bone is exposed, we cover it with a special glue to harden the bone. Then we can put on a cast just as a doctor puts a cast on a broken leg to hold the bone in place. Once the bones are all protected and labeled, they are sent to the laboratory at Princeton University where they can be studied more carefully.

Northern Montana is so far north that the summer sun doesn't set until about 10:30. After we finish work in the late afternoon, we still have almost six hours of daylight. Last year we camped near the Teton River. Often we would go fishing or swimming or floating downriver on a rubber raft. Sometimes we took short hikes to explore the area, looking for better hunting places. By sundown we would build a campfire. Then we would just relax or talk about what had gone on during the day or sometimes sing together.

Now that I have told you what dinosaur hunting is like, I should also tell you about one of our discoveries. One of the

Name _____

mysteries about dinosaurs is why so few fossils of young animals have been found. Therefore, it was especially exciting in the summers of 1978 and 1979 when we found 15 baby dinosaurs and parts of 30 dinosaur eggs. Here is how it happened.

We had been camped north of Rudyard when we received word from Marion Brandvold that she had found parts of a dinosaur near the mountains in Teton County. People often make mistakes, thinking that any old bone is a dinosaur fossil—but not this time. Mrs. Brandvold had parts of a dinosaur called **Corythosaurus.** We talked with her about her dinosaur and were all ready to leave when she asked us to look at some smaller bones she had found.

That was instant excitement. The small fossil looked like the leg bone of a duck-billed dinosaur—only a small one. We guessed correctly that it came from a young animal. No one had ever found a baby dinosaur in North America, and no one had ever found a baby duck-billed dinosaur anywhere in the world. When we saw where the bones had come from, we set up camp and went to work. We found about 3,000 more. There were enough in one place to reconstruct 15 baby dinosaur skeletons. Many of the bones, together with some pieces of eggshells, came from a bowl-like depression in hard rock, about 9 feet across. We think it was a nest. There were other nest-like places with parts of 30 eggs still in them.

Our discovery turned out to be important because it told something about dinosaurs which no one had expected. We think there were 15 baby dinosaurs, all the same size, in that one nest. What does it mean to find 15 growing-up dinosaurs in one nest? We think it means that one or both of the parents must have been taking care of them. Maybe those dinosaurs were not just big, dumb, cold-blooded lizards as they have been pictured in the past.

Now you know why I hope to go on hunting dinosaurs.

Exercise. Answer each of the questions below. Write your answers on the blanks provided.

a. What is Robert Makela's profession?
   He is a science teacher.
   _____

b. What does he do during the summer?
   He hunts dinosaurs.
   _____

c. Do you think he is qualified to tell you about dinosaur hunting? Why or why not?
   Yes. He has a background in science and he has experience hunting
   dinosaurs.
   _____

Copyright © 1984 by Harcourt Brace Jovanovich, Inc. All rights reserved

d. Is the following a statement of fact or of opinion? "I teach science at Rudyard High School, which is very close to the Canadian border in northern Montana."
Statement of fact

e. Is the following a statement of fact or of opinion? "No one had ever found a baby dinosaur in North America, and no one had ever found a baby duck-billed dinosaur anywhere in the world."
Statement of fact

f. Is the following a statement of fact or of opinion? No one will ever find a baby duck-billed dinosaur in Europe.
Statement of opinion

g. The following is a mixed statement of fact and opinion. "Our camp life is full and exciting, for we never know what we will find or what will happen next." Write the part of this statement that is an opinion on the blank below.
Our camp life is full and exciting.

h. Find one fact that supports the following statement. "Hunting dinosaurs takes sharp eyes and lots of patience."
Every rock that looks somewhat strange must be examined carefully.

i. Find one fact that supports the following statement. "The hard work comes after finding part of a bone sticking out of the ground."
After this, the digging starts.

j. Robert Makela says that the scientists think they found "15 baby dinosaurs, all the same size, in that one nest." What conclusion do the scientists draw from this evidence?
One or both of the parents must have been taking care of the baby

dinosaurs.

Chapter 4
Inferences

We all make guesses, but some guesses turn out to be more accurate than others. These guesses are based on evidence. **Intelligent guesses based on evidence are called inferences.** In this chapter, you will learn how to make inferences.

Lesson 1
Making Inferences Based on Evidence

An inference is an intelligent guess based on evidence. To infer means "to make an inference." You make inferences all the time. For example, imagine that you are home on a weekday morning. The telephone rings, you pick it up, and in the background you hear the clatter of many typewriters. Before you even know who the caller is, you make the inference that the person is calling from an office. You base this inference on evidence—the time of day and the clatter of many typewriters in the background.

In the comic strip below, Dagwood doesn't say directly that he doesn't like the chicken pot pie. However, you probably had no trouble inferring that Dagwood thinks the chicken pot pie is terrible. You based your inference on evidence—the look on Dagwood's face as he eats the pie.

BLONDIE by Young and Gersher

Copyright © 1984 by Harcourt Brace Jovanovich, Inc. All rights reserved

81

Exercise. Each item below contains evidence that helps you make an inference. Read each item. Then put an *X* in the blank next to the inference that best fits the evidence.

a. When you open the door to Daniel's room, he is sitting on his bed waxing his skis. You notice a copy of a skiing magazine on the floor and a brochure for a skiing resort in Vermont on the desk. Daniel says, "Great news! I'm going away with my parents for the weekend." On the basis of this evidence, what inference do you make about Daniel's plans for the weekend?

   _____ Daniel plans to go hiking.
   __X__ Daniel plans to go skiing.
   _____ Daniel plans to go snowshoeing.

b. The Villela family has just moved in next door. You decide to visit Cathy Villela, a girl about your age. When you see Cathy, she is reading a book by Isaac Asimov called *On Numbers*. She is wearing a sweat shirt that says, "Hug a mathematician today." She has a poster on her wall of Charles Dodgson, who wrote under the name of Lewis Carroll. Dodgson, in addition to writing *Alice in Wonderland*, was a famous mathematician. When Cathy asks you about after-school clubs, what inference do you make?

   _____ Cathy will be interested in the fantasy club.
   __X__ Cathy will be interested in the math club.
   _____ Cathy will be interested in the literature club.

c. Each year the eighth-grade class has a theme party. You missed the meeting where the class decided on the theme. You call your friend Frank, who attended the meeting. Frank says, "Well, I'm wearing a Frankenstein costume and Phil's going as Dracula. Louise got some old movie posters for *The Invisible Man*, *Bride of Frankenstein*, *The Werewolf*, and *The Thing*. We'll use these to decorate the gym. I think you should go as King Kong." What inference do you make about the theme of the party?

   _____ The theme of the party is "Hollywood Today."
   _____ The theme of the party is "Silent Movies."
   __X__ The theme of the party is "Old Horror Movies."

d. Every month the cooking club chooses one country and learns to prepare dishes from this country. This month the members of the club are preparing veal piccata, shrimp scampi, lasagna, ravioli, and other pasta dishes. What inference do you make about the country they selected?

   _____ They selected Spain.
   __X__ They selected Italy.
   _____ They selected France.

e. While shopping, you meet Mrs. Ferguson. She tells you that her niece Jayne is coming for a month-long visit. Mrs. Ferguson wants to pick up a few things for Jayne so that Jayne will feel at home. Mrs. Ferguson has just come from the record department. Now she is standing on line to buy a nightgown with a picture of a rock group on it. Before she leaves you, she asks if you know where she can buy some guitar strings. What inference do you make about Jayne?

_____ Jayne plays the piano.

_____ Jayne is a musician in a rock group.

___X__ Jayne is interested in music.

Lesson 2
Making Inferences About Characters

Characters are the people in stories, plays, and movies. When you make an inference about a character, you make an intelligent guess about what this character is like or what this character is thinking or feeling. You base your inference on evidence. This evidence includes what the character does and what the character says. It also includes body language: What expression is on the person's face? Does the person's body look relaxed or tense?

Read the comic strip below. On the basis of what Kudzu says when Juney compliments him, you can infer that Kudzu is shy and insecure. An insecure person would look for a criticism behind a compliment.

KUDZU by Marlette

Now read the four paragraphs below from "Putting It On for Juanita" by Piri Thomas.

> During introductions, she smiled at George and in a voice that put nightingales to shame, sang, "*Cómo estás, Jorge? Encantada de conocerte.*" (How are you, George? I am delighted to know you.)
>
> George wished he had on his Sunday best with a bunch of flowers to offer her. He started to put out a hand but quickly pulled it back as being too grimy with street dirt. Instead, he just nodded his head and said, "*Yo también estoy muy encantado de conocerte*, Juanita." (I too am very delighted to know you.)
>
> She replied in lilting English. "Please call me Jenny. I don't like Juanita too much. Back home, there are dozens of Juanitas running all over the place."
>
> Juan junior went to relieve his father of the weight of Juanita's suitcase. But before he could reach for it, George had it in his possession with a personal wink to his friend. It was his passport to allow him to walk along with Juanita.

The author doesn't tell you directly that George immediately likes Juanita. However, it is easy to make this inference. Let's look at the evidence. George wishes "he had on his Sunday best with a bunch of flowers to offer her." He thinks his hand is too grimy to shake her hand. He carries her suitcase so that he can walk home with her.

Exercise. As you read the following selection, "Doc Brackett" by Damon Runyon, pay special attention to clues that help you make inferences about characters. Then answer the questions that follow. Write your answers on the blanks provided.

> Doc Brackett didn't have black whiskers.
> Nonetheless, he was a fine man.
> He doctored in Our Town for many years. He doctored more people than any other doctor in Our Town but made less money.
> That was because Doc Brackett was always doctoring poor people, who had no money to pay.
> He would get up in the middle of the coldest night and ride twenty miles to doctor a sick woman, or child, or to patch up some fellow who got hurt.
> Everybody in Our Town knew Doc Brackett's office over Rice's clothing store. It was up a narrow flight of stairs. His office was always filled with people. A sign at the foot of the stairs said: DR. BRACKETT, OFFICE UPSTAIRS.
> Doc Brackett was a bachelor. He was once supposed to marry Miss Elvira Cromwell, the daughter of old Junius Cromwell, the banker, but on the day the wedding was supposed to take place Doc Brackett got a call to go out into the country and doctor a Mexican child.

Name _____

Miss Elvira got sore at him and called off the wedding. She said that a man who would think more of a stranger's child than of his wedding was no good. Many women in Our Town agreed with Miss Elvira Cromwell, but the parents of the Mexican child were very grateful to Doc Brackett when the child recovered.

For forty years, the lame, and the halt, and the blind of Our Town had climbed up and down the stairs to Doc Brackett's office.

He never turned away anybody.

He lived to be seventy years old, and then one day he keeled over on the sofa in his office and died. By this time his black hair had turned white.

Doc Brackett had one of the biggest funerals ever seen in Our Town. Everybody went to pay their last respects when he was laid out in Gruber's undertaking parlors. He was buried in Riverview Cemetery.

There was talk of raising money to put a nice tombstone on Doc Brackett's grave as a memorial. The talk got as far as arguing about what should be carved on the stone about him. Some thought poetry would be very nice.

Doc Brackett hated poetry.

The matter dragged along, and nothing whatever was done.

Then one day George Gruber, the undertaker, said that Doc Brackett's memorial was already over his grave, with an epitaph and all. George Gruber said the Mexican parents of the child Doc Brackett saved years ago had worried about him having no tombstone.

They had no money themselves, so they took the sign from the foot of the stairs at Doc Brackett's office and stuck it over his grave. It read:

> **DR. BRACKETT, OFFICE UPSTAIRS.**

Questions

a. When you read this story, you probably inferred that Doc Brackett was a generous man. On what evidence did you base this inference?
Doc Brackett took care of poor people who had no money to pay.

b. You probably inferred that Brackett was a dedicated doctor. On what evidence did you base your inference?
"He would get up in the middle of the coldest night and ride twenty miles to doctor" someone.

Copyright © 1984 by Harcourt Brace Jovanovich, Inc. All rights reserved

c. Why did Miss Elvira call off her wedding to Doc Brackett?
She got angry because he went into the country to take care of a child on their wedding day.

d. On the basis of this action, what inference do you make about Miss Elvira?
You can infer that she was a selfish woman.

e. You probably inferred that the townspeople greatly respected Doc Brackett. On what evidence did you base your inference?
They felt that the sign "Doc Brackett, Office Upstairs" was an appropriate gravestone since it indicates that he has gone to heaven.

Lesson 3

Making Inferences About Motives

A motive is the reason a character does a certain thing or acts a certain way. When you make an inference about a character's motives, you make an intelligent guess about the reasons behind his or her actions.

For example, read this paragraph below from "Ironman Gregory" by Dick Gregory.

> Every day when school let out at three o'clock, I'd get into an old pair of sneakers and a T-shirt and gym shorts and run around that block. In the beginning, I'd just run for an hour, then go and take a hot shower. And then one day two girls walked by and one of them said: "What's he think he's doing?" And the other one said: "Oh, he must be training for the big races." I just kept running that day, around and around the block, until every time I hit the pavement pain shot up my leg and a needle went into my side, and I kept going around and around until I was numb and I didn't feel anything any more. Suddenly, it was dark and the track team had all left. I could hardly walk home my feet hurt so much, but I couldn't wait until the next day to get out there again.

This paragraph is from a book Dick Gregory wrote about his life. At first, Gregory ran for just an hour. Then two girls see him run, and one says that "he must be training for the big races." After that, Gregory keeps running and running, even though pain shoots up his leg. Why does Gregory keep running? What is his motive? Perhaps he wants to impress the girls. Perhaps he wants to be important and he knows that his running will get him noticed.

Name _____

Exercise. The selection below is from "Down the Drain" by Zoltan Malocsay. While two boys are scuba diving, each is separately caught by a current and dragged under the ledge, into the throat of some underground river. The river pushes them inside a waterfall where they fall into a churning pool and are trapped. Read the selection carefully. Then answer the questions at the end of it.

Below me, 60-foot trees reached up like black fingers, still rooted in chunks of rock that used to be the jungle floor before it all collapsed to form this pool. It was an eerie place, with green algae covering everything like fur. Yet I could see for at least a hundred feet in every direction and Warren wasn't anywhere to be seen. He just wasn't with me any more.

No bubbles either, so wherever he was, he wasn't breathing!

He must be under that ledge, must've hit his head. I dived down fast, let the camera hang around my neck so I could use both hands to make sure that I wouldn't hit my head also. I thought he'd be right there at the edge, but all I could see were shadows stretching darker and darker under the island. Then, by the time I felt the current, it was too late.

I lunged to get away, but the current had me, dragged me deeper under the ledge, into the dark, into the throat of some underground river. Rolling, I clawed at the ceiling, but my fingernails couldn't hold in the slime. My tanks clonked and scraped, my knees hit rock, my elbows, and suddenly there was nothing but blackness and the rush of water. I was going the same way Warren did, right down the drain.

The water's roar intensified until suddenly I was sliding down a flume, then off an edge and falling, falling amid water, inside a waterfall that splashed into flickering light. Light! Light from someplace flashed in my mask as I rolled in the churning pool, above water now.

Then somebody grabbed my arm. "Over here!" Warren choked, dragging me up to a piece of ground above the stream.

Panting too hard to speak, I pulled off my mask and squinted around. The light came from a chimney high in the ceiling, a single beam that showed me the waterfall and the raging pool, the stream that rushed out again through a rock-studded passage that looked like toothy jaws. Behind us rose a short stack of rocks that reached for the ceiling, but apparently there weren't enough rocks to finish it, for over to one side lay two human skeletons, no telling how old. Maybe centuries.

Warren and I looked at each other, both of us shivering with the notion that the last people who got trapped in here never made it out.

For a while we both tried shouting out the chimney, but it was small and high and the waterfall was loud. Warren tried to

Copyright © 1984 by Harcourt Brace Jovanovich, Inc. All rights reserved

act confident. "They'll be looking for us."

"Yeah, but we're under that, that rock of an island. It's too steep to climb from the water, so how would they ever get up there and why would they try? They can see we're not up there."

"Dad's got another tank," Warren said, looking worried now. "He'll come diving . . ."

"And then we'll all be trapped."

Warren looked away. His eyes led mine toward the rocky jaws where the stream plunged deeper into the earth. "Well," he nodded, "we could always just . . . keep going."

"Where to? Through some underwater meat grinder? No, there's no telling where this comes out—the ocean, in some mangrove swamp miles from shore. It might never come out. For years!"

"Well, we can't go back the way we came, and we can't reach that." He thumbed toward the chimney. "So we can try it now, or wait till we're weak from hunger."

"No, let's think."

"That's what those guys did," he grumbled. "For the rest of their lives! Can we do better?"

"Let's think," I said, studying their stack of rocks. Not enough rocks, not enough boost, even if I stood on Warren's shoulders up there. *Must be a way*, I thought, and then I looked at the waterfall and I grinned. "Come on. Help me move these rocks."

"What for?"

"Block up the passage leading out," I grunted, hefting a big flat one. "That'll make the water rise, clear up to the level of the lake outside. That might be enough."

At first Warren didn't want to, but he finally decided that he didn't want to be swept farther underground either. So we stacked all the rocks against the toothy jaws. The water rose fast, but we used our tanks and blinked my camera's strobe to finish the work underwater. Then we shed all the gear, even our watches, and we trod water, waiting to see how high it would take us.

But it didn't work. It drowned the waterfall, filled the cavern, but we still couldn't reach the chimney. I tried to fin hard enough to boost Warren, but it was no use.

"Some idea!" he choked. "Now we'll drown for sure!"

I shuddered, fingers slipping on the wall. We tried the mosquito float, but even at that we got so tired that giving up began to sound like a good idea. Then, finally, it hit me and I found the strength to laugh. "Golly, we're dumb! We—we're not trapped any more!"

"What?"

"Think! We're up to the level of the lake outside. No water going out—and no more water coming in. Don't you see? There's no current now!"

The flush of understanding spread a smile on Warren's face.

"Then let's get out of here!"

We dived down into the black, feeling for our gear. It took a couple of tries, but once I had a mouthpiece, I had air and time to find the strobe, and that showed us the rest. The dam must've leaked a little because there was a little current, but nothing to hold us back.

I flashed the strobe and together we swam up to the hole that used to spout a waterfall. Then we made our way along the water-worn tunnel that led out to the ledge.

It sounds corny to say that sunlight never looked so good, but that's all I could think when I saw that glimmer ahead. When we broke the surface, we both laughed nervously and shook hands.

"I guess that cave won't swallow any more swimmers!" Warren grinned.

"Just the same," I panted, "let's get out of here."

Questions

a. When he pulls off his mask, why does the boy squint?
He squints because his eyes are unused to the light.

b. Why do the boys begin shouting up the chimney?
They hope someone will hear them and rescue them.

c. Warren hopes that his father will find them. When his friend says, "And then we'll all be trapped," why does Warren look away?
Warren doesn't want his friend to see the fear in his eyes.

d. Warren suggests that the boys keep moving in the hope that they will find a way out. Why does his friend suggest they stop and think before doing anything?
His friend thinks they will have more of a chance of surviving if they have a plan.

e. At the end of the selection, the boys escape. Warren is glad that the cave won't swallow up any more swimmers. Why does his friend say, "Just the same, let's get out of here."
The boy doesn't want to test their luck.

Lesson 4

Making Inferences About Past and Present Events

When you make an inference about past events, you make an intelligent guess about what has happened in the past. For example, imagine it is late Saturday afternoon. The weather is bright and sunny. Your brother comes home wearing a tennis outfit and carrying a tennis racket. He goes into the kitchen and splashes cold water on his face. Then he collapses in a chair and says, "Boy, am I beat!" He doesn't tell you he has been playing tennis, but on the basis of these clues, you make this inference.

When you make an inference about present events, you make an intelligent guess about what is happening now. For example, while walking home from school, you notice that a street is blocked off. You see many movie cameras around a house. Many people carrying microphones and other equipment walk about. A group of three people stand in front of this house. In this group you see a movie actor you recognize. No one tells you that a movie is being filmed, but on the basis of these clues, you make this inference.

In the comic strip below, Hagar is just coming home. Look at Hagar's boat. There are arrows stuck in it, holes in the side of it, and tears in the sail. Do you think Hagar has had a good day? Obviously not. From the look of the boat and the crew, you can tell that Hagar has been in a battle. Now look at Hagar's family. The village is flooded. They are huddled on the roof of their house. Do you think they are having a good day? Obviously not. From the look of their surroundings, you can tell that they are having a very bad day, indeed!

HAGAR THE HORRIBLE by Dik Browne

Exercise. Read the five passages below. Three inferences about past or present events follow each passage. Choose the inference you can make on the basis of the information in the passage. Put an X in the blank next to this information.

a. You are standing in line at the movies waiting to see a new comedy. The previous show lets out. As the audience for this show walks past, you notice that most of the people have very grim

looks on their faces. No one is smiling, and certainly no one is laughing.
What do you think happened?

___ The audience demanded its money back.

___ The audience liked the movie.

_X_ The audience did not like the movie.

b. As you are hiking in the woods with your friends, you notice a shallow pit dug in the earth. A pile of rocks encircles this pit. There are charred pieces of wood in the pit and some chicken bones. The ground in the pit is still warm. Some logs seem to have been moved near the pit.
What do you think happened?

_X_ Some people recently cooked a meal here.

___ Some campers recently ate sandwiches here.

___ Some people spent the night at this site.

c. You are watching your five-year-old brother Pat while your parents are at the movies. Pat has played with his blocks all evening. He particularly liked building tall structures and knocking them down. At nine o'clock, you put Pat to bed, but he complains that he doesn't want to go to sleep. He tries to get out of bed, but you stop him. You turn off the lights, leave the room, and shut the door. Later that night you hear a loud crashing sound from Pat's room.
What has happened?

___ Someone has broken a window.

___ Pat has fallen out of bed.

_X_ Pat has been playing with his blocks.

d. You want to surprise your parents by cooking an anniversary dinner. On the way home from school, you shop for groceries. You buy greens and tomatoes for salad, brown rice, and steaks. At home, you wash the greens and toss the salad. You boil the water for the rice. Then you put the steaks in the oven to broil. Suddenly the phone rings. It is your best friend, Rhonda, who wants to tell you about the party she is planning. She is very excited, and as you talk to her, you get excited, too. Since you enjoy talking to Rhonda, time passes quickly. Suddenly, you hear the loud screech of the smoke detector.
What is happening?

_X_ The steaks are burning.

___ A fire has started in the next room.

___ The water is boiling.

e. After school, you ride your bike over to your friend Danny's house. Danny's little brother Mike answers the door. Mike is dressed like a rabbit. Behind him stand a five-year-old clown and a six-year-old pirate. In the next room you see three little children dressed as an elf, a cat, and a goblin.
What is happening?

_____ Your friend Danny is having a costume party.

_____ Your friend Danny is minding his brother.

___X__ Danny's brother Mike is having a costume party.

Lesson 5
Making Inferences About Future Events

When you make an inference about a future event, you make an intelligent guess, based on evidence, about what will happen in the future. For example, read the following paragraph from "Moon Change" by Ann Warren Turner.

> One night when the moon shone full in the sky, the boy said again half to himself, "I wish I were a cat." His mother and father hardly noticed it; she continuing her sewing by the fire, he mending a bridle beside her. Only Selena heard, and with a switch of her tail, she left the farmhouse and went out into the garden. It seemed an invitation, and the boy followed.

When you read the paragraph above, you probably made the inference that the boy will get his wish. There seems to be something magical about the cat Selena. She understands human talk and invites the boy to follow her into the garden. Most likely she will help the boy turn into a cat.

Read the next two paragraphs, from *Sea Glass* by Laurence Yep.

> The week after that was the hardest of all. It didn't look like I'd ever make friends again with Uncle or Kenyon, or get Dad to act more like himself. Even so, I forced myself to keep trying. If I could work that hard in a game with the kids, I ought to be able to give some of the same energy to making up with my friends—no matter how clumsy I might be.
>
> But that Saturday, things began to turn around finally. Uncle was out on the porch like the last time, still giving me the silent treatment. But this time when I asked him if he wanted me to take his groceries inside, he managed to shrug his shoulders.

When you read the two paragraphs above, you probably made the inference that the boy will make up with his uncle. The boy forces himself to keep trying. He promises that he will devote a lot of energy to making friends again with his uncle and Kenyon. By the end of this passage, the uncle still isn't speaking to the boy. However, when the boy asks if he can take the uncle's groceries inside, the uncle shrugs his shoulders. This is a sign of progress.

Name _____

Now read the comic strip below.

BLONDIE by Young and Gersher

Obviously, Dagwood will find a pair of shoes when he opens his lunch box.

Exercise. Read the five passages below. Three inferences about the future follow each passage. Choose the inference you can make on the basis of the evidence in the passage. Put an X in the blank next to this inference.

a. Bob received a pair of skis for his birthday in April. Since it was spring, he put the skis away in his closet. Bob's closet was somewhat crowded, so eventually the skis got shoved into a corner. Bob started hanging his shirts from the tips of the skis. He started using the foot grips of the skis to hold his shoes.
What do you think will happen by ski season next winter?

_____ Bob's skis will be in perfect condition.

_____ Bob will lose interest in skiing.

__X__ Bob's skis will need repairs.

b. Carmen often window-shops on the way home from school. Last week she saw a blue cashmere sweater that she thought very beautiful. It cost $49.95. Every day after school she looks in the window at that sweater. A big dance is coming up this weekend. As a treat, Carmen's mother gives her fifty dollars to buy something special to wear to the dance.
What do you think Carmen will buy?

_____ She will buy a new pair of jeans.

_____ She will buy a pair of shoes.

__X__ She will buy the blue sweater.

Copyright © 1984 by Harcourt Brace Jovanovich, Inc. All rights reserved

93

c. Christine wants to visit Mexico. She reads about a trip sponsored by the Girl Scouts. When she asks her parents about the trip, they say that she can go next year on one condition. They will give her three quarters of the money for the trip if she saves the other quarter. Christine starts baby-sitting to earn the money for the trip. She baby-sits at least twice a week. She opens an account at the bank, and each week deposits her baby-sitting money.
What do you think will happen at the end of the year?

　　_____ Christine will lose interest in going to Mexico.

　　_____ Christine will decide she wants to teach nursery school.

　　__X___ Christine will go to Mexico.

d. Mr. Johnson loves his son Mark dearly. He always tries to do what is best for him. When Mark was born, Mr. Johnson opened a savings account so that he would have money to send Mark to college. Mr. Johnson is an engineer, and he wants Mark to follow in his footsteps. Mark, however, would like to become a writer, not an engineer. Mark tells his school counselor about his father's wishes. His counselor asks Mr. Johnson to meet with him. During the meeting, the counselor explains that Mark has a natural talent for writing. His best subjects are English and history; his worst are math and science. The counselor explains that Mark doesn't want to do anything that will make his father unhappy, but Mark will be unhappy if he has to choose engineering instead of writing. What do you think Mr. Johnson will decide?

　　__X___ Mr. Johnson will decide to help his son become a writer.

　　_____ Mr. Johnson will decide to force his son to become an engineer.

　　_____ Mr. Johnson will decide that Mark should not go to college.

e. In social studies class today, Maura's teacher announces that a term paper is due in a month and a half. Each student has to prepare a paper on an important event that occurred during the year. Maura isn't certain which event she will choose. After school, she goes to the library to gather ideas for the topic of her paper. By the end of the week, she chooses the event for the topic of her paper. Then she sets aside a half an hour a night to work on her paper. By the end of the second week, she completes her outline. By the end of the fourth week, she writes the first draft of her paper. During the fifth week, she works on her second draft.
What will happen by the end of a month and a half?

　　__X___ Maura will complete her paper.

　　_____ Maura will receive an A+ on her paper.

　　_____ Maura will ask her teacher to give her extra time.

Name _____

Lesson 6
Making Inferences About Time

When you make an inference about time, you make an intelligent guess about when the events occur. One type of time you infer is the time of day. For example: Are the events occurring in the morning, the afternoon, the evening, or the night? Read the comic strip below.

NANCY by Ernie Bushmiller

Nancy's aunt makes the inference that it must be almost 3 o'clock. She bases her inference on evidence. The dogs are all waiting for their owners to come home on the school bus. From this evidence, you can also infer that it must be a weekday, not a Saturday or Sunday.

Another type of time you infer is the time of year. For example: Are the events occurring in the spring, the summer, the autumn, or the winter? Read the two paragraphs below from *Jimmy Yellow Hawk* by Virginia Driving Hawk Sneve.

> One evening after school, when he'd been trapping about two months, it was so bitterly cold and windy that Little Jim's mother didn't want him to go out to check his traps. But Little Jim was sure that he would have caught something important because he had noticed unusual tracks, different from a rabbit's, around his traps.
>
> He bundled up in his parka and set out. The wind was blowing hard on his back as he rode and he was glad that he didn't have to ride into it. His first trap was empty, so he guided the pony on through the deep snow to the next trap. He had almost reached the brush where he had set it when he smelled the strong stink of skunk.

When you read the two paragraphs above, you probably made the inference that the time is winter. You based your inference on evidence—it is bitterly cold and windy, Little Jim wears a parka, and deep snow covers the ground.

Copyright © 1984 by Harcourt Brace Jovanovich, Inc. All rights reserved

Another type of time you infer is time period. For example: Are the events occurring in the present, the past, or the future? Now look at the painting below.

You probably made the inference that the event in this painting occurred in the past. You based your inference on clues—the clothing the man is wearing and the skates he has on.

Exercise 1. Write *Yes* next to each detail that helps you make the inference that the events in a story are occurring in the winter. Write *No* next to each detail that does not help you make this inference.

a. __Yes__ a frozen lake   f. __No__ children on the beach
b. __No__ a nightingale singing g. __Yes__ children wearing mittens
c. __No__ the first daffodils   h. __Yes__ snow plows
d. __Yes__ a blizzard   i. __Yes__ icicles
e. __Yes__ heavy woolen socks   j. __Yes__ people skiing

96   Copyright © 1984 by Harcourt Brace Jovanovich, Inc. All rights reserved

Name _____

Exercise 2. Each passage below contains details that help you make an inference about time. Read each passage carefully. Then answer the questions at the end of each passage. Write your answers on the blanks provided.

    Hannah Drummond made up her mind. She leaned over the pond and tossed her muffin tray into the middle! The muffins scattered over the pond and floated; the bullets sank unnoticed into the water. "No Britisher eats my food!" shrilled Hannah.
    Ephraim shivered. The Redcoats would kill them all now. But at least some of the bullets were lost to them. He hoped Hannah would not stamp her foot again. "Don't you hurt my sister!" he yelled at the officer. He jumped between Hannah and the angry, hungry soldiers.
    "Nobody is going to hurt anybody," said their father.
    And nine hungry Redcoats turned around to see twelve American muskets pointed right at them! (from "Hannah and the Redcoats" by Carolyn B. Cooney)

  a. Does this story take place in the present, the past, or the future?
    Past

  b. List details that help you make this inference.
    The Redcoats, twelve American muskets

    . . . There is a small hut, lighted inside. Smoke is curling up out of a stove pipe through the roof, and sparks fly off into the dark night air. . . . they follow the old people down the bank toward a path through the snow on the frozen river. (from "Crossing" by Richard E. Kim)

  c. Does this story take place in summer, fall, winter, or spring?
    Winter

  d. List details that help you make this inference.
    Smoke curling up out of the stove pipe, snow, frozen river

Jumping down off the fence, the pirate and the ghost ran through the field of pumpkins. They were full-grown and really ripe for harvest. Soup stopped in his tracks, lifting up his black patch as if he didn't believe his other eye. I looked where he pointed, and sure enough, there was the biggest old pumpkin in the whole State of Vermont. I wanted to say something, but the words that came to mind just weren't big enough or orange enough to fit the size.

"That's some vegetable," said Soup.

"You know, Soup . . . if God were to carve a jack-o-lantern, that there is the one pumpkin He'd pick."

"Let's pick it," said Soup.

"And do what with it?"

"Take it to the party." (from *Soup and Me* by Robert Newton Peck)

e. Does this story take place in summer, fall, winter, or spring?
Fall

f. List details that help you make this inference.
Costumes, pumpkins, harvest

Mother had a standing rib roast cooking in the oven, because it's Uncle Douglas' favorite, and the kitchen smelled wonderful with it. Uncle Douglas and John were out in the old barn working on John's space suit, but the rest of us were in the kitchen. I don't suppose we're what you would call an enormous family, Mother and Daddy and the four of us children and the animals, but there are enough of us to make a good kind of sound and fury. Mother had the phonograph on, Brahms's *Second Piano Concerto*, kind of loud to drown us out. Suzy was performing an appendectomy on one of her dolls. She was doing this at the same time that she was scraping carrots, so the carrot scraper was a scalpel as well as a scraper.

Rob was supposed to be helping her, both with the appendectomy and the carrots, but he'd become bored so he was on the floor with a battered wooden train making loud train noises, and Colette, our little gray French poodle, was barking at him and joining in the fun. Mr. Rochester, our Great Dane, was barking at one of the cats who was trying to hide behind the refrigerator. I was being angelically quiet, but this was because I was doing homework—a whole batch of math problems. I was sitting near the fireplace and the fire was going and I was half baked (that's for sure, John would say) on one side, but I was much too cozy to move. (from *Meet the Austins* by Madeleine L'Engle)

g. Does this story occur in the morning, the evening, or at night?
Evening

h. On what evidence did you base your inference?
Rib roast cooking in the oven, homework, fire in the fireplace

Could it be the sun? Was he so far from Earth? No—that was impossible. Some nagging memory told him that the sun was very close—hideously close—not so distant that it had shrunk to a star. And with that thought, full consciousness returned. Sherrard knew exactly where he was, and the knowledge was so terrible that he almost fainted again.

He was nearer to the sun than any man had ever been. His damaged space-pod was lying on no hill, but on the steeply curving surface of a world only two miles in diameter. That brilliant star sinking swiftly in the west was the light of *Prometheus*, the ship that had brought him here across so many millions of miles of space. She was hanging up there among the stars, wondering why his pod had not returned like a homing pigeon to its roost. In a few minutes she would have passed from sight, dropping below the horizon in her perpetual game of hide-and-seek with the sun. (from "Summertime on Icarus" by Arthur C. Clarke)

i. Does this story occur in the past, the present, or the future?
Future

j. On what evidence did you base your inference?
Man far from Earth, space-pod, space ship

Lesson 7
Making Inferences About Place

When you make an inference about place, you make an intelligent guess about where the events in a story occur. For example, imagine you turn on the radio just after a short play has begun. You hear two characters say:

"Oh, look at that boa constrictor! It must be ten feet long."

"I like that golden brown snake curled in the corner of the next cage."

"Do you see the little green one sliding along the glass? I didn't know any snakes were green."

"Let's go to the elephant house next."

As you hear this conversation, you make an inference about place. You infer that the place is the snake room or house at a zoo. You base your inference on evidence. The people are not frightened, as they might be if they saw a boa constrictor in the jungle. The snakes are in cages. There is an elephant house in the area.

In the cartoon below, Queenie has figured out where the man has been by the evidence on his shoulder.

QUEENIE by Interlandi

"What makes you think I've been goofing off in the park?"

Exercise. Read each passage below. Then answer the questions at the end of each passage.

It was hard to understand Barney with the air tubes up his nose. It made his voice sound funny and he couldn't talk very loud. There was a cast on one arm and one leg too and bandages on the others. And his hands were still—that was the worst of it. Barney had long, nervous hands that were usually drumming out a tune or scratching his arm or doing something, but now they were quiet. They didn't seem to belong to him.

I just stood in the doorway because I didn't want to bother Barney if he was about to take a nap. But I didn't like looking at him too much so I looked around the ward. Almost every other patient there had flowers or baskets of fruit or little transistor radios or their own little electric clocks: something that made the space around their bed their own. And most everyone had some visitors with them. Even the oldest guys in there had some friends visiting them. But Barney had nothing and no one, except for me. (from *Child of the Owl* by Laurence Yep)

a. Does this story take place in Barney's house, in a hotel, or in a hospital?
Hospital

b. On what evidence did you base your inference?
Air tubes, cast, bandages, ward, other patients

Name _____

Eskimos had taken the wolves from their den when they were puppies and given them to us. We penned them at night but never tamed or trained them. By day they roamed the tundra with us, a boundless expanse flowing for thousands of square miles, uninhabited except for a few Eskimo families camped ninety miles away. (from "The Wolves in Our Tent" by Lois Crisler)

c. Does this story take place in Norway or in Alaska?
Alaska

d. On what evidence did you base your inference?
Eskimos, wolves, tundra

Our building was just like all the others there, with families crowded into a few rooms, and I guess there were twenty-five or thirty kids about my age in that one building. Of course, there were a few of us who formed a gang and ran together all the time after school, and I was the one who brought T. J. in and started the whole thing.

The building right next door to us was a factory where they made walking dolls. It was a low building with a flat, tarred roof that had a parapet (wall) all around it about head-high and we'd found out a long time before that no one, not even the watchman, paid any attention to the roof because it was higher than any of the other buildings around. So my gang used the roof as a headquarters. We could get up there by crossing over to the fire escape from our own roof on a plank and then going on up. It was a secret place for us, where nobody else could go without our permission. (from "Antaeus" by Borden Deal)

e. Does this story take place in the city or in the country?
City

f. On what evidence did you base this inference?
Apartment building, factory, fire escape

"I wonder who'll be honorary marshal for the Fourth of July parade this year?" Max mopped his face with his shirttail.

Josh shrugged. "Last year it was old Doc Thomas, because he's been a doctor here for fifty years."

"You going to the fireworks display at the park after the parade, Josh?" (from "The Safety Corporation" by Jane K. Priewe)

g. Does this story take place in Canada or in the United States?
The United States

h. On what evidence did you base your inference?
Fourth of July parade, fireworks

Copyright © 1984 by Harcourt Brace Jovanovich, Inc. All rights reserved

Two hundred yards below, a huge beaver dimpled the surface of a dammed-up pool. Bunders watched steadily as the beaver climbed out of the water onto the dam and started fussing with an aspen stick. Bunders' eyes strayed back to the cabin beside the pool.

It was a square cabin, the uncut ends of the logs of which it was built protruding past the corners like ragged fangs. A curl of blue smoke waved out of the chimney. Beside the cabin Bunders counted seven black bear pelts stretched on wooden frames. (from "Code of the Underworld" by Jim Kjelgaard)

i. Does this story take place in town, in the woods, or in the jungle?
   The woods

j. On what evidence did you base your inference?
   Dammed-up pool, beaver, cabin, bear pelts

Lesson 8
Making Inferences About Realistic and Fantastic Details

Realistic details are drawn from life. For example, a girl's finding an animal in her backyard is a realistic detail. **Fantastic details are unreal or highly unusual and difficult to explain.** For example, a girl's finding a creature from outer space in her backyard is a fantastic detail.

Exercise. Read the selection below from "Lights Over Loon Lake" by Monica Hughes. Then follow the directions at the end of the selection.

The sun shimmered on the rocks and the air quivered with heat. There were no trees up here, but there *was* a shadow in the glare of the southern slope.

"Over there, Elaine. But do be careful. You could easily twist your ankle on those loose rocks."

They found that the shadow was a cave, cool and dark and dusty. They sat in the opening—neither of them felt comfortable about actually going *inside*—and they shared out the sandwiches and oranges and drinks of water, now very warm. Chris was just screwing the top back on the bottle when a low moaning sound shivered out of the darkness behind them. Elaine screamed. Chris almost dropped the bottle and jumped to his feet.

"What was *that*?"

"In the cave! Oh, Chris, it came from inside the cave."

"I wish we'd got a flashlight with us."

"We've got matches. It's not angry. You can tell by the sound. It's hurting.

"Hurt animals can be really dangerous. Come on. We'll go and tell Dad. He'll know what to do."

"We just can't go away and leave it." Elaine wasn't really listening to him. Her teeth were chattering and her fingers shook so that the first match went out. She screwed the paper bag the sandwiches had been in into a tight stick and lit the end. She held it up and peered into the darkness.

The cave was deeper than she'd imagined it would be. She had to walk slowly forward into the shadows until the flames flickered off the back wall and she could see, they could both see, the small figure on the floor at the very back. It was like a fish, she thought, a silvery fish with arms and legs, a shining fish that moaned piteously and seemed to be trying to tell them something.

The twisted paper bag burned down to Elaine's fingers. "Ow!" She dropped it and put her fingers in her mouth. The dark was now much blacker than it had been before. She fumbled for another match.

"No, don't." Chris caught her wrist. "Wait a minute. Our eyes will adapt. It's just the sun made it seem so dark."

He was right. Slowly the blackness turned to grey with shadows in it. It was terrifying waiting, wondering what they were going to see. Neither of them spoke. There was only a faint whimper from the shadowy thing on the floor of the cave.

As soon as she could see properly, Elaine knelt down and timidly put out her hand. Touching it was scary at first. She had thought it might be slimy, like a fish, but it wasn't at all. The silveriness was only a kind of cloth that covered the creature completely except for its face and hands. Once she had touched it she wasn't afraid any more, but ran her hands carefully over its body. When she touched its left ankle it cried out and tried to move away.

"Oh, I'm sorry I hurt you. Chris, look. Can you tell if it's broken?"

"I don't know. Isn't it tiny? But it looks awfully swollen next to the other. I'll see if I can find some straight sticks down in the bush to make splints."

When Chris got back, Elaine held the foot as gently as she could while Chris tied it up with bandages out of the first-aid kit.

"Its leg feels cold, Chris. Like ice!"

"Perhaps it's in shock. And it's really chilly back here. I think we ought to get it into the sun."

"Do you think we *should* move it?"

"We'll have to risk it. Suppose it died of cold?"

They lifted the creature out into the sunlight. It moaned when they first moved it, then went limp.

"Oh, my goodness!" Elaine stared. The creature was almost her height, but as thin as a twig, with the ugliest face she had ever seen. Its nose was flat against its cheeks, its mouth a wide, lipless oblong. It was as pale as its silver suit and its slitty eyes were closed.

There was just a little water left in the bottle. Elaine soaked a cloth and gently washed the dust off the ugly little face. The eyelids, as hairless as a lizard's, suddenly opened, and a narrow, pointed purple tongue flickered out of the lipless mouth.

"Oh, it's coming alive again!" She couldn't help drawing back a little. It was so very ugly.

The yellow eyes stared past them at the sun, and, as clearly as if it were written in them, Elaine saw fear and despair. The little creature struggled to sit up, wincing at the pain. Then its eyes shut, its mouth made a square and it began to cry, large tears jumping from its eyes and running down its flat, pale cheeks.

Elaine forgot to be afraid. "Why, you're only a baby!" She put her arms around it. "Please don't cry. It'll be all right." She rocked it gently until the wails became hiccups and the tears stopped.

"Who are you? Where have you come from?"

Almost as if it understood—but how could it!—the silver child pointed up at the sky, and then, with a finger as thin as a drinking straw, began to draw in the dirt at the edge of the cave. It drew circles and stars and a path between them.

"You're from out there? From another planet?" Elaine knew she should be surprised—even not believe it—but once having seen the silver child, where on earth could it come from, except *not* from Earth? "I'm Elaine and this is my brother Chris. Who are you?" She put her hand gently on its chest, and it responded with a clicking snort that she couldn't begin to imitate. "I'm going to call you Starchild," she told it. "I wish I knew where you were from and what you're doing here." Then, "Ow, don't . . . !" She winced and put her hand to her head.

"What's the matter?"

"When he shouted like that my head hurt dreadfully."

"He didn't shout. He didn't make a sound." Chris stared. "Elaine, are you all right?"

"I think so. The pain's gone. Why didn't you hear it? It was an awful noise, as if he were angry."

"Perhaps it was telepathy. Inside your head, you know. Only he doesn't know how to do it properly."

"That's a terrific idea." Elaine put both her arms around Starchild and tried to make her own thoughts calm and soothing, instead of scared to death and full of frantic questions. At first it didn't seem to work, but after a while all kinds of strange pictures began to flit into her mind, things she would never have thought of by herself. She saw cliffs, high and blue, with tall, willowy trees of purple and grey, and huge birds with tail feathers streaming every colour of the rainbow. And big people, as ugly as Starchild, but in some way very special and dear . . .

Directions. In the blank at the right, put *F* next to each detail that is fantastic. Put *R* next to each detail that is realistic.

a. Elaine and Chris eat sandwiches and oranges in front of the cave. ___R___

b. Elaine and Chris hear a moaning sound from within the cave. ___R___

c. The creature in the cave looks like a silvery fish with arms and legs. ___F___

d. Gradually, Elaine's and Chris' eyes adjust to the darkness of the cave. ___R___

e. The creature has no lips on its mouth and no hair on its eyelids. ___F___

f. The creature has a narrow, pointed, purple tongue. ___F___

g. Elaine and her brother Chris introduce themselves. ___R___

h. The creature tells Elaine and Chris that he came from outer space. ___F___

i. The creature can communicate by telepathy. ___F___

j. Elaine's mind is filled with pictures of Starchild's planet. ___F___

Lesson 9
Making Inferences About Tone

Tone is the author's attitude or feeling toward what he or she has written or said. For example, the tone of a selection may be humorous or it may be serious. The tone may be solemn or it may be light-hearted. When you read, you can infer the author's tone by looking carefully at the author's choice of words and details, and by determining the author's purpose. For example, the passage below is from "Who Is I. Dunno?" by Erma Bombeck. It is about Erma Bombeck's family.

Ever since I can remember, our home has harbored a fourth child—I. Dunno. Everyone sees him but me. All I know is, he's rotten.
"Who left the front door open?"
"I. Dunno."

Copyright © 1984 by Harcourt Brace Jovanovich, Inc. All rights reserved

"Who let the soap melt down the drain?"
"I. Dunno."
"Who ate the banana I was saving for the cake?"
"I. Dunno."

Frankly, I. Dunno is driving me nuts. He's lost two umbrellas, four pairs of boots and a bicycle. He has thirteen books overdue from the library, hasn't brought home a paper from school in three years, and once left a thermos of milk in the car for three weeks.

Erma Bombeck's purpose is to amuse you. To do this, she exaggerates, or makes things larger than or more outlandish than they really are. Certainly she doesn't really believe she has a fourth child named I. Dunno living in her home. She includes amusing details. She tells you that I. Dunno has "lost two umbrellas, four pairs of boots and a bicycle." Therefore, we can infer that the tone of this passage is humorous.

The following paragraph from *Who Do You Think You Are?* by Suzunne Hilton tells about finding ancestors.

> Back in the old days—at least thirty years ago—many people searched for their ancestors for snobbish reasons. The results were frustrating. Either they discovered that their ancestors were mostly the hardworking farmers who turned this land into a nation or else they found ancestors who looked so great that the searchers themselves felt like potatoes in comparison—their best parts buried underground.
>
> Today's ancestor hunter is not looking for fame or fortune. He is looking for himself. And he does it by starting with what he knows right now and moving backwards slowly into the past.

The author's purpose is to contrast reasons for finding ancestors yesterday with reasons for finding ancestors today. Her purpose is to inform. Therefore, we can infer that the tone of this passage is serious.

Exercise. Read each passage below. Then decide whether the author's purpose is to inform or to amuse you. Finally, decide whether the author's tone is serious or humorous.

> Not too many people would disagree with the statement that Dracula is the most famous fictional vampire of all time. The black-caped Transylvanian Count, created by author Bram Stoker, has made his chilling undead way through more books, stories, plays, movies, and comic books than any other vampire. Toy cars have been named for him. Play teeth and bats have been modeled after him. His picture has appeared on stickers, notebooks, and even cereal boxes. There are clubs devoted to his memory, and tours booked to his castle in Transylvania. He hasn't yet had his one hundredth anniversary—and won't for more than twenty years—but all signs point to his surviving as a favorite horror character long beyond that

time and in many countries of the world. Before the book *Dracula* was published in 1897, vampires were of many different kinds. After *Dracula*, so powerful was Stoker's tale, all vampires tended to be very like the famous Count. (from *Vampires* by Nancy Garden)

a. What is the author's purpose? *to inform*

b. What is the tone? *serious*

Things that go bump in the night have terrified people for many years. While vampires cannot generally be counted on to go bump in the night—they're more likely to shuffle along in search of more victims—they have been the cause of much terror and fascination over the years. I know that it's often difficult for you to tell whether that shuffling outside your bedroom door is a vampire coming to bite your neck or merely your dad going to get a drink of water. So, I would like to give you a few pointers on how to spot a vampire and what to do when you spot one (or when one spots you!).

First, a little background. Vampires are believed to be "undead." You and I are certainly undead (well, aren't we?), but a vampire is quite another story. All signs seem to indicate that he *is* dead. He has stopped breathing and has been buried in a grave of some sort. However, while a normal human body will begin decomposing in a short time, a vampire's body remains solid, and he continues to seek nourishment. (from "A Field Guide to Vampires" by Paul B. Janeczko)

c. What is the author's purpose? *to amuse*

d. What is the tone? *humorous*

The bookstore was bulging with books on how to save money. It seemed strange to me that they were on a table marked Current Fiction.

Leading the list was the current best seller, *How to Dress a Chicken* (From Separates to Basic Weekenders), followed by *How to Perform Home Surgery Using Sewing Basket Notions*, and my favorite, *How to Build a Summer Cabin Using Scraps Ripped Off from the Neighborhood Lumber Yard*.

I didn't want to get too specific. I just wanted a general book on how to save money by doing things around the house myself. The clerk recommended one that had been selling briskly called *Living Cheap*.

The book cost $23.95, but she said if I followed the advice in the first chapter alone, I'd recoup my original investment in a week. (from "Living Cheap" by Erma Bombeck)

e. What is the author's purpose? *to amuse*

f. What is the tone? *humorous*

Like riding a bike or driving a car, learning to handle money is something you learn by *doing*. You have learned a great deal already, in fact.

Ten years ago, your idea of what to do with money involved putting shiny pennies in a piggy bank! Over time, however, your decisions about money have become increasingly complex. Yesterday's question of "Which yo-yo?" has become today's problem of saving for college *vs.* spending for a vacation, or new clothes *vs.* a new bicycle.

Money offers a kind of independence. The better you handle your finances, the better your chances of living your life the way you want to live it. The challenge is to get a grip on your money—before it gets away from you! (from "The Buck Stops Here: Learning to Manage Money")

g. What is the author's purpose? *to inform*

h. What is the tone? *serious*

Communication is one of the most important skills that we learn. There is hardly an area of life not touched by communication. Salespeople who sell must communicate, or they don't sell. Teachers must communicate, or they don't teach.

When you apply for a job, you must communicate. Some people who want a summer job can and do walk right in and ask the owner of a business if he's going to need help. One of the problems is that he really may not know what his needs are next summer. So you probably are better off mailing him a resume showing your education and work experience. (from "Communications")

i. What is the author's purpose? *to inform*

j. What is the tone? *serious*

Lesson 10

Practice

While you read the following selection, pay special attention to clues that help you make inferences. Then complete the exercise at the end of it.

Johanna
Jane Yolen

The forest was dark and the snow-covered path was merely an impression left on Johanna's moccasined feet.

If she had not come this way countless daylit times, Johanna would never have known where to go. But Hartwood was familiar to her, even in the unfamiliar night. She had often picnicked in the cool, shady copses and grubbed around the tall oak trees. In a hard winter like this one, a family could subsist for days on acorn stew.

Still, this was the first night she had ever been out in the forest, though she had lived by it all her life. It was tradition—no, more than that—that members of the Chevril family did not venture into the midnight forest. "Never, never go to the woods at night," her mother said, and it was not a warning as much as a command. "Your father went though he was told not to. He never returned."

And Johanna had obeyed. Her father's disappearance was still in her memory, though she remembered nothing else of him. He was not the first of the Chevrils to go that way. There had been a great-uncle and two girl cousins who had likewise "never returned." At least, that was what Johanna had been told. Whether they had disappeared into the maw of the city that lurked over several mountains to the west, or into the hungry jaws of a wolf or bear, was never made clear. But Johanna, being an obedient girl, always came into the house with the setting sun.

For sixteen years she had listened to that warning. But tonight, with her mother pale and sightless, breathing brokenly in the bed they shared, Johanna had no choice. The doctor, who lived on the other side of the wood, must be fetched. He lived in the cluster of houses that rimmed the far side of Hartwood, a cluster that was known as the "Village," though it was really much too small for such a name. The five houses of the Chevril family that clung together, now empty except for Johanna and her mother, were not called a village though they squatted on as much land.

Usually the doctor himself came through the forest to visit the Chevrils. Once a year he made the trip. Even when the grandparents and uncles and cousins had been alive, the village doctor came only once a year. He was gruff with them and called them "Strong as beasts," and went away never even offering a tonic. They needed none. They were healthy.

But the long, cruel winter had sapped Johanna's mother's strength. She lay for days silent, eyes cloudy and unfocused, barely taking in the acorn gruel that Johanna spooned for her. And at last Johanna had said: "I will fetch the doctor."

Her mother had grunted "no" each day, until this evening. When Johanna mentioned the doctor again, there had been no answering voice. Without her mother's no, Johanna made up her own mind. She *would* go.

If she did not get through the woods and back with the doctor before dawn, she felt it would be too late. Deep inside she knew she should have left before, even when her mother did not want her to go. And so she ran as quickly as she dared, following the small, twisting path through Hartwood by feel.

At first Johanna's guilt and the unfamiliar night were a burden, making her feel heavier than usual. But as she continued running, the crisp night air seemed to clear her head. She felt unnaturally alert, as if she had suddenly begun to discover new senses.

The wind moulded her short dark hair to her head. For the first time she felt graceful and light, almost beautiful. Her feet beat a steady tattoo on the snow as she ran, and she felt neither cold nor winded. Her steps lengthened as she went.

Suddenly a broken branch across the path tangled in her legs. She went down heavily on all fours, her breath caught in her throat. As she got to her feet, she searched the darkness ahead. Were there other branches waiting?

Even as she stared, the forest seemed to grow brighter. The light from the full moon must be finding its way into the heart of the woods. It was a comforting thought.

She ran faster now, confident of her steps. The trees seemed to rush by. There would be plenty of time.

She came at last to the place where the woods stopped, and cautiously she ranged along the last trees, careful not to be silhouetted against the sky. Then she halted.

She could hear nothing moving, could see nothing that threatened. When she was sure, she edged out onto the short meadow that ran in a downward curve to the back of the village.

Once more she stopped. This time she turned her head to the left and right. She could smell the musk of the farm animals on the wind, blowing faintly up to her. The moon beat down upon her head and, for a moment, seemed to ride on her broad, dark shoulder.

Slowly she paced down the hill toward the line of houses that stood like teeth in a jagged row. Light streamed out of the rear windows, making threatening little earthbound moons on the greying snow.

She hesitated.

A dog barked. Then a second began, only to end his call in a whine.

A voice cried out from the house furthest on the right, a woman's voice, soft and soothing. "Be quiet, Boy."

The dog was silenced.

She dared a few more slow steps toward the village, but her fear seemed to precede her. As if catching its scent, the first dog barked lustily again.

"Boy! Down!" It was a man this time, shattering the night with authority.

She recognized it at once. It was the doctor's voice. She edged toward its sound. Shivering with relief and dread, she came to the backyard of the house on the right and waited. In her nervousness, she moved one foot restlessly, pawing the snow down to the dead grass. She wondered if her father, her great-uncle, her cousins had felt this fear under the burning eye of the moon.

Name _____

The doctor, short and too stout for his age, came out of the back door, buttoning his breeches with one hand. In the other he carried a gun. He peered out into the darkness.

"Who's there?"

She stepped forward into the yard, into the puddle of light. She tried to speak her name, but she suddenly could not recall it. She tried to tell why she had come, but nothing passed her closed throat. She shook her head to clear the fear away.

The dog barked again, excited, furious.

"My God," the doctor said, "it's a deer."

She spun around and looked behind her, following his line of sight. There was nothing there.

"That's enough meat to last the rest of this cruel winter," he said. He raised the gun, and fired.

Exercise. Answer each of the questions below. Write your answers on the blanks provided.

a. When Johanna's father went into the woods at night, he never returned. Which other members of the Chevril family had never returned?
A great-uncle and two girl cousins had never returned.

b. Why does Johanna go into the woods on this particular evening?
Johanna's mother is ill and needs a doctor.

c. When Johanna runs through the woods, she feels unnaturally alert. Find one other detail that makes you suspect something unnatural or strange is happening to Johanna.
She begins to feel graceful and light.

d. Find a second detail that makes you suspect something strange is happening to Johanna.
She feels neither cold nor winded.

e. Find a third detail that makes you suspect something strange is happening to Johanna.
She begins to see well in the dark.

f. Why do the dogs bark as Johanna draws near?
Johanna has turned into a deer.

g. At the end of the story, why can Johanna no longer remember her name?
She is losing her human identity.

Copyright © 1984 by Harcourt Brace Jovanovich, Inc. All rights reserved

h. The name Chevril is based on a French word that means "roe deer." What do you think happened to the other missing members of the Chevril family?
Probably they turned into deer, too.

i. When the doctor visited members of the Chevril family, he always said they were as "Strong as beasts." How does this statement turn out to be truer than the doctor originally meant?
The members turn into beasts—deer.

j. This story contains both realistic and fantastic details. Find one fantastic detail.
Students' answers will vary, but the most obvious answer is that Johanna turns into a deer.

Name _____

Chapter 5
Main Idea

What is the main idea of a paragraph? The main idea is the most important idea. It is the main point that the author wants to make. Sometimes the main idea is stated. Sometimes it is implied, or suggested. In this chapter, you will learn several strategies for finding the main idea.

Lesson 1
Identifying Topics

The subject of a paragraph is called the topic. The topic is what the paragraph is about. Usually, the topic is stated in one word or in a very few words. For example, read the paragraph below from "Eggs" by George Frame.

> Eggs, like birds, come in all different sizes. A finch egg is the size of a marble and weighs only about one gram. An ostrich egg is nearly as large as a football and may weigh as much as two kilograms. One ostrich egg is big enough to hold two or three dozen chicken eggs.

The topic of this paragraph is eggs. Notice that the word *eggs* appears in the first sentence. The word *egg* also appears in every other sentence in the paragraph. In fact, the word *egg* appears twice in the last sentence.

Now read the next paragraph from "Eggs" by George Frame.

> When I looked closely at an ostrich egg, I saw hundreds of tiny dark holes, or pores. Oxygen for the chick to breathe enters through these holes. The waste carbon dioxide gas leaves the egg through the same holes. Later, upon comparing an ostrich egg with other kinds of eggs, I discovered that the pores of chicken eggs and finch eggs are almost too tiny to see.

The word *egg* appears six times in this paragraph. But this paragraph is not about any kind of egg, but a special kind of egg—the ostrich egg. Therefore, the topic of this paragraph is: *ostrich eggs*.

Copyright © 1984 by Harcourt Brace Jovanovich, Inc. All rights reserved

Exercise. Read each paragraph below. Then write the topic of each paragraph in the blank provided. Remember: The topic may be expressed as one word or as a group of words. The topic is not a complete sentence.

a. Do you dig through a dish of mixed nuts and pick out the cashews? Have you noticed how many others do the same thing? Those delicious, kidney-shaped nuts seem to be everybody's favorite. But did you know that the cashew, fresh off the tree, is poisonous? And did you know that the cashew is a relative of the poison ivy plant? (from "Cashewing In" by Mary Gores)

Topic: ***Cashews***

b. There are several types of hearing aids: *Body aid, ear-level aid,* and *glasses aid.* A body aid may be worn on top of or inside a person's clothing. It looks like a small transistor radio with earplugs. An ear-level aid is worn behind the ear. A glasses aid is built into the "wing" of the person's glasses where it fits over the ear. Ear-level aids and glasses aids are small and hard to see. You might not even know a person is wearing one of these. (from "The Better to Hear You With, My Dear" by Carol Pado)

Topic: ***Hearing aids***

c. A raspberry patch is sometimes difficult to start, but once the plants have taken root, a patch will produce for thirty years, and it will double in size every two years (if the farmer lets it). Many farmers tie the canes to fences so that they will have paths in which to walk while they are harvesting. Children usually prefer wild patches so they can hide and eat the berries. (from "Nature's Medicines" by Lois Wickstrom)

Topic: ***Raspberry patches***

d. I decided to call the snake "King." It suited him. I kept an eye out for King during the next few days. I was very careful not to bother him. His black and white pattern made him easy to see. He spent a lot of evenings patrolling around the barn. Sometimes during the hottest part of the day I'd see him resting under the peach tree. I kept wishing another snake would come into the yard. I wanted to see what would happen. I also read everything I could find about king snakes. It gave me an idea of what King's earlier life might have been like. (from "King and the Copperhead" by Betty N. Meisner)

Topic: ***King***

e. What's the name of your favorite "funnies"? *Quincy, Nancy, Wee Pals, Garfield,* or *Big George*? Well, comic strips or "funnies," as they are sometimes called, are a form of entertainment that children all over the world enjoy. Some comic strips make you laugh just reading about the funny adventures of the characters, while others tell an exciting adventure story. The characters in comic strips can be grown-ups, animals, kids, detectives, and even whole families. (from "Ray Billingsley Is Lookin' Fine" by Debra M. Hall)

Topic: *Comic strips*

Lesson 2

Distinguishing Between the Topic and the Main Idea

The subject of a paragraph is called the topic. Usually, the topic is stated in one word, or in a very few words. For example, the topic of a paragraph may be *camping* or *building a fire*.

The main idea of a paragraph is the most important idea a paragraph gives about a topic. The main idea is usually stated as a complete sentence. For example, the main idea of a paragraph about *camping* might be: *Camping can be lots of fun.* The main idea of a paragraph about *building a fire* might be: *You can learn to build a fire in several easy steps.*

The following paragraph is from "A Bird That Cannot Fly" by Eve Merriam. The topic of the paragraph is *the ostrich*. The main idea is: *The ostrich will eat anything.*

Sometimes, when a person has a small appetite, we say that he "eats like a bird." That bird is definitely not the ostrich! An ostrich will eat anything under the sun. Once, when an ostrich died in a zoo, an examination of the bird was made. Here are some of the things that the bird had swallowed: the winder of an alarm clock, three pieces of wood, an electric cable, part of a film roll, a nail, a screw, a pencil, some string, a French coin, three handkerchiefs, three gloves, four pennies, part of a chain—and eighteen pieces of wire!

Exercise. Read each paragraph below. Then answer the questions that follow each paragraph.

a. One of the earliest libraries ever discovered was started by the Babylonians around 2000 B.C. Instead of books, Babylonians collected information they wanted to save by pressing symbols into wet clay and forming tablets. These symbols represented a form of writing called cuneiform. The letters were wedge-shaped and read from right to left, instead of left to right, the way you read the English language. Most of these tablets contained poems, records of taxes and trades, and other writings. (from "Libraries Long Ago" by Mary C. Lewis)

(1) The topic of this paragraph is:

_____ Poems

_____ Tax records

__X__ Libraries

(2) The main idea of this paragraph is:

__X__ The Babylonians were one of the first people to develop libraries.

_____ The Babylonians used a form of writing called cuneiform.

_____ The Babylonians wrote their records of taxes and trades on tablets.

b. Some animals have very special uses for their tails. The white-tailed deer uses its tail for a danger signal, and so does the beaver. A beaver's wide, flat tail whacks the water to warn other beavers. The deer's tail is brown on top but white underneath. When alarmed, he raises it like a white flag to alert the other deer in the herd. (from "A Tale of Tails" by Shirlie Burriston)

(3) The topic of this paragraph is:

_____ The deer's tail

_____ The beaver's tail

__X__ Animals' tails

(4) The main idea of this paragraph is:

__X__ Some animals use their tails in special ways.

_____ Deer signal danger with their tails.

_____ Beavers whack the water with their tails to signal danger.

Name _____ 117

  c.   Ben labored to keep going. Step, slide, step, slide, fall. Flounder in the snow. Struggle upright. Pain coursed through his legs, and his lungs protested with each inhalation of frosty air. Ben took note of a landmark and made it his next goal. The uphill slope strained his legs and slowed his progress. He struggled on. Only the occasional downward slopes gave relief from falls and forced one long, slender ski ahead of the other. (from "Ben's Battle" by Carole Osborne Cole)

    (5) The topic of this paragraph is:

        _____ Skiing

        _____ Snow

        __X__ Ben's struggle

    (6) The main idea of this paragraph is:

        _____ Skiing can be dangerous.

        _____ Traveling uphill on skis can be very difficult.

        __X__ Ben had to work very hard to keep moving through the snow.

  d.   Cooking was probably discovered by accident. Perhaps someone dropped a piece of meat into a fire lit for warmth; it smelled appetizing and tasted delicious. Or maybe a hunter found the still-warm body of an animal caught in a forest fire. He might have tasted the cooked meat and thoroughly enjoyed the experience. (from "Fresh Is Best" by M. Regina Lepore)

    (7) The topic of this paragraph is:

        __X__ Cooking

        _____ Hunters

        _____ Meat

    (8) The main idea of this paragraph is:

        __X__ Most likely, the discovery of cooking was an accident.

        _____ Meat tastes better cooked than raw.

        _____ Food smells good when it is cooking.

Copyright © 1984 by Harcourt Brace Jovanovich, Inc. All rights reserved

e. No one honestly likes camels. True, they're very useful animals. But their faces look bored and disagreeable and scornful and altogether stuffy. That's just how a camel is. He has no friendliness or affection, and no one can make a pet of a camel. He is bad-tempered and not a bit interested in people. (from "Bad-tempered—But Useful" by Alec Dickinson)

(9) The topic of this paragraph is:

__X__ Camels

_____ Unpleasant animals

_____ Animals people like

(10) The main idea of this paragraph is:

_____ Camels are very useful animals.

_____ Camels do not make good pets.

__X__ Since camels are unfriendly and not interested in people, no one really likes them.

Lesson 3

Finding the Topic Sentence of a Paragraph

Some paragraphs have a topic sentence. The topic sentence tells the main idea of the paragraph. The topic sentence often appears at the beginning of the paragraph, but it may appear in or near the middle or at the end of the paragraph. All the other sentences add information about the main idea expressed in the topic sentence.

The following paragraph is from "Is Weight Lifting for You?" by Jean Barbieri. In this paragraph, the first sentence is the topic sentence. It is printed in **boldface.** The other sentences in the paragraph add information about the main idea expressed in the topic sentence.

There are many advantages to improving your muscle strength for sports. As you strengthen your muscles, you are automatically improving your quickness, speed, coordination, agility, balance, and power. You will not, therefore, tire as quickly and will be able to endure the sport. The chance of injury is reduced, and the amount of fun is increased, because you will feel more powerful to challenge your opponent.

The next paragraph is from "Are You a Bore?" by Sharon Carter. In this paragraph, the topic sentence appears near the middle.

Admittedly, being a bore is a difficult trait to acknowledge in oneself. **How can you tell if you are one?** There are obvious signs: People start dodging into doorways when they see you coming. They edge off once it appears you're determined to talk. They avoid eye contact.

In the next paragraph, from "Our Mysterious Past" by M. Regina Lepore, the topic sentence appears at the end.

Archaeologists have found a number of Egyptian mummies with false teeth very much like the kind our modern dentists use. Mayan skulls from the coast of Jaina in Campeche, Mexico, show fillings still in place after many centuries. **Where did these ancient people learn dentistry?**

Exercise. Read each of the following paragraphs carefully. Draw a line under the topic sentence in each paragraph.

a. There are enough fishing rods on the market to confuse you, but here are some basic guidelines to help you pick the good ones. First, consider the manufacturer, and choose a well-known name so you will know where to send it if it needs repairs. Pick a spinning or casting rod with ceramic guides. Single-piece rods give the best action. If you need a rod that breaks down into sections for travel, look at the ferrules that hold the sections together. These should be made of fiber, not metal, for the best rod action. (from "Equipment for a Lifetime" by George Laycock)

b. In many Asiatic countries, a top badminton player is treated the way Americans treat professional football or baseball heroes. For example, an Indonesian named Rudy Hartono has won the world badminton championship eight times. Perhaps the most popular athlete in Asia, he has streets, statues, and babies named after him. The Indonesian government has even issued a stamp with Hartono's picture on it. (from "Competitive Badminton" by Donna Judd)

c. Have your grandparents ever complained that their joints are stiff or painful or that their joints feel as though they are grating together when they move? If so, your grandparents may have arthritis. Lots of people get arthritis when they get older. This form of arthritis—known as *osteoarthritis*—is caused by wear and tear on the joints—especially the joints of the hands, hips, knees, neck, and back. (from "Arthritis: It's Not Just a Grownup Disease" by Dr. Thomas A. Blumenfeld)

Copyright © 1984 by Harcourt Brace Jovanovich, Inc. All rights reserved

d. <u>Our popularity with the neighbors had sunk to an all time low when Dad bought his drums.</u> He had taken lessons for about a year, and at first he owned only a set of bongos. They are kind of small, and since you play them with your hands, the noise isn't too bad. The worst part was when he drove up in the station wagon and unpacked a whole kit. There was a bass drum, snare drum, tom-toms, cymbals, and even a conga! Poor Mom almost fainted. It hadn't taken the neighbors long to gang up on us. A few had resorted to hammering on the front door and threatening us with all sorts of violence if the noise didn't stop. (from "My Dad, the Drummer" by Joan E. Lynn)

e. A medical papyrus from ancient Egypt tells of a fungus that grew on still water. Doctors used this fungus for the treatment of wounds and open sores. <u>Were the ancient Egyptians using penicillin 4,000 years before it was discovered by Sir Alexander Fleming?</u> (from "Our Mysterious Past" by M. Regina Lepore)

Lesson 4

Finding Supporting Details When the Main Idea Is Stated

Supporting details are facts or ideas that back up, or support, the main idea of a paragraph. For example, the paragraph below, from "Midnight" by Sam Savitt, begins with a topic sentence. The rest of the sentences in the paragraph contain details that support the main idea expressed in the topic sentence.

The horse has had a full-time job ever since people discovered that they could slap a saddle on him and ride, or hitch him to a wagon and drive him. He has charged into battle to the din of clashing steel, and dragged caissons through murderous shellfire. He has pulled a stagecoach over seemingly impassable mountain trails, and carried the United States mail. He has also achieved moments of fame by winning a Kentucky Derby or a Grand National, and shared the spotlight with such famous movie cowboys as Gene Autry and Roy Rogers. But, in spite of his varied duties and changing roles, the horse has remained the servant, people the masters. Most horses accept this readily and happily.

The main idea of this paragraph is stated in the topic sentence: *The horse has had a full-time job ever since people discovered that they could slap a saddle on him and ride, or hitch him to a wagon and drive him.* The rest of the sentences in this paragraph contain supporting details that back up the main idea. These sentences tell you about the jobs the horse has had. (1) The horse has "charged into battle." (2) The horse has pulled stagecoaches. (3) The horse has "carried the United States mail." (4) The horse has competed in races—the Kentucky Derby and the Grand National. (5) The horse has acted in movies and on television with such cowboy actors as Gene Autry and Roy Rogers. The last two sentences in the paragraph comment on these jobs. They tell you that the horse has done these jobs willingly, letting people be the masters while the horse remains the servant.

Exercise 1. Read the topic sentence below. Then read the sentences below the topic sentence. Write *Yes* next to each sentence that contains a detail supporting the main idea. Write *No* next to each sentence that does not.

Topic Sentence: *Although it may seem like a strange idea, some people enjoy keeping insects as pets.*

a. In China, for example, some people keep crickets as pets in beautiful little cages. ___Yes___

b. The Chinese like the crickets and enjoy the insects' musical chirping. ___Yes___

c. On farms, some people keep new-born pigs as pets. ___No___

d. They find that pigs can be surprisingly affectionate. ___No___

e. The praying mantis, a strange-looking insect found in the United States, is sometimes kept as a pet, too. ___Yes___

f. Some children like to keep a caterpillar in a cage or bottle, feeding it fresh leaves. ___Yes___

g. The caterpillar is not friendly or musical, but after it has gone through several changes, it provides a wonderful sight—butterfly wings. ___Yes___

h. Children who keep a calf as a pet often find it difficult to give it up when it becomes a full-grown cow. ___No___

i. Some people keep ants in special glass or plastic structures called ant houses. ___Yes___

j. They enjoy watching the ants build hills and tunnel through the earth. ___Yes___

Exercise 2. Read the topic sentence below. Then read the sentences below the topic sentence. Write *Yes* next to each sentence that contains a detail supporting the main idea. Write *No* next to each sentence that does not.

Topic Sentence: *Poisonous snakes present a real danger to people who camp in the United States.*

a. In the United States, the most famous poisonous snake is the rattler. — *Yes*

b. Of the several different types of rattlers, some people feel, the most dangerous is the diamondback. — *Yes*

c. Although rattlesnakes often make a rattling sound with their tails before striking—watch out!—they do not always do so. — *Yes*

d. In the West Indies, many people fear the poisonous fer-de-lance. — *No*

e. You can identify the fer-de-lance by its brown and gray markings. — *No*

f. Campers in swampy areas of the southern United States must watch out for the venomous water moccasin. — *Yes*

g. When it is frightened, the water moccasin, also known as the cottonmouth, opens wide its mouth. — *Yes*

h. Someone unlucky enough to be standing in front of a frightened water moccasin gets a clear view of the cotton-white inside of its mouth. — *Yes*

i. The hiss of the cobra from India can make a person's blood run cold. — *No*

j. Common garden snakes are not poisonous, and people should not be afraid of them. — *No*

Lesson 5

Paraphrasing

Paraphrasing is stating the author's ideas in your own words. Paraphrasing is a good test of reading comprehension. If you can state someone else's ideas in your own language, you have understood what you have read. For example, read the following paragraph from "Equipment for a Lifetime" by George Laycock.

> Saving up to buy a fine piece of outdoor equipment makes real sense. It is going to cost less in the long run than cheaper equipment, replaced several times. And, the longer you own a favorite rod, tent, or backpack, the more you come to appreciate the job it does for you. Each time you pick it up, it brings back pleasant memories. Here are some of the items that can last and last, providing you choose good ones in the beginning.

Name _____ 123

The main idea is stated in the topic sentence. "Saving up to buy a fine piece of outdoor equipment makes real sense." You can judge how well you understand the main idea by paraphrasing it; that is, stating it in your own words. One paraphrase might be: It is a wise decision to buy a good piece of outdoor equipment instead of a cheaper piece, even if you have to save up to do so.

Exercise. The paragraphs below are from "Equipment for a Lifetime" by George Laycock. In each paragraph, the topic sentence is printed in **boldface.** Read each paragraph. Think about the main idea expressed in the topic sentence. Then paraphrase the main idea.

a. **Your sleeping bag makes a fine camp bed, but remember that it does not *provide* heat, it only *holds in* your body heat, and some sleeping bags are better at this than others.** Goose down is the best lightweight insulation for a sleeping bag. It is also the most costly. Whether you choose goose down or a synthetic filler depends partly on how you will go camping. If you expect to backpack where every ounce counts, you need a down-filled bag.

Paraphrase: *Although all sleeping bags hold in heat, some are more effective than others.*

b. **A good pair of binoculars can help you with a lifetime of bird watching, football games, backpacking in the mountains, or all of the above.** The most popular binoculars are either 7 × 35 or 8 × 40. The first figure tells the magnification. More powerful ones are harder to hold steady. It is a sound idea to invest in the best binoculars you can afford. The quality ones have fine lenses, and the lens elements are not so easily jarred out of line as in cheap ones. Check the literature packed with the binoculars to see that all lens surfaces are coated.

Paraphrase: *A good pair of binoculars can last for a lifetime.*

c. **Whatever your outdoor equipment, from canoes to pocketknife, it is going to last longer, and do a better job, if you give it proper care.** Banging any kind of equipment around does nothing to improve it. Neither do dirt and excess moisture. Parts need to be kept secure and well-adjusted. This calls for a few minutes of care at the end of a trip, and an inspection before storing equipment at the end of the season. But good care has its rewards. Treat your outdoor equipment right, and it is going to last.

Paraphrase: *Any outdoor equipment will last longer and do a better job if you take care of it.*

d. **Match the choice of tent to the way you will camp.** If you camp by automobile, weight is not much of a problem. But for backpacking or canoeing, where you may have to portage, you need a lightweight tent. Backpackers want tents that weigh no more than six or seven pounds for a two-person shelter. The modern material for lightweight tents is nylon, the kind that "breathes," so moisture doesn't condense on the inside. Tubular aluminum frames are strong and lightweight. If you can, set up the tent before making your purchase, and see if it is easy to set up and take down. Check to see that it has heavy zippers, a stitched-in waterproof floor, and screened windows for cross ventilation. The material should be folded together and double-stitched at the seams. Remember, light colors reflect more sunlight and are cooler.

Paraphrase: *Consider how you plan to camp when you choose your tent.*

e. **Your new backpack should be lightweight, strong, roomy, and adjustable.** Today's lightweight materials let us choose a backpack with frame made either of tubular aluminum or tough, light plastics. Metal parts used in backpacks should be welded together, and the manufacturer should guarantee his welds. The backpack should be equipped with shoulder pads and a padded hip belt, and a ventilated back band that fits the load to the contours of your back. Select a backpack with small outside pockets so you can reach cameras or lunch without unloading the pack. The pack should close tight enough to protect its contents from rain and dust.

Paraphrase: *When you buy a backpack, make sure it doesn't weigh too much, is sturdy, has enough room, and can be adjusted.*

Lesson 6
Finding the Implied Main Idea

The main idea is the most important idea about a topic. Sometimes the main idea is stated directly in the topic sentence. Sometimes, though, a paragraph does not have a topic sentence. The main idea is implied, or suggested. You have to read closely, add up all the details, and state the main idea in your own words.

For example, in the following paragraph, the main idea is implied.

In the middle of the night, the boy heard something crying in the backyard. He looked through his window and saw a puppy shivering in the cold. He woke up his parents, and they all went downstairs to bring the puppy inside. In the kitchen light, they saw that the puppy was extremely thin. Its skin was stretched tightly over its bones. It was so weak it could barely stand on its legs. It cried piteously. When the boy brought it food, the puppy ate greedily. The boy found dog tags around the puppy's neck. Since it was so late, the boy and his family decided to call the puppy's owners first thing in the morning.

This paragraph is about what the boy finds in his backyard. Let's look at the details. The boy finds a puppy. What is important about this puppy? It is extremely thin. Its skin is stretched tightly over its bones. It is weak. It cries piteously. When it is fed, it eats greedily. These details lead us to assume that the puppy is starving.

What else do we know about the puppy? It is wearing dog tags. Therefore, probably it is lost. These details add up to the main idea of the paragraph: *The boy finds a lost puppy that is starving.*

Exercise. Read each paragraph below. Then, for each paragraph, choose the statement that best expresses the main idea.

    a. In the desert, the sun rages by day and temperatures over a hundred degrees Fahrenheit wring water from your body. At night it's so cold you shiver. The only sign of life is an occasional lizard or snake; despite shimmering mirages on the sand, no real water is visible. What do you do? (from "How Can You Survive" by Gurney Williams III)

__X__ Surviving in the desert can be difficult unless you know what to do to protect yourself.

_____ Surviving in temperatures over a hundred degrees Fahrenheit can be difficult unless you know what to do to protect yourself.

_____ It can be difficult to find food in the desert.

    b. Kudzu also climbs over fences and spreads onto highways, covering and hiding highway signs. Sometimes it grows up utility poles, shorting out electricity by crossing from one wire to the next. The weight of the relentless plant can break telephone lines. (from "Mile-a-Minute Vine" by George Laycock)

_____ Kudzu grows very quickly.

_____ Kudzu can break telephone lines.

__X__ Kudzu can be both troublesome and dangerous.

c. Robin tried to imagine what it was going to be like, coming out on the stage and facing all those eyes. What if he made a mistake, as he had at the first rehearsal? What if he fell and ruined the play? He could not even remember how the dance began. He tried frantically to remember, but his brain seemed to have turned to lead. (from "The Wonderful Winter" by Marchette Chute)

__X__ Robin is nervous about acting in the play.

_____ Robin is upset that he made a mistake during rehearsal.

_____ Robin is eager to get onstage.

d. I caressed the shawl again. Its turquoise color ran together with shades of orange and rust. It had white fringes. Tears begged inside me—please, hurry and take me home. I walked into the trading post and placed the Pendleton shawl back on the wall. I stood and looked as it hugged the wall. Then I remembered that Grandmother wanted new shoestrings. I found a pair and left my money on the counter. (from *Morning Arrow* by Nanabah Chee Dodge)

_____ The girl must buy shoestrings for her grandmother.

__X__ Although the girl very much wants the shawl, she cannot buy it.

_____ The girl thinks the shawl is very beautiful.

e. Those moccasins? Mine. Though I never wore them. Had them on just once to see if they fitted. They did. A bit tight but I could get them on. Don't touch them. The leather's old and dry and the stitching rotted. Ought to be. They've been hanging there a long time. Look close and you can see the craftsmanship. The best. They're Nez Percé moccasins. Notice the design worked into the leather. It's faint now but you can make it out. Don't know how they did that but the Nez Percé could really work leather. A professor who studied such things told me once that design means they're for a chief. For his ceremonial appearances, sort of his dress-up footwear. Said only a chief could use that design. But it's there. Right there on those moccasins. (from "Jacob" by Jack Schaefer)

_____ The man doesn't wear the moccasins because they are very old.

_____ The moccasins were made by Nez Percé Indians.

__X__ The man values the moccasins.

Name _____

Lesson 7

Stating the Implied Main Idea

Many times the main idea of a paragraph is implied, not stated. You have to read carefully, study the supporting details, and state the main idea for yourself. For example, read the paragraph below from "Moon Madness" by P. A. Haddock.

> Cavemen and cavewomen cut marks on mammoth ivory, reindeer bone, and cave walls to mark solar days and new and full moons. Archaeologists have found thousands of early lunar calendars, dating from 40,000 to 8,000 B.C. You know that Stonehenge was probably used to keep track of the Moon's movement. The Anasazi Indians of New Mexico built a similar structure on a butte in Chaco Canyon. The Moslem, Hebrew, and Chinese calendars are still lunar-based.

What do all the details in the paragraph above have in common? They all tell you about calendars. What do these calendars have in common? They all keep track of the movement of the moon. Let's state the main idea. *Since the earliest times, people have measured time by lunar calendars.*

Exercise. Read each paragraph below. Pay special attention to the details in each paragraph. Then, for each paragraph, write a statement expressing the main idea.

a. In the second century A.D., the Roman writer Lucian sent his hero to the Moon on a water spout. More than a thousand years later, another fictional astronaut was pulled to the Moon by a flock of swans. One of the strangest ideas involved tying bottles of dew to a person's waist. Since dew rises in the morning, the theory went, it would carry the person to the Moon with it. (from "Moon Madness" by P. A. Haddock)

Main Idea: ***Over the centuries, people have made up stories about traveling to the moon.***

b. It was a cow that led her owner to the discovery of Howe Caverns in New York. A hunter followed a wounded bear to a cave and found the entrance to Mammoth Cave in Kentucky. In New Mexico, a cowboy investigated what he thought was a column of smoke and found a cave, out of which thousands of bats were flying. The cave is now known as Carlsbad Caverns. (from "The World Under Our Feet" by Renee Bartowski)

Main Idea: ***Some caverns were discovered by accident.***

Copyright © 1984 by Harcourt Brace Jovanovich, Inc. All rights reserved

c. Bedouins of the desert believed that staring at a full moon could make strong men mad, and Germans believed that it could make people careless and clumsy. In the 1600s, the British court declared that "lunacy" was caused by the full moon. By the end of the 1800s, a definition of lunacy was incorporated into British law. Under the law, a "lunatic" had monthly bouts of madness, whereas someone who was "insane" was hopelessly mad. (from "Moon Madness" by P. A. Haddock)

Main Idea: *In many countries people believed that the moon can affect the mind.*

d. Over the years, towns began to pass fire prevention laws. Some towns organized the people into *bucket brigades*. They passed water buckets hand-to-hand from their water source to the fire. Other towns started fire-watch patrols. People walked up and down streets all night. If they spotted a fire, they rang the church bells. Everyone rushed out of bed and helped to put out the fire. (from "Fighting Fires! New Equipment to the Rescue" by Carol G. Vogel and Kathryn A. Goldner)

Main Idea: *Over the years, towns have developed ways to prevent and protect themselves against fires.*

e. At first, Andy couldn't see anything. But then, when he looked a little longer, straining his eyes to see beyond the darkness of the trees and the night itself, he did see what Frank was pointing at. Far away, beneath the trees, and almost hidden by the densely clustered trunks, yet spread clearly over a vast distance from one side of them to the other, was a gentle glow. Gentle it seemed, but gentle only because of its distance. Somehow the glow, as faint as it was, had a glint of fierceness, particularly when he could see, every now and again, a flickering and sudden brightness in the glow. And Andy could smell something. For the first time, he noticed a breeze was blowing. It didn't seem very much, down here on the ground; but up above them the trees were making much more noise than before—much more than a mere rustling. At times it was almost a roar, or a long sigh, as though the trees were in agony. As the trees rolled their tops with great long gasps, the smell was even stronger in his nostrils. Above them the trees rolled and rolled, as though trying to escape, like animals straining against tethers. But down here on the ground, only occasional gusts of wind reached them. Another gust and he knew what he could smell. Smoke! The smoke of brush on fire. (from "The Fire" by G. M. Glaskin)

Main Idea: *A forest fire has started.*

Lesson 8

Identifying Supporting Details When the Main Idea Is Implied

Supporting details back up the main idea of a paragraph. For example, in the paragraph below, the main idea is implied. It can be stated as follows: *Betty leads a very busy life.*

> My sister Betty's job is very demanding. She often works long hours of overtime. In addition, Betty belongs to an amateur acting group. This month she has been attending rehearsals for their new play three nights a week. Moreover, Betty is taking a night course at the local college. Even Betty's Saturdays are busy. On Saturdays Betty does volunteer work at the hospital.

Each of the sentences in the paragraph above contains a detail that supports the implied main idea. Each sentence shows how Betty's life is very busy.

Exercise 1. A paragraph has an implied main idea. It can be stated as follows: *By following several steps, you can improve your grades on tests.* Write *Yes* next to each statement below that supports this main idea. Write *No* next to each statement that does not.

__Yes__ a. Get a good night's sleep before the day of a test.

__No__ b. I always get nervous before a test.

__Yes__ c. Since test directions are very important, make sure you read all the directions carefully.

__Yes__ d. Spend the most time answering the questions that are worth the most points.

__Yes__ e. Spend the least time answering the questions that are worth the fewest points.

__No__ f. Dorothy forgot to eat breakfast before her history test.

__No__ g. It seems to me that math tests are harder than any other tests.

__No__ h. My sister never reads the directions.

Copyright © 1984 by Harcourt Brace Jovanovich, Inc. All rights reserved

__Yes__   **i.** When you start the test, read through it quickly, answering all the questions you think are easy.

__Yes__   **j.** If you have time, go over all your answers before you turn in your test.

Exercise 2. A paragraph has an implied main idea. It can be stated as follows: *Bicycling is an enjoyable form of exercise.* Write Yes next to each sentence below that supports this main idea. Write No next to each sentence that does not.

__No__   **a.** My cousin Jim prefers running.

__No__   **b.** He often runs five miles a day.

__No__   **c.** Many doctors recommend exercising.

__Yes__   **d.** When I'm riding my bicycle, I enjoy looking at the scenery.

__Yes__   **e.** Often I notice things while bicycling that I miss while riding in a car.

__Yes__   **f.** Bicycling is a good way of strengthening your leg muscles.

__Yes__   **g.** I like the fact that I can ride my bicycle at my own pace.

__No__   **h.** Sharon claims that riding a horse is a better form of exercise.

__Yes__   **i.** When I'm riding a bicycle, I like the feel of the wind sweeping through my hair.

__No__   **j.** Next year, maybe I'll take up skiing.

Exercise 3. For each item below, write two sentences containing details that support the implied main idea.

a. Implied main idea: *A great deal of work goes into having a successful party.*

(1) *Students' answers will vary.*

(2) *Students' answers will vary.*

b. Implied main idea: *Costume parties are a lot of fun.*

(1) *Students' answers will vary.*

(2) *Students' answers will vary.*

c. Implied main idea: Students should vote in school elections.
   (1) *Students' answers will vary.*

   (2) *Students' answers will vary.*

d. Implied main idea: *Raising a pet teaches you responsibility.*
   (1) *Students' answers will vary.*

   (2) *Students' answers will vary.*

e. Implied main idea: *Many people get nervous when they have to speak in front of an audience.*
   (1) *Students' answers will vary.*

   (2) *Students' answers will vary.*

Lesson 9
Ordering the Importance of Ideas

When you order the importance of ideas, you decide which idea is the most important and which ideas are less important. For example, read the three statements below.

1. Jeremy displayed his coat of arms at all family occasions.
2. Jeremy was very proud of his family's coat of arms.
3. Jeremy's stationery has his family's coat of arms on it.

The most important idea is that Jeremy was very proud of his family's coat of arms. The other two sentences are less important. They contain details that back up, or support, the main idea.

Exercise. Read the selection below, "A Family Coat of Arms" by Beth Schapira. Then follow the directions at the end of it.

In the twelfth century, European soldiers ready for battle wore heavy armor which kept them from being easily hurt by the enemy. But this armor also made it quite difficult for soldiers to recognize each other, because the armor covered a soldier's face and head. It became the tradition to wear a "coat of arms," a shirt-like garment worn over the armor. Symbols displayed on this coat helped to identify the wearer, in much the way that numbers printed on jerseys help to identify football players.

Soon these symbols became more and more detailed, and the symbols themselves became known as the coat of arms. Soldiers found it hard to remember which symbol represented what lord or family. Armies heading into battle started taking with them men called "heralds." The herald's function was to identify and record which coat of arms represented each lord or family. The herald became quite an important person, and was often paid handsomely by both sides involved in the war. So important was he, that the term "heraldry" came to mean the study of the coats of arms of old families.

Today symbols like those once used on coats of arms are often known as family crests. While they are no longer carried into battle, many families still use them as decorations.

The coat of arms consisted of many parts. The shield was the heart of the coat of arms, and is the part most common today. Within the shield were symbols and colors that represented a particular family. Above the shield was a wreath and a helmet, symbolizing the warriors that wore the original coats of arms. Also above the shield was the crest, a symbol or animal that served as a family mascot. The motto completed the coat of arms. This sentence, often in Latin, expressed a family's ideal or goal and was written on a banner across the bottom of the shield.

There were many different types of shields, with varying shapes, colors, and symbols. The principal colors used on shields had special heraldic names: gules (red), azure (blue), sable (black), vert (green), and purpure (purple). Gold and silver were colors used to represent metal.

Many different symbols were found on the shields. At first, most of the symbol patterns were simple shapes. Today, however, families often design complex shields with pictures that illustrate the family interests.

In the past, European fathers passed their coats of arms on to their eldest sons. Other sons had to add special symbols to the arms to indicate their younger position in the family. An unmarried daughter displayed her father's shield on a diamond shape, which was called a lozenge.

Coats of arms are now often used as symbols by governments, businesses and universities, and they are usually known as seals. The seals are often designed in much the same way as were the coats of arms in ages past. Some professional organizations and college clubs use shields or seals as decorations on stationery and as symbols to represent their groups.

Name _____ 133

Directions. Below are five groups of statements. For each group, write M next to the statement that expresses the most important idea. Write L next to the statements that express the less important ideas.

a. __L__ The soldier began wearing a coat of arms so that he could be identified.

__M__ In the twelfth century, the European soldier had to find a way of making his identity known to other soldiers.

__L__ Since the soldier wore armor covering his face and head, it was difficult for friends or foes to recognize him.

b. __L__ In the battle, many soldiers could not remember which lord or family wore which coat of arms.

__L__ As time went on, each coat of arms became more and more complicated.

__M__ To prevent confusion, the position of herald was created so that someone would be with the armies to identify the complicated symbols on each coat of arms.

c. __M__ Today many families still use coats of arms as decorations.

__L__ Some families place their coat of arms above their mantelpiece.

__L__ Some families have cards printed bearing their coat of arms.

d. __L__ The shield contains the colors and symbols representing a particular family.

__M__ A coat of arms has several parts.

__L__ The wreath and helmet represent the family's original warriors.

e. __M__ Today the use of coats of arms is not limited to families.

__L__ Businesses often have their own crests.

__L__ Many universities have seals, or coats of arms, that they use on their stationery.

Copyright © 1984 by Harcourt Brace Jovanovich, Inc. All rights reserved

Lesson 10

Finding the Main Idea in Dialogue

In a play, the story is usually told through dialogue. When you read dialogue, try to find the point, or main idea. For example, the passage below is from "Dr. Heidegger's Experiment," a play by Steven Otfinoski based on a short story by Nathaniel Hawthorne.

(1) **Narrator:** The scene is the study of the notorious Dr. Heidegger. Around a table sit four old friends. The clock strikes midnight.
(2) **Medford:** This room gives me the creeps.
(3) **Killigrew:** Some say it's haunted.
(4) **Gaston:** Nonsense! The doctor is a man of science.
(5) **Widow:** Maybe so. But he has been known to dabble in magic.

What is the main idea of this passage? The main idea is: *Although Dr. Heidegger is a man of science, he has been known to experiment with magic.*

Exercise. Finish reading "Dr. Heidegger's Experiment." Then answer the questions at the end of it.

(6) **Medford:** Well, I wish he'd hurry up and get here.
(7) **Gaston:** Why did he call us here at this ungodly hour anyway?
(8) **Killigrew:** Probably to look at a cobweb through a microscope or something equally thrilling.
(9) **Widow:** His silly experiments!
(10) **Narrator:** Dr. Heidegger enters the room. He is as old and bent as his friends. He smiles.
(11) **Heidegger:** I doubt if you will find *this* experiment silly or boring.
(12) **Medford:** What is it?
(13) **Heidegger:** Instead of telling you about it, I'll show you.
(14) **Narrator:** The doctor hobbles across the room and takes a large black book from a shelf. From its musty pages he lifts out a dried-up rose. It seems ready to crumble in his hand.
(15) **Heidegger:** This rose blossomed 50 years ago. Would you believe it could ever bloom again?
(16) **Gaston:** Of course not!
(17) **Killigrew:** What do you take us for—fools?
(18) **Widow:** You might as well ask if my wrinkled face could bloom again!
(19) **Heidegger:** Please watch closely.
(20) **Narrator:** The doctor places on the table a bowl filled with what looks like sparkling water. He tosses in the faded rose.
(21) **Killigrew:** Bah! It's just floating.

(22) **Medford:** No, look! It's turning!
(23) **Widow:** Its stalk is green again!
(24) **Gaston:** The petals are . . . red!
(25) **Killigrew:** A marvelous trick, Doctor. How did you do it?
(26) **Heidegger:** I assure you, Colonel, what you've seen is no trick.
(27) **Medford:** Oh, come now! You can't expect us to believe that!
(28) **Heidegger:** Have you ever heard of the Fountain of Youth?
(29) **Widow:** You mean the one the Spanish explorers never found?
(30) **Heidegger:** Yes.
(31) **Gaston:** It never existed.
(32) **Heidegger:** Ah, but it does! A friend of mine recently found it and sent me this liquid—water that's supposed to restore youth!
(33) **Killigrew:** For a rose, perhaps. But what about human beings?
(34) **Heidegger:** I'm not sure. I'd have to perform some experiments. . . .
(35) **Medford:** Then there's no question—we're going to drink the water to find out.
(36) **Gaston:** And become young again?
(37) **Widow:** Of course!
(38) **Heidegger:** Oh, no. You see, my friend explained that there are some consequences after drinking it and—
(39) **Killigrew:** And what? There's only one way to find out—and that's to drink the water.
(40) **Heidegger:** But we're not certain of the results!
(41) **Widow:** What's to be certain? The rose revived, didn't it?
(42) **Heidegger:** But I cannot allow you to risk your lives.
(43) **Medford:** Nonsense, Doctor. Besides, think of the good we can do. I swear to you, if I am made young again, I will go into business. I will share my wealth with the poor.
(44) **Killigrew:** And I'll be the kind of soldier who fights for peace, not for love of war and glory.
(45) **Gaston:** I will enter politics—not to gain power and money, but to truly serve the public.
(46) **Widow:** And I'll serve the world by being a good wife and mother. The selfish, vain flirt who lived only for herself will be no more!
(47) **Heidegger:** But I must protest!
(48) **Killigrew:** There's nothing to protest, Doctor. We shall perform an experiment for you.
(49) **Narrator:** Gaston begins pouring the liquid into some glasses.

(50) **Gaston:** And what about you, Doctor? Aren't you going to join us in the experiment?
(51) **Heidegger:** No. I'm not sure what will happen. Besides, I have had so much trouble in growing old, I am in no hurry to grow young again. I will merely watch.
(52) **Killigrew:** Suit yourself.
(53) **Medford** (*raising his glass*): Well, here goes nothing!
(54) **Gaston:** Down the hatch!
(55) **Widow:** Hmmm. What a funny taste!
(56) **Narrator:** A remarkable change begins to take place. The wrinkles on their faces smooth out. Their cheeks change from ashen gray to rosy red. They feel more lighthearted than they have in years.
(57) **Medford:** Give me more of this wonderful water!
(58) **Widow:** I am younger!
(59) **Gaston:** But still too old!
(60) **Killigrew:** Quick, Gaston, fill the glasses again!
(61) **Heidegger:** No, no, please, my friends. You have been a long time growing old. Surely you can wait—
(62) **Narrator:** But the four friends insist on more water immediately. So Gaston refills the glasses.
(63) **Gaston:** Look! The gray is gone from my hair!
(64) **Killigrew:** And I don't need my glasses to see anymore!
(65) **Medford:** My dear widow, you are beautiful!
(66) **Widow:** Ah! My figure is coming back! But I am still not young enough. Please, Gaston, another glass.
(67) **Heidegger:** Please, please, no more!
(68) **All Four:** We are young! We are young!
(69) **Gaston:** Ha! Look at our baggy clothes!
(70) **Killigrew:** How silly they look!
(71) **Medford:** Now I will show them all how great a businessman I am! I'll make millions!
(72) **Heidegger:** But you'll earn them honestly, I hope.
(73) **Medford:** As honestly as the next fellow. You can be sure of that!
(74) **Heidegger:** But what about the poor?
(75) **Medford:** Yes, well, I'll give to the charities. It always *looks* good.
(76) **Heidegger:** How quickly you forget.
(77) **Killigrew:** I haven't forgotten! I remember the cry of battle, the bullets whizzing by my ears!
(78) **Heidegger:** But you said you would not love war this time.
(79) **Killigrew:** Every soldier must love war. How else could he win?
(80) **Heidegger:** What about peace?
(81) **Killigrew:** There will be no peace until all enemies are destroyed!
(82) **Gaston:** You are too rash, Colonel. War is a waste of human life and money. When I am governor, I will see that the money is spent at home.

Name _____

(83) **Heidegger:** Ah! At least one of you will keep his promise!
(84) **Gaston:** The people will love me so much, I will be made President. And then I can do anything I like. All power will be mine!
(85) **Heidegger:** So you let me down too, Gaston.
(86) **Widow:** We will keep our word, Doctor. But you must be patient. I'll marry and be a proper wife. But what's the rush?
(87) **Heidegger:** You want to flirt first?
(88) **Widow:** Of course! I am far too beautiful to give myself away to the first man that comes along.
(89) **Heidegger:** You have not changed a bit. It's the water. You shouldn't have taken it.
(90) **Widow:** Come, sweet old man. Dance with me.
(91) **Heidegger:** You must excuse me. I am old and feeble. My dancing days were over long ago.
(92) **Killigrew:** Dance with me, Clara!
(93) **Gaston:** No, no. I will be her partner!
(94) **Medford:** She promised me her hand!
(95) **Narrator:** Like spoiled children, the three men fight each other for the Widow Wallace. She enjoys every moment of it.
(96) **Heidegger:** Gentlemen, please! Stop this foolishness!
(97) **Killigrew:** Watch out! The table!
(98) **Gaston:** Grab the bowl!
(99) **Medford:** Too late!
(100) **Narrator:** And so it is. The bowl falls and shatters into pieces. The Water of Youth flows across the floor.
(101) **Widow:** Oh, no! Now how can we become younger?
(102) **Heidegger:** Wait! Look at the rose! It's fading!
(103) **Widow:** It's getting older and uglier than it was before!
(104) **Narrator:** Suddenly the four people shiver.
(105) **Widow:** My skin! I can feel it shriveling!
(106) **Medford:** We're growing old again!
(107) **Gaston:** You must help us, Doctor!
(108) **Heidegger:** There's nothing I can do. In your foolishness you have rushed into what you didn't know. And now you have spilled the water.
(109) **Killigrew:** Then you must send to your friend for more!
(110) **Medford:** Much more!
(111) **Widow:** Enough so we can drink of it morning, noon, and night.
(112) **Gaston:** Then we will stay young forever!
(113) **Heidegger:** Never! You would ruin the world between the four of you!

(114) **Widow:** But you don't realize! We cannot live like this.

(115) **Killigrew:** We would all be better off dead!

(116) **Heidegger** *(horrified)*: Look at all of you. You're growing far more aged than you were before! I think I know now the consequences of drinking the water. You saw what happened to the rose—it crumbled to dust. The potion must carry a reaction. It sends you forward in time as many years as it sent you back!

(117) **Narrator:** The four once-youthful people begin to shrink. The widow's ring slips from her withered finger. Medford's clothes swim and bag on him. Gaston's skeleton of a figure grows smaller in his chair. Killigrew no longer has the strength to sit upright. Dr. Heidegger now sees four corpses before him—all 120 years old.

(118) **Heidegger:** The experiment is over, my friends. *(softly)* All over.

Questions

a. What is the main idea of paragraphs 6-9?
The people are impatient and wonder why Dr. Heidegger has called them together.

b. What is the main idea of paragraphs 10-24?
The doctor has found a way to restore youth to a rose.

c. What is the main idea of paragraphs 25-27?
Killigrew and Medford think that the doctor is trying to trick them.

d. What is the main idea of paragraphs 28-32?
Heidegger claims that the water is from the Fountain of Youth.

e. What is the main idea of paragraphs 33-48?
Despite Heidegger's protests, the group insist on drinking the water, claiming that this time they will use their youth wisely.

f. What is the main idea of paragraphs 49-55?
The group drink the water.

g. What is the main idea of paragraphs 56-70?
The water makes them young.

h. What is the main idea of paragraphs 71-95?
Now young, the group ignore their promises to be better people.

i. What is the main idea of paragraphs 96-101?
They break the bowl containing the water.

j. What is the main idea of paragraphs 102-118?
The final effect of the water is fatal.

Name _____

Lesson 11
Practice

Pay special attention to main ideas as you read the following selection. Then complete the exercises at the end of it.

Using Solar Energy: It's Not All That Easy!
Jack Myers

(1)   Everyone knows that we must learn how to use other sources of energy in place of oil and gas. One source of energy that anyone can see is the solar energy which comes to us every day as sunlight. No one has to pay for sunlight. It is free. So why don't we use a lot of solar energy right now in place of oil and gas?

(2)   There are a whole lot of problems in using solar energy for our different energy needs. One of the easiest ways to use solar energy is for heating houses. Most houses receive enough sunlight energy each day to do the job. There are three problems that need to be solved. First, we must change the light energy into heat. Then we must get the heat inside the house. And finally, we need to store some of the heat to keep the house warm at night. We have learned to solve all of these problems and solar-heated houses are being built today.

(3)   Even though we know how to build them, not many of our present houses are designed for solar heating. The reason is that it costs more to build one. I think that within the next few years we will learn a lot about solar heating. As it becomes easier to use, solar heating will be built into more and more of our houses.

(4)   Now that we have thought about solar houses, how about using sunlight for our many other energy needs? Scientists and engineers are working on ways to do that. They have a great deal of work ahead of them because there are a whole lot of problems.

(5)   The most difficult problem is that there is not nearly so much energy in sunlight as there seems to be. Sunlight looks very bright, but that is partly because our eyes are so sensitive. Sunlight provides the energy that all green plants use to make their food. But most plants make many leaves to catch lots of sunlight, and even they do not grow very fast.

(6)   Here is a practical way to think about how much energy there is in sunlight. First, let's think about a common card table, the kind with folding legs. Let's suppose that we set up the card table out in your backyard or some-

place where it will be in the sun all day. The top of the card table has an area usually a little less than one square yard. How much energy falls on that card table during a sunny day?

(7) One way to answer the question is to think about sunlight as if it were coal dust. How much coal dust would have to fall on your table each day to give the same amount of energy as the energy of sunlight? If you swept off the table once each day, you would get less than a quart of coal dust. We know how to use coal as a source of energy. So how much money would that coal dust be worth to us for its energy? The answer is surprising: only about three cents.

(8) Because of the low energy content of sunlight, practical use of solar energy always requires some kind of collecting system. One way is to collect the light itself by using a lens or a focusing mirror to make a very hot spot. Another way is to collect the energy in some other form that has been made from light.

(9) Let's think about using wood as a form of stored chemical energy. A tree makes its wood by collecting chemicals made in its many leaves with the help of sunlight. A lot of energy from sunlight has to be collected to make wood.

(10) If you want to heat your house by burning wood, you need to cut down many trees and collect their wood. It may take a lot of energy to cut down the trees and chop them up and carry them to your house. If you are not careful, you might spend more energy collecting than you can get back by burning the wood.

(11) Many people have asked me why we don't solve our energy problem right away by using sunlight. I think the answer is that sunlight really does not have a very high energy concentration. And we have to solve a lot of practical problems in learning how to collect it.

(12) I am sure that we will find ways to make better use of solar energy. We need a lot of research to learn how to solve its problems. One of my teachers once told me: "The problems of science and engineering are never easy. If they were, someone would already have solved them."

Exercise 1. Answer each of the questions below.

a. What is the main idea of paragraph 1?
We might be able to use solar energy in place of oil and gas.

b. What is the main idea of paragraph 2?
The use of solar energy presents several problems.

c. What is the main idea of paragraph 3?
Although most houses today are not designed for solar energy, this will probably change in the future.

Name _____

d. What is the main idea of paragraph 4?
Although there are problems involved, scientists are working on ways to use solar energy to fulfill our other energy needs.

e. What is the main idea of paragraph 5?
The major difficulty lies in the fact that sunlight provides less energy than you would expect.

f. What is the main idea of paragraph 6?
The card table experiment can show how much energy there is in sunlight.

g. What is the main idea of paragraph 7?
Only about three cents' worth of energy would fall on that table.

h. What is the main idea of paragraph 8?
Since sunlight has a low energy content, a collecting system is necessary.

i. What is the main idea of paragraph 9?
In order for a tree to make wood, it must collect a lot of sunlight.

j. What is the main idea of paragraph 10?
Since collecting wood takes a lot of energy, you may expend more energy collecting than you would save burning wood.

Exercise 2. Answer each of the questions below.

a. What is the main idea of paragraph 11?
There are several reasons why we do not make better use of solar energy today.

b. Find one detail that supports the main idea in paragraph 11.
Sunlight has a low energy concentration.

c. Find a second detail that supports the main idea in paragraph 11.
We have to learn how to collect sunlight efficiently.

d. What is the main idea of paragraph 12?
We will find better ways to use solar energy.

Copyright © 1984 by Harcourt Brace Jovanovich, Inc. All rights reserved

Name _____

Chapter 6
Dictionary

Why use a dictionary? A dictionary tells you the meaning of a word you do not know. But a dictionary tells you other information as well. For example, it tells you how to pronounce the word, how to use it in a sentence, how to spell it, and what part of speech it is.

In this chapter you will learn how to interpret the information in a dictionary. Of course, dictionaries differ slightly. For more information about your particular dictionary, look at the section called "How to Use Your Dictionary" in the front pages of it.

Lesson 1
Using Guide Words

Two guide words appear at the top of every dictionary page. They name the first and last words that appear on that page. For example, imagine that the guide words at the top of the page are *receive* and *report*. All words in alphabetical order that come between *receiver* and *report* also appear on this page. Guide words help you to find a word quickly.

In the comic strip below, you may not know the meaning of the words *determination* and *temptation*. First let's look up the word *determination* in a dictionary.

GARFIELD by Jim Davis

[Garfield comic strip:
Panel 1: "I, GARFIELD THE CAT, RESOLVE TO SPEND THE ENTIRE WEEK IN BED"
Panel 2: "OH SURE, THE GOING MAY GET TOUGH AT TIMES..."
Panel 3: "BUT MY SHEER WILL AND DETERMINATION SHOULD RESIST THE TEMPTATION TO GET UP"]

Copyright © 1984 by Harcourt Brace Jovanovich, Inc. All rights reserved   143

The guide word on the left shows the *first word* defined on that page.

The guide word on the right shows the *last word* defined on that page.

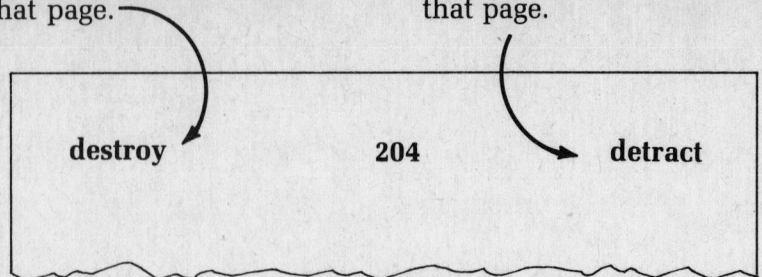

destroy   204   **detract**

You can see that *determination* is on page 204. It falls alphabetically between the words *destroy* and *detract*.

The dictionary tells you that *determination* means "firmness of purpose."

Now let's look up the word *temptation*.

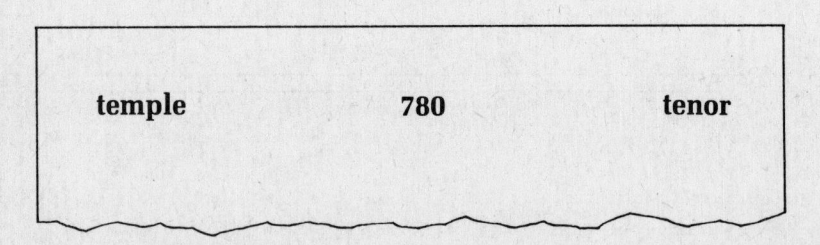

temple   780   **tenor**

You can see that *temptation* is on page 780. It falls alphabetically between *temple* and *tenor*. The dictionary tells us that *temptation* means "the condition of being tempted or persuaded to do something wrong or foolish."

You don't have to know the meaning or the pronunciation of the guide words in order to use them. Simply look carefully at the first few letters of each guide word to see if your word fits on that page.

Exercise 1. The guide words at the top of the dictionary page are *home* and *hubcap*. Which of the words below would be found on this page? Write *Yes* next to those words that would be found on this page. Write *No* next to those words which would not.

a. hobo   *No*
b. hug   *No*
c. homesick   *Yes*
d. homer   *Yes*
e. hole   *No*
f. hogwash   *No*
g. hubbub   *Yes*
h. huddle   *No*
i. hot rod   *Yes*
j. hull   *No*

Name _____ 145

Exercise 2. Look carefully at each word below. If you do not understand the word or do not know how to pronounce it, you may want to look it up later. Your job now is to put an X next to the guide words that show on which page the *italicized* word would be found.

a. *Giggle* would be found on the page with the guide words:

_____ gesture/gift

__X__ gifted/given

_____ gizzard/glint

b. *Yo-yo* would be found on the page with the guide words:

_____ yesterday/yet

_____ yam/yellow

__X__ yoga/yule

c. *Ooze* would be found on the page with the guide words:

__X__ one/opera

_____ operation/orange

_____ orangeade/organ

d. *Pneumonia* would be found on the page with the guide words:

_____ play/plight

_____ plop/plural

__X__ plus/pocket

e. *Nothing* would be found on the page with the guide words:

_____ north/notch

__X__ note/nowhere

_____ nozzle/nurse

Lesson 2

Understanding an Entry

An entry word is a word or term defined in the dictionary. The entry is the information about the entry word. A great deal of information is given in each entry, such as definitions, pronunciation, part of speech, and other forms of the word.

Copyright © 1984 by Harcourt Brace Jovanovich, Inc. All rights reserved

Look at the entry below for the entry word *realize*.

re•al•ize (rē′ə-līz′) *v.*: **realized, realizing.** 1. To understand fully. She *realized* the seriousness of the problem. 2. To make real or bring about. Nancy *realized* her dream of becoming a ballerina. 3. To obtain or gain. Malcolm *realized* a profit on his investment. 4. To bring in as profit as a result of a sale. The Newtons *realized* a profit on the sale of their house. [French *réaliser*, fr. Late Latin *reālis*, real.] **re′al•iz′a•ble**—*adj.* **re′al•iz′er**—n.

Each section of the entry is coded by the letters *A, B, C,* etc.

re•**A**ize (rē′ə**B**iz′) *v*.**C** realized **D**ealizing. 1. To understand fully. She *realized* the seriousness of the problem. 2. To make real or bring about. Nancy *realized* her dream of becoming a ballerina. 3. To ob**E**in or gain. Malcolm *realized* a profit on his investment. 4. To bring in as profit as a result of a sale. The Newtons *realized* a profit on the sale of their house. [French *réaliser*, fr**F** Late Latin *reālis*, real.] **re′al-iz′a**•**G**ble—*adj.* **re′al-iz′er**—n.

Part *A* shows you the entry word, *realize*. It tells you how to spell this word and how to divide it into syllables. Some dictionaries use a dot (•) to divide words, some a hyphen (-), and others just leave a space between the syllables.

Part *B* shows how to pronounce each syllable of the word and which syllable to stress or accent. For example: (rē′ə-līz′).

Part *C* tells you the part of speech of the first definition. The abbreviation *v.* means verb. Other abbreviations for parts of speech are *n.* (noun), *pron.* (pronoun), *adj.* (adjective), *adv.* (adverb), *prep.* (preposition), *conj.* (conjunction), and *interj.* (interjection). The abbreviation *pl.* means plural.

Part *D* shows you other forms of the entry word. Since *realize* is a verb, Part *D* shows the principal parts of this verb. When the entry word is a noun, Part *D* shows the plural form of the word, if the dictionary makers think someone might not know it or might have difficulty spelling it. Sometimes Part *D* also shows the pronunciation of the plural form. For example, **leaf** (lēf) *n., pl.* **leaves** (lēvz). When the entry word is an adjective, Part *D* shows you the comparative and superlative forms. For example, **lean** (lēn) *adj.*: **leaner, leanest.**

Part *E* contains the definitions. Most words in English have more than one meaning. In the entry each different definition is numbered. Sometimes a sample sentence follows the definition to show you how the word is used. For example, the entry for *realize* shows four different meanings for *realize* and gives a sentence showing how each meaning is used.

Part *F* shows the origin, or history, of the entry word. This information is enclosed in brackets [ ]. Sometimes the symbol < is used to mean *comes from*. *Realize* comes from the French word *réaliser*, which came from a Late Latin word *reālis*, which means "real."

Part *G* shows related forms of the entry word. *Realizable* is the adjective form of *realize*, and *realizer* is the noun form.

Name _____

Exercise 1. Read the entry below. Then answer the questions that follow it.

> **par•ty** (pär′tē) *n., pl.* **parties.** 1. A social get-together for entertainment or amusement. *Jeff attended his friend's costume party.* 2. A group of people gathered together to take part in an activity or task. *The sailing party will leave from Southampton at seven in the morning.* 3. A permanent political group organized to support and promote certain common ideals and certain candidates. *Our party supported Willis in the last election.* 4. A participant; a person who takes part in an action. *The police found that Smith was a party to the crime.* [Middle English *partie*, part, party, fr. Old French *partir*, to divide, fr. Latin *partire, pars,* part.] **par′ty**—*adj.*

a. The word *party* is made up of two syllables. Which syllable is stressed? — *first*

b. The word *party* is what part of speech? — *noun*

c. How do you spell the plural of *party*? — *parties*

d. How many meanings does this entry list for *party*? — *four*

e. What is the adjective form of *party*? — *party*

Exercise 2. Read the entry below. Then answer the questions that follow it.

> **speed•y** (spē′dē) *adj.:* **speedier, speediest.** 1. Marked by very swift movement; rapid. *The speedy runner won the race.* 2. Done without delay; prompt; ready; quick. *The store is known for its speedy service.* **speed′i•ly**—*adv.* **speed′i•ness**—*n.*

a. If you break the word *speedy* into two syllables, between which two letters can you break it? — *d and y*

b. The word *speedy* is what part of speech? — *adjective*

c. The comparative form of *speedy* is *speedier*. This is the form you use to compare two things. What is the superlative form—the form you use to compare three or more things? — *speediest*

d. What is the adverb form of *speedy*? — *speedily*

e. What is the noun form of *speedy*? — *speediness*

Lesson 3

Using a Pronunciation Key

You can find out how to pronounce a word by looking it up in the dictionary. In parentheses after the entry word, you will find the word spelled with pronunciation symbols. For example, **quar•ter•back** (kwôr′tər-băk′).

The key to these symbols appears in the front of the dictionary. The key lists each pronunciation symbol used in the dictionary. It illustrates the sound each symbol stands for with a word whose pronunciation most people know. The important parts of this key are usually printed at the bottom of every other page in the dictionary.

Look at the following key. It tells you that the symbol ă stands for the *a* sound you hear in *pat*, and the symbol ā stands for the *a* sound you hear in *pay*. Notice the last symbol, ə, which looks like an upside-down e. It is called a *schwa*, pronounced *shwa*. This sound is never stressed. The pronunciation key shows that ə is pronounced like the *a* in *about*, the *e* in *item*, the *i* in *edible*, the *o* in *gallop*, and the *u* in *circus*.

Pronunciation Key

ă	p**a**t	h	**h**at	ŏ	p**o**t	t	**t**ight
ā	p**ay**	wh	**wh**ich	ō	t**oe**	th	**th**in, pa**th**
âr	c**are**	ĭ	p**i**t	ô	p**aw**, f**o**r	th	**th**is, ba**the**
ä	f**a**ther	ī	p**ie**	oi	n**oi**se	ŭ	c**u**t
b	**b**i**b**	îr	p**ier**	ŏŏ	t**oo**k	ûr	**ur**ge
ch	**ch**ur**ch**	j	**j**u**dge**	ōō	b**oo**t	v	**v**al**v**e
d	**d**ee**d**	k	**k**i**ck**	ou	**ou**t	w	**w**ith
ĕ	p**e**t	l	**l**id, need**le**	p	**p**o**p**	y	**y**es
ē	b**ee**	m	**m**u**m**	r	**r**oa**r**	z	**z**ebra, di**s**mal, e**x**ile vi**s**ion
f	**f**i**fe**	n	**n**o, sud**den**	s	**s**au**ce**		
g	**g**a**g**	ng	thi**ng**	sh	**sh**ip, di**sh**	zh	
						ə	**a**bout, it**e**m, ed**i**ble, gall**o**p, circ**u**s

Look again at the pronunciation of *quarterback* (kwôr′tər-băk′). There are three syllables. For the first syllable (kwôr), the key tells you that the k sounds like the k in *kick*, the w sounds like the w in *with*, the ô sounds like the o in *for*, and the r sounds like the r in *roar*.

For the second syllable (tər), the key tells you that the t sounds like the t in *tight*, the ə sounds like the a in *about*, and the r sounds like the r in *roar*.

For the third syllable, (băk), the key tells you that the b sounds like the b in *bib*, the ă sounds like the a in *pat*, and the k sounds like the k in *kick*.

Name _____

Many long words have two accent marks. In the word *quarterback* (kwôr′tər-băk′), the first syllable receives the heavier, or primary, stress. The third syllable receives the lighter, or secondary, stress. The second syllable is not stressed at all.

Exercise 1. Use the pronunciation symbols to pronounce each word below. Then write the syllable that receives the primary, or heavier, stress in the first blank at the right. In the second blank, write the syllable that receives the secondary, or lighter, stress. If no syllable receives a secondary stress, write *No* in the second blank. An example is done for you.

		Primary	Secondary
Example: quick•sil•ver (kwĭk′sĭl′vər)		quick	sil
a.	qua•sar (kwā′zär′)	*qua*	*sar*
b.	qua•ran•tine (kwôr′ən-tēn′)	*qua*	*tine*
c.	quet•zal (kĕt-säl′)	*zal*	*No*
d.	ques•tion•naire (kwĕs′chə-nâr′)	*naire*	*ques*
e.	quo•tient (kwō′shənt)	*quo*	*No*

Exercise 2. Use the pronunciation symbols to pronounce each word below. Then circle the correct answer. (You may want to check your answers against a dictionary.) An example is done for you.

Example:

The first *i* in *quicksilver* (kwĭk′sĭl′vər) has the same sound as the *i* in

(1) **list** (2) mine (3) sigh

a. The first *a* in *quasar* (kwā′zär′) has the same sound as the *a* in
(1) fan (2) far (3) **date**

b. The first *a* in *quarantine* (kwôr′ən-tēn′) has the same sound as the *a* in
(1) fame (2) rack (3) **sausage**

c. The sound spelled by the letters *qu* in *quetzal* (kĕt-säl′) is the same as the sound spelled by *qu* in
(1) quake (2) **unique** (3) request

d. The first *e* in *questionnaire* (kwĕs′chə-nâr′) has the same sound as the *e* in
(1) **chess** (2) decoy (3) being

e. The *o* in *quotient* (kwō′shənt) has the same sound as the *o* in
(1) body (2) **code** (3) moss

Copyright © 1984 by Harcourt Brace Jovanovich, Inc. All rights reserved

Lesson 4
Finding Principal Parts in a Dictionary

A verb is a word that expresses an action or a state of being. A verb has four principal parts you should know. These principal parts are the present infinitive, the past, the past participle, and the present participle.

Present Infinitive	Past	Past Participle	Present Participle
rise	rose	(have) risen	(is) rising
mix	mixed	(have) mixed	(is) mixing

You can use a dictionary to find the spelling of the principal parts of a verb. First look up the present infinitive, or dictionary, form of the verb; for example, *rise*. You will find the following information:

rise (rīz) *v.*: **rose, risen, rising.**

The first word after the abbreviation *v.* is the past, the second is the past participle, and the third is the present participle.

Sometimes the past and the past participle are the same. When this happens, you will find only two words after the *v.* For example:

mix (mĭks) *v.*: **mixed, mixing.**

The past and past participle are both *mixed*.

Exercise. As you read the following selection from "Nerves" by Kim Solworth Merlino, pay special attention to the verbs printed in **boldface.** Then follow the directions at the end of the selection.

> Your eyes, ears, nose, tongue and skin are information-gathering organs. Each sense organ has tiny nerve endings in it called *receptors*. In your eye, for example, receptors are at the back of the eyeball. Eye receptors are sensitive to light and colors. The brain understands that all messages from the eye are about lights or colors.
> Your skin **has** several kinds of receptors. There are five kinds of touches that can be relayed to the brain. That's why a light tickle feels different from heat or a sharp pain. You might ignore the ticklish feeling, but you will pull away the instant a pin pricks your finger.
> Did you ever bang your elbow and **get** an aching, trembling pain up and down your arm? You hit your funny bone! The funny bone is not a bone at all, but a long nerve. It **runs** from your fingertips up your arm. The nerve is well protected every-

where in your arm except that one spot. When you hit your elbow, you squeezed the nerve against a bone in your arm. The pressure caused the pain.

How did it get the name "funny bone"? Could it be because the name of the bone next to the nerve is the *humerus*? That sounds the same as the word *humorous*, which means funny. But who's laughing?

Did you ever grab something that you **thought** was cold . . . but it wasn't? Before you **knew** it, the hot potato was on the floor. Only a couple of seconds later did you realize what had happened. Then your hand **began** to hurt. Why did you drop it before you **felt** the heat? Your body **had** a *reflex action*.

Reflexes are actions that your nervous system **does** very fast. They are important because sometimes a little extra speed can save your life. How can reflexes be faster than thinking? Because the brain is not involved. The hot message travels from your hand to the spinal cord. Decision-making neurons in the spinal cord instantly **send** a signal back to your hand muscles to pull away.

Reflexes save time because the message doesn't have to travel all the way to the brain. Other examples of reflex actions are sneezing and blinking. Doctors test the speed of your reflexes. When they tap you below the knee with a rubber hammer, your leg **springs** forward. That's a reflex action.

Directions. The present infinitive, or dictionary, form of each **boldface** word is given below. Look up each present infinitive form in your dictionary. For each word, list the past, past participle, and present participle form.

Present Infinitive	Past	Past Participle	Present Participle
a. have	had	had	having
b. get	got	gotten	getting
c. run	ran	run	running
d. think	thought	thought	thinking
e. know	knew	known	knowing
f. begin	began	begun	beginning
g. feel	felt	felt	feeling
h. do	did	done	doing
i. send	sent	sent	sending
j. spring	sprang	sprung	springing

Lesson 5
Using a Dictionary to Find Parts of Speech

You can use a dictionary to identify which part of speech a word is. In a dictionary, the parts of speech are abbreviated as follows:

n.	(noun)	*prep.*	(preposition)
pron.	(pronoun)	*conj.*	(conjunction)
adj.	(adjective)	*interj.*	(interjection)
v.	(verb)		
adv.	(adverb)		

Look at the entry below.

ea·sel (ē′zəl) *n.*: A frame on which something, often a piece of art, is displayed. [Dutch *ezel*, fr. Common Germanic *asiluz*, fr. Latin *asinus*.]

The abbreviation *n.* appears after the pronunciation symbols. It tells you that *easel* is a noun.

Sometimes a word can be used as more than one part of speech. For example, look at the entry below.

dance (dăns) *v.:* **danced, dancing.** 1. To move in rhythm to music. *She danced across the floor.* 2. To leap about in an excited fashion. 3. To perform a particular dance. — *n.:* 1. A series of steps set to music. 2. The art of dancing. 3. A party at which people dance. *The dance was held in the school gym.* 4. A particular form of dance. [Middle English *dansen, dauncer*, fr. Old French *danser, dancier.*]

This entry shows three definitions for *dance* when it is used as a verb. It shows four definitions for *dance* when it is used as a noun.

Exercise 1. Read the following selection from "The Wonders Our Eyes Can See" by Roger Caras. Pay special attention to the words printed in **boldface.** Then follow the directions at the end of the selection.

There is a very old story about a **farmer who** went to the zoo for the first time. He wandered around looking at animals that **although** strange to him looked something like animals he had known on his farm. The wolves looked rather like big dogs and the water buffalo looked something like his **cattle.** Porcupines he had seen before, and raccoons, of course, and even some of the antelope looked a little like goats—but then he came to the pen that held the giraffes.

The old man's jaw fell open, and he stared **at** the **huge** bull giraffe that towered above him. He looked at the bright markings of the animal's coat. He gazed at the enormous neck and

Name _____ 153

the strange bumps on the bull's head and watched with wonder as the giraffe's long blue-gray tongue curled out and grasped some hay. Finally, they say, the man made up his mind. He shook his head and said, "There is no such animal." Satisfied with his decision, he moved along to pass **judgment** on the other animals.

But, you see, there was such an animal, even if the old man couldn't **believe** his own eyes. And the giraffe, as **improbable** as it is, however strange its design, is only one of the wonders that **await** the curious mind beyond the gates of the zoo. But, of course, you have to be prepared to believe what you see.

Directions. Use your dictionary to find the part of speech of each of the words below. Write your answers in the blanks.

a. farmer   _noun_
b. who   _pronoun_
c. although _conjunction_
d. cattle   _noun_
e. at   _preposition_

f. huge   _adjective_
g. judgment   _noun_
h. believe   _verb_
i. improbable _adjective_
j. await   _verb_

Exercise 2. Each word below can be used as more than one part of speech. Look up each word in your dictionary. Then, for each word, write the parts of speech it can be used as. The first one is done for you.

Example:
very: _adverb and adjective_

a. time: _noun, adjective, and verb_
b. wolf: _noun and verb_
c. farm: _noun, verb, and adjective_
d. before: _adverb, preposition, and conjunction_
e. little: _adjective, adverb, and noun_
f. stare: _verb and noun_
g. gaze: _verb and noun_
h. wonder: _noun and verb_
i. if: _conjunction and noun_
j. mind: _noun and verb_

Copyright © 1984 by Harcourt Brace Jovanovich, Inc. All rights reserved

Lesson 6

Dividing Words into Syllables

A syllable is a part of a word having only one vowel sound. A syllable is used to show how a word is pronounced or how it can best be hyphenated at the end of a line. Some words have only one syllable; for example, *young, book, dance*. Many words, though, contain more than one syllable; for example, *newspaper* (news•pa•per), *attempt* (at•tempt), and *multiplication* (mul•ti•pli•ca•tion). In general, the more syllables a word has, the harder it is to read.

Sometimes you may not recognize a long word when you read it, even though you know the word when you hear it. One strategy for reading long words is to break them into syllables. This helps you to pronounce the long words, and so may help you to understand them.

In the comic strip below, Becky uses several long words to describe a college student.

DRABBLE by Fagan

Let's break these long words into syllables. *Enormously* has four syllables (e•nor•mous•ly). It means "immensely" or "to a very great degree." *Intelligent* has four syllables (in•tel•li•gent). It means "very smart or bright." *Energetic* has four syllables (en•er•get•ic). It means "full of energy." *Sophisticated* has five syllables (so•phis•ti•cat•ed). It means "worldly and cultured." *Brilliant* has two syllables (bril•liant). It means "extremely intelligent."

Exercise. Read the selection below from "March of the Army Ants" by Julia Fellows. Pay special attention to the words printed in **boldface**. Then follow the directions at the end of the selection.

It's early morning in the rain forest of southern Mexico. A few rays of sunlight **filter** down through the huge trees onto the shadowy forest floor. Water drips from the wet ferns. On the ground, lines of long-legged army ants begin their search for food.

Name _____

The ants follow each other closely, touching **antennae** often as they hurry along. Hundreds move forward in each line. Unlike most ants, army ants are blind. Each follows a **chemical** trail laid down by the first few ants. The big soldier ants are on the outside of the line. The smaller workers walk in the middle.

Grasshoppers and other insects **scuttle** away from the hungry ants. Ant birds swoop down to eat the insects that the ants scare from the forest floor.

The ants attack whatever food they may come across: beetles, **tarantulas, scorpions,** roaches or the larvae of wasps. Sometimes they eat lizards, snakes or even nestling birds. But there's no need to worry about the ants' eating humans; their jaws aren't big enough. The ants might give you a nasty sting, though.

Now the ants have found a **katydid,*** their first prey of the morning. Suddenly a swarm of ants is crawling over the **katydid.** The ants numb their prey with **poisonous** stings. Then the half-inch-long soldiers tear the **katydid** apart with their huge, pincerlike jaws.

Next the workers carry pieces of the **katydid** back to the ant colony's central camp. Leaves **rustle** as the ants run quickly back and forth along the column.

At the camp the **katydid** is eaten by the other workers, by the larvae, and by their queen. When the ants have finished eating, the column of ants moves forward again.

Directions. Look up each word below in your dictionary. Then divide it into syllables. Write the syllables on the line provided.

a. filter — *fil•ter*
b. antenna — *an•ten•na*
c. chemical — *chem•i•cal*
d. grasshopper — *grass•hop•per*
e. scuttle — *scut•tle*

f. tarantula — *ta•ran•tu•la*
g. scorpion — *scor•pi•on*
h. katydid — *ka•ty•did*
i. poisonous — *poi•son•ous*
j. rustle — *rus•tle*

***katydid** (kā′tē-dĭd′) n.: A type of insect.

Lesson 7
Finding the Correct Meaning

In English, many words have more than one meaning. This means that a dictionary entry will contain several definitions for one entry word. For example, look at the entry below.

note (nōt) n.: 1. A short written record of something one wants to remember. *Good students often take notes during class.* 2. A short written message. *She left a note for the baby-sitter.* 3. A written explanation of a passage of a text printed to the side of the passage, at the bottom of the page, or at the end of the text. *Andy found the author's notes on the play helpful.* 4. In music, a tone of a certain pitch. *The singer hit the wrong note.* 5. In music, the symbol representing such a tone. *In music class, she copied the notes for the first bar of music.* 6. The song of a bird. *The air was filled with the notes of the nightingale.* 7. One of the keys on a piano. *The pianist played the wrong note.* 8. A mark or sign by which something may be known. *There was a note of sadness about the stranger.* 9. Importance. *Nothing of note happened during the meeting.* 10. Notice. *Marla took note of the blue sedan which seemed to be following her.* —v.: **noted, noting.** 1. To notice or become aware of. *The painter noted the way the light shined through the trees.* 2. To write down; record. *On his pad, the reporter noted the time the train departed.* 3. To make particular mention of. *In his speech, Jackson noted Miss Conklin's contribution to the success of the project.* [Middle English *note*, fr. Latin *nota*, mark, sign.] **not'er**—n.

Now read the sentence below.

When Jayne auditioned for the part, she sang every *note* perfectly.

The fourth meaning of *note* listed under the entry above fits this sentence.

Now look at the comic strip below.

SNUFFY SMITH by Fred Lasswell

When you read the first frame, you probably thought Ma was going to leave Pa a short, written message. Instead, she left him a symbol representing a tone of a certain pitch.

When you read, you must choose the meaning that fits the sentence, or context. You may have to change the definition slightly to match the form of the word used in the sentence. For example, read the sentence below.

Reporters keep good *notes* while they are working on a story.

Since *notes* is plural, you have to make the definition plural.

Reporters keep good *written records of what they want to remember* while they are working on a story.

If a verb is used in the past tense, you should rewrite its definition in the past tense.

While speaking before the student body, the adviser *noted* the importance of taking part in after-school clubs.
While speaking before the student body, the adviser *made particular mention of* the importance of taking part in after-school clubs.

Exercise. Read the following selection from "Making a Dirt House" by Ardath Hunt. Pay special attention to the words printed in **boldface.** Use your dictionary to write a definition for each boldface word that fits the sentence it is in.

How would you like to **live** in a house made from dirt? Half of the people in the world do. In the **dry** southwestern United States people learned that adobe, a sun-dried mixture of mud and straw, can be just about **perfect** for building houses. It is not expensive, can last hundreds of years, and keeps inside temperatures pleasant even when outside temperatures **seesaw** from hot to cold.

Why don't adobe houses crumble as the castles you build in the sand do? If you have ever made a mud ball and let it dry in the sun, you already know that dirt can be molded and then baked into a very hard, rocklike material.

Historic Adobe Houses

Prehistoric Pueblos, known as the *cliff dwellers*, **built** their great apartments of stones held together by adobe mortar. Later Pueblos and their Navajo neighbors built **complete** houses with adobe. In those days the whole family usually worked together to make the house, using the dirt **right** on the **spot.** After raking away the top layer of weeds, sticks, and so on, they dug out the top few inches of dirt and mixed it with water. The best adobe was made by mixing sand, clay, water, and straw.

Often the women and children stomped the muddy mixture with their **bare** feet to mix it thoroughly. Sometimes horses or mules were walked around and around, mixing the adobe. This mixing was hard work, but it must also have been fun to feel the mud squishing between your toes.

The adobe mixture was packed into molds or frames like shallow boxes without bottoms. After drying in the sun, these became bricks. It took about 1,000 bricks to make a one-room house.

The adobe bricks were laid flat, making walls at least sixteen inches thick. More often, two rows of adobes were laid side by side to make walls that were twice as thick. Such thickness gave walls the strength to support upper stories and a roof. It also **insulated** because the daytime heat and nighttime cold came inside only very gradually.

Definitions

a. Live means: *reside*
b. Dry means: *characterized by little rain*
c. Perfect means: *lacking nothing essential*
d. Seesaw means: *move back and forth*
e. Built means (look up build): *constructed*
f. Complete means: *whole; entire*
g. Right means: *exactly*
h. Spot means: *a particular place*
i. Bare means: *uncovered*
j. Insulated means (look up insulate): *protected against changes in temperature*

Name _____

Lesson 8
Finding Homophones

Homophones are words that sound alike but have different meanings and different spellings. For example, the words *maize* and *maze* are homophones. *Maize* means "a type of corn." *Maze* means "a network of paths through which it is hard to find one's way."

The words *pause* and *paws* are homophones. *Pause* means "a temporary stop in action or activity." *Paws* means "the feet of an animal." Probably you have heard the expression "a pause in the night." In the caption below, the author uses the homophone for *pause* in a clever way.

Paws in the night

A tiger cat pads carefully along the tops of a pile of pumpkins near Durham, Conn. — a reminder of the season.

Copyright © 1984 by Harcourt Brace Jovanovich, Inc. All rights reserved

159

Sometimes you need to look up homophones in the dictionary. For example, look at the words *stationary* and *stationery*. Do you know which means "fixed, not moving" and which means "writing paper and envelopes"? If you don't, the following sentence may give you trouble.

Steve had a *stationary* store.

By looking up the homophones in a dictionary, you can see that Steve had a store that was fixed, or not moving. He didn't have a store that sold writing paper.

Exercise 1. Read each sentence below. Then use your dictionary to find the meaning of each homophone in parentheses. Choose the one that fits the sentence. Write it in the blank at the right.

a. The gold miners located the mother (load, lode).   *lode*

b. The hiker carried a heavy (load, lode) on his back.   *load*

c. May went to the shopping (mall, maul) to buy a birthday gift.   *mall*

d. The tiger tried to (mall, maul) its trainer.   *maul*

e. Jeff bought a (mask, masque) for the Halloween party.   *mask*

f. In the seventeenth century, a popular form of entertainment was the (mask, masque).   *masque*

g. A rose is often thought of as a (cymbal, symbol) for love.   *symbol*

h. Max fell asleep during the early part of the orchestra's performance, but he awoke with a start when the (cymbals, symbols) clashed.   *cymbals*

i. Pat's grandfather was a (colonel, kernel) in the army.   *colonel*

j. He ate every (colonel, kernel) of corn on his plate.   *kernel*

Exercise 2. Try again. Read each sentence below. Then use your dictionary to find the meaning of each homophone in parentheses. Choose the one that fits the sentence. Write it in the blank at the right.

a. The rabbit dug the (carrot, karat) out of the ground.   *carrot*

b. The necklace is eighteen (carrot, karat) gold.   *karat*

c. Caroline used her (missal, missile) to follow the church mass.   *missal*

d. The submarine carried (missals, missiles) for destroying enemy ships.   *missiles*

e. When making bread, it is necessary to (knead, need) the dough.   *knead*

f. Since it was warm outside, he did not (knead, need) his sweater.   *need*

g. There is a large (naval, navel) base in San Diego.   *naval*

h. She ate a (naval, navel) orange with her lunch.   *navel*

Name _____

i. She received a (medal, meddle) for her service to her country.   _____ *medal*

j. Beverly tried not to (medal, meddle) in other people's business.   _____ *meddle*

Lesson 9
Finding Derivatives in the Dictionary

A derivative is a word formed or built from another word. For example, the word *designer* is a derivative of the word *design*. *Designer* is a noun form built by adding -er to the end of *design*. The word *designable* is a derivative of *design*. It is an adjective form built by adding -able to the end of *design*.

Often derivatives of the entry word are listed at the end of the entry. For example, notice the two derivatives of *design* listed at the end of the entry below.

> **de•sign** (dĭ-zīn′) *v.*: **designed, designing.** 1. To form and carry through a plan. *Malcolm designed the inside of the new building.* 2. To make a drawing that serves as a model for something. *The dress was designed by Christo Arletti.* 3. To intend or plan to be used for a certain purpose. *The clothes are designed for summer activities.* —*n.*: 1. A drawing or sketch that will be used as a pattern. *The store buyer bought our designs for the new sportswear line.* 2. A plan. *The producer liked our design for the stage set.* 3. A decorative work or pattern. *The dress is made from material with an interesting paisley design.* [Old French *designer*, fr. Latin *dēsignāre*, to mark out.] **de•sign′a•ble**—*adj.* **de•sign′er**—*n.*

Exercise. Read the selection below, "Jed and the Gray Jay" by Robert H. Redding. Pay special attention to the words printed in **boldface**. Then follow the directions at the end of the selection.

> Jed Smith paused. The spruce forest was dark and **quiet**. Too quiet. He shivered and walked quickly along the trail. He was supposed to meet his father at Upper Camp in half an hour.
> As the sun sank below the treetops, it threw long shadows into the northern woods. In an hour it would be dark. Jed glanced nervously over his shoulder. Nothing there. He stared into the woods around him. Nothing there either. Why did he feel so **uneasy**?
> Jed picked up his pace until he was running. Suddenly he heard a soft *coo-coo* and stopped, panting for breath. A plump

Copyright © 1984 by Harcourt Brace Jovanovich, Inc. All rights reserved   **161** gray bird, a bit bigger than a robin, fluttered to a tree limb just ahead. It cocked a **bright** eye at Jed and scolded him, as if it expected something.

It was an old friend—a gray jay, or Canada jay, as it is often called. Jed almost laughed, he was so relieved. He had made friends with many of these birds back at the house. Here in Canada the jays were very tame. They seemed to **know** that people meant *food*, and they often flew into Jed's yard to look for some.

In the fall, the gray jays ate lots of wild berries. But they loved hand-outs from people too. Jed often left scraps of bread for the jays in his yard.

When Jed's family went on hikes, the jays usually came along. No one dared to leave a sandwich unwrapped when these thieves were around. The jays would steal anything, even soap! That's how the birds got their nickname—*camp robbers*.

When the jay Jed was watching flew off down the trail, the boy was disappointed. Now he was alone in the dark forest again. But he hadn't gone more than a few yards when the camp robber appeared once more. This time there were two of them, watching every **move** he made.

Reaching into his pocket, Jed brought out half of a sugar cookie. He crumbled it and stretched out his hand. The birds flew to another tree, then broke into a **loud** cackling.

After placing some cookie crumbs on a log, Jed walked away to a place where he could watch for a minute. The jays cackled but wouldn't come get the food.

It surprised Jed that these jays were acting **shy,** since camp robbers usually were very **bold** around people with food. Around the lumber camp where Jed's father worked, the camp robbers would steal food off the men's plates or even out of a frying pan! They would also snitch bait from animal traps.

Finally the two jays Jed had been watching got up their nerve. They swooped down, snatched the food, and disappeared into the forest.

They're probably storing the cookie crumbs somewhere, Jed thought.

Now that the birds had left, Jed realized how late it was getting. It was almost dark. Watching the camp robbers had made him **forget** how creepy he had felt. He'd better get to Upper Camp in a hurry!

The gray jays came back and followed Jed, cooing and cackling as they fluttered from tree to tree. He was **glad** to have their company.

When he got to Upper Camp, his father was waiting for him.

"Where have you been?" Jed's father asked. "I was getting worried about you. . . . It's dark out there."

"Oh, I was fine," said Jed with a smile. "I just ran into a couple of friends along the way."

Name _____

Directions. Look up each word below in your dictionary. For each word, find one derivative and its part of speech. Write it in the blank provided. If you do not find a derivative at the end of the entry, check the entry words above and below the one you looked up. They may be derivatives.

Students' answers will vary. Here are some possible answers.

a. quiet _____*quietly-adv.*_____   f. loud _____*loudly-adv.*_____

b. uneasy _____*uneasiness-n.*_____   g. shy _____*shyness-n.*_____

c. bright _____*brightness-n.*_____   h. bold _____*boldness-n.*_____

d. know _____*knowledge-n.*_____   i. forget _____*forgetfulness-n.*_____

e. move _____*movement-n.*_____   j. glad _____*gladly-adv.*_____

Lesson 10

Finding the Correct Spelling of a Word

The dictionary shows the correct spelling for each entry word. However, when you do not know the spelling of a word, you need a strategy for finding it in the dictionary.

Many dictionaries include a spelling chart in their front pages. This chart shows you all the letters that spell a certain sound. For example, look at the spelling chart below.

Sound	As In	Possible Spelling
ă	add	**c**at, pl**ai**d, **c**alf, l**augh**
ā	ace	m**a**te, b**ai**t, g**ao**l, g**au**ge, p**ay**, st**ea**k, sk**ei**n, w**eigh**, pr**ey**
â(r)	care	d**a**re, f**ai**r, pr**ay**er, wh**e**re, b**ea**r, th**ei**r
ä	palm	d**a**rt, **ah**, s**e**rgeant, h**ea**rt
b	bat	**b**oy, ru**bb**er
ch	check	**ch**ip, ba**tch**, righ**te**ous, bas**ti**on, struc**tu**re
d	dog	**d**ay, la**dd**er, calle**d**
ĕ	end	m**a**ny, **ae**sthete, s**ai**d, s**ay**s, b**e**t, st**ea**dy, h**ei**fer, l**eo**pard, fr**ie**nd, **Oe**dipus
ē	even	C**ae**sar, qu**ay**, sc**e**ne, m**ea**t, s**ee**, s**ei**ze, p**eo**ple, k**ey**, rav**i**ne, gr**ie**f, ph**oe**be, cit**y**
f	fit	**f**ake, co**ff**in, cou**gh**, hal**f**, **ph**ase
g	go	**g**ate, be**gg**ar, **gh**oul, **gu**ard, va**gue**
h	hope	**h**ot, **wh**om
hw	where	**wh**ale
ĭ	it	pr**e**tty, b**ee**n, t**i**n, s**ie**ve, w**o**men, b**u**sy, g**ui**lt, l**y**nch
ī	ice	**ai**sle, **ay**e, sl**ei**ght, **ey**e, d**i**me, p**ie**, s**igh**, g**ui**le, b**uy**, tr**y**, l**ye**
j	joy	e**dge**, sol**di**er, mo**du**late, ra**ge**, exa**gge**rate, **j**am
k	cool	**c**an, a**cc**ost, sa**cch**arine, **ch**ord, ta**ck**, a**cqu**it, **k**ing, tal**k**, li**qu**or
l	look	**l**et, ga**ll**
m	move	drach**m**, phleg**m**, pal**m**, **m**ake, li**mb**, gra**mm**ar, conde**mn**
n	nice	**gn**ome, **kn**ow, **mn**emonic, **n**ote, ba**nn**er, **pn**eumatic
ng	ring	si**nk**, so**ng**, meri**ngue**
ŏ	odd	w**a**tch, p**o**t
ō	open	b**eau**, y**eo**man, s**ew**, **o**ver, s**oa**p, r**oe**, **oh**, br**oo**ch, s**ou**l, th**ough**, gr**ow**
ô	order	b**a**ll, b**a**lk, f**au**lt, d**aw**n, c**o**rd, br**oa**d, **ough**t
oi	oil	p**oi**son, t**oy**

164

Name _____

Sound	As In	Possible Spelling
ou	out	**ou**nce, b**ough**, c**ow**
o͞o	pool	**rheum**, d**rew**, m**o**ve, can**oe**, m**oo**d, gr**ou**p, thr**ough**, fl**u**ke, s**ue**, fr**ui**t
o͝o	took	w**o**lf, f**oo**t, c**ou**ld, p**u**ll
p	pit	ma**p**, ha**pp**en
r	run	**r**ose, **r**hubarb, ma**rr**y, dia**rrh**ea, **wr**iggle
s	see	**c**ite, di**ce**, **ps**yche, **s**aw, **sc**ene, **sch**ism, ma**ss**
sh	rush	o**ce**an, **ch**ivalry, vi**ci**ous, **psh**aw, **s**ure, pres**c**ience, **sch**ist, nau**se**ous, **sh**all, pen**s**ion, fi**ss**ion, ti**ss**ue, po**ti**on
t	talk	walk**ed**, though**t**, **p**tarmigan, **t**one, **Th**omas, bu**tt**er
th	thin	**th**ick
th	mother	**th**is, ba**th**e
ŭ	up	s**o**me, d**oe**s, bl**oo**d, y**ou**ng, s**u**n
yo͞o	fuse	b**eau**ty, **eu**logy, q**ueue**, p**ew**, **ewe**, a**dieu**, v**iew**, f**u**se, c**ue**, **you**th, **yu**le
û(r)	burn	y**ear**n, f**er**n, **err**, g**ir**l, w**or**m, j**our**nal, b**ur**n, G**uer**nsey, m**yr**tle
v	eve	o**f**, Ste**ph**en, **v**ise, fli**vv**er
w	win	c**h**oir, q**u**ilt, **w**ill
y	yet	on**i**on, hallelu**j**ah, **y**earn
z	zoo	wa**s**, **sc**i**ss**ors, **x**ylophone, **z**est, mu**zz**le
zh	vision	rou**ge**, plea**s**ure, inci**s**ion, sei**z**ure, gla**z**ier
ə		**a**bove, fount**ai**n, dark**e**n, clar**i**ty, parl**ia**ment, cann**o**n, porp**oi**se, vi**c**i**ou**s, loc**u**st

Imagine you *hear* the following sentence: *They had a picnic on the knoll.* Because you are not quite certain what *knoll* means, you want to look it up in your dictionary. Since the word is pronounced nōl, you look it up under the n's. You can't find it. What do you do? Check the spelling chart. This chart tells you that the sound /n/ can be spelled gn, kn, mn, n, nn, or pn. You can eliminate n since you have already tried it, and nn since no word begins with a double n. That leaves you four choices. When you try the second one, you will find the correct spelling of *knoll*, which means "a small, rounded hill."

Copyright © 1984 by Harcourt Brace Jovanovich, Inc. All rights reserved

Exercise. Study the spelling chart. Then answer the questions that follow. Write your answers in the blanks at the right.

a. The sound /ă/ can be spelled *a, ai, al,* and _____?   *au*

b. The letters *ae, ay, e, ea, ee, ei, eo, ey, i, ie, oe,* and *y* all spell the first sound you hear in what word?   *even*

c. The first sound you hear in *hope* can be spelled by *h* or _____?   *wh*

d. The letters *hm, gm, lm, m, mb, mm,* and *mn* all spell what sound?   /m/

e. The letters *n, ng,* and *ngue* all spell the final sound you hear in what word?   *ring*

f. The vowel sound you hear in *odd* can be spelled by two letters. One is *o* as in *pot.* What is the other?   *a*

g. The first vowel sound you hear in *order* can be spelled by *a, au, aw, o, oa,* and _____?   *ough*

h. The vowel sound you hear in *took* can be spelled by *o, oo, ou,* and _____?   *u*

i. The letters *th* spell the sound you hear in *thin* and in _____.   *mother*

j. The /v/ you hear in *eve* can be spelled *f, ph, v,* and _____.   *vv*

Lesson 11

Practice

While you read the following selection, pay special attention to the words printed in **boldface.** Then complete the exercise that follows.

The Two Kings
Helen Pierce Jacob

In the **dense** Burmese jungle there lived a huge white tiger. He was king of the beasts. When he went hunting, the whole jungle trembled—for he was swift and **cunning.** He preyed on deer and buffalo and other large beasts. He held all small things in **contempt.**

One fine evening he was resting after having eaten, when something tickled him. He reached up with a mighty paw and swept an ant from his nose. He held the ant carelessly between two claws and roared, "**Impudent** ant, how dare you crawl on the nose of the King of the Jungle? Prepare to die."

The ant, half-crushed by the tiger's great paw, replied, "I am small, but I am also a king, just as you are."

"A king?" **scoffed** the white tiger. "You are too small to have a brain."

"I am King of the Ants." The ant bowed as best he could.

"Prove you are a king by pleasing me with one wise statement," said the white tiger.

"Though small, ants are many; and though big, tigers are few."

"A fair start," said the white tiger. He twitched his claws a little, and the King of the Ants breathed a bit easier. "Please me with another wise statement."

"The powerful can be merciful; the small can be powerful."

"You have pleased me again," said the white tiger. He moved his paw again and held the King of the Ants by just two legs. "Say one more thing that pleases me, and you shall go free."

"Better to spare the life of another than to owe your life to another." The white tiger roared his approval. "You speak like a true king. Go. But remember that you owe your life to me."

The King of the Ants dropped to the ground, bowed, and walked away with great **dignity.**

The tiger slept well. The next day he went hunting. He had **pursued** his prey into a deep cave when an earthquake shook the land, and the roof of the cave fell in. The tiger was trapped. He roared his anger, and all the beasts of the jungle gathered around.

First the elephants tried to free the tiger king, but they were too big to enter the cave. The water buffalo tried, but their horns were too wide to enter the cave. The monkeys tried, but they were too weak to remove the tons of dirt. The smaller beasts were afraid of the tiger king and would not enter the cave to try to free him. The animals sadly shook their heads. They could do nothing to help their king. At last they went away.

The King of the Ants heard of the tiger king's **peril.** He called for all his **subjects.** The jungle turned black as the ants gathered to hear their king.

"We must free the tiger king," said the King of the Ants. He sped into the cave and took one grain of dirt, turned, raced to the entrance of the cave, and dropped his grain outside. Instantly the walls, the sides, and the floor of the cave were covered with **scurrying** ants. Grain by grain they labored till morning. Then the wall of dirt was gone, and the great white tiger came out blinking his eyes.

At the cave entrance, on top of a mountain of dirt, sat the King of the Ants. The tiger saw the mound of dirt and knew that the King of the Ants had saved his life.

"I shall never scoff at anything small again. I once gave you your life; now you have given me mine. We are equal kings."

And the two kings bowed again and went their ways.

Copyright © 1984 by Harcourt Brace Jovanovich, Inc. All rights reserved

Exercise. Look up each of the words below in your dictionary. Then copy the complete dictionary entry for each word.

a. dense
Students' answers will vary.

b. cunning
Students' answers will vary.

c. contempt
Students' answers will vary.

d. impudent
Students' answers will vary.

e. scoffed
Students' answers will vary.

f. dignity
Students' answers will vary.

g. pursued
Students' answers will vary.

h. peril
Students' answers will vary.

i. subjects
Students' answers will vary.

j. scurrying
Students' answers will vary.

Name _____

Chapter 7
Context

The context of a word is the group of words or sentences surrounding the word. In this chapter you will learn several strategies for using context clues to find the meaning of words you do not know. In addition, you will learn to choose the meaning of a word that fits the context.

Lesson 1
Understanding Context

The context of a word is the group of words or sentences surrounding the word. Often the context contains clues that help you figure out the meaning of an unfamiliar word. For example, look at the sentence below.

> The scientist checked the results of the experiment *assiduously*, or with extreme care.

You may not know the meaning of the word *assiduously*. The context, that is, the words surrounding *assiduously*, should help you figure out that *assiduously* means "with extreme care."

Now look at the following paragraph.

> The scientist prepared a table to show the results of the four experiments. She put the results of Experiment A in the first column, of Experiment B in the second column, of Experiment C in the third column, and of Experiment D in the fourth column. When she finished *tabulating* the results, she showed them to the head of her department.

You may not know the meaning of the word *tabulating*. Look at the context, the rest of the sentences in this paragraph. The scientist prepares a *table*. She arranges *results* in *columns*. The context should help you see that *tabulating* means "arranging facts or results in the form of a table."

Copyright © 1984 by Harcourt Brace Jovanovich, Inc. All rights reserved   **169**

Exercise. Read the selection below from "The Earth Moves" by Dennice DiGirolamo. Use the context to help you figure out the meaning of each **boldface** word. Write these definitions in the blanks following the selection. Then check your definitions against a dictionary.

Before Christopher Columbus sailed to America, many believed our earth to be flat, but it is not. It is a **sphere** like a baseball. People also once believed that the earth was perfectly solid, but it isn't. Earth scientists known as *geologists* and earthquake scientists known as *seismologists* are studying our earth very carefully to find out how it was made. They look for the causes and reasons for occurrences of earthquakes and volcanoes. Here are some of the known facts about our planet Earth.

It is made of three layers—the **core,** the **mantle,** and the **crust.** Deep, deep inside, at the very center of the earth, is the **core,** which has two zones. The first is a hard, round mass of metals such as iron and nickel. This is surrounded by a second zone also made of metals that are so hot they have melted into liquid, just as ice melts into water when it is warmed.

The **mantle,** which surrounds the core, forms the second earth layer. The mantle is mostly rock. Geologists once believed that the rock in the mantle was liquid. Now many believe that most of the rock is solid, but that it often gets so hot that the rocks actually melt. Melted rock is called *magma.*

The third and final earth layer is the **crust.** It surrounds and contains the mantle just as the crust of a pie holds its filling. The earth's crust is very thick in some places, very thin in others. Where the crust is thick we have continents—the land we live on. Where the crust is thin, there are deep basins filled with the oceans' waters.

Fruit juices bubble up through the crust while a pie is cooking. The earth's crust, just like the piecrust, has holes and cracks (volcanoes and faults) in it. Volcanoes are openings that reach through the earth's surface to the mantle below. Through them, melted rock (magma) reaches the earth's surface. These eruptions of magma are called *lava.* Lava flows can be seen near active volcanoes such as Mount Lassen in California or Mt. St. Helens in Washington.

There are also long cracks in the earth's surface. These cracks or faults are so long that they actually divide the surface into many separate pieces. These pieces of crust are called *tectonic plates.* We wouldn't even know about them except for one thing: Tectonic plates move. Because they move they rub and bump against one another. You might say that they get in one another's way. A terrible tension builds up among them, just as tension and anger build between two people who are getting ready to fight.

Sooner or later this tension or energy must be released. When it is, it is in the form of **seismic** waves and vibrations that travel through the earth. *Seismic* comes from a Greek word *seismos,* which means earthquake or earthshaking. If we could see these seismic waves, they would look just like the ripples that move slowly through the water after you throw a rock into a pond.

Definitions

a. sphere: *a ball; a three-dimensional shape having all its points the same distance from the center*

b. geologists: *scientists who study the earth*

c. seismologists: *scientists who study earthquakes*

d. core: *innermost part*

e. mantle: *second earth layer*

f. crust: *third earth layer*

g. magma: *melted rock*

h. lava: *eruptions of magma*

i. tectonic plates: *separate pieces of earth's crust*

j. seismic: *having to do with earthquakes*

Lesson 2

Finding the Meaning That Fits the Context

The English language contains many words that have more than one meaning. When you read, you must choose the meaning that fits the context. For example, the word *lesson* has several meanings. It can mean (1) an exercise or assignment; (2) instruction given during a class period; (3) something one must learn for the sake of one's safety, well-being, happiness, etc.; (4) a reading from the Bible. Now look at the following sentence.

Penny learned a new song during her guitar *lesson*.

Only the second meaning of *lesson* fits this sentence.

Copyright © 1984 by Harcourt Brace Jovanovich, Inc. All rights reserved

171

Now look at the comic strip below.

GARFIELD by Jim Davis

> WELL, GARFIELD, THAT'S THE LAST TIME THE HAMILTONS EVER ASK US OVER

> I HOPE YOU LEARNED A LESSON FROM THIS EVENING
>
> I SURE DID

> NEVER SHARPEN YOUR CLAWS ON A WATER BED

Jon hopes Garfield has "learned a lesson." Only the third meaning of *lesson* fits this context.

Exercise. Read the selection below, "What the Outdoors Means to Me" by Ron Guidry. Pay special attention to the words printed in **boldface.** Then, for each boldface word, choose the meaning that fits the context. Put an X next to this definition.

    My friends think I'm crazy when I tell them that sitting alone in a duck **blind,** watching the sun rise, can be as enjoyable as pitching in the World Series.

    When I talk about my love of the outdoors with friends, or with sportswriters, they'll often say, "You mean you'd rather shiver in a cold duck **blind** all by yourself than pitch in a World Series with all the **color** and excitement and millions of people watching?" That's when I try to explain that the enjoyment I get from hunting is not "better" than the enjoyment I get from baseball. It's "different," and I wouldn't trade one for the other.

    The rewards of the outdoors are **personal** and, therefore, not always easy to explain.

    If I strike out the final batter to win an important **game** and 50,000 fans give me a standing ovation, that makes me feel good. I know I've helped my team, and I know the fans appreciate my effort. I know that I've done my job. But when I'm alone in a duck blind, creatures of nature—not man—are my sole audience. The only noise I may hear is the rustling of reeds in the early morning breeze or the fluttering wings of a fast-flying mallard. There's no applause from 50,000 people. There are no teammates patting me on the back. There are no headlines. Only the personal satisfaction that I receive from being one-on-one with nature. For me, that's worth just as much.

    If I pass up shots at ducks or other game because I think they are out of **range** and I don't want to risk crippling them, I know that no one else will ever know about it. No sportswriters will write about what an ethical hunter I am. But, personally, I

172   Copyright © 1984 by Harcourt Brace Jovanovich, Inc. All rights reserved

know that I did the **right** thing. Even if I go home empty-handed from a hunt, I'll still go home happy because I know I've played the game according to the rules—even though there was no umpire standing near me calling "fair" or "**foul**."

The **time** that I spend in the outdoors during the off-season not only helps me to relax and to recharge my batteries for the next season, it also helps to remind me who Ron Guidry really is. All of the media attention that comes from playing for the N.Y. Yankees can sometimes make a guy feel more important than he really is. But I noticed that the ducks didn't fly any slower for me when I became a Yankee, and they didn't crowd around my blind when I won the Cy Young Award. A day or two in the outdoors sort of puts things in **perspective.** I'm no different from anyone else.

Twenty years from now when the Yankee Stadium scoreboard asks, "Can you name the Yankee pitcher who won the Cy Young Award in 1978 with a record of 25-3, while setting a Yankee record of 248 strike-outs?" many boys and girls will never have heard of Ron Guidry.

But my hunting buddies will still be my hunting buddies, and sunrise in my favorite duck blind will still be as enjoyable as pitching in the World Series.

Hunting and the outdoors have provided me with many enjoyable experiences since my father and grandfather introduced me to the outdoors nearly 20 years ago. The outdoors remains an important part of my life, and I look forward to visiting my favorite hunting **spots** with my favorite hunting friends for many years to come.

That's what the outdoors means to me.

Definitions

a. In this selection *blind* means:

_____ without the sense or use of sight

__X__ a shelter for concealing hunters

b. In this selection *color* means:

__X__ vividness; liveliness

_____ hue, such as red, blue, yellow

c. In this selection *personal* means:

__X__ private

_____ done in person

d. In this selection *game* means:

_____ a way of amusing oneself; a pastime

__X__ a single instance of a sports activity

e. In this selection *range* means:

   __X__ the furthest distance one can shoot

   _____ a series of mountains

f. In this selection *right* means:

   __X__ correct; appropriate

   _____ the opposite of left

g. In this selection *foul* means:

   _____ very wicked

   __X__ not fair; landing outside the foul lines

h. In this selection *time* means:

   __X__ the period spent doing something

   _____ the rate of speed

i. In this selection *perspective* means:

   _____ distant view

   __X__ point of view that helps one judge the true relation of one thing to another

j. In this selection *spots* means:

   __X__ particular places

   _____ stains or blots

Lesson 3
Understanding Direct Context Clues

Definitions are direct context clues. They tell you directly what a word means. Writers sometimes give definitions of words they think their readers may not know. These definitions may be signaled by words or by punctuation marks. Words that sometimes signal definitions include *means, called, are, is, were, was*. For example, read the sentences below.

> A *flamingo* is a large tropical bird with bright pink or red feathers.
> *Dodos*, which are now extinct, were large birds with hooked bills and short necks and legs.

Punctuation marks that signal definitions include commas, dashes, and parentheses. For example, read the sentences below.

> They tried to *pacify*, or quiet, the baby.
> They became *frantic*—wild with worry—when they found the dog was missing.
> Their house was destroyed by the deluge (heavy rainfall).

Name _____

In the comic strip below, Hagar gives a definition of an island. Why does his friend ask if an island has eyes?

HAGAR THE HORRIBLE by Dik Browne

Exercise. Read "How to Drill an Oil Well" by Bob Winston. Pay special attention to the words printed in **boldface.** Then use direct context clues to find the meaning of these words. Write their meanings on the blanks provided at the end of the selection.

Suppose you had to dig a hole a mile deep. How would you do it? Just think how far a mile is! To walk a mile you would go from one end of a football field to the other 17 times.

Most of our oil is at least that deep in the ground. In fact, a lot of it is more than two or three miles down. The very deepest well in the United States is 31,441 feet, almost six miles. It was drilled in western Oklahoma in 1974.

Where Do You Dig?

You might ask, "How do we know where to drill an oil well and how deep it will have to be?" That is a very good question. We can't tell for sure, but by bouncing a sort of echo off the rock layers far below the earth's surface **geologists** (persons who study soils and rock formations) can detect changes in the earth's structure where oil might be trapped. "Might be" is just as uncertain as it sounds. Oil or gas is found in only about one in every nine exploratory wells.

When the spot has been selected, a crew moves in with a bulldozer and levels a place for the drilling platform. Then they make a big pit to hold the special mud that will be an important part of the drilling.

Next the big tower, or **derrick,** is set up. It may be from 60 to over 200 feet high, depending on how deep the well is to be and what lengths of pipe will be used.

Along with the derrick comes all the other heavy equipment that will be needed: big diesel engines to drive the mud pumps and turn or raise the drill pipe, cables and pulleys, pipe racks, and special tools.

At one side of the drilling platform there is a little cabin where the superintendent watches the instruments and charts that tell how fast the drill is moving, how deep it is, and what kind of rock formation it is passing through. The **roughnecks**—the rest of the crew—are stationed around the rig to see that everything is running properly.

Before **spudding in**—starting to drill—the crew may drill a mousehole 50 feet or so deep at one side of the well. What do you suppose it is for? We shall see in a moment.

Now, we are ready to start the drilling. Here's how it is done. The **drill bit,** or pointed tip, which is attached to one end of a section of drill pipe, has three wheel-like pieces at the bottom, each with several rows of sharp spikes, set at angles to each other. As the whole thing is turned, these spiked wheels **rotate**—spin—against each other, chopping out little pieces of rock as the drill goes slowly into the ground.

The top of the drill pipe is attached to a section of heavy square pipe, called the **kelly,** which passes through a square hole in the turntable on the drilling platform. The **turntable** is the rotating disk. This arrangement serves to turn the drill, while letting it slide through the square hole as it goes deeper into the ground.

But what happens when the square section is as far down as it can go? That is when the roughnecks go into action, for it is time to add another section of the round drill pipe. For this, the whole drill assembly must be pulled up until the bottom end of the square section can be unhooked from the top of the drill pipe. Next the square piece is attached to the top end of the new section, which is sitting upright in—you guessed it—the mousehole. The square piece with the new section attached is then raised some more, until the bottom end of the new section can be screwed into the top of the drill pipe sticking out of the well.

Section By Section

With the new section now in place, the whole thing is lowered until the drill bit reaches the bottom. Drilling can continue for the length of the new section, which may be 30 to 90 feet. Then the whole process must be repeated.

When the bit gets dull, all the pipe must be taken out and stacked, then put back together with a new bit. "Making a round trip," as it is called, takes six hours or more for a hole a mile or two deep. In this operation, the kelly is stored in another hole off to one side—called the "rat hole" and the pipe is stacked vertically.

Sound a bit complicated? It's not, really. It is one of those things that are easier to do than to tell about. But it is very hard and dangerous work! The sections of pipe weigh 500 pounds or more, and the huge machines move them around as we would handle soda straws.

Special Mud?

So that is how the long trip into the ground proceeds—a section of pipe at a time. But what about the special mud? It is pumped down inside the drill pipe and comes out through holes in the bit, where it cools and **lubricates,** which means "makes slippery," the cutting edges. Then, because it is pumped in with high pressure, it flows back up, outside the drill pipe, and out the top. One of the reasons a special mud is used is that it must be more dense than the rock cuttings so it will carry them out.

The other purpose for the mud is to keep the oil and gas sealed in when the drill reaches them. You may have heard of gushers that blew oil hundreds of feet high, tearing up derricks and other equipment. A **gusher** is an oil well with a heavy natural flow. They were exciting, but dangerous and very wasteful. Modern rotary drilling with mud has just about eliminated the gushers. The pressure is contained by the mud until pipes can be cemented in place and capped with the "Christmas tree" of valves to control the flow. Then the heavy mud is carefully pumped out, and the final steps to put the well into production are started.

All this work of drilling an oil well is going on in many places. In the United States, about 2,700 drilling rigs are working, most of them day and night.

Directions. Define each of the words below.

a. geologists: *persons who study soils and rock formations*
b. derrick: *the big tower*
c. roughnecks: *the rest of the crew*
d. spudding in: *starting to drill*
e. drill bit: *drill's pointed tip*
f. rotate: *spin*
g. kelly: *section of heavy square pipe*
h. turntable: *rotating disk*
i. lubricates: *makes slippery*
j. gusher: *oil well with a heavy natural flow*

Lesson 4
Understanding Indirect Context Clues

The context often contains indirect clues that help you make an intelligent guess about the meaning of an unfamiliar word. These clues do not tell you exactly what the unfamiliar word means. However, by studying these clues carefully and using your common sense, you should be able to figure out the meaning of the unfamiliar word. For example, read the sentence below.

> After the Eskimos loaded the *umiak* with supplies, they climbed into this boat and paddled it down the river.

You probably do not know the meaning of the word *umiak*. However, look at the context clues—Eskimos, boat, paddled down the river. These clues should help you figure out that an *umiak* is an Eskimo boat propelled by paddling.

Now look at the next sentences.

> After the sheriff rounded up the outlaws, he seized their guns. The outlaws felt helpless now that their weapons had been *confiscated*.

You probably do not know the meaning of the word *confiscated*. However, the context should help you figure out that *confiscated* means "seized by authority."

When you read, look for indirect context clues to help you figure out the meaning of an unfamiliar word. Be sure, though, to check your guesses against a dictionary.

Exercise. Read the selection below from "How to Survive a Fire" by James Lincoln Collier. Pay special attention to the **boldface** words. Then use indirect context clues to find the meaning of each boldface word.

> If you or your family are ever caught in a fire, knowing what to do may be a matter of life and death. The problem is that in a fire you are suddenly plunged into a strange, confused world. When we think of fire, we think of flames, but in fact what we experience mostly is smoke, billowing everywhere, blinding us, making us gasp for air. Smoke, not flame, is what kills most victims of fire: It is **lethal** to breathe it. Moreover, even in broad daylight, the smoke usually reduces **visibility** to nothing, so that a flashlight may penetrate only six inches into it.
>
> Says fireman Smith, "When the smoke fills up, everything seems to be in the wrong spot. The smoke **distorts** your thinking. You get worried about breathing and you can't think straight."
>
> The first rule, then, is to stay away from smoke. If you can get out of the building, do so after warning the other inhabitants. Peter Bondy, a big-city fireman who has been cited for bravery three years in a row, says, "Don't wait to call the fire

department. Warn the other inhabitants and leave. Run to a neighbor's and call the fire department from there. And don't try to fight the fire yourself. In doing so you may be breathing carbon monoxide which could cause you to go unconscious right there."

Once you get out, stay out. Too many people suddenly remember **valuables,** especially pets, and go back after them. Peter Bondy witnessed one such incident. "We had a woman who'd gotten out. Then she remembered her cat, and ran back into the building. We were lucky to save her, but she got badly hurt. The thing is, in a fire a pet'll panic just like a human being. A dog will try to hide, or maybe scratch or bite when you try to pick it up. So don't go back. It isn't worth risking your life for a pet."

However, in many cases it is impossible to get out of a building, especially an apartment building when the fire is on a lower floor and the halls are filled with heat, flames, and the smoke. Says Ray Smith, "In a modern, fireproof building, if the fire isn't in your apartment, especially if it's on another floor, you want to avoid going out into smoky halls. Also, avoid running upstairs. A stairwell can act like a flue, and suck the smoke and heat right up after you."

Peter Bondy says, "We once had a fire in a third floor hallway. There were a couple of kids in an apartment on that floor. They went out into the hall to go up to the roof and the smoke and heat followed them right on up and caught them at the top. If they'd stayed in the apartment, they'd have been okay. That terrible hotel fire out in Las Vegas a couple of years ago—the people were running out into the hallways and the smoke got them."

Ray Smith continues, "There are really three things to do. One is to keep the doors closed and seal off the smoke as best you can with towels or whatever. The second is to open a window, crouch and breathe outside air. The third thing is to remain **visible** so people outside can see you. Above all, don't jump. Even a one-story drop of ten or fifteen feet can badly hurt you. We'll get to you within three to five minutes, and we'll get you out of there."

Directions. Define each of the words below. Check your answers against a dictionary.

a. lethal: *deadly*
b. visibility: *ability to see*
c. distorts: *alters*
d. valuables: *important possessions*
e. visible: *able to be seen*

Exercise 2. Write a sentence using each of the words below.

a. lethal: *Students' sentences will vary.*

b. visibility: *Students' sentences will vary.*

c. distorts: *Students' sentences will vary.*

d. valuables: *Students' sentences will vary.*

e. visible: *Students' sentences will vary.*

Lesson 5
Understanding Words Used As Nouns and Verbs

A noun is a word that names a person, a place, a thing, or an idea. For example, the words *sister, town, necklace,* and *friendship* are nouns. **A verb is a word that expresses action or a state of being.** For example, the words *create* and *were* are verbs. Some words can be used as either nouns or verbs. Look at the following sentences.

He did not want to *alarm* his neighbors.
He was frightened when the smoke *alarm* went off.

In the first sentence *alarm* is a verb that means "frighten." In the second sentence *alarm* is a noun that means "a device that warns of danger." The meaning of a word in a sentence depends on whether it is used as a noun or as a verb.

Exercise 1. Read the selection below from "Eland: Africa's Biggest Antelope" by George W. Frame. Pay special attention to the words printed in **boldface**. Then follow the directions at the end of the selection.

Tick birds sitting on the eland's back squawked in **alarm.** Then, as they flew away, the eland stopped eating and nervously looked around. Where was the danger? Was a lion nearby?
Slowly, I drove closer. One wheel went into a hole hidden by the long grass, and my car bounced with a **thump.** The big bull eland looked toward me, but he seemed not to **care.** He had

seen the cars of tourists every day for years, and my car didn't look much different. He knew cars would not **hurt** him.

When I got closer, I stopped the engine and sat quietly, watching the big bull. His short fur was grayish brown. And his dewlap, a long loose **fold** of skin, hung far below his neck. He looked big and strong, but not clumsy. The eland is the largest of all African antelopes, and this one probably weighed about three-quarters of a ton. I think that he must have stood six feet tall at the shoulder.

Directions. Find each word below in the selection you have just read. First tell whether the word is used as a noun or as a verb. Then write a definition of the word that fits the context.

a. alarm: *noun—sudden fear*
b. thump: *noun—a muffled sound*
c. care: *verb—mind, be bothered by*
d. hurt: *verb—harm*
e. fold: *noun—a layer of skin formed by creasing the skin*

Exercise 2. Follow the directions below.

a. Write a sentence using *alarm* as a verb.
   Students' answers will vary.

b. Write a sentence using *thump* as a verb.
   Students' answers will vary.

c. Write a sentence using *care* as a noun.
   Students' answers will vary.

d. Write a sentence using *hurt* as a noun.
   Students' answers will vary.

e. Write a sentence using *fold* as a verb.
   Students' answers will vary.

Exercise 3. Read another paragraph from "Eland: Africa's Biggest Antelope" by George W. Frame. Pay special attention to the words printed in **boldface.** Then follow the directions at the end of the selection.

> One problem with eland ranching is that elands, like all antelopes, are very good jumpers. From a standing **start,** elands can easily **jump** over a fence five feet tall. When running, they can jump over each other, and over **objects** as much as eight feet tall. If these huge antelopes are left untended on a **ranch,** the **fences** must be tall to keep the elands from jumping over them.

Directions. Find each word below in the paragraph you have just read. First tell whether the word is used as a noun or as a verb. Then write a definition of the word that fits the context.

a. start: *noun—position*

b. jump: *verb—spring; leap*

c. objects: *noun—items*

d. ranch: *noun—a large farm*

e. fences: *noun—structures that serve as barriers*

Exercise 4. Follow the directions below.

a. Write a sentence using *start* as a verb.
   Students' sentences will vary.

b. Write a sentence using *jump* as a noun.
   Students' sentences will vary.

c. Write a sentence using *objects* as a verb.
   Students' sentences will vary.

d. Write a sentence using *ranch* as a verb.
   Students' sentences will vary.

e. Write a sentence using *fences* as a verb.
   Students' sentences will vary.

Name _____

Lesson 6
Using Context to Choose the Correct Synonym

A synonym is a word that means the same or almost the same as another word. For example, a synonym for *evil* is *wicked*. A synonym for *sparkling* is *flashing*.

Many words have more than one meaning. A synonym for one meaning of a word will not be a synonym for another meaning of a word. For example, the word *right* has several meanings. One meaning is "in keeping with certain standards of behavior." A synonym for *right* when it is used with this meaning is "correct" or "proper." For example:

> He did the *right* thing when he gave his winnings to charity.
> He did the *correct* thing when he gave his winnings to charity.

A second meaning of *right* is "something that puts one at an advantage." A synonym for *right* when it is used with this meaning is "favorable" or "advantageous." For example:

> She got the job because she was in the *right* spot at the *right* time.
> She got the job because she was in an *advantageous* spot at an *advantageous* time.

Notice that *correct* is not a synonym for *right* when it is used with this second meaning. *Correct* would not fit the sentence above.

A third meaning for *right* is "suitable for a certain purpose." A synonym for *right* when it is used with this meaning is "fitting" or "perfect." For example:

> Maria is just *right* for this role.
> Maria is just *perfect* for this role.

When you read, it is important to choose a synonym that fits the context.

Exercise. Read the following selection from "Leave Room for the Grizzly" by George Laycock. Pay special attention to the **boldface** words. Then follow the directions at the end of the selection.

> The first **wild** grizzly bear I ever saw surprised both of us. I was waiting quietly with my luggage and fishing tackle on the edge of a **remote** grass landing strip in northern Canada for a friend to arrive in his single-engine plane. I was alone. At least, I **thought** I was alone.
> Then the bushes at the end of the runway moved, and I knew that a large animal was poking around. The wind was

Copyright © 1984 by Harcourt Brace Jovanovich, Inc. All rights reserved

blowing from my direction toward the hidden animal and I remember thinking, "He'll smell me!"

As I sat motionless, waiting, there arose from the bushes about 75 yards away, perhaps the most beautiful—and frightening—creature I had ever seen . . . a grizzly. The huge bear was immediately recognizable. It was covered with heavy light brown fur and I could see the bear's famous hump above its **powerful** shoulders.

He seemed unable to locate where the foreign odor was coming from. While he sniffed the wind he remained **quiet.** So did I.

What would I do if he came toward me? There was no tree close enough to save me and there was nobody around to help. Suddenly the question was answered for me. The bear and I had similar thoughts; we both wanted to avoid **trouble.** He dropped silently to all four feet and vanished into the heavy brush. The encounter had lasted perhaps a minute, but that moment is etched in my memory more vividly that anything else that happened on the trip.

Directions. Locate each word below in the selection. Then choose the synonym that fits the context. You may use your dictionary to help you. Circle the correct answer.

a. wild

　((1) undomesticated)　　　　(2) reckless

b. remote

　((1) out-of-the-way)　　　　(2) uninterested

c. powerful

　((1) mighty)　　　　(2) effective

d. quiet

　(1) tranquil　　　　((2) still)

e. trouble

　((1) conflict)　　　　(2) malfunction

Name _____

Lesson 7

Understanding Dialect

Dialect is a regional variety of language. It is recognized by differences in pronunciation, grammar, and vocabulary. When authors write about people from a specific region, they often have these people speak in dialect. For example, read the sentence below.

Nothin's goin right today.

Many people drop the g from words ending in *ing*. Of course, this sentence means:

Nothing's going right today.

Now read the next sentence.

I usta work at the bakery.

Of course, this sentence simply means:

I used to work at the bakery.

If you have trouble reading dialect, look carefully at the context. It often can help you figure out the meaning of the words.

Exercise. In the story below, "The Lucky Stone" by Lucille Clifton, the characters speak in dialect. Read the story carefully. Then follow the directions at the end of it.

When I was a girl we lived all together in a house with a big wrap-around porch: me, my Mama and Daddy, and my Great-grandmother, Mrs. Elzie F. Pickens. The F stood for Free. She was about seventy-some years old, my Great-grand. We used to sit out on that porch in good weather, and she would tell me stories about when she was a girl and the different things that used to happen.

Oh, I loved it so, I loved her so! Tee, she would call me. Sweet Baby Tee. Some of my favorite stories were her favorites, too. Oh, how we both loved telling and hearing about the Lucky Stone!

Great-grand was rocking slowly on the porch one afternoon when I brought her a big bunch of dogwood blooms, and that was the beginning of this story:

Ahhh, now that dogwood reminds me of the day I met your Great-granddaddy, Mr. Pickens.

It was just this time, spring of the year, and me and my best friend Ovella Wilson was goin to join the Silas Greene. Usta be a kinda show went all through the South, called it the Silas

Copyright © 1984 by Harcourt Brace Jovanovich, Inc. All rights reserved

185

Greene Show. Somethin like the circus. Me and Ovella wanted to join that thing and see the world. Nothin wrong at home or nothin, we just wanted to travel and see new things and have high times. Didn't say nothin to nobody but one another. Just up and decided to do it.

Well, this day we plaited our hair and put a dress and some things in a crokasack and started out to the show. Spring day like this.

We got there after a good little walk, and it was the world—such music and wonders as we never had seen! They had everything there, or seemed like it.

Me and Ovella thought we'd walk around for a while and see the show before goin to the office to sign up and join.

While we was viewin it all we come up on this dancin dog. Cutest one thing in the world next to you, Sweet Tee—dippin and movin and head bowin to that music. Had a little ruffly skirt on itself and up on two back legs twistin and movin to the music. Dancin . . . dancin . . . dancin till people started throwin pennies out of they pockets.

Me and Ovella was caught up too and laughin so. She took a penny out of her pocket and threw it to the ground where that dog was dancin, and I took two pennies and threw 'em both.

The music was faster and faster, and that dog was turnin and turnin. Ovella reached in her sack and threw out a little pin she had won from never being late at Sunday school. And me, laughin and all excited, reached in my bag and threw out my lucky stone!

Sweet Tee, you know how lucky that stone is—how it saved old Miss Mandy from bein starved, and how it saved her daughter Vashti from bein struck down by lightning. Now, it was mine, and I didn't want to lose that stone, no way possible.

Soon as it left my hand it seemed like I reached back out for it to take it back. But the stone was gone from my hand, and Lord, it hit that dancin dog right on his nose!

Well, he lit out after me, poor thing. He lit out after me, and I flew! Round and round the Silas Greene we run, through every place me and Ovella had walked before, but now that dancin dog was a runnin dog, and all the people was laughin at the new show, which was us.

I felt myself slowin down after a while, and I thought I would turn around a little bit to see how much gain that cute little dog was makin on me. When I did I got such a surprise! Right behind me was the dancin dog, and right behind him was the finest fast runnin hero in the bottoms of Virginia.

And that was Mr. Pickens when he was still a boy! He had a length of twine in his hand and he was twirlin it around in the air just like the cowboy at the Silas Greene and grinnin fit to bust.

While I was watchin how the sun shined on him and made him look like an angel come to help a poor sinner girl, why, he twirled that twine one extra fancy twirl and looped it right around one hind leg of that dancin dog and brought him low.

I stopped then and walked slow and shy to where he had picked up that poor dog to see if he was hurt, cradlin him and talkin to him soft and sweet. That showed me how kind and gentle he was, and when we walked back to the dancin dog's place in the show he let the dog loose and helped me to find my stone. I told him how shiny black it was and how it had the letter A scratched on one side—A for Amanda. We searched and searched, and at last he spied it.

Ovella and me lost heart for shows then, and we walked on home. And a good little way, the one who was gonna be your Great-granddaddy was walkin on behind. Seein us safe. Us walkin kind of slow. Him seein us safe.

Great-grand's voice trailed off softly, and I noticed she had a little smile on her face. "Grandmama, that stone almost got you bit by a dog that time. It wasn't so lucky, was it?"

Great-grand shook her head and laughed out loud. "That was the luckiest time of all, Tee Baby. It got me acquainted with Mr. Amos Pickens, and if that ain't luck, what could it be! Yes, it was luckier for me than for anybody, I think. Least mostly I think it."

I laughed with her though I didn't exactly know why. "I hope I have that kind of good stone luck one day," I said.

"Maybe you will someday," Great-grand said.

And we rocked a little longer and smiled together.

Directions. Some people have trouble reading stories that contain dialect. If you have trouble, one strategy that will help you is to rewrite each sentence containing dialect in standard English. Try this strategy now. Rewrite each sentence below in standard English.

a. "It was just this time, spring of the year, and me and my best friend Ovella Wilson was goin to join the Silas Greene."
It was just this time, spring of the year, and my best friend Ovella Wilson and I were going to join the Silas Greene.

b. "Usta be a kinda show went all through the South, called it the Silas Greene Show."
It used to be a kind of show that went all through the South. They called it the Silas Greene Show.

c. "Nothin wrong at home or nothin, we just wanted to travel and see new things and have high times."
Nothing was wrong at home. We just wanted to travel and see new things and have high times.

d. "She took a penny out of her pocket and threw it to the ground where that dog was dancin, and I took two pennies and threw 'em both."
She took a penny out of her pocket and threw it to the ground where that dog was dancing, and I took two pennies and threw them both.

e. "And a good little way, the one who was gonna be your Great-granddaddy was walkin on behind."
And a good little way, the one who was going to be your Great-granddaddy was walking on behind.

Lesson 8

Using Context to Understand Jargon

Jargon is the language—special words and phrases—used by a particular group of people to talk about their particular job, sport, or hobby. It is a colorful way of expressing ideas that involve that group on a regular basis. However, jargon can give you trouble if you are not part of that particular group.

BEETLE BAILEY by Mort Walker

188

Name _____

Sometimes context can help you figure out the meaning of jargon. For example, read the sentence below.

> The computer cards that were used to record and store data for electronic transfer have pretty much been replaced by **floppy discs,** which look like flimsy 45 records and are easily transported.

Although you may not have known what a floppy disc is, the sentence gives you enough clues to figure out the meaning: "A record-shaped item on which electronic information is recorded and stored for use in computers."

Exercise. Use context to define each of the **boldface** words and phrases below.

a. Greta applied her **pancake** skillfully and quickly. Then she studied her face carefully in the mirror of her dressing room to be sure all of the skin outside her costume was evenly made up.
stage make-up

b. The director called, "Greta, curtain time in five minutes! Remember, that audience out there wants to love you. **Break a leg!**"
good luck; do a good job

c. She drew herself up and took a deep breath. She was a professional, but she was still nervous. Last night's **dress rehearsal** had not gone well; the real opening, tonight, was more important.
final uninterrupted run-through, with costumes and props

d. As she left her dressing room, she saw stage hands feverishly rushing to and fro, getting together the **props** needed for each act. An old wooden table, two chairs, and an umbrella stand had already been placed on the stage for the opening scene.
things or property used on stage in a play to help set the scene

e. Marlow, the male lead, was pacing nervously. Greta thought him too vain and conceited. She hoped he would not try to **upstage** her in the scenes where the audience was supposed to be intent on her lines.
distract audience attention from, as by standing in front of

f. The crew brought down the **backdrop,** which showed the back wall of a poor Russian hut. The illusion was complete—the stage was set for 1880 Russia.
painted curtain hung at the back of a stage set

Copyright © 1984 by Harcourt Brace Jovanovich, Inc. All rights reserved

189

g. The curtain went up. Greta counted to ten, took a deep breath, then made her entrance, and crossed to **stage right.** She peered out before her, somewhere above the heads of people sitting on the left side of the auditorium.
the right side of the stage as you face the audience

h. Marlow entered, and they began the dialogue. "**Cheek out,** Marlow!" Greta thought crossly, willing him to turn more toward the audience as he spoke to her, so his words would not be lost.
act of turning half to face audience, half to face actor to whom one is speaking

i. The play went all too quickly. The curtain fell for the final act, and all the actors breathed a sigh of relief and gladness. It had gone well. They took **curtain call** after curtain call before the cheering audience.
appearance of performers after the performance in response to audience applause

j. On her way to the final cast party, Greta paused on the set. Stage crew were already beginning to **strike** the set. The pounding of their hammers and the noises of heavy props scraping across the floor as they were hauled out gave her a sense of finality. "Goodbye," she thought fondly. "It was magic. But now it's time for a new production."
to break up and clear away parts of a set when a play is finished

Lesson 9

Practice

Pay special attention to context clues as you read the selection below. Then complete the exercise that follows.

from *Lame Deer: Seeker of Visions*
John (Fire) Lame Deer and Richard Erdoes

It was said that I didn't take after my grandpa Good Fox, whom I loved, but after my other grandfather, Crazy Heart, whom I never knew. They said I picked up where he left off, because I was so daring and full of the devil. I was told that Crazy Heart had been like that. He did not care what happened to other people, or to himself, once he was on his way. He was hot-tempered, always **feuding** and on the warpath. At the same time he saved lots of people, gave wise counsel, urged the people to do right. He was a good speech-maker. Everybody who listened to him said that he was a very encouraging man. He always advised patience, except when it came to himself. Then his temper got in the way.

I was like that. Things I was told not to do—I did them. I liked to play rough. We played **shinny ball,** a kind of hockey game. We made the ball and sticks ourselves. We played the hoop game, shot with a bow and arrow. We had foot races, horse races and water races. We liked to play *mato kiciyapi,* the bear game, throwing sharp, stiff grass stems at each other. These could really hurt you and draw blood if they hit the bare skin. And we were always at the *isto kicicastakapi,* the pit-slinging game. You chewed the fruit from the rosebush or wild cherries, spit a fistful of pits into your hand and flung them into the other fellow's face. And of course I liked the Grab-Them-by-the-Hair-and-Kick-Them game, which we played with two teams.

I liked to ride horseback behind my older sister, holding onto her. As I got a little bigger she would hold onto me. By the time I was nine years old I had my own horse to ride. It was a beautiful gray pony my father had given me together with a fine saddle and a very colorful Mexican saddle blanket. That gray was my favorite companion and I was proud to ride him. But he was not mine for long. I lost him through my own fault.

Nonge Pahloka—the Piercing of Her Ears—is a big event in a little girl's life. By this **ceremony** her parents, and especially her grandmother, want to show how much they love and honor her. They ask a man who is respected for his bravery or wisdom to pierce the ears of their daughter. The grandmother puts on a big feed. The little girl is placed on a blanket surrounded by the many gifts her family will give away in her name. The man who does the piercing is much admired and gets the most valuable gift. Afterward they get down to the really important part—the eating.

Well, one day I watched somebody pierce a girl's ears. I saw the fuss they made over it, the presents he got and all that. I thought I should do this to my little sister. She was about four years old at the time and I was nine. I don't know anymore what made me want to do this. Maybe I wanted to feel big and important like the man whom I had watched perform the ceremony. Maybe I wanted to get a big present. Maybe I wanted to make my sister cry. I don't remember what was in my little boy's mind then. I found some wire and made a pair of "ear rings" out of it. Then I asked my sister, "Would you like me to put these on you?" She smiled. "*Ohan*—yes." I didn't have the sharp bone one uses for the ear-piercing, and I didn't know the prayer that goes with it. I just had an old awl I thought would do fine. Oh, how my sister yelled. I had to hold her down, but I got that awl through her earlobes and managed to put the "ear rings" in. I was proud of the neat job I had done.

When my mother came home and saw those wire loops in my sister's ears she gasped. But she recovered soon enough to go and tell my father. That was one of the few occasions he talked to me. He said, "I should punish you and whip you, but I won't. That's not my way. You'll get your punishment later." Well, some time passed and I forgot all about it. One morning my father announced that we were going to a powwow. He had hitched up the wagon and it was heaped high with boxes and bundles. At that powwow my father let it be known that he was doing a big **otuhan**—a give-away. He put my sister on a rug, a pretty Navajo blanket, and laid out things to give away—quilts, food, blankets, a fine shotgun, his own new pair of cowboy boots, a sheepskin coat, enough to fit out a whole family. Dad was telling the people, "I want to honor my daughter for her ear-piercing. This should have been done openly, but my son did it at home. I guess he's too small. He didn't know any better." This was a long speech for Dad. He motioned me to come closer. I was sitting on my pretty gray horse. I thought we were both cutting a very fine **figure**. Well, before I knew it, Dad had given my horse away, together with its beautiful saddle and blanket. I had to ride home in the wagon and I cried all the way. The old man said, "You have your punishment now, but you will feel better later on. All her life your sister will tell about how you pierced her ears. She'll brag about you. I bet you are the only small boy who ever did this big ceremony."

That was no **consolation** to me. My beautiful gray was gone. I was heart-broken for three days. On the fourth morning I looked out the door and there stood a little white stallion with a new saddle and a silver-plated bit. "It's yours," my father told me. "Get on it." I was happy again.

Exercise. In the blanks provided, write the meaning of each **boldface** word as it was used in the selection. Check your answers against a dictionary.

a. feuding: *quarreling*
b. shinny ball: *a kind of hockey game*
c. mato kiciyapi: *the bear game*
d. isto kicicastakapi: *the pit-slinging game*
e. nonge pahloka: *the piercing of her ears*
f. ceremony: *ritual*
g. ohan: *yes*
h. otuhan: *a give-away*
i. figure: *impression*
j. consolation: *comfort*

Name _____

Chapter 8
Structure

A root word is the base from which other words are built. A root word may be the word itself or a word stem that comes to us from another language. To this root word we can add prefixes and suffixes to build new words. We can also combine two words to form compound words and contractions.

Lesson 1
Identifying Root Words

A root word is the base from which other words are built. Identifying the root word often gives you a clue to the meaning of the longer words built from it. For example, look at the following words: *rewrap, wrappable*. The root word of each of these words is *wrap*. When you *rewrap* something, you wrap it again. Something that is *wrappable* is able to be wrapped.

Look at the next group of words: *governor, governorship, government, ungovernable*. The root of each of these words is *govern*, which means "to control or direct" or "to exercise political control." A *governor* is a person who governs. A *governorship* is the office of governor. A *government* is the system by which a political unit is governed. Something that is *ungovernable* is not able to be governed.

Sometimes the spelling of the root word changes slightly when you use it to form a new word. For example, the root of *valuable* is *value* (the final *e* is dropped). The root of *merciful* is *mercy* (the *y* changes to *i*).

Exercise 1. In the space provided, write the root word of each of the following words.

a. graceless   *grace*   f. drummer   *drum*
b. powerful   *power*   g. discovery   *cover*
c. unkind   *kind*   h. grippingly   *grip*
d. knowledge   *know*   i. mysterious   *mystery*
e. difference   *differ*   j. recoverable   *cover*

Copyright © 1984 by Harcourt Brace Jovanovich, Inc. All rights reserved

Exercise 2. Read the following selection from "Life Is a Dance" by Karen Odom. Pay special attention to each **boldface** word. Then follow the directions at the end of the selection.

Marla, Mary, Mark, and Matthew all have something in common—something besides having names beginning with the letter "m," that is. They all make their **living** the same way. You could say they're dancing their way through life.

That may sound like fun—to dance for a living. And although Marla, Mary, Mark, and Matthew do enjoy their work, it's not as easy as it seems. They work very hard.

Take Marla, for instance. She's a *professional* dancer. She is a member of a dance troupe that travels around the world giving **performances.** Marla's friends think she has a **glamorous** job.

Even though some parts of Marla's life may seem glamorous, there's more to being a dancer than traveling and being on stage. Actually, Marla works very, very hard and puts in many long hours.

It has taken Marla years and years of studying dance to become a professional dancer. Marla started her first ballet class when she was only eight years old. She took lessons two days a week. Then when she was about 13 years old and had **definitely** decided dancing was what she wanted to do for the rest of her life, she started taking lessons every single day.

For years, Marla worked at this exhausting schedule and practiced, practiced, and practiced, until now, at 21, Marla is a full-time professional dancer. And that means even more work than ever. Now Marla has classes in the mornings, followed by **rehearsals** for the performances which last the rest of the day. Marla can finally go home at about 6:30 p.m. which leaves her just enough time to eat dinner, relax, and get ready for the same kind of schedule the next day. When Marla gets home in the evenings, she's worn out and her feet hurt, but because Marla loves what she does, it makes it all worthwhile.

When people think of a career in dance, they usually think of being a dancer like Marla, but performing on stage isn't the only thing a professional dancer can do. Mary is a professional dancer, too, but she doesn't dance on stage like Marla. She creates the steps that dancers like Marla perform. Mary is what is known as a *choreographer* (kôr′ē-ŏg′rə-fər). Mary does her hard work behind the scenes.

Mary is doing something different all the time. Sometimes she creates dances for dance companies, sometimes she choreographs for Broadway **musicals,** and one time she even choreographed the dancer's part in a movie. Every dance you've ever seen, no matter how big or small it may have seemed, had a person behind it who made it up. That's exactly what Mary does.

Mary spends many hours alone in the dance studio, trying to think of just the right steps. She starts with an idea or a story

Name _____

and then has to create a dance that brings it to life. That isn't easy, because Mary has to tell a story or communicate an emotion through dance—no words, just body **movement.** While creating a dance, Mary tries lots of ideas, arranges and **rearranges** them until she finds the **mixture** of steps and movements that she thinks are just right. Mary really gets excited then, because she knows half of her work is over.

That doesn't mean there won't be changes later on. Once the dancers start learning the movements Mary has created, some parts of Mary's dance may turn out to be not so right after all and she will have to think of something else.

Directions. Find the root word of each word below. Write it on the blank provided. You may use your dictionary to help you.

a. living _____*live*_____   f. rehearsals _____*rehearse*_____
b. professional _____*profession*_____   g. musicals _____*music*_____
c. performances _____*perform*_____   h. movement _____*move*_____
d. glamorous _____*glamor*_____   i. rearranges _____*arrange*_____
e. definitely _____*definite*_____   j. mixture _____*mix*_____

Lesson 2
Understanding Prefixes That Show Number

A prefix is a letter or group of letters added to the front of a word or word root. A prefix adds a new meaning to the original word. Some prefixes tell you number or quantity. For example, the prefix *mono-* adds the meaning "one," and the prefix *bi-* adds the meaning "two." Read the sentence below.

Chris flew a *monoplane*, while Pat flew a *biplane*.

A *monoplane* has one pair of wings, while a *biplane* has a double pair of wings.

Copyright © 1984 by Harcourt Brace Jovanovich, Inc. All rights reserved

The table below shows some common prefixes that add number.

Prefix	Meaning	Example
mono-	one	*monoplane*—an airplane with a single set of wings
uni-	one	*unidirectional*—having one direction only
bi-	two	*bifocals*—glasses that correct both near and far vision
tri-	three	*tricolor*—a flag that has three colors
quad-, quadr-	four	*quadrangle*—a four-sided figure with four angles
penta-, pent-	five	*pentagon*—a figure with five sides and five interior angles
oct-, octo-	eight	*octopus*—a marine creature with eight tentacles
deca-, dec-	ten	*decade*—a period of ten years
deci-	1/10th	*decimeter*—1/10th of a meter
centi-, cent-	1/100th	*centimeter*—1/100th of a meter
mill-, milli-	1/1000th	*millimeter*—1/1000th of a meter

Be careful. These letters do not always spell prefixes. Sometimes they are simply part of the original word. For example, the letters *deci* in *decide* and the letters *uni* in *unite* are simply part of the original word.

Exercise 1. The five words below begin with a prefix that indicates number. Look up each word in the dictionary. In the first set of blanks, write the meaning of each word. In the second set of blanks, rearrange these words in numerical order. Start with the word beginning with the prefix meaning "one," and end with the word beginning with the prefix meaning "ten."

	Meaning	Numerical Order
a. octet	*a group of eight*	*unicorn*
b. decagon	*a ten-sided figure*	*triangle*
c. unicorn	*a mythical horselike figure with one horn*	*quadruple*

196

Name _____

d. triangle   *a three-sided figure*   octet

e. quadruple   *fourfold*   decagon

Exercise 2. The five words below begin with a prefix that indicates number. Look up each word in the dictionary. In the first set of blanks, write the meaning of each word. In the second set of blanks, rearrange these words in numerical order. Start with the word beginning with the prefix meaning "one," and end with the word beginning with the prefix meaning "ten."

	Meaning	Numerical Order
a. bicycle	*a vehicle with two wheels*	*monogram*
b. monogram	*a design made up of the initials of one's name*	*bicycle*
c. trident	*a three-pronged fork*	*trident*
d. quadrangle	*a four-sided figure*	*quadrangle*
e. decapod	*a crustacean with ten appendages for movement*	*decapod*

Exercise 3. Answer each of the questions below. You may use the prefix table and your dictionary to help you.

a. A *quadrille* is a square dance that is performed by how many couples?   *four*

b. A magazine that comes out *biannually* comes out how many times a year?   *two*

c. A *triade* is a group of how many people?   *three*

d. If your stereo system has *quadraphonic* sound, it has sound coming from how many directions?   *four*

e. If a newspaper is published *triweekly*, it is published how many times a week?   *three*

f. A *monodrama* is a drama written for how many actors?   *one*

g. A *pentagon* has how many sides?   *five*

h. A *millimeter* is what part of a meter?   *1/1000th*

i. A *centigram* is what part of a gram?   *1/100th*

j. A *monocle* is an eyeglass for how many eyes?   *one*

Lesson 3

Understanding Prefixes That Show Position

Some prefixes indicate position. For example, the prefix *trans-* means "across." When you add *trans-* to the word *oceanic*, you form the word *transoceanic*, which means "across or over the ocean."

The chart below shows some common prefixes that can indicate position.

Prefix	Meaning	Example
intra-	in; within; inside of	*intrastate*—within a state
inter-	between; among	*interstate*—between two or more states
sub-	under; beneath	*submarine*—a ship that can travel beneath the surface of the sea
trans-	across; over	*transoceanic*—across the ocean

The prefixes *inter-* and *sub-* have additional meanings. However, in this lesson, we will use these prefixes only with their meanings that indicate position.

Exercise 1. Add the correct prefix to each of the **boldface** words below. Write the complete word in the blank at the right.

a. The foundation of a building is called its _____**structure**. — *substructure*

b. Relationships between two or more nations are called _____**national** relations. — *international*

c. Mountainous territory that is just below the timber line is _____**alpine** land. — *subalpine*

d. A journey across the Atlantic is a _____**atlantic** journey. — *transatlantic*

e. A contest between two or more schools is an _____**scholastic** contest. — *interscholastic*

f. A basketball game that is held between two teams within a school is an _____**mural** game. — *intramural*

g. A trip across the continent is a _____**continental** journey. — *transcontinental*

h. A person who is under the control of another person is a _____**ordinate**. — *subordinate*

i. The time between two sessions of school is called an _____**session**. — *intersession*

j. In a building, a room beneath the basement is called a _____**basement**. — *subbasement*

Name _____

Exercise 2. The puzzle below contains ten words that have prefixes indicating position. These words may be written from top to bottom, from bottom to top, from left to right, from right to left, or diagonally. Find each word in the puzzle. Circle the word. Then look it up in the dictionary. Write the word and its meaning on the line provided.

```
S A E T R E L E N T O M I
U P L S N A T D R S N T N
B K B L A O R L G A M Y T
M G I O G E A O R T O A E
E S S T R A N S P O L A R
R M R Y C T S H R N E M C
G A E U R A P E L Z I A O
E B M E T H A E G N N E N
S U B G L A C I A L T J T
P A U H R T I N O W R N I
N I S F E N F O M R A M N
A N J F R Y I O B L S A E
K E A X L I C I S W T S N
A M N A T R W S E R A M T
A L C I E H X C E V T E A
G I F T I C F O E T E S L
C I N I N T R A M U R A L
D I N T E R S T E L L A R
```

	Word	Meaning
a.	_intercom_	_a communication system between two rooms_
b.	_intrastate_	_within a state_
c.	_interstellar_	_between stars_
d.	_submerge_	_go under water_
e.	_submersible_	_a vessel that can remain under water_
f.	_transpacific_	_across the Pacific_
g.	_intercontinental_	_between continents_
h.	_transpolar_	_across the pole_
i.	_subglacial_	_formed beneath a glacier_
j.	_intramural_	_within a school_

Copyright © 1984 by Harcourt Brace Jovanovich, Inc. All rights reserved

Lesson 4

Understanding Negative Prefixes

A prefix is a letter or group of letters added to the beginning of a word or word root to change its meaning. A negative prefix adds the meaning "not" or "no" or indicates a reversal. For example, *dis-* is a negative prefix. The word *disagreeable* means "not agreeable." The word *disconnect* means "to cut the connection between something." When you disconnect something, you reverse the action of connecting it.

Other negative prefixes are *a-; de-; il-, im-,* or *in-; non-;* and *un-*. Be careful though. These letters do not always spell prefixes. Sometimes they are simply part of the base word.

Exercise 1. Each of the words below contains a negative prefix. Write the meaning of each word in the blank provided. You may use your dictionary to help you.

a. atypical *not typical*

b. deactivate *make harmless*

c. debark *unload*

d. disarm *deprive of arms*

e. illegal *not legal*

f. imprecise *not precise or accurate*

g. imperfect *not perfect*

h. insecure *not secure*

i. nonsense *something that doesn't make sense*

j. unstable *not stable*

Name _____

Exercise 2. Complete the crossword puzzle that follows. Each word in the crossword puzzle has a negative prefix. You may use your dictionary to help you.

Across
1. To unfasten or reverse the process of putting strings on
3. Not helpful
5. Not sincere
7. Not making a profit
9. To reverse the process of arming
10. The condition of not being able to read and write
11. Not capable
13. Not perfect
15. Not polite
16. Not safe
17. To remove bugs, incorrectly functioning elements

Down
2. Not patient
3. Not necessary
4. Not distinct
6. Not possible
8. Not mature
9. To reverse the process of banding together
11. Not complete
12. To reverse the process of coding
14. Not legal

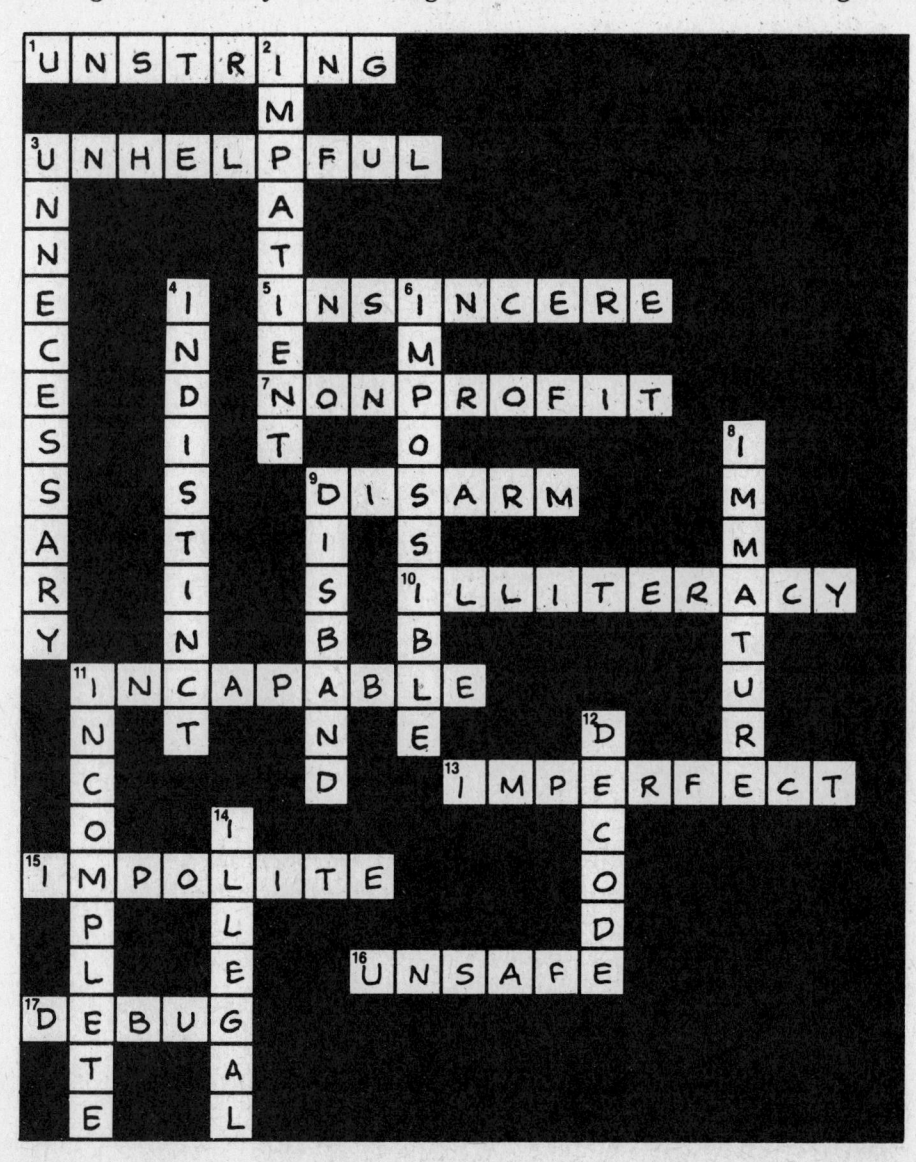

Copyright © 1984 by Harcourt Brace Jovanovich, Inc. All rights reserved

201

Lesson 5

Understanding Comparative and Superlative Suffixes

A suffix is a letter or a group of letters added to the end of a word or word root to change its meaning or its function. Two common suffixes are -er and -est. These suffixes are added to the end of descriptive words to compare things. They signal that a person, place, or thing is being compared with other persons, places, or things.

The suffix -er is called a comparative suffix. It is used to compare two things. For example:

The elephant is *larger* than the gorilla.

The suffix -est is called a superlative suffix. It is used when one thing is compared with two or more things. For example:

The elephant is the *largest* animal at this zoo.

The spelling of the base word may change slightly when you add a suffix. For example:

Your blouse is *pretty*.
Your blouse is *prettier* than mine. (y changes to i)
Your blouse is the *prettiest* one I've seen. (y changes to i)

Your dictionary can help you find the correct spelling.

Exercise 1. Read each word below. If the word has a comparative suffix, it compares two things. Write *Two* in the blank next to the word. If the word has a superlative suffix, it compares three or more things. Write *Three or more* in the blank next to the word.

a. happiest	*Three or more*	f. faster	*Two*
b. redder	*Two*	g. gentlest	*Three or more*
c. kindest	*Three or more*	h. bluest	*Three or more*
d. firmer	*Two*	i. taller	*Two*
e. harder	*Two*	j. strongest	*Three or more*

Exercise 2. Fill in the missing forms in the following chart. You may use your dictionary to help you choose the correct spelling.

	Comparative	Superlative
a. lovely	lovelier	*loveliest*
b. pink	*pinker*	pinkest
c. happy	*happier*	happiest

Name _____

	Comparative	Superlative
d. bouncy	bouncier	*bounciest*
e. short	shorter	*shortest*
f. jazzy	*jazzier*	jazziest
g. sharp	sharper	*sharpest*
h. sweet	sweeter	*sweetest*
i. juicy	*juicier*	juiciest
j. crispy	crispier	*crispiest*

Exercise 3. For some words, the comparative and superlative forms are very different from the original word. Look up each word below in your dictionary. Then complete the chart below.

	Comparative	Superlative
a. good	*better*	*best*
b. bad	*worse*	*worst*
c. little	*less*	*least*
d. many	*more*	*most*

Lesson 6

More About Using Suffixes to Determine Meaning

A suffix is a letter or a group of letters added to the end of a word or word root. One type of suffix adds a different meaning to the base word. For example, look at the suffixes *-ful* and *-less*. A *powerful* person is a person full of power, or with power. A *powerless* person is a person without power.

A second type of suffix changes the function of a word. This type marks a part of speech. For example, the suffixes *-age*, *-ment*, and *-tion* mark nouns. Look at the words *carriage*, *agreement*, and *relation*. The suffixes *-able* and *-ible* mark adjectives. Look at the words *breakable* and *horrible*. The suffix *-ly* marks either an adjective or an adverb. For example, the word *brotherly* is an adjective; *Philadelphia* is known as the city of brotherly love. The word *horribly* is an adverb: Charles behaved horribly in school.

Copyright © 1984 by Harcourt Brace Jovanovich, Inc. All rights reserved

Exercise 1. Read each item below. Add the suffix *-ful* or *-less* to each **boldface** word. Write the new words on the blanks provided. Make sure that your answers make sense.

   a. Amanda was happy and full of **cheer**. Amanda was _**cheerful**_.

   b. Terri was sad and without **cheer**. Terri was _**cheerless**_.

   c. The coat was designed by someone with good **taste**. The coat was _**tasteful**_.

   d. The jacket was designed by someone without good **taste**. The jacket was _**tasteless**_.

   e. The teacher's glance was full of **meaning**. The teacher's glance was _**meaningful**_.

   f. His gesture was without **meaning**. His gesture was _**meaningless**_.

   g. The hero was without **fear**. The hero was _**fearless**_.

   h. The guests in the strange house were full of **fear**. The guests were _**fearful**_.

   i. Their song was full of **joy**. Their song was _**joyful**_.

   j. The rainy day was without **joy**. The day was _**joyless**_.

Exercise 2. Fill in the missing word in each sentence below by adding the suffix *-age*, *-ment*, or *-tion* to each **boldface** word. Use your dictionary to help you choose the correct suffix and the correct spelling of the new word.

   a. When two people **marry**, they enter into a _**marriage**_.

   b. When you **argue** with a person, you have an _**argument**_.

   c. When you **agree** with a person, you have an _**agreement**_.

   d. When you **break** things, the damage due to breaking is called _**breakage**_.

204   Copyright © 1984 by Harcourt Brace Jovanovich, Inc. All rights reserved

e. When you **collect** money, you take up a _collection_.

f. When you **appreciate** something, you show your _appreciation_.

g. When something is **required**, it is a _requirement_.

h. A vehicle that **carries** people is a _carriage_.

i. When you **create** a work of art, you often display your _creation_.

j. An **organized** group is an _organization_.

Exercise 3. Fill in the missing word in each sentence below by adding the suffix -*able* or -*ible* to each **boldface** word. Use your dictionary to help you choose the correct suffix and the correct spelling of the new word.

a. Someone on whom you can **depend** is _dependable_.
b. Something that makes **sense** is _sensible_.
c. Something that can be **accepted** is _acceptable_.
d. Something that can be **debated** is _debatable_.
e. Someone who can be **relied** on is _reliable_.
f. Something that can be **allowed** is _allowable_.
g. Something that can be **divided** is _divisible_.
h. Something that can be **used** is _usable_.
i. Something that **collapses** is _collapsible_.
j. Something that can be **recovered** is _recoverable_.

Exercise 4. Fill in the missing word in each sentence below by adding the suffix -*ly* to each **boldface** word. Use your dictionary to help you choose the correct word and the correct spelling of the new word.

a. Aretha sang in a **joyful** manner. Aretha sang _joyfully_.

b. Carmen was **patient** when she explained the game to her younger sister. Carmen _patiently_ explained the game to her younger sister.

Copyright © 1984 by Harcourt Brace Jovanovich, Inc. All rights reserved

c. Dave was **cautious** when he walked along the balance beam. Dave walked along the balance beam ____*cautiously*____.

d. Rita was **sincere** when she apologized. Rita apologized ____*sincerely*____.

e. It was **surprising** that the party turned out so well. The party turned out ____*surprisingly*____ well.

f. The model is so attractive, she is **striking**. The model is ____*strikingly*____ attractive.

g. The politician smiled in a **winning** manner. The politician smiled ____*winningly*____.

h. The strangers nodded in a **polite** manner when they were introduced. The strangers nodded ____*politely*____ when they were introduced.

i. All of a **sudden,** or in a **sudden** way, it stopped raining. ____*Suddenly*____, it stopped raining.

j. It is **probable** that school will be called off tomorrow because of snow. ____*Probably*____, school will be called off tomorrow because of snow.

Lesson 7

Understanding Latin Roots

A root word is the base from which other words are built. Many root words have come to us from Latin. Some commonly used Latin roots are *anim*, *vid* or *vis*, and *port*. For example, look at the chart below.

Root	Meaning	English Words Built from This Root
anim	live, mind	animate, animal
vid, vis	see	video, televise
port	carry	transport, deport

In general, learning the meaning of Latin roots can help you to figure out the meaning of many English words.

Name _____

Exercise 1. Each word below is based on the Latin root *anim*, which means "live" or "mind." First circle the root in each word. Then look up each word in your dictionary. Write its meaning on the line provided.

a. (anim)ate: *to fill with spirit or life*
b. (anim)al: *a living creature of a class Animalia*
c. un(anim)ous: *of one mind; being in harmony*
d. in(anim)ate: *not having the qualities of a living organism*
e. (anim)osity: *active hatred*

Exercise 2. Each word below is based on the Latin root *vid, vis*, which means "see." First circle the root in each word. Then look up each word in your dictionary. Write its meaning on the line provided.

a. (vid)eo: *pertaining to television*
b. tele(vis)e: *to broadcast by television*
c. (vis)ion: *sight*
d. pro(vis)ion: *the act of supplying, with an eye to the future*
e. pro(vid)ence: *foresight*

Exercise 3. Each word below is based on the Latin root *port*, which means "carry." First circle the root in each word. Then look up each word in your dictionary. Write its meaning on the line provided.

a. trans(port): *carry from one point to another*
b. de(port): *remove from a country*
c. (port)age: *carrying boats overland between waterways*
d. im(port)ation: *the act of carrying in goods from an outside source*
e. ex(port): *send abroad for trade*

Copyright © 1984 by Harcourt Brace Jovanovich, Inc. All rights reserved

Exercise 4. Each of the words from Exercises 1, 2, and 3 can be found in the puzzle below. Find these fifteen words and circle them. The words may read from right to left, from left to right, from top to bottom, from bottom to top, or diagonally.

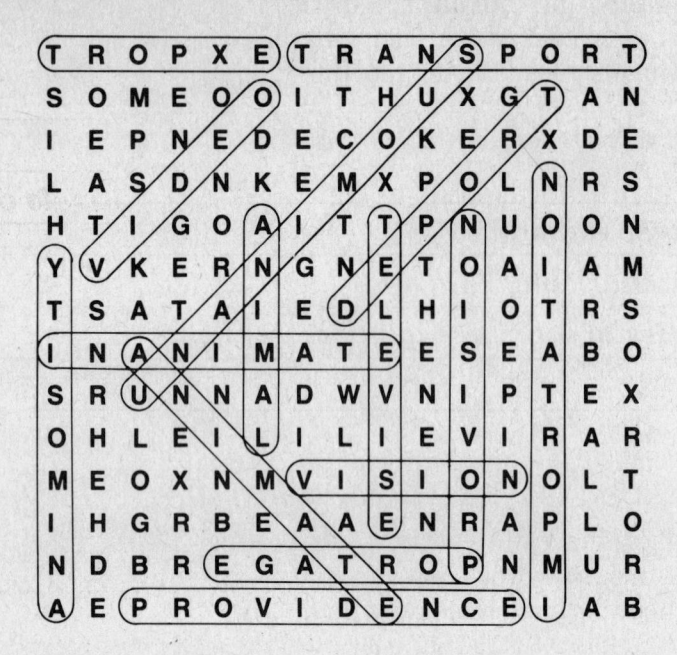

```
T R O P X E T R A N S P O R T
S O M E O O I T H U X G T A N
I E P N E D E C O K E R X D E
L A S D N K E M X P O L N R S
H T I G O A I T T P N U O O N
Y V K E R N G N E T O A I A M
T S A T A I E D L H I O T R S
I N A N I M A T E E S E A B O
S R U N N A D W V N I P T E X
O H L E I L I L I E V I R A R
M E O X N M V I S I O N O L T
I H G R B E A A E N R A P L O
N D B R E G A T R O P N M U R
A E P R O V I D E N C E I A B
```

Lesson 8
Understanding Greek Roots

A root word is the base from which other words are built. Many root words have come to us from Greek. Some commonly used Greek roots are *geo*, *auto*, and *onym*. For example, look at the chart below.

Root	Meaning	English Words Built from This Root
geo	earth	geography, geometry
auto	self	autograph, autocrat
onym	name, word	pseudonym, synonym

In general, learning the meaning of Greek roots can help you to figure out the meaning of many English words.

208   Copyright © 1984 by Harcourt Brace Jovanovich, Inc. All rights reserved

Name _____

Exercise 1. Each word below is based on the Greek root *geo*, which means "earth." First circle the root in each word. Then look up each word in your dictionary. Write its meaning on the line provided.

a. (geo)graphy: *the study of the earth and its features*
b. (geo)metry: *a form of mathematics*
c. bio(geo)graphy: *the biological study of the distribution of plants and animals over the earth*
d. (geo)logy: *the study of the structure of the earth*
e. (geo)centric: *having the earth as its center*

Exercise 2. Each word below is based on the Greek root *auto*, which means "self." First circle the root in each word. Then look up each word in your dictionary. Write its meaning on the line provided.

a. (auto)graph: *a person's own signature*
b. (auto)crat: *an absolute ruler*
c. (auto)matic: *self-moving*
d. (auto)nomous: *independent*
e. (auto)motive: *a vehicle that is self-propelled*

Exercise 3. Each word below is based on the Greek root *onym*, which means "name" or "word." First circle the root in each word. Then look up each word in your dictionary. Write its meaning on the line provided.

a. pseud(onym): *false name; pen name*
b. syn(onym): *a word having the same meaning as another*
c. ant(onym): *a word having the opposite meaning of another*
d. acr(onym): *a word formed from the initial letters of a name*
e. patr(onym)ic: *a name received from ancestors on the father's side of the family*

Exercise 4. Use your dictionary to find the meaning of each of the Greek roots below. Write the meaning on the line provided.

a. pseudo: *false*
b. graph: *writing*
c. metry: *measurement*
d. bio: *life*
e. logy: *study of*

Lesson 9

Understanding Compound Words

A compound word consists of two or more words joined together to form a new word. Many compounds are written as one word; for example, *smokestack, beehive.* Some, though, are joined by hyphens; for example, *small-minded, son-in-law.* Others are written as two words; for example, *cold wave, heat exhaustion.*

In the comic strip below, the children form some interesting compound words.

FOR BETTER OR FOR WORSE **by Lynn Johnston**

You can understand most compound words by breaking them into their parts. For example, a *smokestack* is a stack or chimney through which smoke passes. A *beehive* is a hive where bees live.

Some compounds, however, stretch the meaning of the original words. For example, look at the word *skunkweed.* This weed has nothing to do with skunks. Since it smells bad, though, people say its odor is like that of a skunk. Therefore, they call this ill-smelling weed "skunkweed."

Exercise 1. Below are five groups of words. In each group, three words are compound words. One word is not. Write the word that is not a compound word in the blank at the right.

a. slipknot, slipcover, slippery, slip-stream — *slippery*

b. workable, workout, workshop, workday — *workable*

c. underfoot, undercut, underground, underling — *underling*

d. moonbeam, moonshine, moonstruck, moony — *moony*

e. heart-to-heart, heart attack, heartbeat, heartless — *heartless*

Name _____

Exercise 2. Read the selection below, "Baseball's World Series" by Mike Klodnicki. Then define each of the **boldface** compound words. Use your dictionary to help you.

When October rolls around, so does the World Series. The long **baseball** season—which started with spring training—ends, and the best two teams play each other for the championship.

Each year over 300,000 people go to the **ball park** to watch the **World Series.** Millions more watch the games on television and listen on radio.

The popularity of the World Series goes back to the 1800s. Baseball was a new sport then, but people quickly found it to their liking.

In 1884 there were two major leagues—the National League (NL) and the American Association (AA). The New York Mets were the AA champions and the Providence Grays were the best in the NL.

Mets manager James Mutrie had an idea. Why not play the Grays to see which was the better team? He issued a challenge to Grays manager Frank Bancroft, who accepted it. Three games were played, and Providence won all three. The games were called the Championship of the United States.

The next year Alfred Spink, a St. Louis **sportswriter,** called the contest the World Championship Series. (The word "Championship" was later dropped to make the title shorter.) That year the series was extended to seven games.

The World Series has always featured exciting plays and action. It is the best baseball played by the best **ballplayers.**

In 1956 New York Yankees pitcher Don Larsen proved that true. In a game against the Brooklyn Dodgers, he pitched the first, and only, perfect game in World Series history. Larsen allowed no hits. There were no walks. New York made no errors. Not a single Dodger managed to get on base.

Another famous World Series moment never actually happened. It was New York against Chicago in 1932. **Home-run-hitter** Babe Ruth was at bat. With two strikes, the Babe pointed at the Chicago **dugout** and then toward **center field.** He then hit the next pitch over the center-field fence. Everybody thought Ruth had picked out where he wanted to hit a **home run** and then hit it. It became known as "the called shot."

What had really happened? A Chicago pitcher named Guy Bush was sitting on the bench. He began heckling Ruth when he had two strikes against him. Ruth had then pointed to Bush and then to the pitcher's mound, saying, "Wait until I bat against you." The Babe just happened to hit a home run on the next pitch.

Since its beginning the World Series has had some changes. In the early 1900s, the AA folded and the American League (AL) took its place. Through the years teams have moved to

Copyright © 1984 by Harcourt Brace Jovanovich, Inc. All rights reserved   211

different cities, and old teams have been disbanded, while new teams have taken up the slack. However, the World Series idea has remained the same—to determine a major league baseball champion.

And every fall, while the leaves are changing colors, the weather is getting cool, and you're busy getting out your **schoolbooks,** baseball fans are enjoying the World Series.

Definitions

a. baseball: *a type of game played with a ball*

b. ball park: *a park in which a ball game is held*

c. World Series: *a contest for championship*

d. sportswriter: *a writer who writes about sports*

e. ballplayers: *people who play ball games*

f. home-run-hitter: *a person who hits home runs*

g. dugout: *a sunken shelter at the side of a ball field*

h. center field: *the center playing field*

i. home run: *a hit that allows a batter to run home*

j. schoolbooks: *books for school*

Lesson 10

Understanding Contractions

A contraction is a word formed by combining two words. When the two words are combined, some letters are left out and replaced by an apostrophe ('). Many contractions are made up of a verb plus the word *not*. An apostrophe replaces the letter *o* in *not*. For example:

is + not = isn't
was + not = wasn't
had + not = hadn't

Sometimes adding *not* to a verb causes other spelling changes:

can + not = can't
will + not = won't

Other contractions are formed by combining pronouns or nouns with verbs. The apostrophe may replace more than one letter. For example:

One Letter	More Than One Letter
I + am = I'm	who + would = who'd
she + is = she's	he + will = he'll
	she + has = she's
they + are = they're	they + have = they've
Laura + is = Laura's	Tony + will = Tony'll

Notice that the contraction of *she is* and of *she has* is *she's*. The contraction of *he is* and of *he has* is *he's*. The contraction of *who is* and *who has* is *who's*. When you read these contractions, you have to look at the word immediately following the contraction to find which verb is meant. For example:

She's **going** to the party.
She is **going** to the party.

She's **been** working on the decorations committee.
She has **been** working on the decorations committee.

Exercise. Read "The Cake Icing Caper" by Shirley Lee. Pay special attention to the contractions printed in **boldface**. Then, after reading the selection, write the two words that form each contraction. You may use your dictionary to help you.

I never wanted to be in the middle of a crowd. For as long as I can remember, somebody has always been urging me to participate in things.

"Get involved," said my history teacher, Mr. Asbury. "Run for an office. **You're** capable of much more than you attempt, Harold. Why, I can even see you as student body president."

"Uh, thanks for the compliment," I told him, "but I really **don't** think . . ." I used my usual stalling bit.

And then there was Miss Tate, only with her it was art, since **that's** what **she's** involved in. And with her I was given three choices. I should: 1. Join the school art club. 2. Make some posters for school events. 3. Do some work for the school annual.

I hinted that I was too busy helping my dad with a project at home, though why he, a well-known commercial artist, should need the help of a mere amateur, I hoped I **wouldn't** have to explain.

With Mom a freelance writer, it was only natural that I should take to writing as well, so my English teacher, Mrs. Jennings, was the third one this year to plague me with projects.

"With your talent, you should really be a member of the school paper staff and join the Writer's Club," she pointed out to me on returning my latest short-story assignment.

I knew I should be flattered, and I was, but I felt no more desire to be a part of a group than I ever had. I guessed I was a born lone wolf. "I really **don't** have time right now," I muttered regretfully.

Even Mom and Dad had given up on trying to talk me into doing things I really **didn't** want to, and contented themselves with letting me go along at my own pace.

I'm no great athlete. I play games for the fun of it. And parties and social events never did turn me on. So I **hadn't** even planned to attend the class banquet.

Now, **don't** get me wrong. I *do* love to eat. That was one reason I enjoyed spending nearly two months visiting Uncle Earl and Aunt Belle last summer, and helping out in their small retail bakery. I learned to fry doughnuts and mix up cake batter in the big electric mixer, and to ice and decorate cakes. And Uncle Earl taught me to handle the decorating tubes enough to write messages, do simple borders and make roses and leaves. But I never told anyone.

There were two or three guys I hung around with at lunchtime. Since they **weren't** the sort to jump into school activities either, it was surprising that we even got around to mentioning the banquet. Except that Jim Thompson had a twin sister, Jody, who was gung-ho for school events.

"**It's** too bad about the banquet cakes," he muttered, sliding his long legs under the table and digging into his Spanish rice.

"**How's** that?" I asked.

"They **can't** get anybody to decorate them this year."

"Why not?"

"Because the cafeteria lady who did their decorating moved to another town. Mrs. Muffet, **who's** in charge, says **we'll** just have to make do with plain cakes this year."

"Really? I thought nearly anyone who cooked for a living could decorate cakes."

Jim gave me a funny look. "What makes you think so?" he asked. My mom does lots of baking, but she **can't** do fancy things like cake decorating."

"Huh." I said, "Maybe it runs in my family or something."

"What are you talking about?" Pete Fenton had been listening all this time without making a comment.

"Why, cake decorating, of course," I answered, shoving back my empty plate. "I learned how at my uncle's bakery last summer. **It's** not hard."

"You what?" Jim stared at me. "Well, why **don't** you tell them? **They're** looking all over for someone to do it. Jody came home and talked about it all last evening."

It was my turn to stare. "You know how I feel about volunteering. No, thanks."

Suddenly I remembered something urgent I had to do in the school library and took off with just a casual word and wave.

I did my best to forget the whole thing, but the next day was the day before the banquet. **You'd** be surprised how hard everyone was taking a simple little thing like undecorated cakes. It seemed **we'd** be the first class since the school opened to have cakes without the usual junk all over them—the emblem, the name, the motto and all the trim. So who cared? Just about everybody, and especially Jody Thompson, who was class historian and wanted color photos to put in the scrapbook.

I tried to concentrate on the prism I was making in plastics class, but I kept hearing Jody talking to her friend Samantha, where they were lined up over at the buffer.

"I just **don't** know what **we're** going to do," Jody moaned. "The cakes are being baked today, but nobody offered to decorate them. **They're** going to look just awful plain white."

I turned back to my work. What a nerd! Did she really think it mattered all that much what kind of cakes the class had?

"I might try to do it myself," she was saying in a funny little voice. "I might go over to the cafeteria after school. Mrs. Muffet says there will be plenty of white icing to work with, and **she's** got the coloring and even the bags and tubes."

Samantha was shocked. "But you **don't** know the first thing about it. **You'll** probably make a big mess of it."

"It's better to light one candle than to curse the darkness," said Jody decisively.

I sneaked a look at Jody. **Hadn't** anyone ever taught her the meaning of the word quit? I admired her staying power, but I shuddered to think of the way those cakes might turn out.

There were two classes left—English and math—and I tried to think only about what I was doing in them. But horrible pictures kept coming to mind—Jody with icing smeared from head to toe . . . the cakes lying broken upon the concrete floor. I found myself giving in to the inevitable. **I'd** have to drop by and see the worst, but **I'd** be careful nobody saw me.

I knew the back way into the kitchen, and I managed to open the door quietly. The cafeteria help was gone, and the place was quiet and closed-up looking. Down the hall I heard voices and saw a couple of overhead lights on. I moved to the door and peeked inside. Jody was there, talking to Samantha. On the stainless steel table before her stood two enormous crockery bowls full of blue frosting, and spread out all around were metal icing tubes and canvas bags. On the table behind her were four large "sheet" cakes.

Jody was trying to stuff huge gobs of icing into one of the bags with a giant metal spoon, but it was oozing out over the top. "If I can teach myself to use these things," she was saying, "then I can make some blue and gold and put on some sort of design."

"Oh, no!" I **couldn't** help an involuntary groan. It had taken me a couple of weeks to get that far along even with Uncle Earl's expert instructions.

I heard a step behind me, turned, and bumped into Jim. All he said was "Well?"

But I read between the lines. He meant "Well, why **don't** you break down and help her?"

Then, before I knew it, I was in the midst of things. Coloring frostings, filling bags—putting on curlicue borders, drawing on the class emblem, and writing on the name and the motto. I did all four cakes in a little more than an hour.

After a few exclamations of surprise and some amazed looks, the others helped, handing me equipment, and helping me get the cakes onto the racks in the refrigerator. I insisted on carrying them myself as I **didn't** want to see all my hard work wind up on the floor.

When we finally finished I took a deep breath and reached for my jacket. Mom would be wondering what had happened to me.

"It was wonderful of you to help us, Harold," Jody was saying earnestly. "**I'll** never be able to thank you enough. And think how proud **you'll** be at the banquet tomorrow when we tell the class what you did."

"But I **won't** be there," I started to say, then stopped and looked at Jim, who shrugged and nodded.

"Well, that will be great," I told her with a grin.

It felt nice to be the center of attention and I really felt proud that I had helped the class out. I **wouldn't** think too far ahead about it just now, but I **wasn't** at all sure I wanted to go on with my nonparticipation schedule. I mean, joining the Writer's Club might prove an inspiration to me, and drawing a poster or two certainly **wouldn't** be all that difficult. And what was it that Mr. Asbury had said? Well, maybe the student body *could* have a worse president than me!

Directions. On the blank provided, write the two words that form each contraction below.

a. you're	*you are*	n. who's	*who is*
b. don't	*do not*	o. we'll	*we will*
c. that's	*that is*	p. they're	*they are*
d. she's (involved)	*she is*	q. you'd	*you would*
e. wouldn't	*would not*	r. we're	*we are*
f. didn't	*did not*	s. you'll	*you will*
g. I'm	*I am*	t. I'd	*I would*
h. hadn't	*had not*	u. we'd	*we would*
i. weren't	*were not*	v. couldn't	*could not*
j. it's (too bad)	*it is*	w. I'll	*I will*
k. she's (got)	*she has*	x. wasn't	*was not*
l. how's	*how is*	y. he'd	*he had*
m. can't	*cannot*		

Name _____

Lesson 11
Practice

Pay special attention to word structure as you read the selection below. Then complete the exercise that follows it.

How To Improve Your Vocabulary
Tony Randall

Words can make us laugh, cry, go to war, fall in love.

Rudyard Kipling called words the most powerful drug of mankind. If they are, I'm a hopeless addict—and I hope to get you hooked, too!

Whether you're still in school or you head up a corporation, the better command you have of words, the better chance you have of saying exactly what you mean, of understanding what others mean—and of getting what you want in the world.

English is the richest language—with the largest vocabulary on earth. Over 1,000,000 words!

*Y*ou can express shades of meaning that aren't even *possible* in other languages. (For example, you can differentiate between "sky" and "heaven." The French, Italians and Spanish cannot.)

Yet, the average adult has a vocabulary of only 30,000 to 60,000 words. Imagine what we're missing!

Here are five pointers that help me learn—and remember— whole *families* of words at a time.

They may not *look* easy—and won't be at first. But if you stick with them you'll find they *work!*

What's the first thing to do when you see a word you don't know?

1. Try to guess the meaning of the word from the way it's used

You can often get at least *part* of a word's meaning—just from how it's used in a sentence.

That's why it's so important to read as much as you can— different *kinds* of things: magazines, books, newspapers you don't normally read. The more you *expose* yourself to new words, the more words you'll pick up *just by seeing how they're used*.

For instance, say you run across the word "manacle":

"The manacles had been on John's wrists for 30 years. Only one person had a key—his wife."

You have a good *idea* of what "manacles" are—just from the context of the sentence.

Copyright © 1984 by Harcourt Brace Jovanovich, Inc. All rights reserved

217

But let's find out *exactly* what the word means and where it comes from. The only way to do this, and to build an extensive vocabulary *fast*, is to go to the dictionary. (How lucky, you *can*—Shakespeare *couldn't*. There *wasn't* an English dictionary in his day!)

So you go to the dictionary. (NOTE: Don't let dictionary abbreviations put you off. The front tells you what they mean, and even has a guide to pronunciation.)

2. Look it up

Here's the definition for "manacle" in *The American Heritage Dictionary of the English Language*.

man-a-cle (măn′ə-kəl) *n.* Usually plural. **1.** A device for confining the hands, usually consisting of two metal rings that are fastened about the wrists and joined by a metal chain; a handcuff. **2.** Anything that confines or restrains—*tr. v.* **manacled, -cling, -cles.** **1.** To restrain with manacles. **2.** To confine or restrain as if with manacles; shackle; fetter. [Middle English *manicle*, from Old French, from Latin *manicula*, little hand, handle, diminutive of *manus*, hand. See **man-²** in Appendix.*]

The first definition fits here: A device for confining the hands, usually consisting of two metal rings that are fastened about the wrists and joined by a metal chain; a handcuff.

Well, that's what you *thought* it meant. But what's the idea *behind* the word? What are its *roots*? To really understand a word, you need to know.

Here's where the detective work—and the *fun*—begins.

3. Dig the meaning out by the roots

The root is the basic part of the word—its heritage, its origin. (Most of our roots come from Latin and Greek words at least 2,000 years old—which come from even earlier Indo-European tongues!)

Learning the roots: 1) Helps us *remember* words. 2) Gives us a deeper understanding of the words we *already* know. And 3) allows us to pick up whole families of *new* words at a time. That's why learning the root is the *most important part of going to the dictionary*.

Notice the root of "manacle" is *manus* (Latin) meaning "hand."

Well, that makes sense. Now, other words with this root, man, start to make sense, too.

Take manual—something done "by hand" (manual labor) or a "handbook." And manage—to "handle" something (as a manager). When you emancipate someone, you're taking him "from the hands of" someone else.

When you manufacture something, you "make it by hand" (in its original meaning).

And when you finish your first novel, your publisher will see your—originally "handwritten"—manuscript.

Imagine! A whole new world of words opens up—just from one simple root!

The root gives the *basic* clue to the meaning of a word. But there's another important clue that runs a close second—the *prefix*.

4. Get the powerful prefixes under your belt

A prefix is the part that's sometimes attached to the front of a word. Like—well, prefix! There aren't many—less than 100 major prefixes—and you'll learn them in no time at all just by becoming more aware of the meanings of words you already know.

Here are a few. (Some of the "How-to" vocabulary-building books will give you the others.)

PREFIX		MEANING	EXAMPLES	
(Lat.)	(Gk.)			(Literal sense)
com, con, co, col, cor	sym, syn, syl	with, very, together	conform sympathy	(form with) (feeling with)
in, im, il, ir	a, an	not, without	innocent amorphous	(not wicked) (without form)
contra, counter	anti, ant	against, opposite	contravene antidote	(come against) (give against)

Now, see how *prefix* (along with the context) helps you get the meaning of the italicized words:

● "If you're going to be my witness, your story must *corroborate* my story." (The literal meaning of *corroborate* is "strength together.")

● "You told me one thing—now you tell me another. Don't *contradict* yourself." (The literal meaning of *contradict* is "say against.")

● "Oh, that snake's not poisonous. It's a completely *innocuous* little garden snake." (The literal meaning of *innocuous* is "not harmful.")

Now, you've got some new words. What are you going to do with them?

5. Put your new words to work at once

Use them several times the first day you learn them. Say them out loud! Write them in sentences.

Should you "use" them on *friends*? Careful—you don't want them to think you're a stuffed shirt. (It depends on the situation. You *know* when a word sounds natural—and when it sounds stuffy.)

How about your *enemies*? You have my blessing. Ask one of them if he's read that article on pneumonoultramicroscopicsilicovolcanoconiosis. (You really can find it in the dictionary.) Now, you're one up on him.

So what do you do to improve your vocabulary?

Copyright © 1984 by Harcourt Brace Jovanovich, Inc. All rights reserved

Remember: 1) Try to guess the meaning of the word from the way it's used. 2) Look it up. 3) Dig the meaning out by the roots. 4) Get the powerful prefixes under your belt. 5) Put your new words to work at once.

That's all there is to it—you're off on your treasure hunt.

Now, do you see why I love words so much?

Aristophanes said, "By words, the mind is excited and the spirit elated." It's as true today as it was when he said it in Athens—*2,400 years ago!*

I hope you're now like me—hooked on words forever.

Exercise. Decide whether the following statements are true or false. Write *T* by each statement that is true. Write *F* by each statement that is false.

a.	English has the smallest vocabulary of any language.	F
b.	Shakespeare used the dictionary often when he wrote his plays.	F
c.	Most of our roots come from Latin and Greek.	T
d.	The word *manacle* is based on the Latin word *manus*, which means "hand."	T
e.	The word *manuscript* is based on a Greek word which means "machine."	F
f.	A prefix is attached to the end of a word or word root.	F
g.	If a snake is poisonous, it is *innocuous*.	F
h.	In the word *corroborate*, the prefix *cor-* means "together."	T
i.	In the word *contradict*, the prefix *contra-* means "against."	T
j.	Never guess at the meaning of words.	F

220   Copyright © 1984 by Harcourt Brace Jovanovich, Inc. All rights reserved

Name _____

Chapter 9
Word Origins

Words, like people, have interesting histories. In this chapter you will learn some of these histories. You will look at words based on the names of real people and real places. You will see how words have changed in meaning as they have grown older. You also will learn about words that came into English from other languages.

Lesson 1
Understanding Words Based on Place Names

The origin of a word is the source from which the word came into our language. Many English words are based on the names of cities, regions, or even countries. For example, each of the cats below is named after a certain place.

SIAMESE: originally from Siam and Burma

ANGORA: from Ankara, Turkey

MANX: from the Isle of Man

CALICO: from Calicut, India

Copyright © 1984 by Harcourt Brace Jovanovich, Inc. All rights reserved

221

The origins of words tell us interesting stories. Long ago, when sailors were hard to find, men were often kidnapped and dragged on board ship. When they woke up, they were often far out at sea, often on a boat going to Shanghai, China. Today, the word *shanghai* means: (1) to kidnap someone and force this person to serve on board a ship, and (2) to force someone to do something through deceit.

Usually the origin of a word can be found in the dictionary at the end of the entry. Look for the explanation in brackets [. . .]. Here is the dictionary entry for *shanghai*.

> **shang·hai** (shăng-hī′) *v*.: **shanghaied, shanghaiing.** 1. To kidnap someone and force this person to serve on board a ship. 2. To force someone to do something through deceit. [After Shanghai (city), based on the former practice of kidnapping people to sail on board ships destined for Shanghai.]

Exercise 1. Each word below is named after a specific place. Look up each word in your dictionary. Then use your dictionary to find out the country in which each place is located. Write the name of the country on the blank provided.

		Place	Country
a.	Airedale	Airedale, a valley in Yorkshire	*England*
b.	limousine	Limousin	*France*
c.	damask	Damascus	*Syria*
d.	canopy	Canopus	*Egypt*
e.	cheddar	Cheddar, a village in Somerset	*England*

Exercise 2. Below is a list of English words. Each is based on the name of a specific place. Look up each word in your dictionary. Write the name of the specific place on which the word is based in the blanks provided.

		Meaning	Place
a.	afghan	A colorful knitted or crocheted blanket. The word is based on the name of the country where these blankets were first made.	*Afghanistan*
b.	canary	A yellow songbird. The word is based on the name of one of the group of islands to which these birds are native.	*Canary Islands*
c.	gauze	A thin see-through fabric that is often used for curtains or as a surgical dressing. It is probably based on the name of the city near the Mediterranean Sea where it was first made.	*Gaza*

	Meaning	Place
d. palace	The place where a royal person lives. In ancient Rome, the palaces of the emperors were built on a certain hill. The word *palace* is based on the name of this hill.	*Palatine Hill*
e. bedlam	A noisy and confusing situation. The word is based on the name of a hospital that at one time served the mentally ill.	*Hospital of St. Mary of Bethlehem*

Exercise 3. For each word below, write a sentence using it.

a. afghan: *Students' sentences will vary.*

b. canary: *Students' sentences will vary.*

c. gauze: *Students' sentences will vary.*

d. palace: *Students' sentences will vary.*

e. bedlam: *Students' sentences will vary.*

Lesson 2

Understanding Words Based on People

The origin of a word is the source from which the word came into our language. A great many English words come from the names of people. For example, the songbird called the *Baltimore oriole* is named after Lord Baltimore, the founder of Maryland. The coat of the male Baltimore oriole is orange and black. These were the colors of Lord Baltimore's coat of arms.

Samuel A. Maverick was a Texas cattleman who lived from 1803 to 1870. Unlike other cattlemen, he refused to brand his cattle. His name, *maverick*, is used to describe any unbranded range calves. Today we also use the word *maverick* to describe anyone who refuses to conform to the group.

You can find the origins of words in the dictionary. Look for the explanation within brackets. For example, people think that the word *husky* is based on the name of the whole group of people who use these dogs, the Eskimos. Here is the information you would find in the dictionary.

[Probably a shortened form of *Eskimo*.]

Exercise. Each word below is based on the name of a person or a group of people. Look up each word in your dictionary and write the name of the person or the group in the blank at the right.

a. guillotine — During the French Revolution, a French doctor invented a machine to behead people. — *Joseph Ignace Guillotine*

b. silhouette — This man had a hobby of cutting profile pictures out of black paper. — *Etienne de Silhouette*

c. macabre — This word means "gruesome" or "ghastly." The word is probably based on the name of a group of people who were slaughtered. — *Maccabees*

d. mackintosh — A *mackintosh* is a type of raincoat made of heavy rubberized cloth. The word is based on the name of its inventor. — *Charles Macintosh*

e. Yankee — During the War Between the States, this word was used to describe someone who lived in the northern part of the United States. The word is based on the Dutch name for *John*. What is this name? — *Janke*

f. cardigan — This type of sweater opens down the front. Who is it named after? — *James Thomas Brudenell, Seventh Earl of Cardigan*

g. daguerreotype — A *daguerreotype* is an early photographic process. It is also the photograph created by this process. The word is based on the name of the inventor of the process. — *Louis J. M. Daguerre*

h. dahlia — A *dahlia* is a type of flower. Its name is based on the name of a Swedish botanist. — *Anders Dahl*

i. bloomers — *Bloomers* are a type of loose-fitting pants that are gathered around the ankles. The word is based on the name of a woman who fought to obtain the right to vote for women. — *Amelia Bloomer*

j. groggy — This word means "unsteady" or "dazed." It is based on the nickname, Old Grog, of an admiral who ordered that his sailors be served watered-down rum. — *Edward Vernon*

Name _____

Lesson 3

Understanding That Words Have Changed in Meaning

Over the years, the meaning of a word may change or grow. For example, look at the word *hobby*. Originally the word meant "a small horse." Then the word came to mean "a hobbyhorse," like the kind children ride with a toy horse's head attached to a long pole. Today the word also means "an activity you do in your spare time for pleasure."

The word *comfort* originally meant "to strengthen" or "to make strong." For example, think about this meaning in the famous words from the Bible, "Thy rod and Thy staff they *comfort* me." Today the word means "to console" or "to relieve pain."

Exercise 1. Read the selection below from *Listening to America* by Stuart Berg Flexner. Then answer the questions that follow it.

Colonists were calling city blocks laid out on the grid plan *squares* by the 1760s (the term is often associated with Philadelphia but did not originate there). By 1832 men used *square* approvingly to refer to the natural, even gait of a good horse in such expressions as a *square-gaited* horse or a *square trotter*. By 1836 *square* meant full or complete, as a *square meal*, though people didn't talk about *three squares a day* until 1882. By the 1850s *to square* meant to put a matter straight and later to pay a debt.

As early as 1804, however, *square* had come to mean fair, honest, as in *square fight*, with *square talk* coming in 1860, *square deal* appearing as a card player's term in the 1880s, and *square shooter* in 1920. However, it was Theodore Roosevelt who popularized the term *square deal* in its general sense. He used it against business trusts soon after he succeeded the assassinated President McKinley in 1901, then made a *Square Deal* his slogan during his successful 1904 Presidential campaign. His use of the term made it the forerunner of Franklin D. Roosevelt's 1933-37 *New Deal* and Truman's 1949-52 *Fair Deal*.

Questions
a. What does *square* mean in the expression "the village square"?   *block*

b. What does *square* mean in the expression "a square-gaited horse"?   *natural, even*

c. What does *square* mean in the expression "a square meal"?   *full, complete*

d. What does *square* mean in the expression "to square with someone"?

to put matters straight; to settle a debt

e. What does *square* mean in the expression "a square fight"?

fair, honest

Exercise 2. Read the selection below from *Listening to America* by Stuart Berg Flexner. Then answer the questions that follow it.

Colonists ate their big hot meal of the day, actually served lukewarm in the style of the times, between noon and 2 or 3 P.M. This meal was called *dinner* (a 13th-century English word, via French *diner*, from Latin *dis-*, away + *jejunus*, fast) and the hour at which it was eaten was called *dinner time* (a 14th-century English term). On eastern farms and southern plantations family and fieldhands might be summoned to dinner by a large *dinner bell* (1809) or *dinner horn* (1836), and later, on western ranches, the hands might be summoned by either a *dinner horn* or a *dinner gong* (1900).

Until the late 1820s and early 1830s the last meal of the day was always called *supper* (also a 13th-century English word, via the French, and related to *soup* and *sip*). This supper was much humbler than dinner and originally was a farm laborers' meal of bread dunked in soup or milk.

Lunch and *luncheon* both originally meant a hunk or thick piece of something in the 16th century (perhaps from Spanish *lenja*, slice, hunk), but in the 17th century, *luncheon* came to mean only a slice or hunk of something to eat as a midmorning snack. Americans began to talk of eating *luncheon* (soon shortened back to *lunch*) as the midday meal in the 1820s and 30s, when the increasing number of city workers began to find it necessary to eat a quick, cheap midday meal at or near work rather than going home for a large dinner or buying one in an expensive restaurant. Of course, some workers managed to eat a hot dinner at work by taking one along in a *dinner pail* (1856) or *dinner bucket* (1901), which always held hot dinners (cold lunches were carried in *lunch pails*, which became the *lunch box* of the late 1850s). Thus, during the six-day work week the big hot midday dinner gave way to the quicker lunch, but Americans continued to eat a big midday dinner on the one day a week they could, calling it *Sunday dinner*. However, the quick workingman's lunch of the 1820s and 30s put off the main meal or "dinner" of most days until suppertime—and it could now be called either *supper* or *dinner*, with working-class families being more apt to call it *supper*. In fact, if you're like most American families, you eat *breakfast*, *lunch*, and *supper*, but when guests come or you have something extra fancy, and use the best silverware, etc., you call that "supper" *dinner*.

226

Copyright © 1984 by Harcourt Brace Jovanovich, Inc. All rights reserved

Name _____

Questions

a. In Colonial times was dinner a *hot, lukewarm,* or *cold* meal?
   Dinner was a lukewarm meal.

b. In Colonial times when was dinner served?
   It was served between noon and 2 or 3 P.M.

c. Before the 1830s what was the last meal of the day called?
   It was called supper.

d. Originally what did supper consist of for farm laborers?
   Originally it consisted of bread dunked in soup or milk.

e. Originally luncheon consisted of what?
   Originally luncheon consisted of a hunk or thick piece of something.

f. What did *luncheon* come to mean in the seventeenth century?
   It came to mean a slice or hunk of something to eat as a midmorning snack.

g. When did Americans start talking about *luncheon* as the midday meal?
   Americans started doing this in the 1820s and 1830s.

h. In the mid-1800s, in what would a person carry a hot dinner to work?
   A person would carry a hot dinner to work in a dinner pail.

i. What would a worker carry in a lunch box?
   A worker would carry a cold lunch in a lunch box.

j. Today what do Americans commonly call the last meal of the day when it isn't extra fancy?
   They call it supper.

Lesson 4

Understanding Words from the American Indians

Many words we use today came into English from the languages of the American Indians. Settlers arriving in this country long ago learned the American Indian words for many of the animals and other natural features of the country. We still use many of these words, although the spellings and pronunciations may have changed somewhat.

A single American Indian word often carried as much meaning as a whole sentence. For example, look at the word *caribou*. This word comes from the Micmac word *khalibu*, which means "that which paws the snow." *Raccoon* comes from the Algonquin word *arahkunen*, which means "that which scratches with his hands."

Exercise. Look up each word below in your dictionary. Then tell the American Indian language the word comes from.

a. moose — *Algonquin*
b. chipmunk — *Algonquin*
c. tepee — *Dakota*
d. toboggan — *Micmac*
e. canoe — *Cariban*

f. skunk — *Algonquin*
g. hogan — *Navaho*
h. wigwam — *Algonquin*
i. sequoia — *Cherokee*
j. woodchuck — *Algonquin*

Lesson 5

Understanding Words from Foreign Languages

English words have come from nearly every language on earth. For example, some people eat *yogurt* with their lunch. Do you know what language this word comes from? It comes from Turkish. Some people eat sandwiches made from bagels. Do you know what language *bagel* comes from? It comes from Old High German by way of Yiddish. In other words, it came into English from Yiddish.

You can find information about the origin of a word in your dictionary. Let's look at the information a dictionary would give you about the word *bagel*.

> [Yiddish *beygel*, fr. Middle High German *bouc*, ring, fr. Old High German *boug*.]

The first language *bagel* comes from is Old High German. Then the word entered Middle High German, where it was spelled *bouc* and meant "ring." Next the word entered Yiddish, or became a Yiddish word. Finally the word entered English.

Some dictionaries use abbreviations to indicate foreign languages. Some of these abbreviations are:

ME	(Middle English)
OE	(Old English)
G	(German)
L	(Latin)
Gk	(Greek)
F	(French)
Sp	(Spanish)

Exercise 1. Look up each word below. Write the name of the language from which the word came into English.

		Original Meaning	Language
a.	aardvark	earth pig	*Afrikaans*
b.	poodle	splashing dog	*German*
c.	dodo	stupid	*Portuguese*
d.	bronco	rough, wild	*Mexican Spanish*
e.	orangutan	man of the forest	*Malay*
f.	porcupine	spiny pig	*Middle English*
g.	alligator	lizard	*Spanish*
h.	mustang	stray	*Mexican Spanish*
i.	piranha	toothed fish	*Portuguese*
j.	squirrel	shadow tail	*Middle English*

Exercise 2. Read the story below, "The First Light" by Susan Goldsmith. Pay special attention to the **boldface** words. Then follow the directions at the end of the story.

When I realized I was going to be late getting home that first night of **Chanukah,** I got scared. Grandpa would be **furious** and Mom would take his side. It wasn't really my fault I was late—all the kids were at the Rec Center. We were playing ping pong, dancing, just fooling around. I lost track of time. And anyway, I didn't want to be the only one who had to leave. Now, as I raced along the sidewalk, I knew I'd be in trouble.

Sure enough, when I reached the house, the **menorah** with two candles flickering, the *shamos* and the first light, stood in the big bay window. So I missed Grandpa's candle-lighting ceremony. Big deal. A bunch of words in a language I don't understand to commemorate something that happened 5000 years ago.

Grandpa was sitting in the big overstuffed chair in the living room. He looked at me sadly as I came in. I leaned over and kissed his dry cheek. "Hi, Gramps. Happy Chanukah. I'm sorry . . ."

"So," he said, fixing me with a baleful stare. "So you do remember it's Chanukah."

"I'm sorry but I just didn't realize . . ."

Suddenly he stood up. He wasn't much taller than I but his anger made him seem huge. "That, my granddaughter, is true.

You don't realize." He turned and **shuffled** into the kitchen, an old man in a shapeless blue sweater. Just then, my mother came downstairs.

"I see you finally made it home, Rebecca." As soon as she called me Rebecca instead of Becky I knew she was as angry as Grandpa.

"Oh, Mom, so I missed his lighting a candle. There are seven more nights. I just don't understand . . ."

Mom stopped at the bottom step. "Have you ever tried?" she asked.

"Has he? He acts like some kind of king around here. He doesn't care if I have any friends, if I have any fun, just as long as I go along with what he preaches. His thousand-year-old miracles. What does any of that have to do with me or my life?" I started to brush past her up the stairs, tears of anger and self-pity stinging my eyes, when a thundering voice from behind me stopped me in my tracks.

"You are a Jew!"

I turned to see my grandfather standing across the room from where I stood with my mother.

"Poppa," she said, making a move toward him.

"No," he said, brushing a hand over his eyes. Mom stopped, one hand still reaching toward him. "You are a Jew," he repeated but softly this time.

"I know that, Grandpa, and I know about tradition and **heritage** and all that." I was trying hard not to cry. "What terrible thing did I do? I missed the first candle."

"Rivka," Grandpa said, using my Jewish name, "come. Sit here. Let us talk, you and I, about tradition and heritage and all that. Lillian," he said to my mother, "you may stay, too."

I looked at my mother. She gave me a little shove toward Grandpa. Resigned, I sat on the couch next to him.

"It is true," he said in his accented English, "that the miracle of Chanukah took place thousands upon thousands of years ago. What has this to do with your life here today, you ask. A fair question. In 1939, I left Poland. I took with me your mother, my eldest child, who was then still a child. But she had learned a little English so she came. We boarded a ship and sailed, in discomfort, for thirteen days to land in America. We were to work here to bring over my wife, my son. We arrived in New York on August 23. One week later, Poland fell before the German **onslaught.** My wife, my son, everyone we left behind was lost to us forever."

"Grandpa, I know all that . . ."

"You know? You know what you read in your books; what you see in your movies. You know that you sit and talk each night about what college you want to go to; what career you want for yourself. It is easy. And you know your tradition. That, too, is easy . . ."

"But Grandpa . . ."

"Please let me finish. Yes, you have heard the story. But you have not heard the feelings. We left Poland, your mother, me, millions like us, because we were poor, yes. Because America offered promise, yes. But also because we were Jews. As Jews, we could not discuss to what college we would go. As Jews, we could not go to any. Do you remember, Lillian, the Chanukah that your grandfather was beaten as he returned from the Temple?"

I looked at my mother, who nodded silently. Her hands lay **twisted** in her lap; tears ran slowly down her cheeks. I looked back at my grandfather.

"My own father," he said, "was walking home from the Temple thinking of the Chanukah *latkes* my mother would be cooking. Suddenly he was set upon by some young boys who pulled at his beard and taunted him. They tore his prayer book to bits. When he got home, my mother cried. 'Don't cry,' he said to her that night. He looked to where I sat holding your mother, a small frightened child of six or seven. 'Remember, my son,' he said to me, 'even should you want to forget you are a Jew, the world will remember for you.' We lit candles that year, and many other years, in **secret.** Which was worse—the fear under which we lived there? Or the fear with which we came here to a foreign land, poor, alone, ignorant of the customs, the language? But here we didn't have to live in secret."

Grandpa leaned back and closed his eyes. I didn't know if he was finished or not but I was unable to move. He opened his eyes slowly. "You think I don't care if you have friends. This is not true. But friends who cause you to forget your duties and responsibilities, these are not friends. Friends who make you ashamed of your heritage, these are not friends. There is a tradition in Judaism, yes. But there is also responsibility. I will not tell you that you must carry the burden for thousands of years of persecution. Nor must you believe wholeheartedly in a miracle thousands of years old. We light the Chanukah candles now for a miracle much newer, more relevant, as your generation says. We are here. We are together. We are Jews who are allowed to live in freedom. Who may place our menorah proudly in the window for all to see. As I walked from the Temple tonight, I passed a **priest.** 'Merry Christmas, Father,' I said to him. 'Happy Chanukah,' he said to me. This, Rebecca, is the modern day miracle for which we light the candles."

"Grandpa," I managed to say before the lump in my throat closed off my voice completely. He simply nodded at me and closed his eyes.

That was last year. Grandpa is sick now and it's doubtful that he'll live much past the beginning of the year. Last night was the first night of Chanukah. Mom and I brought the menorah up to Grandpa's room so he could light the candle. With trembling fingers, he lit the *shamos* and was about to light the first candle from it. But instead he looked at me and said in a voice so low I had to lean close to hear him. "Rivka, last year you missed the first night candle. This year, you light it." I put my hand over his and together we lit the first candle. Then I recited with Grandpa the **prayer** he had taught me.

Directions. Look up each word below in your dictionary. In the blank provided, write the language from which the word originally came.

a. Chanukah   *Hebrew*   f. onslaught   *Middle Dutch*
b. furious   *Latin*   g. twist   *Old English*
c. menorah   *Hebrew*   h. secret   *Latin*
d. shuffle   *Low German*   i. priest   *Greek*
e. heritage   *Latin*   j. prayer   *Latin*

Lesson 6
Practice

Read the selection below. Then complete the exercises that follow.

**from *Words from the Myths*
Isaac Asimov**

The Greeks did not do a great deal in their myths as far as the creation of man was concerned. The nearest thing to such an account involves the Titan, *Prometheus* (pruh-mee'thyoos). His name comes from Greek words meaning "forethought," and he had a brother, *Epimetheus* (ep'i-mee'thyoos), whose name meant "hindthought." In other words, Prometheus was wise, seeing the results of actions in advance, while Epimetheus was foolish, understanding results only after they had come about.

Both were the sons of the Titan Iapetus, and therefore brothers of Atlas. However, when the Titans and Olympians were at war, with Atlas leading the Titans, Prometheus, foreseeing that the Olympians would win, abandoned the Titans and persuaded Epimetheus to do likewise. As a result these two brothers were spared the punishment that fell on the Titans generally.

After the war with the Titans was over, men were created by Prometheus at the order of Zeus. Or, as some versions have it, ordinary mortal human beings were the descendants of Prometheus and Epimetheus.

In either case, Zeus, who did not entirely trust Prometheus, disliked men, while Prometheus, on his part, did his best to help men against the Olympians. When Zeus tried to destroy mankind with a huge flood, Prometheus managed to warn one man, *Deucalion* (dyoo-kay'lee-on), supposedly the son of Prometheus, according to some of the mythmakers. Deucalion built a ship in which he and his wife, *Pyrrha* (pir'uh), supposedly a daughter of Epimetheus, escaped.

As mankind struggled back from that catastrophe, they were neglected by the Olympians and allowed to live lives of misery and savagery. Prometheus took pity on the men he had created, or fathered, and taught them various arts and sciences that might help them to an easier life. To top things off, he stole fire from the sun and taught mankind how to use it. (This may indicate that he was the pre-Greek god of fire, replaced by Hephaestus after the Greek invasion.)

All this was in defiance of Zeus, so that any act which is very daring and defiant, or very original and creative, is called "promethean."

In revenge, Zeus created a beautiful woman to whom all the gods gave gifts of beauty, grace, wit, melody and so on. She was called *Pandora* (pan-daw'ruh) from Greek words meaning "all-gifted." She was then given to Epimetheus for a wife. Because of her beauty, Epimetheus accepted her although Prometheus had warned him against taking any gift from Zeus.

Along with Pandora, Epimetheus received a box which Pandora was forbidden to open. However, at her first opportunity, she opened the box to see what was in it and out flew the spirits of old age, death, famine, sickness, grief, and all the other ills that plague human beings. Only hope was left at the bottom of the box and, when finally let out, was all that kept human beings alive under the weight of their misery.

Thus, anything which is harmless when undisturbed, but which lets loose many troubles when interfered with, is called a "Pandora's box."

Not satisfied with having his revenge on humanity, Zeus also punished Prometheus directly. He chained him to a rock in the Caucasus Mountains which, to the ancient Greeks, represented the eastern end of the world. There he was continually tortured by an eagle.

The story of Pandora is actually a moral tale, a kind of fable intended to teach men how to behave. For instance, Epimetheus is a warning against careless action taken without due consideration of possible consequences. Pandora herself is a warning against foolish curiosity.

Many mythical warnings were against the kind of pride which made people consider themselves above the law. Such pride led to insolent behavior and a disregard of the rights of others. In the Greek myths, it usually involved defying the gods—the sort of pride the Greeks called "hubris."

When that happened, the gods saw to it that the proud individual was dealt with by *Nemesis*, the goddess of retribution. The name comes from Greek words meaning to "distribute." In other words, Nemesis sees to it that matters are distributed evenly. If a person has so much good fortune that he becomes boastful, proud and insolent, she sees to it that he has a corresponding amount of bad fortune to even things out.

Since most of the Greek myths involve matters evened out by bad fortune, rather than by good fortune, "nemesis" has come to mean, in our language, an unavoidable doom.

Pride is still considered the most serious of the seven deadly sins. It was through pride that Lucifer fell. We still have this old Greek feeling about pride when we speak of "the jealous gods" who won't allow anyone to be too lucky. That is why we say that "pride goeth before a fall" and why we knock wood when we talk about how fortunate we are, or how well off. That is supposed to keep off Nemesis.

An example of such a pride-goeth-before-a-fall myth is the story of *Arachne* (uh-rak'ne). She was a girl of the kingdom of Lydia (in western Asia Minor) who was very skilled at weaving. She was so proud of her skill that she boasted that even Athena, the goddess of the practical arts, including that of weaving, could do no better, and challenged Athena to a contest. (There was hubris.)

Athena accepted the challenge and both wove tapestries. Athena wove into hers all sorts of glorious stories about the gods while Arachne wove into hers unflattering stories about them. Arachne's work was excellent but Athena's was perfect. In anger at Arachne's subject matter, Athena tore Arachne's weaving to shreds and Arachne, struck with terror, hanged herself. (There was nemesis.)

Athena, who was not a cruel goddess, didn't want things to go that far, so she loosened the rope and changed Arachne into a spider. As a spider, Arachne continued spinning threads and weaving beautiful webs, and she also continues to hang from a strand of gossamer as though still trying to hang herself. Of course "arachne" is the Greek word for "spider" and the idea of the myth surely came from watching spiders at work. But it does teach a moral: avoid hubris.

In zoology, the name of the girl lives on, since spiders and their relatives are put in the class "Arachnida."

Furthermore, anything as filmy and delicate as a spider's web is said to be "arachnoid." For instance, the brain and spinal cord are enclosed by a double membrane for protection. In between the two parts of the double membrane is a third membrane which is very thin and filmy. This is called the "arachnoid membrane."

Another example of this sort of myth is that of *Phaëthon* (fay'uh-thon), the mortal son of Helios. He was so proud of being the son of the sun god, that he felt he could drive the sun (which was pictured as a gleaming chariot drawn by wild, gleaming horses) across the sky. He tricked his father into promising to let him do so. (That was hubris.)

Phaëthon drove the sun but found he could not control the horses, which went out of their course and swooped too near the earth. The Greeks supposed the burning sands of the Sahara showed where the swooping sun chariot had scorched the earth and felt that the dark color of the African natives was also the result of it. To save the earth from destruction, Zeus was forced to kill Phaëthon with a thunderbolt. (That was nemesis.)

The word "phaeton" (usually without the "h" and pronounced "fay'uh-ten") can be applied to any reckless driver. The word has also applied to a carriage or automobile without top or sides. These were light vehicles, you see, that could be driven more quickly than ordinary heavier ones. Both uses are out of date, now.

One case of hubris and nemesis struck father and daughter separately. It begins with *Tantalus*, a mortal son of Zeus. He was a great favorite of his father and the other gods. He was even allowed to join the banquets of the gods and eat *ambrosia* (am-broe'zhee-a) and drink *nectar* (nek'ter). This is the food of the gods. "Ambrosia" comes from a Greek word meaning "immortal" and "nectar" from one meaning "death-defeating." As a result of such food, the veins of gods are filled with *ichor* (eye'kor) instead of blood, so that the gods are immortal.

Nowadays, in more practical times, nectar and ambrosia are used to describe any delightful food. Nectar, particularly, can refer to any sweet liquid. The sugary fluid in flowers, used by bees to make honey, is called nectar, for instance. A type of smooth-skinned peach has been named "nectarine" for its sweet taste.

To return to Tantalus, however—He felt so puffed up at the gods' friendship that he acted as though his food and drink were his in actual fact and took some back to earth with him to give to his friends. Furthermore, he boasted about this.

Nemesis followed. He was killed by Zeus and condemned to a special torture in Tartarus, one which involved food and drink. He was forced to stand forever in water up to his neck. Every time he bent to drink, however, the water sank downward and swirled away. When he stood up, the water rose to his neck again. Meanwhile, delicious fruit dangled near his face, but when he reached out for it, the wind blew it out of his reach. Thus, with food and drink continually near, he suffered eternal hunger and thirst.

For this reason, we have the word "tantalize" referring to any action which is designed to give someone false hope which is snatched away just as it seems on the point of coming true. In the same way, a glass cabinet in which bottles of wine may be locked away is called a "tantalus" because the wine can be seen but, without the key, cannot be touched.

In 1814, the tantalized Tantalus entered the list of elements. Twelve years earlier, a Swedish chemist named Anders Gustaf Eckeberg discovered a new metal. Strong acids did not affect it. It could stand in strong acid without "drinking" it; that is, without reacting with it and using it up. In 1814, therefore, the

Swedish chemist Berzelius decided that this was like Tantalus standing in water but not drinking. He named the element "tantalum" and that is now its name.

Niobe (nie'o-bee) was the daughter of Tantalus, but she did not learn humility from his fate. She had fourteen children, seven sons and seven daughters, and was so proud of their good looks and accomplishments that she felt no other mother could be as lucky. Even Leto, she boasted, only had one daughter and one son.

Of course these children were Apollo and Artemis and, on hearing their mother sneered at, they took revenge. Apollo killed the seven sons with his arrows and Artemis killed the seven daughters with hers.

Niobe, in whose arms the last daughter died, wept ceaselessly for her lost children and eventually, out of pity, the gods turned her into a stone out of which a spring of water continued to run.

Niobe, like her father, Tantalus, also entered the list of chemical elements. In 1801, an English chemist, Charles Hatchett, thought he had located a new element in a rock that had first been found in Connecticut. He named the new element "columbium" after Columbia, a poetic name for the United States.

However, some argument arose as to whether columbium wasn't actually identical with tantalum, which was discovered at about the same time. It wasn't until 1846 that a German chemist, Heinrich Rose, showed that columbium was similar to tantalum but not identical. For the sake of its similarity, however, he suggested that it be named after a close relative of Tantalus; to wit, after his daughter, Niobe. For a long time, American chemists called the element columbium, while the European chemists called it "niobium." A few years ago, the American chemists gave in. The official name everywhere is now niobium.

The moral of "beware hubris" was not the only one the Greeks could draw. There is a well-known myth which has a moral of an entirely different sort. This involves Midas, the son of Gordius. Gordius was the first king of Phrygia (a kingdom in Asia Minor).

Gordius was greeted as king when he rode into the capital city in an ox-cart. It seems an oracle had advised the citizens to accept the next man to enter the city on such a vehicle.

Gordius's first act was to tie the yoke of the ox-cart with the reins in a very complicated knot, to show that he would never have to use that ox-cart again. He announced that anyone who untied that knot would conquer all Asia, and then went on to be king in the city, now renamed "Gordium." Though many tried to untie the knot, none ever succeeded. From that, we still have our phrase "a Gordian knot" to represent a very tangled and insoluble problem.

The legend was mythical but the knot actually existed. At least when Alexander the Great passed through Phrygia in 333

B.C. he was shown the Gordian knot. He made no attempt to untie it. Instead, he drew his sword and calmly cut through it, then went on to conquer all those parts of Asia he could reach with his armies, without once being defeated. From this comes the phrase "to cut the Gordian knot," meaning to solve a complicated problem by direct and unexpected action.

But it was *Midas*, the son of Gordius, whose actions pointed a particular moral. He grew quite wealthy but had his mind entirely fixed on the desire to grow still more wealthy. Because of a favor Midas had done for Dionysus, that god offered Midas a free wish for anything he wanted. At once Midas wished that everything he touched should turn to gold.

We still speak of this as the "Midas touch" or the "golden touch" and use it to refer to anyone who is particularly successful in business. Everything he touches, so to speak, turns to gold.

However, although most people still admire and envy this ability, the Greeks pointed out the opposite moral. Midas found that his entire palace and all its furnishings turned to gold, as he touched object after object, but that made everything rather monotonous and ugly. Everything he tried to eat and drink turned to gold as soon as he touched it so that he was threatened with starvation. Finally (in a late version of the myth) his daughter ran to him, and turned to gold when he embraced her.

He had to beg Dionysus to withdraw the gift, and Dionysus did. Apparently the moral is one well known to us, whether we believe it or not. It is that "money isn't everything."

The Greeks would not have been human if they weren't interested in romance. It is natural, therefore, that many of their myths should have been what we would call today "love stories." Some of them are very touching and have remained famous for nearly three thousand years.

There is, for instance, the story of *Orpheus* (or'fyoos), the son of Apollo and Calliope, chief of the Muses. With such parents, it is not surprising that Orpheus should be a sweet singer. At his singing, the very rocks would move closer while wild beasts would lie down tamely to hear.

So famous was he in this respect that "Orphean" still means melodiously enchanting. Similarly, various music halls were called "Orpheum" in his honor, and the name passed on to vaudeville theaters and movie houses.

Orpheus married *Eurydice* (yoo-rid'i-see), but after a short period of happiness, Eurydice was bitten by a snake and died. Orpheus was inconsolable and decided to go down to Hades and get her back. Playing his lyre and singing, he went down to the underworld. So enchanted by his playing was Charon that he took him across; and Cerberus bowed his heads and let Orpheus pass. The shades flocked around, remembering sadly their past lives at the sound of the music, and the tortures in Tartarus stopped while the demons paused to listen.

Tears came even to the iron face of Hades at the approach of Orpheus and he gave the sweet singer back his Eurydice, on one condition: that he never look back to see her until he reached the world above.

Back upward traveled Orpheus, still playing his lyre, still singing. And when he was almost out of Hades, when the light of the sun could already be dimly seen, he could bear it no longer. He turned to see if Eurydice was really following. She was, but when he turned, she suddenly drifted away with a sad cry, holding out her arms helplessly.

Orpheus rushed back downward but now no one would listen. Charon barred him from the boat. Cerberus on the other side growled terribly, and Hades, in the distance, shook his head stonily.

Eurydice was lost!

Orpheus was later made the center of a mystery religion. He had after all been in the underworld and returned. His was one of the most famous mysteries, in fact, and "Orphic" still means "mystical."

Another story is that of a mountain nymph, called *Echo* (from a Greek word meaning "sound"). She had offended Hera with her chattering tongue and had been condemned to almost complete silence. She could only repeat the last words anyone said to her.

Echo fell in love with a handsome young man named *Narcissus*, but she could not make her feelings plain because she could only repeat his last words. Narcissus treated her with unfeeling harshness and scorned her. This was a kind of hubris, and nemesis followed. Narcissus saw his own reflection in the water. He had never seen it before and did not know it was himself he saw. He fell in love with the reflection.

Naturally, that did him no good and it was his turn to be rejected. He pined away and died, turning into a flower which is still called the "narcissus" in his honor. And we still call anyone who is extremely conceited "narcissistic."

As for Echo, she pined away, too, until nothing was left of her but her voice, which is still to be heard in the mountains of which she was nymph. Her voice is still called an "echo."

Then there was the case of *Alcyone* (al-sie′o-nee), a woman happily married to *Ceyx* (see′iks). Unfortunately, Ceyx died in a shipwreck and Alcyone, wild with grief, threw herself into the sea when she heard the news.

The gods, in pity, turned her and her dead husband into kingfishers so that their happiness might continue, even if not in human form. The kingfisher is still called "halcyon" in poetry. (The reason for the initial "h" is that Greek words sometimes started with a sound that doesn't occur in Latin or in English. It somewhat resembles an "h" sound, and words that start with it, as *Alcyone* does, may be spelled without an initial "h" or with one, in English, depending on taste. For instance, the kingfishers are referred to by zoologists as the "Alcyonidae" (without the initial "h").

Actually, the halcyon of the Greeks is not a real kingfisher but an imaginary bird who the Greeks believed made her nest on the sea and hatched out her chicks there. This was supposed to be done during the two weeks following December 15. At this time, the gods were supposed to keep the ocean dead calm for the sake of the chicks. For this reason, any time of great peace and security is referred to as "halcyon days."

(One last word; the brightest of the Pleiades is called "Alcyone" but this honors a different Alcyone, and not the wife of Ceyx.)

It would seem that the Greek love stories run to tragedy and so they do. Love stories generally do, for sad stories seem to move people more than happy ones do.

Still, love stories with a "happy ending" are to be found among the myths. I'll mention only one, the most famous one, even though it is not really Greek, but was invented by a Roman named Lucius Apuleius about A.D. 150. It is the story of Cupid and *Psyche* (sie'kee).

Psyche was a princess so beautiful that all men fell in love with her. She was considered even more beautiful than Venus. Venus, growing jealous, sent her son Cupid to use his arrows of love to cause her to fall in love with a beggar and thus punish her; nemesis for hubris, in the usual way. (Notice that it is Venus and Cupid here, not Aphrodite and Eros, for the story is Roman, not Greek.)

Cupid is, in this story, pictured as a young man, instead of the usual child. He flew down on his task and as he was about to shoot Psyche, he accidentally wounded himself on one of his own arrows and fell in love with her himself.

He wooed her at night and married her, but never allowed her to see him (for he didn't want the news to get back to Venus). He even forbade her to make any attempt to see him. Psyche's sisters, jealous of this romantic affair, teased Psyche and told her that her husband was really an ugly monster and that was why she was not allowed to see him. Psyche was sufficiently worried about this to bring a lamp secretly to the bed where Cupid was sleeping. She leaned over to look at him and oil from the lamp dropped on his face and woke him. Sorrowfully, he left her.

The rest of the story concerns the manner in which Psyche wanders through the world, and even down into Hades, going through great troubles and hardships imposed on her by the angry Venus; but searching, always searching, for her Cupid. Eventually, her faithfulness won her the forgiveness of Venus. Psyche was made immortal and joined Cupid forever in heaven.

Now this is more than just a love story. Psyche is the Greek word for "soul" and behind the actual events of the story lay a deeper meaning. (A story with a deeper meaning hidden behind the surface meaning is an "allegory.") The soul (Psyche), originally in heaven where all is love (Cupid), is condemned for a period to wander through the earth, undergoing misery and hardship. Still, if it is faithful and true, the story points out, it will eventually return to heaven and be reunited with love.

The situation is like that of the ugly caterpillar which, after a while, seems to die and be buried in a cocoon like a man in a tomb. But then it breaks out as a beautiful butterfly, just as a man's soul breaks out into a better life. It is with this thought in mind that artists usually picture Psyche with the wings of a butterfly. (The popularity of the Psyche story later led to having fairies drawn in the same way.) There is even a group of moths with the family name of "Psychidae," showing that zoologists are acquainted with the myth, too.

The word "psyche" in its meaning of mind or soul is also part of our language. "Psychology" is the study of the mind and a "psychiatrist" is a doctor who specializes in mental disorders. A person who is supposed to sense things with his mind, rather than with his eyes, ears, or other ordinary senses, is said to be "psychic."

Psyche lives in the heavens literally, too, for the sixteenth asteroid to be discovered was named "Psyche."

Exercise 1. Match each word or phrase below with its modern meaning. Write the numbers for the correct meanings in the blanks at the left.

a. __3__ promethean (1) the kind of pride that makes people boastful and insolent

b. __4__ Pandora's box (2) anything filmy and delicate

c. __1__ hubris (3) any act which is very daring and defiant, or very original and creative

d. __5__ nemesis (4) anything which is harmless when undisturbed but which lets loose many troubles when interfered with

e. __2__ arachnoid (5) an unavoidable doom

Name _____ 241

Exercise 2. Write the modern meaning of each word or phrase below on the blanks provided.

a. phaeton: *a reckless driver*
b. nectar: *any sweet liquid*
c. tantalize: *any action which is designed to give someone false hope but is snatched away just as it seems on the point of coming true*
d. a Gordian knot: *a very tangled and insoluble problem*
e. Midas touch: *the ability to make everything turn out successfully*
f. Orphean: *melodiously enchanting*
g. narcissistic: *extremely conceited*
h. halcyon days: *any time of great peace and security*
i. psychology: *the study of the mind*
j. psychic: *a person who is supposed to sense things with his or her mind*

Exercise 3. In the past, people used terms like men to refer to both men and women. Today, our outlook has changed somewhat, and therefore, so has our language. For each term below, write the word or words we would use today to refer to both men and women.

a. men *people; men and women*
b. mankind *human being; humankind*
c. man's fate *human fate*
d. manned *defended; operated*
e. manhunt *hunt for a person*

Copyright © 1984 by Harcourt Brace Jovanovich, Inc. All rights reserved   241

Name _____

Chapter 10
Figurative Language

What is figurative language? Figurative language is a vivid and colorful way of expressing your thoughts. Figurative language creates a picture in your reader's mind. This picture gets your thought across in a strong and sometimes startling way.

Figurative language is not meant to be taken literally. The words in figurative language take on a new meaning all their own. That's why the comic strip below is funny. When the boy says, "I just can't seem to get moving this morning," he is using figurative language, or a figure of speech. He means that he is having trouble getting started or beginning his day. When Winthrop hears his friend say these words, he takes them literally. Therefore, he shakes his friend to get him moving.

WINTHROP by Dick Cavalli

[Comic strip: Panel 1 - "I JUST CAN'T SEEM TO GET MOVING THIS MORNING." Panel 2 - "HERE...I'LL HELP YOU GET STARTED." Panel 3 - "DON'T YOU KNOW A FIGURE OF SPEECH WHEN YOU HEAR ONE?" © 1982 NFA Inc. TM Reg US Pat & TM Off]

Lesson 1

Identifying Figurative and Literal Language

In literal language, words mean exactly what they say. For example, read the following sentence.

> When he pulled out the plug, all the water went down the drain.

In the sentence above, each word is used with its usual dictionary meaning. The water really did go down the drain, which is a pipe or tube.

Copyright © 1984 by Harcourt Brace Jovanovich, Inc. All rights reserved 243

In figurative language, words do not mean exactly what they say. Figurative language suggests a new meaning for the words in a vivid, or colorful, way. For example, read the next sentences.

Although I worked all summer, I didn't save any money. All my earnings went down the drain.

Here, the words *down the drain* are used figuratively. The earnings didn't really go down a pipe that draws off water. The words are simply a colorful way of saying that the earnings were spent in a wasteful, or careless, manner.

In the cartoon below, Dennis takes his father's comment literally.

DENNIS THE MENACE by Ketcham

"YOU REMEMBER **WHICH** DRAIN ALL THAT MONEY WENT DOWN LAST YEAR?"

Exercise. In the selection below, Rob and his friend Luther, also known as Soup, set out to catch a wild turkey. Read the selection, from *Soup and Me* by Robert Newton Peck. Then follow the directions at the end of it.

Until today, I was thinking as we chased that bird, I never knew that a turkey could run so speedy. It didn't fly. But it sure did cover the ground, in and out of the pines, heading toward the County Road. Sometimes we were fast enough to keep that old turkey in sight, and sometimes not. Once or twice we thought he'd got away. But then we spied him again and gave chase. I was puffing.

"I'm pooped," said Soup. He leaned against the trunk of a sassafras in order to wait for his wind. Another tree was handy, so I hugged it to hold me up.

"I see him," I said.
"Who cares?" said Soup.
"Aren't we going to catch him?"
"Not according to him," said Soup. "I don't guess that old turk wants to be caught."
"You give up awful easy," I said.
"Look," said Soup, "it ain't that we give up easy. That there turkey just gives up awful hard."
"We can corner him."
"Fine," said Soup, "if we had a corner."
"Come on," I said.
"There he goes!" Soup pointed.

There was suddenly a small stone inside my right shoe, but not big enough of a tribulation to stop for. Not when that old turk was so much in our vicinity. It would sure be a crying shame to wash out now, just when we were gaining on that bird.

Ahead was a culvert.

This I knew, because I'd once been to Ally Tidwell's house (which was nearby) and the two of us had caught a frog at the mouth of one end. The culvert was just a big old tube that went under the County Road like a tunnel, from one ditch to the other. Veering over to the shoulder of the road as I ran, I caught a look at the turkey, who just ducked into one end of the culvert. Soup and I both got the flash of an idea at the same time.

"I'll take this side," I yelled.
Soup said, "And I'll head him off on the other end."
He was trapped!

Jumping clear of the road, I ducked down to look into the culvert and there was that turkey, halfway through the tunnel. A second later I saw the happy face of Luther Vinson. Between us was the turkey, looking first at me and then at Soup. He knew he was in a pickle. Back when Ally Tidwell and I caught the frog, it was May or early-on June, and there had been a few inches of water flowing under the dirt road from one side to the opposite. But now it was November; the water was gone. The culvert was bone dry from one end all the way through to the other.

"We got him," said Soup. His voice came through the culvert real funny, sort of like he was down in the bottom of a well. I could see him as he was at a squat in the circle of light.

"Sure have," I said to Soup.

The turkey ran down toward where Soup was waiting. Soup made a noise and clapped his hands, sending that big white bird back toward me. He sure was big. Almost filled up the culvert like a cork. He looked to be near big as a pony. Coming close up to me, I was afraid he was fixing to take a peck at my face.

Copyright © 1984 by Harcourt Brace Jovanovich, Inc. All rights reserved

245

"Yah!" I said. He turned and showed me the big white puff of his rump and his yellow feet. "Soup, when he comes your way, grab him."

"No thanks."

"Whaddaya mean, no thanks?" I said.

"I don't want to. You do it. Or are you scared?" asked Soup.

"Well, not really. I just never took much to turkeys."

"Me neither," said Soup, "and this turkey looks like he don't cotton too much for me."

The old turkey let out a *gobble, gobble,* and I've got to admit I jumped, hitting my head a crack on the rim of the culvert. It sure did smart. We continued to talk back and forth in our funny hollow voices that bounced around inside the culvert.

"What'll we do?" I said.

"One of us," said Soup, "will have to volunteer."

"What's *volunteer* mean? Is it like a fireman?"

"Sort of. It's when you volunteer for a dangerous mission, like the Green Hornet."

"Oh," I said.

"Rob?"

"Yeah."

"Do you want to volunteer?"

"Not a whole lot. You?"

"Nope," said Soup. "But I just got another idea."

"Yeah? Like what?"

"We'll use strategy."

"Is it something like volunteer?"

"In a way."

"What's your plan?" I said.

"Someone has to crawl into the culvert and grab the turkey."

"You thought of it first."

"So I get to pick the volunteer. My job is to create a diversion."

Only one volunteer on Soup's roster possessed the skill, the courage, not to mention the stupidity, to enter a culvert and have it out with a turkey that was becoming increasingly annoyed, running from Soup to me to Soup to me. There was a look in his eye that promised hostility by the carload, hatred by the hatful, discomfort by the lump. This turkey was not chicken. This bird was as big as a goat. And yet all the volunteer had to do was crawl inside the culvert, crawl right up to the turkey, and grab it. Simple. A fool could do it. Only a fool would try.

As I crawled inside the culvert on my hands and knees, I kept asking myself why *I* was doing this, and also why Soup was not. I was hoping Soup would start creating a diversion, whatever that was, but all he did was bang on the iron of the culvert's rim with a stick and yell. He made a racket. The turkey turned his back to Soup, faced me, and stood his ground with yellow feet. Nothing else about him looked very yellow. I bet this old guy weighed close to thirty pounds.

"Here goes," I said.

Well, it all proves at least one thing. People (or turkeys) can look ferocious; but when the chips are down, lots of times they're just as afraid as you are. Pretending I was a dog, I gave a lunge at the turkey as well as a loud and healthy *woof*. I've always been able to bark pretty well. My bark is much worse than my bite, even outdoors. But inside a dark culvert, my bark is sensational. It nearly ruptured my own eardrums. Would it scare a thirty pound turkey? As a matter of record, yes.

So much so that even Soup was caught totally unprepared. The turkey, upon viewing my rush and hearing my bark, turned tail to me and headed in the other direction. Right smack into Soup's arms!

"Grab him, Soup!"

Standing up to run, my head went *thud* into the roof of the culvert and half the canaries of the universe tweeted and twirped, and sang out little silver and gold stars, comets, and planets in the darkness. Stumbling forward, I fell on the turkey. Soup was on the bottom of the hogpile for once in his lucky life. I heard him grunt, either Soup or the turkey. That bird could kick like a mad mule. If he had on horseshoes, that old turkey couldn't have bucked any harder.

"Hold him, Soup. Hold him!"

I had a good purchase on the turkey's neck with both hands. I thought it was his neck until I discovered it was really Soup's. No wonder Soup was so quiet. I was half choking him to death. So I let loose and grabbed another neck, this one being a bit more feathery.

"We got him!" said Soup.

"Hang on," I said. "Grab his other leg."

Just in case you get asked, it sure is fun to chase a turkey. But to tell you the truth, it really isn't a whole lot of fun to catch it. That old bird could kick, scratch, and peck off a bulldog. Two bulldogs, as that was how determined Soup and I were to hang on.

"We really got him, Rob."

"Yeah, and he's got us," I croaked, just as a wing cracked across the bridge of my nose. A nose is sort of a sensitive place, especially *my* nose; and when a nose gets whacked by a turkey wing, it sure gets your attention. I was crying. Not a good old boo-hoo kind of a cry, but my eyes sure did fill up with tears. But then I forgot about my nose and started to think a great deal about my stomach, as that was where the turkey was kicking me.

"I got his leg," yelled out Soup.

"No! You got my finger. Let go!"

My mouth was full of feathers and not a single one tasted too good. But if that turkey had a sorry taste, it smelled even worse.

Directions. Write *L* next to each item in which all the words are used with their literal meaning. Write *F* next to each item in which the words are used with a figurative meaning.

a. "He leaned against the trunk of a sassafras in order to wait for his wind."   **F**

b. "Soup and I both got the flash of an idea at the same time."   **F**

c. "But now it was November; the water was gone."   **L**

d. "The culvert was bone dry from one end all the way through to the other."   **F**

e. "There was a look in his eye that promised hostility by the carload, hatred by the hatful, discomfort by the lump."   **F**

f. "As I crawled inside the culvert on my hands and knees, I kept asking myself why *I* was doing this, and also why Soup was not."   **L**

g. "People (or turkeys) can look ferocious; but when the chips are down, lots of times they're just as afraid as you are."   **F**

h. "Standing up to run, my head went *thud* into the roof of the culvert and half the canaries of the universe tweeted and twirped, and sang out little silver and gold stars, comets, and planets in the darkness."   **F**

i. "Soup was on the bottom of the hogpile for once in his lucky life."   **F**

j. "But then I forgot about my nose and started to think a great deal about my stomach, as that was where the turkey was kicking me."   **L**

Lesson 2

Understanding Figurative Expressions

Figurative expressions contain words and phrases used without their usual, or dictionary, meanings. The words in figurative expressions work together to form a new meaning all their own. For example, read the sentence below.

    Eddie walks around with his head in the clouds.

This sentence means that Eddie is always daydreaming and is impractical.

248   Copyright © 1984 by Harcourt Brace Jovanovich, Inc. All rights reserved

Now look at the comic strip below. When Hagar told Lucky Eddie to "keep on his toes," he meant, "Keep alert!" or "Be ready to act quickly."

HAGAR THE HORRIBLE by Dik Browne

Exercise. In the story below, "The Day It Rained Cats and Dogs" by Linda Allen, Mrs. Jenkins has a curious talent. When she says something, her words have an odd way of coming true. Read the story. Then answer the questions that follow it.

It was a curious thing about Mrs. Jenkins, but every once in a while her words had a strange way of coming true.

"Oh, *blow!*" she said to Mr. Jenkins one day after she had stumbled over something in the road. Immediately the wind began to blow so hard that they had to cling to a tree until it stopped.

"My dear," said Mr. Jenkins, straightening his clothes, "you really will have to be careful what you say when these moods come over you. Let's go home, and I will make you a nice cup of tea."

As Mrs. Jenkins sipped her tea, Mr. Jenkins said, "You just sit here quietly, and I'll do the housework today."

"Thank you," said Mrs. Jenkins gratefully. "I'll do as you say, although it does seem a shame to leave all that work to you. The kitchen is quite full of dirty pots and pans."

No sooner had she spoken than they heard a great clatter in the kitchen. When Mr. Jenkins opened the door, he found that he could scarcely get into the room for all the pots and pans. They were piled up on the table and on the shelves, in the sink and on the chairs, from the floor right up to the ceiling. It was late in the evening by the time poor Mr. Jenkins finished washing them all.

The next day Mrs. Jenkins was her usual self. As the weeks went by, she quite forgot to be careful about what she said. Then one morning, after she had done the washing and hung it outside to dry, she began to feel rather peculiar again. She didn't like to mention it to Mr. Jenkins. I'll just sit down quietly, she thought to herself. Perhaps it will pass.

She was just about to go into the sitting room when she happened to glance out of the window. "Oh!" she shouted angrily. "Look at that! The washing was almost dry, and now look what's happening. It's raining cats and dogs!"

Immediately the black clouds parted, and out of the sky there came an absolute downpour of cats and dogs. Big dogs and little dogs, nice cats and nasty cats—dozens of them falling everywhere—barking and meowing and fighting among themselves as they landed. Some of them splashed into the goldfish pool, and others twanged up and down on the clothesline. They ran up the trees and along the fences. They sat on the window sill and stared in at Mr. and Mrs. Jenkins.

"It's that Mrs. Jenkins again!" cried the neighbors. "She's had one of her spells again. Why can't she be more careful when she feels them coming on? Shoo! Shoo! Go away!"

"It's only a shower," called Mr. Jenkins from an upstairs window. "It will be over in a minute or two."

But it wasn't. All the rest of the morning it rained cats and dogs around the Jenkins's house, until there wasn't a patch of ground or an inch of fence that wasn't being sat upon.

"You've done it this time," said Mr. Jenkins, shaking his head. "You've really done it. Pots and pans were bad enough, but at least we were able to give them away to our friends. Who on earth would want so many damp cats and dogs?"

Just after noon a policeman came to the door. "Are you the owner of these animals?" he asked Mr. Jenkins. "We've had a complaint."

"I'm sorry," apologized Mr. Jenkins. "You see, it's Mrs. Jenkins. She's had one of her spells again."

"I can't help that," said the policeman. "Just keep these animals under control, or we shall have to take action."

"Oh, dear!" wailed Mrs. Jenkins when he had gone. "What can I do? I shall be seeing pink giraffes next!"

There were two great thumps. When Mr. and Mrs. Jenkins looked out of the kitchen window, they saw two pink giraffes sitting on the lawn, looking rather dazed. The cats began to spit, and the dogs put their tails between their legs and howled. For a moment the giraffes just looked at them; then suddenly they trumpeted loudly and began to chase the cats and dogs.

Round and round the garden they went, and out of the gate, and up the road, and the last that Mr. and Mrs. Jenkins saw of them they were disappearing over the hill.

Mrs. Jenkins went out into the garden and brought in her wash. "I hope I never see anything like that again in the whole of my life," she said. Which was a good thing to say, because she never did. And from that day to this she hasn't had another spell.

Not yet.

Questions

a. Mrs. Jenkins is annoyed when she stumbles over something in the road. What does she say to express her annoyance?
   She says, "Oh, blow!"

b. What happens when she says this?
   The wind begins to blow hard.

c. What does Mrs. Jenkins mean when she says, "The kitchen is quite full of dirty pots and pans"?
   There are some dirty pots and pans.

d. What happens when she says this?
   The kitchen fills up with dirty pots and pans.

e. A person cannot really be someone else. What does the following sentence mean: "The next day Mrs. Jenkins was her usual self"?
   She felt as she normally feels.

f. What normally happens when Mrs. Jenkins is not her "usual self"?
   Whatever she says comes true.

g. What does Mrs. Jenkins mean when she says, "It's raining cats and dogs"?
   It's raining heavily.

h. What happens when she says this?
   It actually rains live cats and dogs.

i. What does Mrs. Jenkins mean when she says, "I shall be seeing pink giraffes next"?
   The unexpected will happen.

j. What happens when she says this?
   She actually sees two pink giraffes sitting on the lawn.

Lesson 3

Understanding Similes

A simile is a direct comparison between two essentially, or basically, unlike things. A simile contains the word *like* or *as.* For example, read the paragraph below, from "How Old Stormalong Captured Mocha Dick" by Irwin Shapiro.

> Alfred Bulltop Stormalong was the greatest sailor who ever lived. He stood four fathoms tall in his stocking feet. His eyes were as blue as a calm sea. His hair was as black as a storm cloud. He could whistle shrill like the wind in the rigging; he could hoot like a foghorn; and he could talk ordinary, just like anyone else. Stormalong had one fault. He was always complaining that they didn't make ships big enough for him.

Now let's look at the similes in this paragraph.

"His eyes were as blue as a calm sea."

How were Stormalong's eyes like a calm sea? Both were blue.

"His hair was as black as a storm cloud."

How was Stormalong's hair like a storm cloud? Both were black.

"He could whistle shrill like the wind in the rigging . . ."

How was the way Stormalong whistled like the wind in the rigging? Both sounded shrill.

". . . he could hoot like a foghorn . . ."

How was Stormalong's hoot like a foghorn? Both made a loud, deep, penetrating sound.

Now look at the comic strip below. At first, Dagwood wants to compare the minute steak to the bottom of a shoe because both are tough. Then he decides that the steak is a lot tougher.

BLONDIE by Young and Raymond

Name _____

Exercise 1. Each of the sentences below contains a simile. For each sentence, the two things being compared are underlined. Read each sentence. Then choose the description that tells how the two things being compared are alike. Put an X in the blank next to your choice.

Example

　　Her dress was as colorful as a sunset.
　　__X__ Both have vivid colors.
　　_____ Both are dull.
　　_____ Both are red.

a. Naomi's skin was as dark as ebony.
　　_____ Both are pale.
　　__X__ Both are dark.
　　_____ Both are smooth.

b. His problem followed him like a shadow.
　　__X__ Both stayed with him.
　　_____ Both were dark.
　　_____ Both brought him happiness.

c. Her smile is as cheerful as daffodils on a hillside in spring.
　　_____ Both are yellow.
　　__X__ Both are happy.
　　_____ Both occur in the spring.

d. Melinda was as nervous as a cat walking on snow.
　　__X__ Both are uneasy.
　　_____ Both do not like the snow.
　　_____ Both are young.

e. Julie's smile was like the dawn that follows a storm.
　　_____ Both last for only a short time.
　　__X__ Both are radiant.
　　_____ Both are gloomy.

Copyright © 1984 by Harcourt Brace Jovanovich, Inc. All rights reserved

Exercise 2. Each of the following sentences contains a simile. Read each sentence. Draw a line under the two things being compared. Then choose the description that tells how the two things being compared are alike. Put an X next to your choice.

a. Lloyd's <u>mood</u> was as unpredictable as <u>quicksilver</u>.
   _____ Both are easy to predict.
   __X__ Both are hard to predict.
   _____ Both are silvery.

b. To the mother and father, the new <u>baby</u> was like a <u>rare jewel</u>.
   _____ Both are tiny.
   _____ Both are new.
   __X__ Both are treasured.

c. When she put on ice skates for the first time, <u>Peggy</u> looked like a <u>fawn trying to walk</u>.
   _____ Both are very young.
   __X__ Both are shaky on their legs.
   _____ Both run quickly.

d. The <u>sound of his voice</u> was as comforting as a <u>warm fire on a winter night</u>.
   _____ Both make a crackly noise.
   __X__ Both make a person feel warm and safe.
   _____ Both have a wintry sound.

e. <u>He</u> was as useful as a <u>car without gas</u>.
   _____ Both move quickly.
   _____ Both are useful.
   __X__ Both are useless.

Exercise 3. Complete each of the following similes. Write your answers in the blanks provided.

a. Linda was as pretty as ___*Students' answers will vary.*___

b. Lee was as unmovable as ___*Students' answers will vary.*___

Name _____

c. The clouds looked like *Students' answers will vary.* _____

d. Carl's word is as good as *Students' answers will vary.* _____

e. The dancer was as graceful as *Students' answers will vary.* _____

Lesson 4

Interpreting Similes in Poetry

A **simile** is a direct comparison between two essentially, or basically, unlike things. A simile contains the word *like* or *as*. Often poets use similes in their poetry to express their ideas in a vivid way. For example, in the poem below, "Haiku" by Robert Philips, the poet compares the cat on the bed to peanut butter on bread.

"The cat spreads herself
across my bed, like pea
-nut butter on bread."

In the next poem, "Vulture" by X. J. Kennedy, the poet compares the vulture to a sack.

The vulture's very like a sack
Set down and left there drooping.
His crooked neck and creaky back
Look badly bent from stooping
5 Down to the ground to eat dead cows
So they won't go to waste
Thus making up in usefulness
For what he lacks in taste.

Copyright © 1984 by Harcourt Brace Jovanovich, Inc. All rights reserved

Exercise 1. Read the poem below, "Winter Trees" by Leonard Burch. Then answer the questions that follow the poem.

> Look! Winter trees are so bare.
> Like empty cabinets in a house
> where nobody lives.
>
> Maybe the coming spring will
> 5 bloom them up.
> Buds will burst like dynamite.
>
> Look! Winter trees are so bare.
> Like empty cabinets in a house
> where nobody lives.

Questions

a. To what does the poet compare winter trees?
   He compares them to empty cabinets.

b. How are these two objects alike?
   Both are bare.

c. To what does the poet compare buds in spring?
   He compares them to dynamite.

d. How are these two objects alike?
   Both burst or explode.

e. Do you think the poet prefers winter or spring? Why?
   He prefers spring, which is alive, to winter, which is bare.

Exercise 2. Read the poem below, "The Open Door" by Elizabeth Coatsworth. Then answer the questions that follow it.

> Out of the dark
> To the sill of the door
> Lay the snow in a long
> Unruffled floor,
> 5 And the lamplight fell
> Narrow and thin
> Like a carpet unrolled
> For the cat to walk in.
> Slowly, smoothly,
> 10 Black as the night,
> With paws unseen
> White upon white,
> Like a queen who walks
> Down a corridor,
> 15 The black cat paced
> The cold smooth floor
> And left behind her,
> Bead upon bead,
> The track of small feet
> 20 Like dark fern-seed.

Name _____

Questions

a. Reread ll. 5-8. How is the lamplight like a carpet?
Both are narrow and thin. Both are on the floor.

b. The cat is black with white paws. Find the simile that describes how black the cat is.
It is black as the night.

c. Reread ll. 13-16. How is the cat like a queen?
The cat walks proudly like a queen.

d. To what does the poet compare "the track of small feet"?
She compares them to dark fern-seed.

e. How are these two things alike?
Both are small and dark.

Lesson 5

Understanding Metaphors

A metaphor is an implied, or suggested, comparison between two essentially unlike things. It does not contain the word *like* or *as.* For example, the poem below, "A Modern Dragon" by Rowena Bastin Bennett, contains a metaphor. The poet compares a train to a dragon.

> A train is a dragon that roars through the dark.
> He wriggles his tail as he sends up a spark.
> He pierces the night with his one yellow eye,
> And all the earth trembles when he rushes by.

The next poem, "Snow Toward Evening" by Melville Cane, contains two metaphors. In l. 6, the "invisible blossoming tree" is the sky. In l. 7, the "petals, cool and white" are snowflakes.

> Suddenly the sky turned gray,
> The day,
> Which had been bitter and chill,
> Grew soft and still.
> 5 Quietly
> From some invisible blossoming tree
> Millions of petals, cool and white,
> Drifted and blew,
> Lifted and flew,
> 10 Fell with the falling night.

Copyright © 1984 by Harcourt Brace Jovanovich, Inc. All rights reserved

Sometimes metaphors become part of our everyday language. For example, you say that someone who is very slender is *reed-thin*. We speak of someone who is very quick as being *lightning-quick*. We call loud, rowdy play *horseplay*. We call a rough, tight hug a *bear hug*.

Exercise 1. Each sentence below contains a metaphor. For each sentence, the two things being compared are underlined. Read each sentence. Then choose the description that tells how both things are alike. Put an *X* in the blank next to your choice.

a. The icy wind was a razor slashing our faces.
   __X__ Both are sharp and cutting.
   _____ Both are cold.
   _____ Both are soft and gentle.

b. The new-fallen snow was a velvet carpet under our feet.
   _____ Both are new.
   __X__ Both are soft.
   _____ Both are white.

c. To his enemies, he was a shark.
   _____ Both are fish.
   _____ Both have enemies.
   __X__ Both devour everything in their paths.

258   Copyright © 1984 by Harcourt Brace Jovanovich, Inc. All rights reserved

d. He woke up with a <u>headache</u>—a <u>rock band</u> playing in his brain.

__X__ Both are loud and persistent.

_____ Both cut through wood.

_____ Both make little noise.

e. At night, the <u>bridge</u> is a <u>diamond tiara</u> crowning the river.

_____ Both are made of diamonds.

_____ Both are made of steel.

__X__ Both are bright and richly luminous.

Exercise 2. In the poem below, a mother speaks to her son. Read the poem, "Mother to Son" by Langston Hughes. Then answer the questions that follow it.

> Well, son, I'll tell you:
> Life for me ain't been no crystal stair.
> It's had tacks in it,
> And splinters,
> 5 And boards torn up,
> And places with no carpet on the floor—
> Bare.
> But all the time
> I'se been a-climbin' on,
> 10 And reachin' landin's,
> And turnin' corners,
> And sometimes goin' in the dark
> Where there ain't been no light.
> So boy, don't you turn back.
> 15 Don't you set down on the steps
> 'Cause you find it's kinder hard.
> Don't you fall now—
> For I'se still goin', honey,
> I'se still climbin',
> 20 And life for me ain't been no crystal stair.

Questions

a. The mother uses a metaphor to tell her son about life. She says, "Life for me ain't been no crystal stair." Think about the word "crystal." Do you think the mother means that life has been easy or hard?
It has been hard.

b. What does the mother mean when she says that the stair has had "tacks" and "splinters" in it?
Life has had rough spots or problems.

c. Reread ll. 9–11. What does the mother mean?
In spite of the problems, she hasn't given up.

d. Reread ll. 12–13. What does the mother mean?
At times life has seemed hopeless.

e. What does the mother mean when she tells her son not to "turn back" or "set down on the steps"?
He must not give up.

Lesson 6

Interpreting Figurative Language

In figurative language words do not have their usual dictionary meaning. Figurative language expresses ideas in a vivid and forceful way. For example, the quotations below are from Ray Bradbury's story "Naming of Names." Read the first quotation.

" 'I feel like a salt crystal,' he often said, 'in a mountain stream being washed away. We don't belong here.' "

When the character compares himself to a salt crystal in water, he means that he feels as if his identity is being dissolved. In other words, he is losing his identity, or his sense of self, because he is in a place where he doesn't belong.

Now read the next quotation.

"The morning paper was toast-warm from the 6:00 A.M. Earth rocket."

How warm was the morning paper? It was about the same temperature as toast. The word *toast-warm* creates a vivid impression because it brings to mind good memories of breakfasts at home with your family.

Exercise. Read the selection below from "Naming of Names" by Ray Bradbury. Then follow the directions at the end of it.

The rocket metal cooled in the meadow winds. Its lid gave a bulging *pop*. From its clock interior stepped a man, a woman, and three children. The other passengers whispered away across the Martian meadow, leaving the man alone among his family.

The man felt his hair flutter and the tissues of his body draw tight as if he were standing at the center of a vacuum. His wife, before him, seemed almost to whirl away in smoke. The children, small seeds, might at any instant be sown to all the Martian climes.

The children looked up at him, as people look to the sun, to tell what time of their life it is. His face was cold.

"What's wrong?" asked his wife.

"Let's get back on the rocket."

"Go back to Earth?"

"Yes! Listen!"

The wind blew as if to flake away their identities. At any moment the Martian air might draw his soul from him, as marrow comes from a white bone. He felt submerged in a chemical that could dissolve his intellect and burn away his past.

They looked at Martian hills that time had worn with a crushing pressure of years. They saw the old cities, lost like thin children in their meadows, lying like children's delicate bones among the blowing lakes of grass.

"Chin up, Harry," said his wife. "It's too late. We've come at least thirty-five million miles or more."

The children with their dandelion hair hollered at the deep dome of Martian sky. There was no answer but the racing hiss of wind through the stiff grass.

He picked up the luggage in his cold hands. "Here we go," he said—a man standing on the edge of a sea, ready to wade in and be drowned.

They walked into town.

Directions. Each item below contains figurative language. Rewrite each item in literal language.

Example

"The other passengers whispered away across the Martian meadow, leaving the man alone among his family."
The other passengers walked away in a hush across the Martian meadow, leaving the man alone among his family.

a. "The man felt his hair flutter and the tissues of his body draw tight as if he were standing at the center of a vacuum."
The man felt absolutely alone.

b. "His wife, before him, seemed almost to whirl away in smoke."
His wife seemed to disappear.

c. "The children, small seeds, might at any instant be sown to all the Martian climes."
The children might become part of the land.

d. "The children looked up at him, as people look to the sun, to tell what time of their life it is."
The children looked to him for guidance.

e. "The wind blew as if to flake away their identities."
The wind made them feel anonymous.

f. "At any moment the Martian air might draw his soul from him, as marrow comes from a white bone."
The Martian environment might make him lose his identity.

g. "He felt submerged in a chemical that could dissolve his intellect and burn away his past."
He felt he was losing his identity.

h. "They saw the old cities, lost like thin children in their meadows, lying like children's delicate bones among the blowing lakes of grass."
They saw the ruins of the old cities in the grass.

i. "The children with their dandelion hair hollered at the deep dome of Martian sky."
The yellow-haired children yelled at the Martian sky.

j. " 'Here we go,' " he said—a man standing on the edge of a sea, ready to wade in and be drowned."
He felt he was going to do something that would destroy him.

Lesson 7
Practice

As you read the following selection, pay special attention to figurative language. Then complete the exercise that follows.

The Boy Who Found Fear
A Medieval Tale Collected by Ignaz Künos

Once upon a time there lived a woman who had one son whom she loved dearly. The little cottage in which they dwelt was built on the outskirts of a forest. As they had no neighbors, the place was very lonely, and the boy was kept at home by his mother to bear her company.

They were sitting together on a winter's evening when a storm suddenly sprang up, and the wind blew the door open. The woman started and shivered, and glanced over her shoulder as if she half expected to see some horrible thing. "Go and shut the door," she said hastily to her son. "I feel frightened."

"Frightened?" repeated the boy. "What does it feel like to be frightened?"

"Well—just frightened," answered the mother. "A fear of something—you hardly know what—takes hold of you."

"It must be very odd to feel like that," replied the boy. "I will go through the world and seek fear till I find it." And the next morning, before his mother was out of bed, he had left the forest behind him.

After walking for some hours he reached a mountain, which he began to climb. Near the top, in a wild and rocky spot, he came upon a band of fierce robbers sitting around a fire. The boy, who was cold and tired, was delighted to see the bright flames, so he went up to them and said, "Good greeting to you, sirs," and wriggled himself in between the men, till his feet almost touched the burning logs.

The robbers stopped drinking and eyed him curiously. At last the captain spoke.

"No caravan of armed men would dare to come here; even the very birds shun our camp. Who are you to venture in so boldly?"

"Oh, I have left my mother's house in search of fear. Perhaps you can show it to me?"

"Fear is wherever *we* are," answered the captain.

"But *where*?" asked the boy, looking around. "I see nothing."

"Take this pot and some flour and butter and sugar over to the churchyard, which lies down there, and bake us a cake for supper," replied the robber. And the boy, who was by this time

Copyright © 1984 by Harcourt Brace Jovanovich, Inc. All rights reserved

quite warm, jumped up cheerfully and, slinging the pot over his arm, ran down the hill.

When he got to the churchyard, he collected some sticks and made a fire; then he filled the pot with water from a little stream close by. Mixing the flour and butter and sugar together, he set the cake on to cook. It was not long before it grew crisp and brown. Then the boy lifted it from the pot and placed it on a stone while he put out the fire. At that moment a hand stretched from a grave and a voice said:

"Is that cake for me?"

"Do you think I am going to give to the dead the food of the living?" replied the boy with a laugh. Giving the hand a tap with his spoon and picking up the cake, he went up the mountainside, whistling merrily.

"Well, have you found fear?" asked the robbers when he held out the cake to the captain.

"No; was it there?" answered the boy. "I saw nothing but a hand which came from a grave. It belonged to someone who wanted my cake, but I just rapped the fingers with a spoon, and said it was not for him, and then the hand vanished. Oh, how nice this fire is!" He flung himself on his knees before it and so did not notice the glances of surprise the robbers cast at each other.

"There is another chance for you," said one of the robbers at length. "On the other side of the mountain lies a deep pool. Go to that, and perhaps you may meet fear on the way."

"I hope so, indeed," answered the boy, and he set out at once.

He soon beheld the waters of the pool gleaming in the moonlight. As he drew near, he saw a tall swing standing just over it, and in the swing a child was seated, weeping bitterly.

"That is a strange place for a swing," thought the boy. "But I wonder what the little one is crying about." He was hurrying toward the child when a maiden ran up and spoke to him.

"I want to lift my little brother from the swing," cried she, "but it is too high above me. If you will get closer to the edge of the pool and let me mount on your shoulders, I think I can reach him."

"Willingly," replied the boy, and in an instant the girl had climbed to his shoulders. But instead of lifting the child from the swing, as she could easily have done, she pressed her feet so firmly on each side of the youth's neck that he felt that in another minute he would choke, or else fall into the water beneath him. So, gathering up all his strength, he gave a mighty heave and threw the girl backward. As she touched the ground, a bracelet fell from her arm. This the youth picked up.

"I may as well keep it as a remembrance of all the queer things that have happened to me since I left home," he said to himself. Turning to look for the child, he saw that both it and the swing had vanished, and that the first streaks of dawn were in the sky.

With the bracelet on his arm, the youth started for a little town which was situated in the plain on the farther side of the mountain.

As, hungry and thirsty, he entered its principal street, a merchant stopped him and said, "Where did you get that bracelet? It belongs to me."

"No, it is mine," replied the boy.

"It is not. Give it to me at once, or it will be the worse for you!" cried the merchant.

"Let us go before a judge and tell him our stories," said the boy. "If he decides in your favor, you shall have it; if in mine, I will keep it!"

To this the merchant agreed, and the two went together to the great hall, in which the judge was holding court. He listened very carefully to what each had to say and then pronounced his verdict. Neither of the two claimants had proved his right to the bracelet; therefore it must remain in the possession of the judge till its fellow was brought before him.

When they heard this, the merchant and the boy looked at each other, and their eyes said, "Where are we to find the other one?" But as they knew there was no use in disputing the decision, they bowed low and left the hall of audience.

Wandering he knew not whither, the youth found himself on the seashore. Some distance from the shore, a ship had struck a hidden rock and was rapidly sinking. On deck, the crew were gathered, with faces as white as death, shrieking and wringing their hands.

"Have you met with fear?" shouted the boy. And the answer came back above the noise of the waves.

"Oh, help! help! We are drowning!"

Then the boy flung off his clothes and swam to the ship, where many hands drew him on board.

"The ship is tossed hither and thither and will soon be sucked down," cried the crew. "Death is very near, and we are frightened!"

"Give me a rope," said the boy in reply. He took it and tied one end around his body, and the other to the mast. Then he sprang into the sea. Down he went, down, down, down, till at last his feet touched the bottom, and he stood up and looked about him. There, sure enough, a sea maiden with a wicked expression was tugging hard at a chain which she had fastened to the ship, in order to drag it beneath the waves. Seizing her arms in both his hands, he forced her to drop the chain, and the sailors were able to float the ship off the rock. Then, taking a rusty knife from a heap of seaweed at his feet, he cut the rope from around his waist and fastened the sea maiden firmly to a stone, so that she could do no more mischief. Bidding her farewell, he swam back to the beach, where his clothes were still lying.

The youth dressed himself quickly and walked on till he came to a beautiful shady garden filled with flowers, and with a clear little stream running through it. The day was hot and he was tired, so he entered the gate and seated himself under a clump of bushes covered with sweet-smelling red blossoms. Before long he fell asleep.

Suddenly a rush of wings and a cool breeze awakened him. Raising his head cautiously, the boy saw three doves plunging into the stream. They splashed joyfully about, shook themselves, and then dived to the bottom of a deep pool. When they appeared again they were no longer three doves but three beautiful damsels, bearing a table made of mother-of-pearl. On this they placed drinking cups fashioned from pink and green shells. One of the maidens filled a cup from a crystal flagon, and was raising it to her mouth when her sister stopped her.

"To whose health do you drink?" asked she.

"To the youth who prepared the cake, and rapped my hand with the spoon when I stretched it out of the earth," answered the maiden, "and was never afraid as other men were. But to whose health do you drink?"

"To the youth on whose shoulders I climbed at the edge of the pool, and who threw me off when I tried to drown him," replied the second. "But you, my sister," added she, turning to the third girl, "to whom do you drink?"

"Down in the sea I took hold of a ship and shook it and pulled it till it would soon have been lost," said she. "But a youth came and freed the ship and bound me to a rock. To his health I drink." And they all three lifted their cups and drank.

As they put their cups down, the fearless boy appeared before them.

"Here am I, the youth whose health you have drunk; and now give me the bracelet that matches a jeweled band which of a surety fell from the arm of one of you. A merchant tried to take it from me, but I would not let him have it. When I appealed to the judge, he kept my bracelet till I could show him its fellow. I have been wandering hither and thither in search of it, and that is how I have found myself in such strange places."

"Come with us, then," said the maidens. They led him down a passage into a hall out of which opened many chambers, each one of greater splendor than the last. From a shelf heaped up with gold and jewels, the eldest sister took a bracelet exactly like the one in the judge's keeping, and fastened it to the youth's arm.

"Go at once and show this to the judge," said she, "and he will give you the fellow to it."

"I shall never forget you," answered the youth, "but it may be long before we meet again, for I shall never rest till I have found fear." Then he went his way, and won the bracelet from the judge. After that, he again set forth in his quest.

On and on walked the youth, but fear never crossed his path. One day he entered a large town where all the streets and squares were so full of people that he could hardly pass among them.

"Why have all these crowds gathered?" he asked of a man who stood next to him.

"The king of this country is dead," was the reply, "and as he had no children, it is needful to choose a successor. Therefore each morning one of the sacred pigeons is let loose from the tower yonder. On whomsoever the bird perches, that man shall be our king. In a few minutes the pigeon will fly. Wait and see what happens."

Every eye was fixed on the tall tower which stood in the center of the chief square. The moment the sun was seen to stand straight over it, a door was opened and a beautiful pigeon, gleaming with pink and gray, blue and green, came rushing through the air. Onward it flew, onward, onward, till at length it rested on the head of the boy.

Then a great shout arose: "The King! The King!" But as the boy listened to the cries, a vision, swifter than lightning, flashed across his brain. He saw himself seated on a throne, spending his life trying, and never succeeding, to make poor people rich, miserable people happy, bad people good; never doing anything he wished to do, not even able to marry the girl that he loved.

"No! No!" he cried, hiding his face in his hands. But the crowds who heard him thought he was overcome by the grandeur that awaited him and paid no heed.

"Well, to make quite sure, let fly more pigeons," said they. Each pigeon followed where the first had led, and the cries arose louder than ever:

"The King! The King!" As the boy heard, a cold shiver ran through him.

"This is fear, which you have so long sought," whispered a voice to his ears alone. And the youth bowed his head. As the vision once more flashed before his eyes, he accepted his destiny and made ready to pass his life with fear beside him.

Exercise. Each sentence below contains figurative language. Rewrite each sentence in literal language.

a. "A fear of something . . . takes hold of you."
You become afraid.

b. "Go to that, and perhaps you may meet fear on the way."
Go to that, and you may become afraid.

c. "Turning to look for the child, he saw that both it and the swing had vanished, and that the first streaks of dawn were in the sky."
When he turned to look for the child, he saw that it and the swing were gone, and it was dawn.

d. "On deck, the crew were gathered, with faces as white as death, shrieking and wringing their hands."
On deck, the frightened crew gathered, shrieking and wringing their hands.

e. "Death is very near, and we are frightened!"
We are about to die, and we are frightened!

f. "On and on walked the youth, but fear never crossed his path."
On and on walked the youth, but he never became afraid.

g. "Every eye was fixed on the tall tower which stood in the center of the chief square."
Everyone looked at the tall tower in the center of the chief square.

h. "But as the boy listened to the cries, a vision, swifter than lightning, flashed across his brain."
As the boy listened to the cries, he had a sudden vision.

i. "As the boy heard, a cold shiver ran through him."
As the boy heard, he became afraid.

j. "As a vision once more flashed before his eyes, he accepted his destiny and made ready to pass his life with fear beside him."
As he once again had his vision, he accepted his destiny and prepared to live life afraid.

Name _____

Chapter 11
Imagery

Imagery is language that helps you form a picture of what something is like. Writers try to help you imagine the things they are writing about by using language that appeals to your five senses and that creates vivid pictures in your mind.

In the cartoon below, the girl tries to explain to her brother what happens when she thinks. She translates words into pictures in her mind.

THE FAMILY CIRCUS by Bil Keane

"Thinking is when the picture is in your head with the sound turned off."

Lesson 1
Recognizing Sensory Language

Sensory language contains words and phrases that appeal to one or more of the five senses—sight, hearing, taste, smell, and touch. These words and phrases create vivid images, or word pictures, in your mind.

Copyright © 1984 by Harcourt Brace Jovanovich, Inc. All rights reserved   269

For example, read the following paragraph from *Roll of Thunder, Hear My Cry* by Mildred D. Taylor.

> Spring. It seeped unseen into the waiting red earth in early March, softening the hard ground for the coming plow and awakening life that had lain gently sleeping through the cold winter. But by the end of March it was evident everywhere: in the barn where three new calves bellowed and chicks the color of soft pale sunlight chirped; in the yard where the wisteria and English dogwood bushes readied themselves for their annual Easter bloom, and the fig tree budded producing the forerunners of juicy, brown fruit for which the boys and I would have to do battle with fig-loving Jack; and in the smell of the earth itself. Rain-drenched, fresh, vital, full of life, spring enveloped all of us.

Mildred Taylor uses details that help you experience the arrival of spring. She appeals to your sense of sight. You can clearly see the new calves and the chicks "the color of soft pale sunlight." You can see the wisteria and the dogwood bushes in the yard. She appeals to your sense of hearing. You can hear the calves "bellowing" and the chicks "chirping." She appeals to your sense of taste. You can taste the "juicy, brown fruit" from the fig tree. She appeals to your sense of smell. You can smell the wisteria and the dogwood and the "rain-drenched" earth. She appeals to your sense of touch. You can feel the hard ground that softens in early March.

Exercise 1. Read the paragraph below from *Chappie and Me* by John Craig. Then read the details that follow the paragraph. For each detail, write the sense to which it mainly appeals. (Remember: The five senses are sight, hearing, taste, touch, and smell.)

> The evening of the game we had supper, as usual, in the big kitchen of the house we rented, a block off the main street at the north end of town. I don't suppose my mother thought so as she worked over the wood stove, but it always seemed to me to be cool in that kitchen, even on days when the burning sun turned the asphalt of the streets into spongy gumbo under your bare feet. The table was covered with rose-patterned oil cloth, and on the side by the window there was a permanent cluster of salt and pepper shakers, catsup bottle, covered sugar bowl, and a sealer of homemade sweet pepper relish. I even know what we had to eat—potato soup, which was one of my dad's favorites, and creamed salmon on toast, which certainly wasn't one of mine.

		Sense
a.	burning sun	*touch*
b.	rose-patterned oil cloth	*sight*
c.	homemade sweet pepper relish	*taste*

Name _____

    d. asphalt turning to spongy gumbo under your bare feet   *touch*

    e. creamed salmon on toast   *taste*

Exercise 2. Read the three paragraphs below from *Tuck Everlasting* by Natalie Babbitt. Then read the details that follow the paragraph. For each detail, write the sense to which it mainly appeals.

    It was another heavy morning, already hot and breathless, but in the wood the air was cooler and smelled agreeably damp. Winnie had been no more than two slow minutes walking timidly under the interlacing branches when she wondered why she had never come here before. "Why, it's nice!" she thought with great surprise.

    For the wood was full of light, entirely different from the light she was used to. It was green and amber and alive, quivering in splotches on the padded ground, fanning into sturdy stripes between the tree trunks. There were little flowers she did not recognize, white and palest blue; and endless, tangled vines; and here and there a fallen log, half rotted but soft with patches of sweet green-velvet moss.

    And there were creatures everywhere. The air fairly hummed with their daybreak activity: beetles and birds and squirrels and ants, and countless other things unseen, all gentle and self-absorbed and not in the least alarming. There was even, she saw with satisfaction, the toad. It was squatting on a low stump and she might not have noticed it, for it looked more like a mushroom than a living creature sitting there. As she came abreast of it, however, it blinked, and the movement gave it away.

        Sense

a. heavy morning that is hot and breathless   *touch*

b. air smelling agreeably damp   *smell*

c. interlacing branches of the trees   *sight*

d. the woods full of light   *sight*

e. the leaves forming sturdy stripes between the tree trunks   *sight*

f. flowers that are white and palest blue   *sight*

g. rotten log that is soft with patches of green-velvet moss   *touch*

h. air humming with sounds of unseen beetles and birds   *hearing*

i. toad squatting on a low stump   *sight*

j. toad appearing to be a mushroom   *sight*

Copyright © 1984 by Harcourt Brace Jovanovich, Inc. All rights reserved

Lesson 2

Understanding Image-Making Words

Some words create vivid pictures or images in your mind by appealing to your senses. For example, read the following paragraph from *River Runners* by James Houston.

> Andrew Stewart heard the excited beating of the ship's bell above him on the bridge, then an answering *clang clang clang!* from the engine room below. He heard the ship's twin propellers grind into reverse. That action set the whole ship shuddering from stem to stern. Andrew was almost flung from his upper bunk as the chartered vessel struck something hard. There was a frightening moment of silence, then shouting and the sound of running feet.

The words *clang* and *grind* appeal to your sense of hearing. The words *shuddering*, *flung*, and *struck* appeal to your sense of touch.

Now read the next paragraph, from "The Big Change" by Janey Montgomery.

> As a shy December sun slipped cautiously behind a cloud, Kimera Chung wondered if she would ever see a brilliant California sunset again or feel its golden touch on her olive skin as the Pacific surf roared in her ears and the wind gently slapped a salty spray against her face. Depressed by the incredible appearance of the world outside her window, she pressed her nose against the pane where ice crystals formed geometric patterns unlike anything she had ever seen before. Her voice was sad as she sighed, "Look at it! Snow! Snow everywhere!"

The words *shy December sun* and *brilliant California sunset* appeal to your sense of sight. The word *roared* appeals to your sense of hearing. The words *gently slapped* appeal to your sense of touch. The words *salty spray* appeal to both your sense of taste and your sense of smell.

Exercise 1. The five senses are sight, hearing, smell, taste, and touch. Read each group of words below. Then write the name of the sense to which each group appeals.

		Sense
a.	sour, tart, vinegary, tangy	*taste*
b.	snoring, sneezing, sniffling, sighing	*hearing*
c.	tingly, prickly, tickling, itchy	*touch*
d.	glittering, shimmering, twinkling, glistening	*sight*
e.	ringing, pealing, tinkling, chiming	*hearing*

Exercise 2. The poem below is "Smells" by Christopher Morley. Read the poem. Then follow the directions at the end of it.

>
> Why is it that the poets tell
> So little of the sense of smell?
> These are the odors I love well:
>
> The smell of coffee, freshly ground;
> 5 Or rich plum pudding, holly-crowned;
> Or onions fried and deeply browned.
>
> The fragrance of a fumy pipe;
> The smell of apples, newly ripe;
> And printers' ink on leaden type.
>
> 10 Woods by moonlight in September
> Breathe most sweet; and I remember
> Many a smoky camp-fire ember.
>
> Camphor, turpentine, and tea,
> The balsam of a Christmas tree,
> 15 These are the whiffs of gramarye*—
> A ship smells best of all to me!

Directions. In "Smells" Christopher Morley mentions many details that appeal to the sense of smell. For each detail listed below, write one or two words describing the smell. (Use your dictionary to help you.)

Example

coffee   *sweet, spicy*

a. fried onions   *pungent*

b. apples   *tart, spicy*

c. camp fire   *smoky*

d. pipe   *acrid, fumy*

e. Christmas tree   *balsamy*

*****gramarye** (grăm'ə-rē) n.: Magic.

Lesson 3

Understanding Words That Stand for Sounds

Onomatopoeia (ŏn′ə-măt′ə-pē′ə) is the use of words that sound like or imitate what they describe. For example, the word *ding-dong* describes the sound made by a bell, and the word *hum* describes the sound people make when they sing a tune without saying words or opening their mouths. The word *ha-ha* imitates the sound of laughter, and the word *snip-snip* imitates the sound of scissors.

The poem below is "Bee Song" by Carl Sandburg. Notice the words *drone* and *droning* in this poem. These words imitate the sound of the bee's song.

> Bees in the late summer sun
> Drone their song
> Of yellow moons
> Trimming black velvet,
> 5 Droning, droning a sleepysong.

Exercise 1. The words in Column A imitate the sounds of animals. Match each sound with the name of the animal, in Column B, that produces it. Write the number in front of the name of this animal in the blank at the left.

	A		B
2	a. hee-haw	(1)	dog
4	b. baa	(2)	donkey
8	c. oink	(3)	bird
5	d. croak	(4)	sheep
7	e. honk	(5)	frog
9	f. gobble-gobble	(6)	rooster
6	g. cock-a-doodle-do	(7)	goose
3	h. tweet	(8)	pig
1	i. bow-wow	(9)	turkey
10	j. quack	(10)	duck

Name _____

Exercise 2. The poem below is "Onomatopoeia" by Eve Merriam. Read the poem aloud. Then follow the directions at the end of it.

> The rusty spigot
> sputters,
> utters
> a splutter,
> 5   spatters a smattering of drops,
> gashes wider;
> slash,
> splatters,
> scatters,
> 10 spurts,
> finally stops sputtering
> and plash!
> gushes rushes splashes
> clear water dashes.

Directions. In "Onomatopoeia" Eve Merriam uses verbs that sound like water forcing itself from a rusty spigot, or faucet. Look up each of the words below in your dictionary. Write the definition next to each word.

a. sputter: *to spit out in short bursts*
b. utter: *to say, to speak*
c. splutter: *to make a spitting sound*
d. spatter: *to scatter in small drops*
e. gash: *to cut deeply*
f. slash: *to cut with violent, sweeping strokes*
g. splatter: *to fall with heavy splashes*
h. scatter: *to disperse*
i. spurt: *to gush forth*
j. plash: *to splash lightly*

Exercise 3. In "Onomatopoeia" Eve Merriam uses many rhyming words to capture the rhythm of water forcing itself through a rusty spigot. For each word below, write the word or words in the poem that rhyme with it.

a. sputters: *utters*
b. spatters: *splatters, scatters*
c. gashes: *splashes, dashes*
d. gushes: *rushes*

Copyright © 1984 by Harcourt Brace Jovanovich, Inc. All rights reserved

Lesson 4

Understanding Vivid Verbs

Verbs are the action words in sentences. For example, the words *leap*, *twirl*, and *toss* are verbs. **Some verbs are particularly vivid and sharp. They describe the action exactly.** For example, read the following two sentences:

The man in the audience *interrupted* the speaker.
The man in the audience *heckled* the speaker.

Both sentences contain verbs, but the verb in the second sentence creates a more vivid, or exact, picture. *To heckle* means "to annoy a speaker by interrupting with questions or scornful remarks."

Exercise 1. The poem below is "About Motion Pictures" by Ann Darr. Read the poem. Pay special attention to vivid verbs. Then follow the directions at the end of the poem.

> "Get the verb right
>   and directing is a cinch,"
> he said modestly, gesturing
> toward his newest masterpiece.
>
> 5 The same is said for poetry.
> Strike adjectives, adverbs!
> Red-pencil ands and buts.
> Get the verb right
>   and writing is a cinch.
>
> 10 It's true in living.
>   Move. Scintillate.
>   Grasp. Dodge.
>   Placate.
>   Glow.
> 15 Get the verb right
>   and living is a cinch.
>
> The verb is get.

Directions. Look up each **boldface** verb below in a dictionary. Write its meaning on the line provided. Be sure to use the meaning that fits the poem.

a. scintillate: *flash; sparkle*
b. grasp: *seize; hold firmly*
c. dodge: *shift suddenly*
d. placate: *calm; soothe*
e. glow: *shine brightly*

Exercise 2. The poem below is "Foul Shot" by Edwin A. Hoey. Read the poem. Pay special attention to vivid verbs. Then follow the directions at the end of the poem.

>   With two 60's stuck on the scoreboard
>   And two seconds hanging on the clock,
>   The solemn boy in the center of eyes,
>   Squeezed by silence,
>   5 Seeks out the line with his feet,
>   Soothes his hands along his uniform,
>   Gently drums the ball against the floor,
>   Then measures the waiting net,
>   Raises the ball on his right hand,
> 10 Balances it with his left,
>   Calms it with fingertips,
>   Breathes,
>   Crouches,
>   Waits,
> 15 And then through a stretching of stillness,
>   Nudges it upward.
>   The ball
>   Slides up and out,
>   Lands,
> 20 Leans,
>   Wobbles,
>   Wavers,
>   Hesitates,
>   Exasperates,
> 25 Plays it coy
>   Until every face begs with unsounding screams—
>   And then
>   And then
>   And then,
> 30 Right before ROAR-UP,
>   Dives down and through.

Directions. Look up each verb listed below in a dictionary. Write its meaning on the line provided. Be sure to use the meaning that fits the poem.

a. squeeze: *compress*
b. soothe: *calm; relieve the pain of*
c. drum: *thump or tap rhythmically*
d. measure: *appraise; size up*
e. crouch: *bend knees; squat*

f. nudge: *gently push or shove*
g. wobble: *move erratically from side to side*
h. waver: *swing or move uncertainly*
i. hesitate: *pause before moving; falter*
j. exasperate: *try the patience of*

Lesson 5

Visualizing a Setting

The setting of a story is where and when it takes place. Writers help you visualize, or picture in your mind, the setting by including details that appeal to your senses.

For example, read the paragraph below from "The Crossover" by Edna Corwin.

> Now is later. I'm exploring old Joseph Henderson's land. I am staring at the strangest trees I have ever seen. They are bone-white, crooked and dead . . . dead enough for ghosts to ooze out of the hollows. The twiggy branches twist down, like witches' hands. Mist is coming up, like something breathing. Am I scared? Yes, sir! I saw a movie once where this big plant ate live things. Maybe these trees eat kids. While I'm thinking this I see a funny, humped-up shape moving in the mist. I run fast to somewhere else. When I fall in dry grass, it rattles like a rattlesnake. I lie belly flat and don't think. After a long time I hear boots. When I turn on my back I see Dad.

Notice the specific details in the paragraph above. The author tells you exactly how the trees look. "They are bone-white, crooked and dead." She tells you exactly how the branches look. They are "twiggy," and they "twist down, like witches' hands." She tells you there is mist moving in. She tells you how the dry grass sounds; "it rattles like a rattlesnake." These details create a vivid picture in your mind of the dead woods. They make you feel that you are seeing the woods yourself, and they help you to understand why the person describing these woods is frightened by them.

Exercise. Read the selection below from "The Spanish Smile" by Scott O'Dell. Then answer the questions that follow the selection.

> There was no lighthouse on Isla del Oro, although two ships had gone aground there in the past year and five in my memory. The nearest light stood at Point Firmin, across the channel thirty miles away. On clear nights I could see it from my tower, shining red and then green and then red again.
>
> In place of a lighthouse there were two whistling buoys, one in the shallows at the northernmost point of the island and one to the south where the water was deep. On calm days they made sounds no louder than a curlew's cry, but during a storm, when the gray-back waves came down from Alaska, they moaned and between the moans there were long, drawn-out sighs, as if the land and the sea and the world itself were in mortal pain.
>
> The ship that went aground on Isla del Oro last December, less than a month ago, came from Panama with a cargo of animals and reptiles for the San Francisco zoo. She struck the southern reef in a heavy fog and broke up, spilling some of her cargo on the beach. All of the animals were rescued, except a

Copyright © 1984 by Harcourt Brace Jovanovich, Inc. All rights reserved

quetzal bird, three rare monkeys, and a pair of bushmasters. The monkeys were found later, but the quetzal bird and the two serpents were still roaming around somewhere.

My father, Don Enrique de Cabrillo y Benivides, received a letter just this week from the curator of the zoo describing the quetzal bird and the bushmaster snakes.

"The quetzal, *Pharomachrus mocinna*," he wrote, "is golden-green with scarlet, iridescent plumage and a long, flowing upper tail covert. Prized and worshipped by the ancient Maya Indians, it is a bird of surpassing beauty, extremely rare, and very secret in its habits. Its call is a single, melodious note not unlike that of a thrush."

The curator went on to describe the serpents, which he seemed to value less than the quetzal bird. "The bushmaster, *Lachesis muta*," he wrote, "is a pit viper more than twelve feet in length, marked by black bars and pink shading. Its aggressive nature, its ability, because of its length, to strike human prey in the throat, and its long fangs supplied with copious venom, make the bushmaster the deadliest snake in the world, deadlier than the king cobra or the mamba. Extreme care in handling the bushmaster is suggested. It may be well to remember, however, that this viper is reluctant to attack unless provoked."

Captain Vega and his *pistoleros*, who guard our island night and day, have been given descriptions of the bird and the serpents with instructions to capture the one and kill the others. So far they have not been successful, though they have brought in, as proof of their diligence (careful effort), three of the large but harmless snakes that inhabit Isla del Oro.

Perhaps I should explain a little about Isla del Oro. In 1542, when my ancestor Juan Rodriguez Cabrillo sighted the island, he thought it was two islands, not one, and named it after his caravels (sailing ships), *La Victoria* and *San Salvador*. Nearly a hundred years later another explorer, Sebastián Vizcaíno, sailed by and gave the island a different name. It was my grandfather who, after he discovered gold on the island, gave it still another name, Isla del Oro. That was after the days when Spain owned all the land from Alaska to Peru, including California, Baja and Alta both.

It had been storming for a week, with heavy winds lashing the castle walls and great waves driving down from the Aleutians. You could see the waves looming far away on the horizon. At first they looked like hills, low gray hills on the moon or on a moonlit desert. As they drew near they changed their shape but not their color, and looked like a herd of prehistoric beasts as they stampeded headlong against the island, one after the other.

The walls of my tower, like the walls all through the castle, measured more than four feet in thickness, made of hard blue and white stones hewn from the living ledges of our gold mines. Yet they trembled as waves crashed against the island.

Storms in January usually lasted a week or more, which meant that my plans for the next day—my sixteenth birthday—were very much in doubt. Our ship, the *Infanta*, was big and seaworthy, but with me, his only child, on board would my father allow her to cross the channel in such heavy weather?

I have been on the mainland only once in my lifetime. It was on my ninth birthday, when I went to visit my grandmother, Doña Gertrudis. I was only there from one morning to the next, yet remembering this time it seems more like a month. So many things happened to me that never happened before . . .

Questions

a. On clear nights, what can Lucinda see from her tower?
She can see the light from the lighthouse at Point Firmin.

b. How do the whistling buoys of Isla del Oro sound on calm days?
They make sounds no louder than a curlew's cry.

c. How do they sound during a storm?
They moan as if the world were in mortal pain.

d. Describe the weather the day the Panamanian ship went aground.
There was a heavy fog.

e. The ship was carrying a cargo of animals. Find a sentence in the story describing the way the quetzal looked. Write it below. Use your dictionary to define any words you do not know.
"The quetzal, Pharomachrus mocinna, . . ., is golden-green with scarlet, iridescent plumage and a long, flowing upper tail covert."

f. Find a sentence describing the way the quetzal sounded. Write it below. Use your dictionary to define any words you do not know.
"Its call is a single, melodious note not unlike that of a thrush."

g. Find a sentence describing the bushmaster. Write it below.
"The bushmaster, Lachesis muta, . . ., is a pit viper more than twelve feet in length, marked by black bars and pink shading."

h. Lucinda says that it had been storming for a week. At first, what did the waves look like?
They looked like hills on the moon or on a moonlit desert.

i. What did the waves look like as they came nearer?
They looked like a herd of prehistoric beasts.

j. Find the sentence describing the walls of Lucinda's tower.
"The walls of my tower, like the walls all through the castle, measured more than four feet in thickness, made of hard blue and white stones hewn from the living ledges of our gold mines."

Name _____

Lesson 6
Understanding Connotation and Denotation

The denotation of a word is its dictionary definition. For example, the dictionary definition of *love* is "an intense affectionate feeling for another human being." The connotation of a word is what it suggests to you, and the feelings it arouses in you. For example, the word *love* brings to mind all the people who have cared for you and for whom you have cared.

Poets often use words that carry feelings and associations in addition to their dictionary definitions. For example, read the poem below, "In Time of Silver Rain" by Langston Hughes.

```
      In time of silver rain
      The earth
      Puts forth new life again,
      Green grasses grow
   5  And flowers lift their heads,
      And over all the plain
      The wonder spreads
          Of life,
          Of life,
  10      Of life!

      In time of silver rain
      The butterflies
      Lift silken wings
      To catch a rainbow cry,
  15  And trees put forth
      New leaves to sing
      In joy beneath the sky
      As down the roadway
      Passing boys and girls
  20  Go singing, too,
      In time of silver rain
          When spring
          And life
          Are new.
```

The poet describes the rain as *silver*. The dictionary definition of *silver* is "medium gray." Why didn't the poet simply write: In time of gray rain? Since silver is also a precious metal, the word carries the connotation of something rich and rewarding. In this poem, the poet wants to show how rain helps life to renew itself.

Copyright © 1984 by Harcourt Brace Jovanovich, Inc. All rights reserved

Exercise. The poem below is "Snowy Morning" by Lilian Moore. Read the poem. Then answer the questions that follow it.

>   Wake
>   gently this morning
>   to a different day.
>   Listen.
> 5 There is no bray
>   of buses,
>   no brake growls,
>   no siren howls and
>   no horns
> 10 blow.
>   There is only
>   the silence
>   of a city
>   hushed
> 15 by snow.

Questions

a. In this poem, the poet contrasts the way the city sounds normally with the way it sounds on a snowy morning. Which word does she use to name the sound buses usually make?
bray

b. What does this word mean?
to make a loud, harsh cry, like that of a donkey

c. Does this word create a pleasant or an unpleasant impression?
unpleasant

d. According to this poem, what do brakes usually do?
Brakes growl.

e. What does this word mean?
to make a gruff, angry sound

f. Does this word create a pleasant or an unpleasant impression?
unpleasant

g. According to this poem, what do horns usually do?
Horns blow.

h. Do car horns create a pleasant or an unpleasant sound?
unpleasant

i. What does the snow do to the sounds of the city?
It hushes them.

j. Does the poet prefer the way the city sounds normally? Why?
We know she prefers the way the city sounds on a snowy morning, because she uses only unpleasant words to describe the way it sounds normally.

Name _____

Lesson 7
Finding Imagery in Poetry

Poets use imagery to create vivid impressions. For example, read the poem below, "Colt in the Pasture" by Elizabeth Coatsworth.

>   Colt in the pasture
>   Frolic and run,
>   Kick unshod heels
>   High up toward the sun,
>   5 You've never known saddle
>   Nor bridle nor fear,
>   Frolic and rollick
>   For springtime is here,
>   You will be soberer
> 10 This time next year.
>   Colt in the pasture
>   Roll in green grass,
>   Toss out your mane
>   At the birds as they pass,
> 15 Down by the willows
>   The streamlet runs clear,
>   Splash in the shallows
>   For no one is near,
>   You will be soberer
> 20 This time next year.

The poet creates a vivid impression of colts at play. Look at lines 2-3. The colts are frolicking and kicking up their heels. Look at lines 12-13. The colts are rolling in the grass and tossing out their manes. Look at line 17. The colts are splashing in the shallow water.

However, according to the poet, come next year, the colts will be soberer, or less carefree. Why? Let's look at the vivid details. Up until now, the colts have "never known saddle/Nor bridle nor fear." By this time next year, they will know these things. Up until now, the colts have only known springtime with its green grass. By this time next year, they will know winter.

Exercise. The poem below is "Forest Fire" by Elizabeth Coatsworth. Read the poem. Then answer the questions that follow it.

>   The leaves were yellow, the leaves were red,
>   and bright and dry as the sun overhead,
>   the springs of the earth grew faint and slow,
>   and buckets came empty from wells below,
>   5 the wind went prying, now here, now there,
>   it tossed the dust and the leaves in the air,

Copyright © 1984 by Harcourt Brace Jovanovich, Inc. All rights reserved

it dried up the dew, the mists were driven
far away, and the clouds were riven
and scattered afar, the wind went whining,
10 it cleared the sky where the sun was shining.

Then the fire rose like an asp* from the dust
and the colored leaves, and it ran like rust
along the ground till it took on power
and it rose in the trees in tendril and flower,
15 and the wind gave a yell and the fire ran
with the wind behind it, and ruin began,
and the fire roared and the fire hissed,
and smoke whirled up instead of the mist,
and the sun went down and the moon arose
20 with its light as chill and pale as the snows,
and the fire glowed against that light,
a moving red against tranquil white,
and the wind went on and the fire strengthened,
and the stain of its blackened shadow lengthened,
25 and very low and weak and small
the farm crouched there in the path of it all.

---

*asp (ăsp) n.: A small poisonous snake.

Questions

a. In line 1, the poet describes the color of the leaves. On the basis of this description, what time of year do you think it is?
It is autumn.

b. In line 2, to what does the poet compare the brightness and dryness of the leaves?
She compares the brightness and dryness of the leaves to the sun overhead.

c. In lines 3-4, the poet gives two details that create a vivid impression of the dryness of the earth. What are these two details?
The springs grow faint, and the buckets come up empty from the wells.

d. In lines 5-10, the poet shows you the effect of the wind. In line 5, she uses the vivid words "went prying" to show you what the wind does. Look up the word *pry* in your dictionary. Does this word create a pleasant or unpleasant impression of the wind? Why?
It creates an unpleasant impression since the word suggests both force and furtiveness.

e. In line 9, the poet uses the vivid words "went whining." Look up the word *whine* in your dictionary. Does this word create a pleasant or unpleasant impression of the wind? Why?
It creates an unpleasant impression since the word suggests a high-pitched sound that is annoying.

Name _____

f. In lines 11-13, the poet uses two similes to create a vivid impression of the fire. How is the fire like an asp?
Both are deadly and both run along the grass.

g. How is the fire like rust?
Both have a reddish color and both spread.

h. Reread lines 15-24. Find three details that appeal to your sense of hearing.
Three details are the wind's giving a yell, the fire roaring, and the fire hissing.

i. In lines 15-24, find three details that appeal to your sense of sight.
Three details are the smoke's whirling up, the sun's going down, and the moon's rising.

j. In lines 25-26, the poet says that a farm is in the path of this forest fire. Find four words the poet uses to create a vivid impression of the helplessness of the farm.
The words low, weak, small, **and** crouched **create an impression of helplessness.**

Lesson 8

Practice

Pay special attention to imagery as you read the selection below. Then complete the exercise that follows the selection.

Prairie Fire
Laura Ingalls Wilder

(1) One day Laura and Mary were helping Ma get dinner. Baby Carrie was playing on the floor in the sunshine, and suddenly the sunshine was gone.

(2) "I do believe it is going to storm," Ma said, looking out of the window. Laura looked, too, and great black clouds were billowing up in the south, across the sun.

(3) Pet and Patty were coming running from the field, Pa holding to the heavy plow and bounding in long leaps behind it.

(4) "Prairie fire!" he shouted. "Get the tub full of water! Put sacks in it! Hurry!"

Copyright © 1984 by Harcourt Brace Jovanovich, Inc. All rights reserved

285

(5) Ma ran to the well; Laura ran to tug the tub to it. Pa tied Pet to the house. He brought the cow and calf from the picket line and shut them in the stable. He caught Bunny, the little mule, and tied her fast to the north corner of the house. Ma was pulling up buckets of water as fast as she could. Laura ran to get the sacks that Pa had flung out of the stable.

(6) Pa was plowing, shouting at Pet and Patty to make them hurry. The sky was black, now; the air was as dark as if the sun had set. Pa plowed a long furrow west of the house and south of the house and back again east of the house. Rabbits came bounding past him as if he weren't there.

(7) Pet and Patty came galloping, the plow and Pa bounding behind them. Pa tied them to the other north corner of the house. The tub was full of water. Laura helped Ma push the sacks under the water to soak them.

(8) "I couldn't plow but one furrow; there isn't time," Pa said. "Hurry, Caroline. That fire's coming faster than a horse can run."

(9) A big rabbit bounded right over the tub while Pa and Ma were lifting it. Ma told Laura to stay at the house. Pa and Ma ran staggering to the furrow with the tub.

(10) Laura stayed close to the house. She could see the red fire coming under the billows of smoke. More rabbits went leaping by. They paid no attention to Jack and he didn't think about them; he stared at the red undersides of the rolling smoke and shivered and whined while he crowded close to Laura.

(11) The wind was rising and wildly screaming. Thousands of birds flew before the fire; thousands of rabbits were running.

(12) Pa was going along the furrow, setting fire to the grass on the other side of it. Ma followed with a wet sack, beating at the flames that tried to cross the furrow. The whole prairie was hopping with rabbits. Snakes rippled across the yard. Prairie hens ran silently, their necks outstretched and their wings spread. Birds screamed in the screaming wind.

(13) Pa's little fire was all around the house now, and he helped Ma fight it with the wet sacks. The fire blew wildly, snatching at the dry grass inside the furrow. Ma and Pa thrashed at it with the sacks; when it got across the furrow, they stamped it with their feet. They ran back and forth in the smoke, fighting that fire.

(14) The prairie fire was roaring now, roaring louder and louder in the screaming wind. Great flames came roaring, flaring and twisting high. Twists of flame broke loose and came down on the wind to blaze up in the grasses far ahead of the roaring wall of fire. A red light came from the rolling black clouds of smoke overhead.

(15) Mary and Laura stood against the house and held hands and trembled. Baby Carrie was in the house. Laura wanted to do something, but inside her head was a roaring and whirling like the fire. Her middle shook, and tears poured out of her

stinging eyes. Her eyes and her nose and her throat stung with smoke.

(16) Jack howled. Bunny and Pet and Patty were jerking at the ropes and squealing horribly. The orange, yellow, terrible flames were coming faster than horses can run, and their quivering light danced over everything.

(17) Pa's little fire had made a burned black strip. The little fire went backing slowly away against the wind; it went slowly crawling to meet the racing furious big fire. And suddenly the big fire swallowed the little one.

(18) The wind rose to a high, crackling, rushing shriek; flames climbed into the crackling air. Fire was all around the house.

(19) Then it was over. The fire went roaring past and away.

(20) Pa and Ma were beating out little fires here and there in the yard. When they were all out, Ma came to the house to wash her hands and face. She was all streaked with smoke and sweat, and she was trembling.

(21) She said there was nothing to worry about. "The backfire saved us," she said, "and all's well that ends well!"

(22) The air smelled scorched. And to the very edge of the sky, the prairie was burned naked and black. Threads of smoke rose from it. Ashes blew on the wind. Everything felt different and miserable. But Pa and Ma were cheerful because the fire was gone and it had not done any harm.

(23) Pa said that the fire had not missed them by far, but a miss is as good as a mile. He asked Ma, "If it had come while I was in Independence, what would you have done?"

(24) "We would have gone to the creek with the birds and the rabbits, of course," Ma said.

(25) All the wild things on the prairie had known what to do. They ran and flew and hopped and crawled as fast as they could go to the water that would keep them safe from fire. Only the little soft striped gophers had gone down deep into their holes, and they were the first to come up and look around at the bare, smoking prairie.

(26) Then out of the creek bottoms the birds came flying over it, and a rabbit cautiously hopped and looked. It was a long, long time before the snakes crawled out of the bottoms and the prairie hens came walking.

Exercise. Answer each of the questions below.

a. When Ma looks out the window, why does she at first think it is going to storm?
She sees great black clouds in the sky.

b. What do Ma and Pa do to protect the farm?
Pa plows a furrow between the house and the fire. Ma brings water up from the well and soaks sacks. Then Pa sets fire to the grass on the far side of the furrow and in the furrow, while Ma uses the wet sacks to beat out the flames that cross the furrow.

c. The author creates a vivid impression of the frenzied activity in the face of a prairie fire. How do the prairie animals add to the frenzy?
The animals run frantically for safety.

d. While Pa and Ma work hurriedly, they tell Laura to stay close to the house. What does Laura see under the billows of smoke?
She sees the red fire coming.

e. Reread paragraph 11. How does the author describe the sound of the wind?
She describes it as wildly screaming.

f. In paragraph 12, the author uses a vivid verb to describe the way the snakes move. What is this vivid verb and what does it mean?
The verb is rippled, *which means "moved in a wave-like fashion."*

g. Reread paragraph 14. Find three vivid verbs that describe the way the flames move.
The flames come roaring, flaring, and twisting.

h. Reread paragraph 15. Find two details that appeal to the sense of touch.
Some details are holding hands, trembling, her middle shaking, tears stinging her eyes, smoke stinging her throat.

i. Reread paragraph 16. Find two details that appeal to the sense of hearing.
Two details are Jack howling and Bunny, Pet, and Patty squealing.

j. Write two sentences describing how the backfire saves the farm.
The fire Pa set has made a burned black strip. This fire, the backfire, draws the main fire away from the house.

Name _____

Chapter 12
Flexibility and Study Skills

In this chapter you will learn several skills that will help you to read more efficiently. You will learn how to set a purpose for reading and how to adjust your speed to your purpose. In addition, you will practice several study skills that will help you be more successful with your school work.

Lesson 1
Setting a Purpose for Reading

Setting a purpose for reading helps you to read more efficiently. How do you set a purpose for reading? First, get a general idea of what the selection is about. (The title usually gives you a good idea.) Second, write down several questions to which you want to find answers in this selection. To write these questions, you might use the formula newspaper reporters use to get a story. They ask: Who? What? Where? When? Why? and How?

Exercise. Read "What a Great Report Needs: People" by Anne E. Schraff to answer each of the questions below. Write your answers in the blanks provided.

a. According to Anne E. Schraff, what is the secret ingredient in writing a good report?
The secret ingredient is people.

b. To whom should you talk when you are writing your report?
You should talk to people in your neighborhood who can give you eyewitness accounts.

c. Why should you talk to these people?
They have lived through these events. They can give you first-hand information.

d. Where can you find people to use as resources?
You can find people in your family, in your neighborhood, and in retirement homes.

Copyright © 1984 by Harcourt Brace Jovanovich, Inc. All rights reserved

e. What is the first step in setting up an interview?
Decide whom to interview.

f. When should you *not* use a tape recorder during an interview?
You should not use it when the person you are interviewing does not want you to and when you are unfamiliar with the equipment.

g. What is the last step in conducting an interview?
Thank the people you have interviewed for their help.

h. When you finally begin writing, how should you start your report?
You should start by describing the event.

i. What information should your second paragraph contain?
It should explain what the event meant.

j. How should you end your report?
You should describe the immediate consequences of the event for all Americans.

What a Great Report Needs: People
Anne E. Schraff

Your Social Studies teacher just announced a report due at the end of the month. You join the rest of the class in a deep sigh. Another deadly dull chore ahead! Trips to the library checking out such exciting topics as the Great Depression and inflation. You're afraid you will end up as usual, taking words from a book, switching them around a bit, then grinding out a report. You're pretty sure you won't learn much and you'll be bored to tears.

But wait, there's another way. It's simple, fun and it works for most social science classes. It's people plus, and the secret ingredient is *people*. To you the depression of the 1930's may seem as ancient as Hannibal pushing his weary elephants over the Alps. But your neighborhood is full of people who lived through it. They have eyewitness accounts; make use of them.

There are years of exciting history right in the minds of the people around you. Many of the most important events in human history happened in front of them. Many of them are eager to talk about their experiences.

You can learn first hand what people felt when they heard that Pearl Harbor was attacked. You can capture the stunned sorrow when President Kennedy was assassinated. You can find wonderful stories among our recent immigrants of life in other lands without freedom or opportunity. So how to translate all of this first-hand information into a school report? It's not as difficult as you might think, and it's a lot more interesting than doing all your research in the library.

First, check with your teacher to see if you can include a personal interview in your report. Chances are your teacher will be delighted you want to do something so unique. When I assigned my students to write reports on a country of their choosing, I received about a hundred seventy slightly dry reports from books and magazines. I also got one on Switzerland that included general facts about the country and three delightful interviews with Swiss folk living in America and talking about life in Switzerland. Guess which was the most interesting and received the better grade?

Second, select a topic you can understand, such as "What the Depression Meant to America" or "What Kinds of Sacrifices Did People Make in World War II?" or "Who Is Most Hurt by Inflation?" Read about the topic so you feel comfortable with it. Now you're ready for the people plus.

Third, decide on whom to interview. Older relatives and neighbors are fine. If there's a retirement home nearby, you might interview some of the people there. Introduce yourself and tell them about your paper. Many people are very happy to relate their experiences and help a student at the same time.

Fourth, conduct the interview with a tape recorder if the person is willing and you know how to use the machine. Don't attempt it if you're unfamiliar with the equipment; a pad and pencil works just fine. Jot down ideas, colorful comments, interesting anecdotes. Be sure to tell the person you are interviewing that you'll show him/her a copy of your paper when you're finished. And don't forget to thank those you've interviewed for their help.

Fifth, you now have a notebook or a tape full of good stuff and a paper to write. This is a good way to organize your material: Your first paragraph describes what happened. For example, you describe the attack on Pearl Harbor, using a good source book. Make it brief. Your second paragraph should explain what it meant—the United States was now at war. Then you get to the people ingredient. It might go something like this:

"For Naomi Jones, a young stenographer in 1941, the big black headlines meant her boyfriend might be going to war," or "For Jack Smith, a toolmaker in 1941, news of the war meant going to work making tanks for the Army."

Quote what the person said, paraphrase some of the impressions you got. Use real names with permission or just use initials. Explain how the person felt, how neighbors and friends reacted to the news of Pearl Harbor.

Your concluding paragraph should describe the immediate consequences of the event for all America. And mention how the interview helped to make the event more real to you.

Lesson 2

Adjusting Rate to Purpose

How quickly or slowly you read a selection depends on why you are reading it. For example, if you were reading a chapter in a science textbook to study for a test, you would read it slowly and carefully. If you were reading a chapter to get a general idea of what it was about, you would skim it, or read it quickly. If you were reading to find a specific piece of information, you would scan the chapter, or read it quickly until you came to the information you needed. If you were reading for enjoyment, you would read at the speed you find most comfortable.

Exercise. Below are some purposes you might have for reading "What a Great Report Needs: People" by Anne E. Schraff. Write *Slowly* next to each item where you would read the article slowly. Write *Skim* next to each item where you would read it quickly to get a general idea. Write *Scan* next to each item where you would read it to find specific information. Write *Own Speed* next to each item where you would read it simply for enjoyment.

a. While thumbing through a magazine, you see this article. The bell rings for your next class. You want to get a general idea of what is in this article so that you will know if you should read it later. *Skim*

b. You want to find out the best way to conclude a report. *Scan*

c. Your teacher wants to test how well you read. He gives you this article and tells you he will ask you ten questions about it after you have finished reading it. *Slowly*

d. You want to find out whether or not to use a tape recorder during an interview. *Scan*

e. You have just received your favorite magazine in the mail. This article is in it. You want to sit on the porch, relax, and read. *Own Speed*

Lesson 3

Scanning

Scanning is reading to find specific facts or details. When you scan, you sweep your eyes quickly over the page until you find the specific piece of information you want. You do not read any other information. For example, the article on p. 294 is called "Where Bats Look Like Smoke" by Aubrey B. Haines. Suppose you wanted to find out the place where, according to the author, the bats are so thick they look like smoke. You would sweep your eyes quickly over the page until you found this information. You would ignore all other information. The place is the Carlsbad Caverns.

Name _____

Here are some tips for scanning:

1. Before you start scanning, decide which facts or details you want to find.

2. Start looking for the information you think will be at the beginning of the selection. (Experience will help you become increasingly expert at this.)

3. Run your finger quickly across and down the page. Search for key words for the information you want; for example, people's names or place names (which begin with capital letters) and numerals.

4. When you find the information you are looking for, stop and write it down. If you happen to see some information you will need later, write this down too.

Exercise. Scan "Where Bats Look Like Smoke" to find the following information. Write your answers in the blanks below.

a. How were the Carlsbad Caverns discovered?
They were discovered by accident when a cowboy decided to investigate what he thought was smoke rising from a cave.

b. Where does the free-tailed bat live during the winter?
It lives in Mexico.

c. Are bats born without teeth?
No.

d. How old are bats when they begin to fly on their own?
They are four to five weeks old.

e. How far upward do the bats spiral as they leave the cave?
They spiral 150 to 180 feet upward.

f. Why are bats able to fly and feed in total darkness?
They have a built-in radar system.

g. When bats leave the caverns, they fly in what direction?
They usually fly in a southeasterly direction.

h. When do the greatest number of bats return to the caverns?
The greatest number return just before dawn.

i. How large is the bat colony at the Carlsbad Caverns?
It numbers about 3 million.

j. How large is the colony at some caves on the Edwards Plateau?
Some caves have 20 million bats.

Copyright © 1984 by Harcourt Brace Jovanovich, Inc. All rights reserved

Where Bats Look Like Smoke
Aubrey B. Haines

Have you heard about the Carlsbad Caverns in New Mexico? If so, you may have thought that they were discovered hundreds of years ago. Actually, they were not found until 1901. One night a lone cowboy happened to look in the direction of the caverns and thought he saw smoke rising out of the cave. It seemed strange, so he went to see for himself. What he discovered was the famous caverns. He had seen bats leaving on their nightly search for food.

Each year, from May until fall, millions of these bats make their homes in these famous caves. No one knows exactly when the bats will begin to fly out each night. Usually they fly within fifteen to twenty minutes of the time they left the night before. Sometimes, however, they surprise visitors by leaving as early as 4:30 or as late as 8:00.

The free-tailed bat lives in Mexico during the winter. It usually leaves the Carlsbad Caverns in November and returns the next spring. About June the females give birth to babies. Each mother bears only one infant a year. The baby bat is well developed at birth and weighs about one-fourth as much as its mother.

The first few nights, the mother bats carry their babies with them. Bats are born with full sets of teeth, and large claws with which they cling tightly to their mothers. Within a few nights, the babies have gained too much weight for their mothers to carry them. From then on, until they are ready to fly, the babies must stay behind, hanging from the ceiling of the bat cave.

In four to five weeks, the young bats begin to fly on their own. Leaving the cave each evening, they feed on insects. The hordes of bats fly up out of the entrance in a spiraling, counterclockwise direction. They spiral in order to gain the 150-to-180-foot altitude it takes to come up out of the bat cave. This spiral also allows their eyes to become accustomed to the brighter light as they emerge from the dark caverns.

All bats have eyes and can see. But their eyes are small, so they do not see as well as some other small mammals. Bats do not need eyes, because they can fly and feed in total darkness. They have a built-in radar system that is sensitive to echoes. Bats continually emit high-frequency sounds that travel ahead of them. When the sound waves strike an object in the bat's path, echoes bounce back to be heard and interpreted in the bat's ears and brain.

Usually, when bats leave the caverns, they fly in a southeasterly direction, the shortest route to the Pecos and the Black River Valleys. They fly all through the night and seldom alight. Since they may fly from eight to ten hours, at fifteen miles an hour, they may in one night fly as much as 150 miles. They feed within a radius of about 50 miles of their cavern homes.

The first few bats may return as early as 9:00 the same evening. But most of them straggle in throughout the early morning hours, reaching their greatest numbers just before dawn. A return bat flight is much different from an exit flight. Instead of spiraling slowly back into the caverns, they dive in from great heights with much speed.

Sometimes they approach the entrance from a height of 600 to 1,000 feet, fold their wings, and plummet inside. As they do this, they attain a high rate of speed, and the air begins to vibrate their wings, making a strange noise. When several hundred bats are coming into the caverns at once, the return flight is spectacular and noisy.

The first bats that enter the caverns select a place on the ceiling to roost. All the other bats that come in after that begin to cluster around them.

The bat colony at the Carlsbad Caverns numbers about 3 million. This is not unusual when you consider that some large bat caves on the Edwards Plateau of south central Texas have 20 million bats!

The next time you hear about the Carlsbad Caverns and their strange rock formations, remember that this is but one feature of the place. The strange little Mexican free-tailed bats that inhabit the caverns are a subject of interest in themselves. Indeed, if it had not been for them, the famous caves might not have been discovered even by the year 1901!

Lesson 4

Skimming

Skimming is reading quickly to get a general idea of what a selection is about. Skimming gives you a quick overview of the content. A good technique for skimming is to know first of all *why* you are skimming. For example, do you simply want to find out whether you would like to read this article slowly and carefully later, or do you want to get a general idea about the topic of the article? Once you know your purpose, look at the title of the article. Then read the first and last paragraphs of the article. Next, run your finger down the middle of the page, letting your eyes search the lines of print quickly and letting your mind register key words and impressions. Finally, decide whether you have accomplished your purpose. If you haven't, repeat the procedure.

Exercise. Skim this selection from "Manatees: Gentle Giants of the Sea" by Richard Thiel to get a general idea of its contents. Then decide which of the statements below are true and which are false. In the blanks at the right, put T next to each statement that is true and put F next to each statement that is false.

a. Manatees have whiskers on their faces.   T

b. Because manatees eat up to a hundred pounds of water plants and weeds each day, they are considered pests.   F

c. Like whales and dolphins, manatees must come up to the surface of the water to breathe.   T

d. Unlike most animals, manatees can live in fresh water as well as in salt water.   T

e. Manatees often swim far out into the open sea.   F

f. Manatees prefer cool water to warm water.   F

g. Manatees maintain strong family groups.   T

h. Manatees are fierce animals that often fight one another.   F

i. Manatees have many natural enemies.   F

j. Manatees are in danger of dying out.   T

Manatees: Gentle Giants of the Sea
Richard Thiel

Imagine yourself sitting on a dock along a river in Florida. You're relaxing in the warm sun. Then you glance down into the water at your feet. Staring back at you is something huge that you've never seen before! It has whiskers on its face and looks like a friendly old hound dog.

But this animal is no dog. It has a large, blimp-shaped body with flippers. Its broad, flat tail looks like that of a whale, only smaller. This mysterious creature swims slowly away from you. Finally it dives into the river and disappears.

You have just spotted a rare animal called a manatee (măn′ə-tē′). They are quite a sight to see because they're so large. Manatees may be 12 feet (3.6 m) long and weigh 1,500 pounds (680 kg). Naturally, they are big eaters. They gobble up to 100 pounds (45 kg) of water plants and weeds each day. This hearty appetite makes them useful to the people of Florida. Manatees help clean out rivers and canals by eating the weeds that would otherwise clog them up.

Manatees often feed on grasses growing near the surface of streams. Their peaceful grazing gives them the nickname "sea cows." Manatees use their divided upper lips to fasten onto plants like pliers. On quiet nights, a manatee can be heard feeding 200 yards (182 m) away.

Manatees are related to whales and dolphins. All three are descended from creatures that lived long ago on land. All of them must come to the surface of the water to breathe. Manatees usually come up for a breath every four or five minutes.

Unlike their ocean-dwelling relatives, manatees never go very far into the open sea. Instead, they often swim from the ocean off the southern coast of the U.S. into inland rivers, canals and lakes. Their ability to live in fresh water as well as salt water is rare in the animal world.

Manatees like warm water. In Florida, they can often be found near electric generating plants. There, the hot water used in making electricity is dumped directly into the ocean. And at the time of the year when the sea warms up, some manatees will move up the Atlantic coast to North Carolina. Others will swim along the Gulf of Mexico as far west as Texas.

Despite their odd looks, most people like manatees. They are very graceful swimmers. Manatees are also fun to watch when they play. Sometimes they romp together in what looks like games of tag or follow-the-leader.

Family Life

Manatees have strong family groups. Male and female pairs often stay together for life. When their calf is born, the mother swims beneath to raise it to the surface for its first breath. By the time the little one is 30 minutes old, the mother is teaching it to swim. She nurses her baby and cradles it in her flippers. For over a year, she stays close to the young manatee to protect it.

Manatees are one of the most gentle kinds of creatures on earth. They never fight. Even when a baby is in danger, a manatee mother will not attack to defend her calf. Instead, she puts herself between her child and whatever is threatening it.

It is lucky that the manatees have no natural enemies. They are nearly defenseless. Their weak flippers serve only to walk along the sea floor while grazing, and to put food in their mouths. Manatees do have teeth. But they're used only for chewing soft food, not for defense. And as for eyesight, the manatee can't see past its own flippers.

The lives of manatees are not as peaceful as they may sound. These animals are in danger of dying out. Like whales, they once were hunted for their meat and oil. Finally, laws were passed to protect them from hunters. But today there are only about 1,000 manatees left.

Lesson 5

Reading Intensively

Reading intensively means reading slowly and carefully. It is the opposite of skimming. When you read intensively, you pause after each paragraph to summarize the most important information in that paragraph. You stop to ask yourself a question about an important point in a paragraph.

Exercise. Read intensively the selection below from "Danger—Mudslides!" by John R. Burger. After you read each paragraph, write a sentence summarizing the most important information in it. The first three paragraphs are done for you.

(1) The family had gone to bed for the night. Suddenly, the father was wakened by a roar and felt the jolt of something smashing into his house. He ran to see if his three children—two girls aged four and 14, and a boy, nine—were all right and found that their bedrooms were full of mud. He caught hold of his son's hand. But a powerful stream of mud immediately separated them again. The man helped his wife to safety. But all three children were lost. They died in the mud that engulfed and destroyed their home.

(1) *A man lost his three children when his house was destroyed by a stream of mud.*

(2) Early last January, extremely heavy rains in the San Francisco Bay area of northern California caused at least 28 deaths and hundreds of millions of dollars worth of damage. These tragedies were caused by perhaps the strangest and most powerful destructive forces unleashed by the storm—*mudslides* and *mudflows*.

(2) *Mudslides and mudflows have caused death and destruction.*

(3) What caused the mudslides? This particular storm dropped from five to 18 inches of rain on different parts of the San Francisco area, saturating the clayey soil. Where slopes were steep enough the clay-rich, soil-plus-water combination started to flow like a mass of thick mud, forming *mudslides* (also known as earthflows). In some cases, houses at the top of a slope, pushed along with the mudslides, crashed into and destroyed the houses that were built below it.

(3) *Mudslides occur when rain picks up soil on the slope of a hill, forming mud which flows down the hill with tremendous power.*

What are mudflows?
a. The name "mudflow" sounds alot like "earthflow," but a mudflow starts and moves quite differently from an earthflow (mudslide). On some slopes, the soil can't absorb the rain. So the rain runs off the slope into the canyon below, picking up soil particles, forming mud as it goes. As more and more solid material is added, the mud becomes thicker and thicker. Eventually, the mud may become as thick as freshly made concrete.

a. *Mudflows occur when rain flows off the hill into a canyon, where it picks up soil particles, forming a stream of mud.*

Name _____

When this stream of mud is walled-in by steep-sided canyon walls, it can move downstream with tremendous power—much more power than a stream of water.

b. Why is the mudflow so powerful? Because it is much heavier than an equal volume of water, the mud exerts a much greater force. In fact, mudflows are so powerful that they can carry boulders of 85 tons or more—carry such boulders hundreds of feet down slopes that are so gentle the land is almost flat.

b. *Mudflows are so extremely powerful because mud is much heavier than an equal volume of water and exerts a much greater force.*

c. Something happens to a mudflow when it rushes out of the mouth of a steep canyon onto the more gentle slopes below. It spreads out. It does damage both by the sheer force of its movement and by covering broad areas with a layer of mud perhaps a few centimeters to several meters thick. The advancing front of the flow has a rolling action that mixes the water and sediment. When something gets in the way of the mudflow, the mudflow slows down or stops—temporarily. Meanwhile, water builds up behind the front until the mudflow has enough force to go around the barrier, go over it, or carry it along.

c. *As the mudflow rushes out of the mouth of the steep canyon, it spreads out and does damage both by the force of movement and by covering broad areas with mud.*

d. A mudflow must be at least a certain minimum thickness if it is to move rapidly. When a flow moves through a canyon, the canyon walls confine the mudflow and keep it deep. Outside the canyon, the mudflow usually spreads out and goes more slowly. However, in some cases, a mudflow will build its own confining channel of natural levees (dikes). This happens when water drains off the edges of the unconfined stream of mud. This drying mud is then deposited as a wall along the edges of the flow. Such walls, or natural levees, will then keep the flow in a channel and help keep the mudflow speeding along.

d. *Inside the canyon, the mudflow remains the necessary thickness for it to move rapidly, but outside the canyon, it may spread out and lose force unless the mud itself forms restraining walls.*

e. Mudflows are also a hazard associated with volcanoes. Volcanic ash is turned into mud when it mixes with rainwater. And the mud flows down the sides of the volcano into the valleys below.

e. *Volcanic ash can turn to mud when mixed with rainfall and so create a mudflow.*

Copyright © 1984 by Harcourt Brace Jovanovich, Inc. All rights reserved

Lesson 6
Following Directions

Directions are instructions for how to do something. Directions may be spoken or written. When directions are spoken, you must listen carefully. When directions are written, you must read carefully. If you don't understand directions, you must ask questions.

Here is part of a page from a student's book.

Exercise. Choose a synonym for each **boldface** word below. Write the letter of your choice in the blank at the right.

1. **silent** _____
   ((a) quiet)   (b) peaceful   (c) loud
2. **journey** _____
   (a) discovery   (b) detour   ((c) trip)
3. **adhere** _____
   ((a) stick)   (b) fasten   (c) smooth

This student did not read the directions carefully. The student circled the correct answer. The directions say to write the letter of the correct answer in the blank at the right. If the teacher were using a grid, a piece of paper that covers everything but the answers, to mark this paper, the teacher would think the student hadn't filled in the answers. The student would get a zero even though the student knew all the answers.

Exercise. The selection below is from *The Long Ago Lake* by Marne Wilkins. It gives you directions for making a rush mat. Read this selection carefully. Then follow the instructions at the end of it.

How to Make a Rush Mat

Materials needed: cattail (bulrush) leaves, masking tape, scissors.

Gather young cattail rushes (leaves) and dry them, out of the sun. When you are ready to weave, dampen and wrap them in a towel.

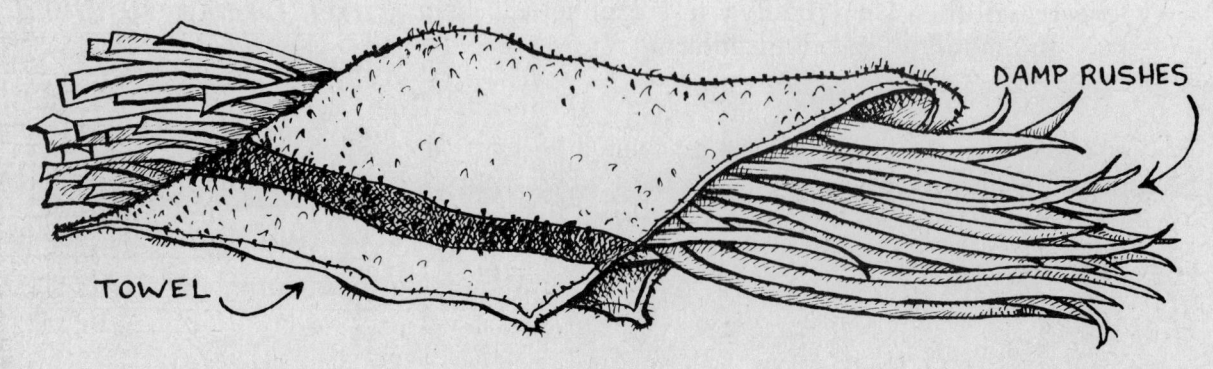

300   Copyright © 1984 by Harcourt Brace Jovanovich, Inc. All rights reserved

Name _____

Use 18 rushes, each about 1 inch wide and 30 inches long for the long side and 14 rushes about 26 inches long for the short side.

Cut the bottom end to the same shape as the top end with scissors. Now lay the long rushes out flat, side by side, with no space in between. You can keep them in place with a piece of masking tape across the ends.

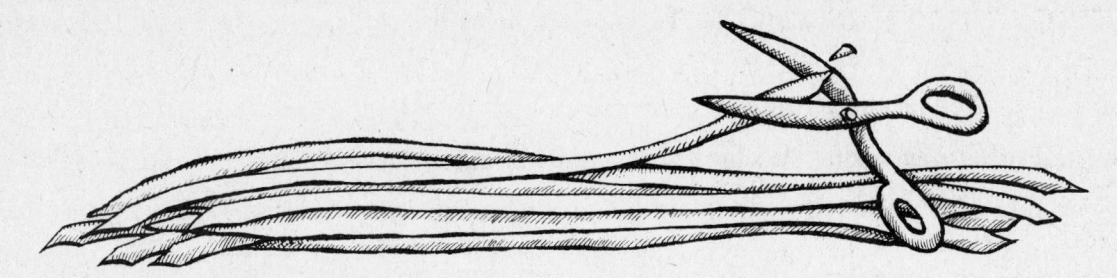

To begin weaving your mat, start at one side with a short rush and work opposite the direction of the long rushes. Put the short one first *over* then *under* the 18 long rushes. The next short rush is placed beside the first short rush, but it starts by going *under* the first long rush, then over, under, over, under.

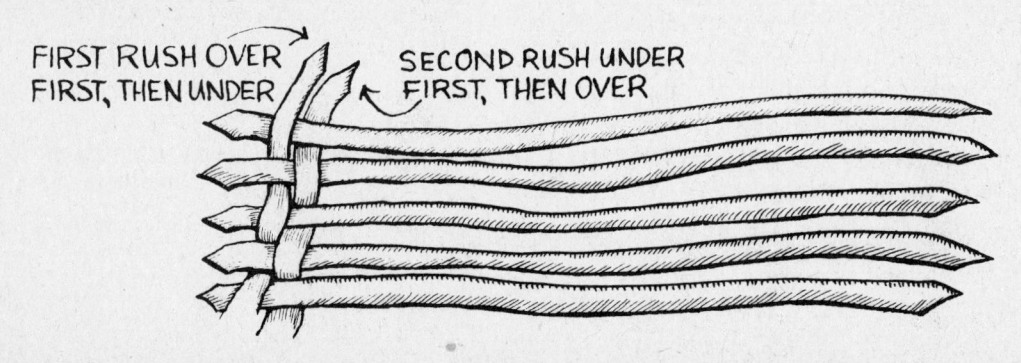

FIRST RUSH OVER FIRST, THEN UNDER
SECOND RUSH UNDER FIRST, THEN OVER

Leave 6 inches sticking out at the top and bottom of the mat and at each end. These are turned back and woven into the other weaving so that the edge of the mat has a solid finish instead of a loose, wiggly one.

If you want to make a square mat, use rushes that are all the same length. If you want to make a thicker one, use two layers and weave them as one.

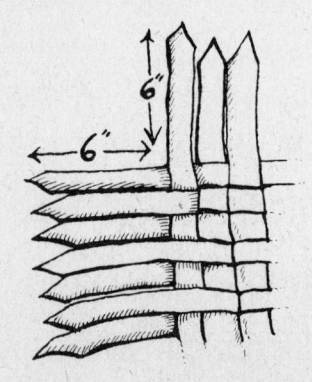

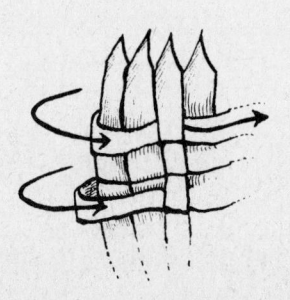

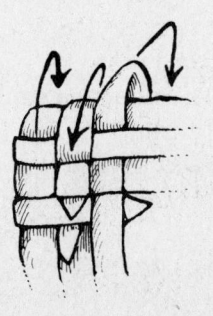

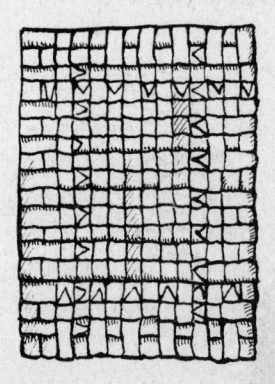

Copyright © 1984 by Harcourt Brace Jovanovich, Inc. All rights reserved

Directions. Now that you have studied carefully the directions for making a rush mat, read the statements below. If the statement contains a correct, or accurate, direction, write C in the blank at the right. If the statement contains a wrong, or inaccurate, direction, write W in the blank at the right.

a. After you gather your cattail rushes, dry them out of the sun.   C

b. Make sure your rushes are completely dry when you weave.   W

c. To make your mat, you need 34 rushes in all.   W

d. The bottom end of the rush should be the same shape as the top end.   C

e. Lay the long rushes on the ground in a crisscross pattern.   W

f. You can hold the long rushes in place with masking tape.   C

g. Weave the first short rush over, then under, the eighteen long rushes.   C

h. Weave the second short rush over, then under, the eighteen long rushes.   W

i. Leave ten inches sticking out of the top and bottom of the mat and at the side.   W

j. Make sure your mat has a wiggly edge.   W

Lesson 7

Outlining

Outlining helps you to remember the information in a selection. **Outlining is organizing a selection so that important information stands out from less important information.**

You can divide most selections containing factual information into several major parts or topics; for example, "Motion Pictures." You can further divide these major topics into subtopics. For example, under the topic "Motion Pictures" you might have the subtopic "Musical Comedies." Then, under the subtopic, you can list specific information found in this part.

The idea of outlining is to divide and organize. First divide the article into major topics. Then divide those topics into subtopics. Indicate the major topics by Roman numerals (I, II, III). Indicate the subtopics by capital letters (A, B, C). Indicate the divisions of the subtopics by Arabic numerals (1, 2, 3).

Name _____

Exercise. Read the items in the box below. Then use these items to fill in the outline skeleton on bats that follows the box.

Roost in groups	Hare-lipped bat
Behavior of bats	Some feed on fish
Horseshoe bat	Weighs one-fourth as much as its mother
Born with closed eyes	Some feed on fruit
Some types of bats	The newborn bat

I. *Some types of bats*

   A. Free-tailed bat

   B. Mouse-tailed bat

   C. Sheath-tailed bat

   D. *Hare-lipped bat*

   E. *Horseshoe bat*

II. Life of bats

   A. Birth

      1. Usually bear only one infant a year

      2. Give birth in the spring

   B. *The newborn bat*

      1. Well developed at birth

      2. *Born with closed eyes*

      3. *Weighs one-fourth as much as its mother*

   C. The adult

      1. Has eyes and can see, though not well

      2. Has built-in radar system

III. *Behavior of bats*

   A. Feeding habits

      1. Most feed on insects

      2. *Some feed on fruit*

      3. *Some feed on fish*

   B. Living habits

      1. Hang upside down in caves or other dark places during day

      2. *Roost in groups*

Lesson 8

Understanding the Parts of a Book

Books contain two sections that you will find helpful. These sections are the frontmatter and the backmatter.

The frontmatter contains the *title page,* the *copyright page,* a *preface* or *foreword,* and the *table of contents.* The *title page* tells you the title of the book, the author, the publisher, and the place of publication. The *copyright page* appears on the reverse side of the title page. It tells you when the book was copyrighted and by whom. If there are any acknowledgments, credits for material used from other books, these also appear on the copyright page. The *preface* or *foreword* is a note to the reader by the author, editor, or another involved person. The *table of contents* lists the titles of each chapter and the page where each chapter begins. Often it also lists major sections within each chapter and the page where each section begins. If the book is divided into units or parts, the titles of these are listed too. For example, look at part of the table of contents of *American Civics, Fourth Edition,* by William H. Hartley and William S. Vincent.

UNIT ONE CITIZENSHIP IN OUR DEMOCRACY	1
1. Civics in Our Lives	3
2. Who Are American Citizens?	6
3. The American People Today	11
Citizenship in Action: Learning About "The Good Old Days"	12
Civics Skills: Using Your Textbook	18

Unit One in this book is called *Citizenship in Our Democracy.* It begins on page 1. Chapter 1 is called *We the People.* It begins on page 2. Chapter 1 is divided into five parts. The part called *Who Are American Citizens?* begins on page 6.

The backmatter may include a *glossary,* a *bibliography,* and an *index.* The *glossary* is a dictionary of words in the book that the reader may not know. The *bibliography* is a list of other books about the topic. The *index* is an alphabetical listing of topics and subtopics and the pages where they appear.

For example, look at part of a page from the index for *Language for Daily Use, Phoenix Edition.*

A and *an,* 162–163, 410, 430, 452–453
Abbreviations
    acronyms, 169
    of days and months, 86–87, 93, 113, 117
    of organizations, 69, 77, 87, 113, 169, 460
    of people's titles, 69, 77, 86–87, 93, 113, 117, 441, 460–461
    of place names, 86–87, 93, 107, 113, 117, 441
    postal, 86–87, 439
    punctuation of, 69, 86, 441, 444
Abstract nouns. *See* Nouns

Information about the topic *A and an* can be found on pages 162-163, 410, 430, and 452-453. The topic *Abbreviations* is divided into seven subtopics. Information about the subtopic *postal* can be found on pages 86-87 and on page 439.

Exercise 1. Below is part of the first page from the table of contents for *English Writing and Language Skills*, Second Course, by W. Ross Winterowd and Patricia Y. Murray. Study this table of contents. Then answer the questions that appear after it. Write your answers in the blanks provided.

1 Keeping a Journal 2

Starting Your Journal **2**
Recording Your Observations **9**
Writing About Your Feelings **13**

2 Writing to Friends 16

Learning About Friendly Letters **16**
Writing an Interesting Letter **18**
Writing to a Pen Pal **20**

a. What is the title of Chapter 1?
Keeping a Journal

b. On what page does Chapter 1 begin?
page 2

c. In Chapter 1, on what page does the section *Recording Your Observations* begin?
page 9

d. What is the title of Chapter 2?
Writing to Friends

e. In Chapter 2, on what page does the section *Writing to a Pen Pal* begin?
page 20

Exercise 2. The part of the index shown below is from *Your Speech* by Francis Griffith, Catherine Nelson, and Edward Stasheff. Study this index. Then answer the questions that appear after it. Write your answers in the blanks provided.

Index

A
"Aardvark," 322-323
Abstract words, 181-182
Accent marks, dictionary listings, 171
Acceptance speech, 248
Accuracy, in giving directions, 51
Acquaintance, between class members, 2
Acting, art of, 345-350
    characterization, 342, 345, 347-348, 350
    concentration, 345, 353
    ensemble, 354
    imagination, 345-347
    improvisation, 345, 349-350
    motivation, 342, 345, 349
    observation, 345-347
    television, 396-397
Address forms, dictionary listings, 183
Addressing:
    informants, when asking information, 49
    older people by first names, 10
Adjournment, meeting, 267, 270, 274
Affected speech, 188
"Ah, Faustus," 315-316
Almanacs, use in preparing a speech, 203

Argument, in debate, 293-294
    by analogy or comparison, 293
    from authority, 293
    from example, 293
    by reasoning, 293
    by statistics, 293
Arnold Matthew, 436-437
Assertion proving, debate, 292-294
Assertions, unsupported, 135
Assignments, debate, to team members, 284
Association of Better Business Bureaus, 84
Astaire, Fred, 412
Audibility:
    in classroom discussions, 38-39
    in discussions, 236-237
Audience:
    discussion, 239
    speech, 197-198
Authoritative statements, accepting as listener, 140-141
Awkward gestures, 151

B
"Bait and switch" techniques, 79
Bandwagon, the, 137
Begging the question, 135-136
Behavior, changed in groups, 107-108
Bell, T. H., 217 fn.
Belloc, Hilaire, 314-315
Benét, Stephen Vincent, 314

a. On what pages would you find information about the topic *"Aardvark"*?
pages 322-323

b. On what page would you find information about the topic *Acceptance speech*?
page 248

c. Look at the topic *Acting, art of*. On what pages would you find information about the subtopic *concentration*?
pages 345 and 353

d. Look at the topic *Addressing*. On what page would you find information about the subtopic *older people by first names*?
page 10

e. On what page would you find information about the topic *Affected speech*?
page 188

Name _____

Lesson 9
Using Reference Books

There are many kinds of reference books. Each kind contains different information. For example, if you want to find out how to spell *Australia*, you would look in a dictionary. If you want to refer to a map of Australia, you would look in an atlas.

Reference	What is in it?	Other facts
Almanac	Records, lists of facts like capitals, and presidents, and sports records. Current information.	New editions come out every year so the facts are up-to-date.
Atlas	Maps, tables, and charts.	
Dictionary	Words—their meanings, spellings, and pronunciations.	Some dictionaries also have the origins of words and place names. Special dictionaries contain words on only one subject, like sports or cooking.
Encyclopedia	Detailed information on a huge range of subjects. May be one book or a set of books.	Some encyclopedias cover only one subject, like sports or science.

Exercise. Decide which reference book would give you the best and quickest answer to each question below. Write the word *almanac*, *atlas*, *dictionary*, or *encyclopedia* in the blank provided.

a. What states border New Mexico? _____atlas_____
b. Which baseball team won the World Series in 1982? _____almanac_____
c. During what years was the pony express in operation? _____encyclopedia_____
d. How do you spell the past participle of *barbecue*? _____dictionary_____
e. How do you pronounce *sociology*? _____dictionary_____
f. Which country is immediately to the west of France? _____atlas_____
g. Who are four jazz musicians? _____encyclopedia_____
h. What is the average rainfall of Florida? _____almanac_____
i. Who are the current senators from New York? _____almanac_____
j. How does an airplane fly? _____encyclopedia_____

Copyright © 1984 by Harcourt Brace Jovanovich, Inc. All rights reserved

Lesson 10
Reading Graphs

A graph is a diagram that shows how two or more sets of facts are related. One type of graph is a bar graph. A bar graph shows this relationship with bars of different lengths. For example, the bar graph below shows job opportunities today and tomorrow. Along the bottom of the graph, you can see job categories; for example, *Professional and Technical Workers, Business Managers and Owners, Clerical Workers*. Along the left side of the graph, you can read the percentage of total workers. Each horizontal black bar represents the percentage of total workers in that category in 1980. Each horizontal white bar represents the expected percentage in that category in 1990.

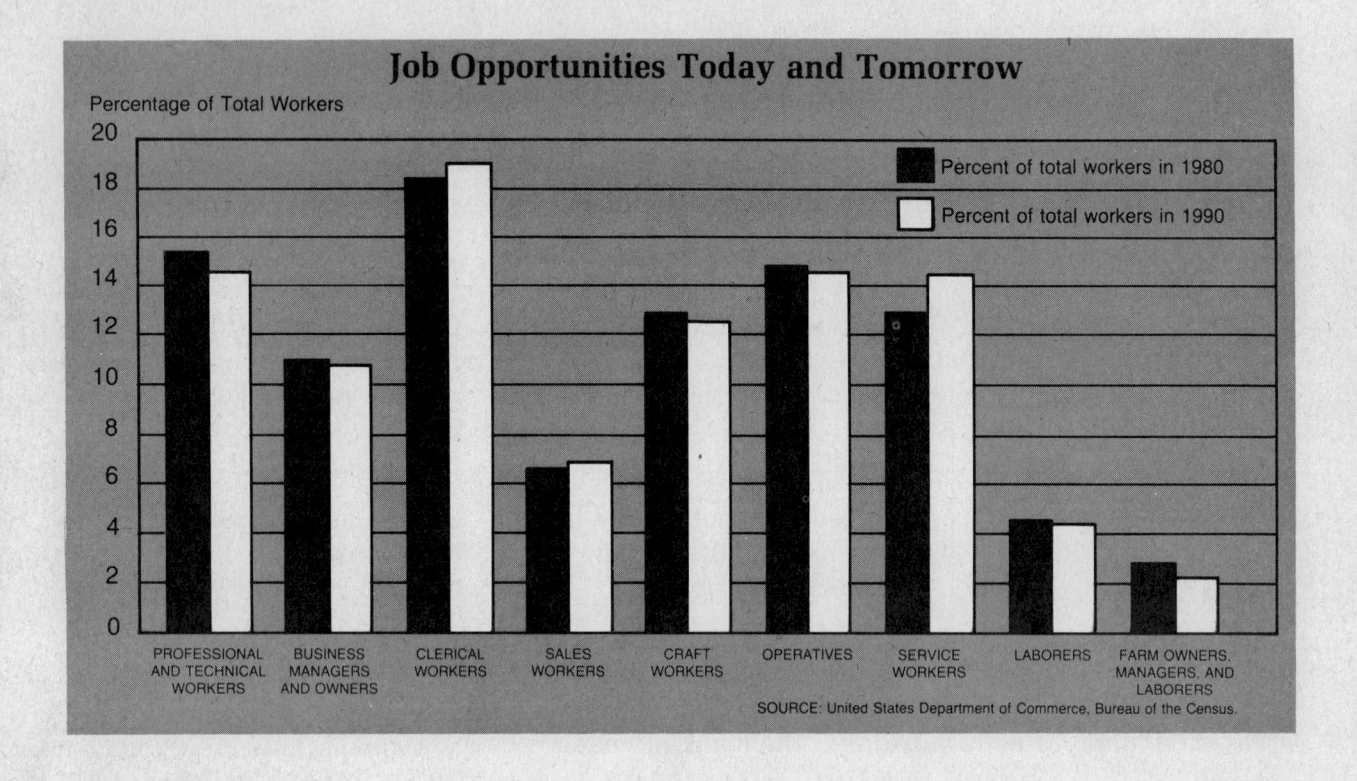

Job Opportunities Today and Tomorrow

Percentage of Total Workers

- Percent of total workers in 1980
- Percent of total workers in 1990

Categories: PROFESSIONAL AND TECHNICAL WORKERS, BUSINESS MANAGERS AND OWNERS, CLERICAL WORKERS, SALES WORKERS, CRAFT WORKERS, OPERATIVES, SERVICE WORKERS, LABORERS, FARM OWNERS, MANAGERS, AND LABORERS

SOURCE: United States Department of Commerce, Bureau of the Census.

Exercise. Use the graph above to answer each question.

a. Which category is expected to have the highest percentage of workers in 1990? *Clerical Workers*

b. Which category had the highest percentage of workers in 1980? *Clerical Workers*

c. Look at the category *Sales Workers*. Is the percentage of total workers in this category expected to rise or fall in 1990? *It is expected to rise.*

d. Look at the category *Craft Workers*. Is the percentage of total workers in this category expected to rise or fall in 1990? *It is expected to fall.*

e. Which category is expected to have the greatest rise in percentage of total workers in 1990? *Service Workers*

Name _____

Lesson 11
Reading Time Lines

A time line is a line on which the dates of certain events are placed in chronological order. Years or other measures of time are measured out equally across the line, so you get a clear picture of how close together or far apart certain things happened.

For example, look at the time line below. It shows some important dates in the early history of motion pictures.

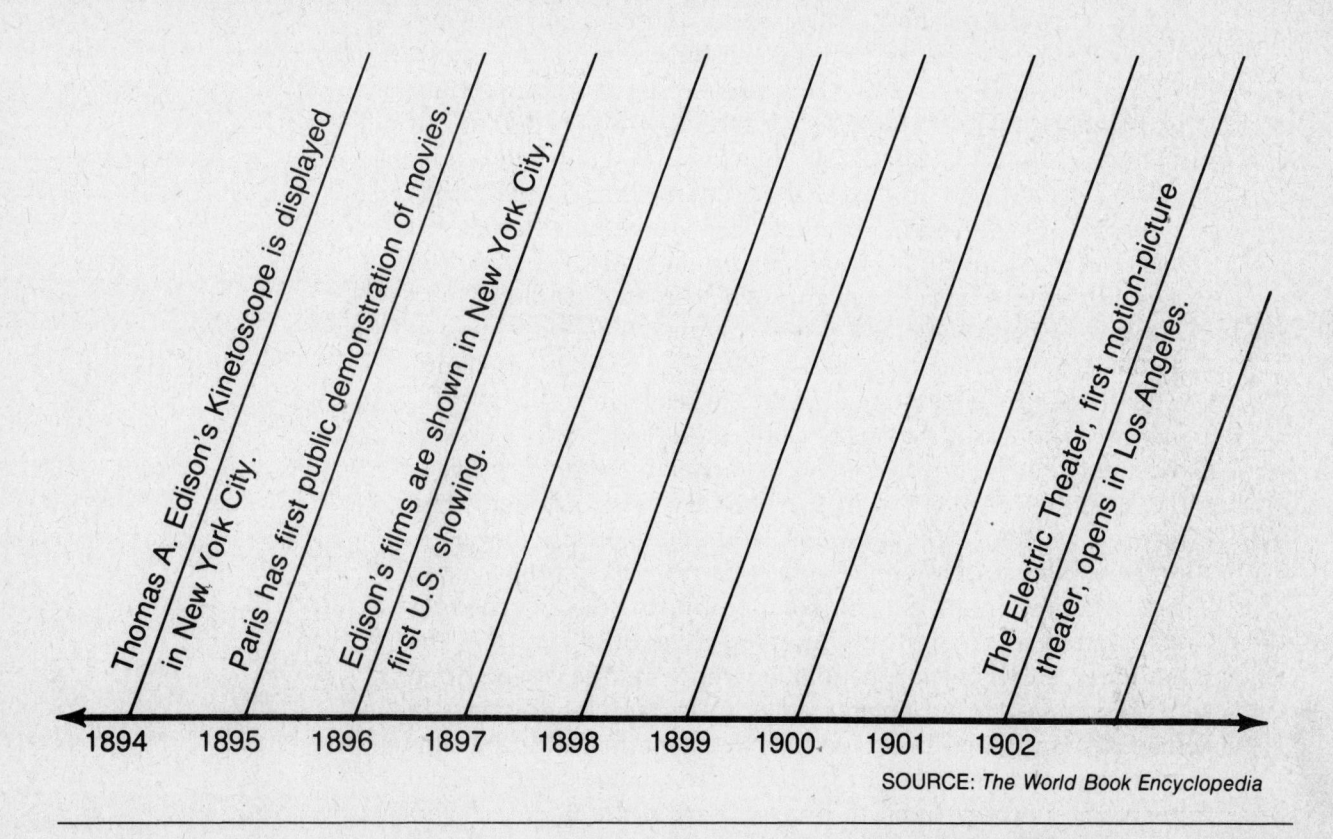

- Thomas A. Edison's Kinetoscope is displayed in New York City. — 1894
- Paris has first public demonstration of movies. — 1895
- Edison's films are shown in New York City, first U.S. showing. — 1896
- The Electric Theater, first motion-picture theater, opens in Los Angeles. — 1902

1894 1895 1896 1897 1898 1899 1900 1901 1902

SOURCE: *The World Book Encyclopedia*

Exercise. Study the time line above to answer each of the following questions.

a. In what year was Edison's kinetoscope displayed in New York City? **1894**

b. In what year were Edison's films first shown in the United States? **1896**

c. In what year did the Electric Theater open in Los Angeles? **1902**

d. In what year did Paris have its first public demonstration of movies? **1895**

e. In what year were Edison's films first shown in New York City? **1896**

Copyright © 1984 by Harcourt Brace Jovanovich, Inc. All rights reserved

Lesson 12
Practice

Read the selection below as though you were going to be tested on it. Then complete the exercise that follows the selection.

The Mystery of Tornadoes
Sandra Henneberger

Picture a giant whirling cloud, shaped like a long black funnel and glowing like a Chinese lantern. Steel and concrete buildings can be twisted apart in seconds by this cloud, yet its action can be gentle and bizarre; a tornado has been known to pluck feathers off chickens without harming the birds.

Tornadoes create the most powerful winds that travel the earth. A tornado once twisted apart a building that had been built to withstand winds of 375 miles per hour (mph). Scientists estimate that funnel clouds often have winds of 500 to 600 mph and can have circulating wind speeds of nearly 800 mph. That's faster than a jet travels while breaking the sound barrier!

One of the worst tornadoes on record traveled at a *forward* speed of sixty mph. Hours later, it had left a path of destruction three-fourths of a mile wide through Missouri, Indiana, and Illinois. It was called the Tri-State Tornado of 1925, and it killed 689 people. Today, because of weather warning systems, the death rate from tornadoes is much lower.

Even ordinary tornadoes contain great destructive power. Fortunately, their power doesn't usually last more than ten to thirty minutes. A funnel will seldom carve a path longer than fifteen miles. Very strange things can happen inside this path. Buildings blow apart, windows burst, even *before* they are hit. A wheat straw can be driven like a nail into wood. Tornadoes often destroy anything they hit, even huge buildings. On the other hand, small objects, people, or whole houses can be lifted into the winds, carried several feet or miles, and let down again gently without harm. In this regard, the tornado that lifted Dorothy's house in *The Wizard of Oz* had some basis in fact. Remember, Dorothy lived in Kansas, part of the famous "Tornado Alley." This name describes a wide area of Kansas, Oklahoma, and Texas where two or more tornadoes occur every year.

Where does such incredible power come from? So far, the answer to that question only creates more puzzles. Weather researchers have long known the "right" conditions for a tornado: A dry, cold air mass, or front, pushes against a wet warm front. People living in Tornado Alley often have these two types of cloud masses clashing in the sky. Thunderclouds form. Luckily, less than one in ten thunderstorms produce tornadoes.

More than luck is at work: Between the cold front near the ground and a thin layer of cold air very high in the sky, warm, wet air becomes trapped. These conditions are common in spring and early summer, as the earth is warming. Tornadoes occur more often during those seasons. Because of its *lower pressure* (which may be thought of as weight), warm air tends to rise. The cloud masses whirl around each other and create an *updraft* of rapidly rising air. The warmer the whirling air becomes—compared with quiet air around it—the faster the updraft rises. Some scientists think that frequent lightning inside a warm thundercloud superheats the trapped air. The extra heat helps the air rise even faster. A funnel of whirling clouds forms.

The updraft inside a funnel cloud is very strong, causing very low air pressure. Like a huge vacuum cleaner, the funnel sucks up everything it touches. But the strength of these rising winds changes from moment to moment. Imagine a real vacuum cleaner turning on and off very suddenly. That is how a tornado can lift things in strange ways.

Why do buildings burst? The air pressure inside a building remains normal. As intense low air pressure in the form of a funnel cloud approaches, the air in the building pushes *out*. The inside air breaks windows or walls as it rushes outward.

Some schoolchildren in Nebraska once had a chance to look inside this mysterious monster for themselves. They were having a picnic in a park. The weather had been hot and muggy for three days. Suddenly someone shouted, "Tornado!" A huge finger-shaped cloud spilled down from gray-green thunderclouds. Before anyone could run, the funnel was hanging directly over their heads. They looked up into it. Inside it was completely black, but flashes of lightning were striking every second in the funnel, letting them see the whirling, inner black clouds. There was a noise like "ten thousand freight trains." The funnel moved off. Several miles away it touched ground, destroying trees and buildings.

From rare "shows" like this we know that nearly constant lightning inside a tornado causes its weird lighting effects. Sometimes at night a tornado will look like a dim lantern in the shape of a funnel cloud. Why the lightning is so frequent is unclear.

Some of a tornado's trickier actions are caused by its rapidly changing updraft of air. The huge force of these winds creates the damage. These winds and the brief life of a funnel cloud prevent balloons or planes from carrying recording instruments inside it. Without exact data, scientists can only estimate where, when, or why a tornado will start.

The exact nature of tornadoes is still a puzzle. The more weather researchers learn about them, the more they discover there is to learn.

Exercise. Decide whether the following statements are true or false. In the blanks provided, write *T* if the statement is true. Write *F* if the statement is false.

a. The most powerful winds that travel the earth are created by tornadoes. _____T_____

b. The death rate from tornadoes is as high today as it was in 1925. _____F_____

c. The "right" conditions for a tornado are a dry, cold air mass pushing against a wet warm front. _____T_____

d. More than 30% of thunderclouds produce tornadoes. _____F_____

e. A tornado starts when cold, dry air becomes trapped between thin layers of warm air. _____F_____

f. Tornadoes occur most often in spring and early summer. _____T_____

g. Warm air tends to rise. _____T_____

h. The updraft inside a funnel cloud causes very low air pressure. _____T_____

i. No one has ever looked inside a tornado and lived. _____F_____

j. The tornado's strange lighting effects are caused by nearly constant lightning within it. _____T_____